AF522316

Commercial Economics: Theories and Methods

Commercial Economics: Theories and Methods

Anand Prakash

RANDOM PUBLICATIONS
NEW DELHI (INDIA)

Commercial Economics: Theories and Methods

ISBN 978-93-5111-809-1

Published in 2016 in India by

RANDOM PUBLICATIONS

4376-A/4B, Gali Murari Lal, Ansari Road
New Delhi-110 002
Phone : +9111-43580356, 011-23289044, 011-43142548
e-mail: sales@randompublications.com,
info@randompublications.com, randomexports@gmail.com

Reprinted 2025

Type Setting by : Friends Media, Delhi-110089
Digitally Printed at: Replika Press Pvt. Ltd.

Preface

Economics is the social science that seeks to describe the factors which determine the production, distribution and consumption of goods and services. The term economics comes from the Ancient Greek hence "rules of the house ". 'Political economy' was the earlier name for the subject, but economists in the late 19th century suggested "economics" as a shorter term for "economic science" to establish itself as a separate discipline outside of political science and other social sciences. Economics focuses on the behavior and interactions of economic agents and how economies work. Consistent with this focus, primary textbooks often distinguish between microeconomics and macroeconomics. Microeconomics examines the behavior of basic elements in the economy, including individual agents and markets, their interactions, and the outcomes of interactions. Individual agents may include, for example, households, firms, buyers, and sellers. Macroeconomics analyzes the entire economy and issues affecting it, including unemployment of resources, inflation, economic growth, and the public policies that address these issues. In the investment field, the term "commercial" is generally used to refer to a trading entity engaged in business activities that are hedged by positions in the futures or options markets. A commercial plays an active role in the futures and forward markets, ranging from the initial production to the final sales. While the term is also widely used in other areas of finance and everyday life, it generally denotes an activity that pertains to business or one that has a profit motive.

– Author

Contents

1

Demand Analysis

DEMAND

This lesson examines demand and its determinants. Demand is the force that drives all business without a demand for its goods or services, a firm is doomed to failure.

MEANING OF DEMAND

In economic science, the term "demand" refers to the desire, backed by the necessary ability to pay. The demand for a good at a given price is the quantity of it that can be bought per unit of time at the price. There are three important things about the demand: 1. It is the quantity desired at a given price. 2. It is the demand at a price during a given time. 3. It is the quantity demanded per unit of time.

DETERMINANTS OF DEMAND

The factors that determine the size and amount of demand are manifold. The term "function" is employed to show such "determined" and "determinant" relationship. For instance, we say that the quantity of a good demanded is a function of its price

$$\text{i.e., } Q = f(p)$$

Where Q represents quantity demanded

- f means function, and
- p represents price of the good.

There are many important determinants of the demand for a commodity:

- Price of the goods: The first and foremost determinant of the demand for good is price. Usually, higher the price of goods, lesser will be the quantity demanded of them.
- Income of the buyer: The size of income of the buyers also influences the demand for a commodity. Mostly it is true that "larger the income, more will be the quantity demanded".

- Prices of Related Goods: The prices of related goods also affect the demand for a good. In some cases, the demand for a good will go up as the price of related good rises. The goods so inter-related arc known as substitutes, e.g. radio and gramophone. In some other cases, demand for a good will comes down as the price of related good rises. The goods so inter-related are complements, e.g. car and petrol, pen and ink, cart and horse, etc.
- Tastes of the buyer: This is a subjective factor. A commodity may not be purchased by the consumer even though it is very cheap and useful, if the commodity is not up to his taste or liking. Contrarily, a good may be purchased by the buyer, even though it is very costly, if it is very much liked by him.
- Seasons prevailing at the time of purchase; In winter, the demand for woollen clothes will rise; in summer, the demand for cool drinks rises substantially; in the rainy season, the demand for umbrellas goes up.
- Fashion: When a new film becomes a success, the type of garments worn by the hero or the heroine or both becomes an article of fashion and the demand goes up for such garments.
- Advertisement and Sales promotion: Advertisement in newspapers and magazines, on outdoor hoardings on buses and trains and in radio and television broadcasts, etc. have a substantial effect on the demand for the good and thereby improves sales.

The need to have clarity in demand analysis makes us adopt a 'ceteris paribus' assumption, i.e. all other things remain the same except one. This enables us to consider the relation between demand and each of the variable factors considered in isolation. For a long period of time economists are much interested to study the relationship of price and sales. An indepth knowledge of such relationship is necessary for the management

LAW OF DEMAND

Among the many causal factors affecting demand, price is the most significant and the price- quantity relationship called as the Law of Demand is stated as follows: "The greater the amount to be sold, the smaller must be the price at which it is offered in order that it may find purchasers, or in other words, the amount demanded increases with a fall in price and diminishes with a rise in price". In simple words other things being equal, quantity demanded will be more at a lower price than at higher price. The law assumes that income, taste, fashion, prices of related goods, etc. remain the same in a given period. The law indicates the inverse relation between the price of a commodity and its quantity demanded in the market. However, it should be remembered that the law is only an indicative and not a quantitative statement. This means that it is not necessary that such variation in demand be proportionate to the change in price.

DEMAND SCHEDULE

It is a list of alternative hypothetical prices and the quantities demanded of a good corresponding to these prices. It refers to the series of quantities an individual is ready to buy at different prices. An imaginary demand schedule of an individual for apples is given below:

Table Demand of a Consumer for apples

Price of apple per unit (in rupees)	Quantity demanded of apples (in dozens)
5	1
4	2
3	3
2	4

Assuming the individual to be rational in his purchasing behaviour, the above schedule illustrates the law of demand. At Rs.5/- per apple, the consumer demands 1 dozen of apples; at Rs.4/- per unit 2 dozens, at Rs.3/- per unit 3 dozens and at Rs.2/~ per unit 4 dozens. Thus the inverse relationship between price and demand is shown in the demand schedule.

DEMAND CURVE

When the data presented in the demand schedule can be plotted on a graph with quantities demanded on the horizontal or X- axis and hypothetical prices on the vertical or Y- axis, and a smooth curve is hypothetical prices on the vertical or Y- axis, and a smooth curve is drawn Joining all the points so plotted, it gives a demand curve. Thus, the demand schedule is translated into a diagram known as the demand curve.

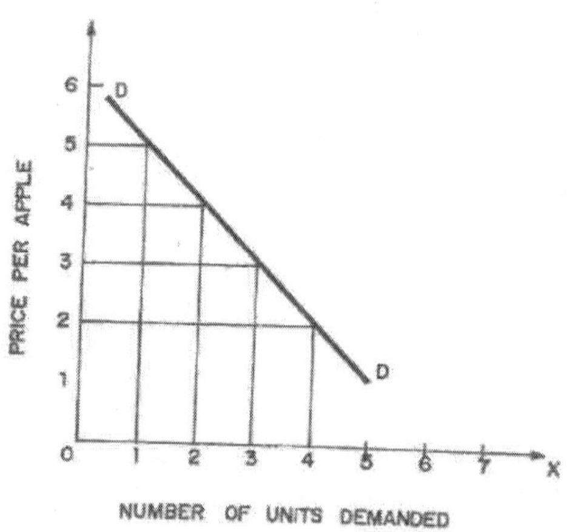

The demand curve slopes downwards from left to right, showing the inverse relationship between price and quantity as in Figure 1.

MARKET DEMAND

The market demand reflects the total quantity purchased by all consumers at alternative hypothetical prices. It is the sum-total of all individual demands. It is derived by adding the quantities demanded by each consumer for the product in the market at a particular price. The table presenting the series of quantities demanded of all consumers for a product in the market at alternative hypothetical prices is known as the Market Demand Schedule. If the data are represented on a two dimensional graph, the resulting curve will be the Market Demand Curve. From the point of view of the seller of the product, the market demand curve shows the various quantities that he can sell at different prices. Since the demand curve of an individual is downward sloping, the lateral addition of such curves to get market demand curve will also result in downward sloping curve.

SHIFTS IN DEMAND CURVE

The price-quantity relationship represented by the law of demand is important but it is more important for the manager of the firm to know about the shifts in the demand function (or curve). For many products, change in price has little effect in the quantity demanded in relevant price ranges. Many other determinants like incomes, tastes, fashion, and business activity have larger effect on demand for such product. Thus, changes or shifts in demand curve rather than movement along the demand curve is of greater significance to the decision-maker in the firm.

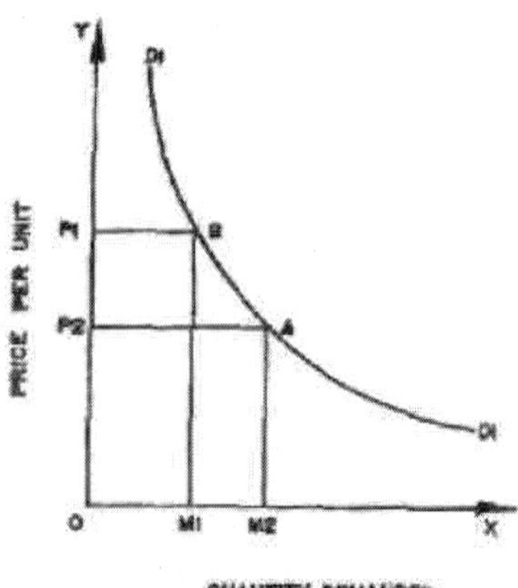

Let us clearly know the difference between movement along one and the same demand curve and shift in demand curve due to changes in demand. When price of a good alone varies, ceteris paribus, the quantity demanded of the good changes. These changes due to price variations alone are called as extension or contraction of demand represented by movement along the same demand curve. Such movement along the same demand curve is shown in Figure.

Price declines from OP1 to OP2 and demand goes up from OM1 to OM2. Here the demand for the good is said to have extended or expanded. This is represented by movement from point A to point B along the demand curve. On the contrary, if price rises from OP2 to OP1 demand falls from OM2 to OM1. Here the demand for the good is said to have contracted. This is represented by movement from point B to point A along the demand curve D1D1. Shifts in demand curve take place on account of determinants other than price such as changes in income, fashion, tastes, etc.

The ceteris paribus assumption is relaxed; other factors than price influence demand and the impact of these factors on demand is described as changes in demand or shifts in demand, showing increase or decrease in demand. This kind of change is shown in Figure.

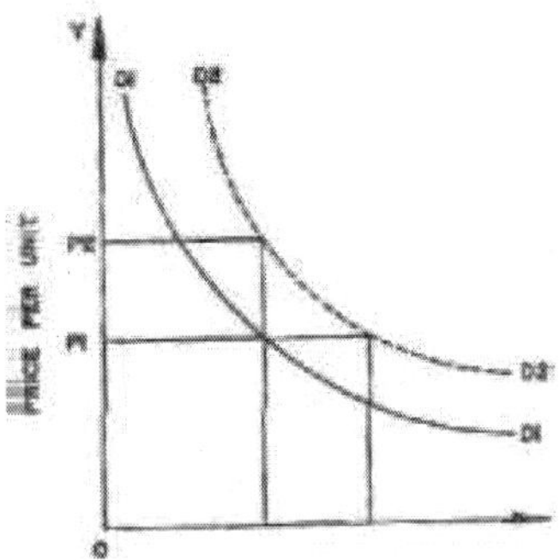

The quantity demanded at OP1 is OM1. If, as a result of increase in income, more of the product is demanded, say OM2 at the same price OP1. Note that OM2 is due to the new demand curve D2D2. This is a case of shift in demand. Due to fall in income, less of the good may be demanded at the same price and this will be a case of decrease in demand. Thus increase or decrease in demand with shifts in demand curves upward or downward are different from extension or contraction of demand. Causes of changes in demand may be due to:

- Changes in the consumer's income.
- Changes in the tastes of the consumer.
- Changes in the prices of related goods (substitutes and complements).
- Changes in exogenous factors like fashion, social structure, etc.

WHY THE DEMAND CURVE SLOPES DOWNWARD OR REASONS FOR THE LAW OF DEMAND

Truly, the demand curve slopes left downward to right, throughout its length although the slope may be much steeper in some parts. It means, demand increases with the fall in price and contracts with an increase in price. There are several reasons responsible for the inverse price demand relationship which has been explained as under:

Law of Diminishing Marginal Utility

The law of demand is based on the law of diminishing marginal utility which states that as the consumer purchases more and more units of a commodity, the utility derived from each successive unit goes on decreasing. It means as the price of the commodity falls, consumer purchases more of the commodity so that his marginal utility from the commodity falls to be equal to the reduced price and vice-versa.

Substitution Effect

Substitution effect also leads the demand curve to slope from left downward to right. As the price of a commodity falls, prices of its substitute goods remain the same, the consumer will buy more of that commodity. For instance, tea and coffee are the substitute goods. If the price of tea goes down, the consumers may substitute tea for coffee, although price of coffee remains the same. Therefore, with a fall in price, the demand will increase due to favourable substitution effect. On the other hand with the rise in price, the demand falls due to unfavourable substitution effect. This is nothing but the application of Law of Demand.

Income Effect

Another reason for the downward slope of demand curve is the income effect. As the price of the commodity falls, the real income of the consumer goes up. Real income is that income which is measured in terms of goods and services. For example, a consumer has Rs.20, he wants to buy oranges whose price is Rs.20 per dozen. It means the consumer can buy one dozen of oranges with his fixed income. Now, suppose, the price of the oranges falls to Rs.15 per dozen which leads to an increase in his real income by Rs.5. In this case, either the consumer will buy more quantity of oranges than before or he will buy some other commodity with his increased income.

New Consumers

When the price of commodity falls, many other consumers who were not consuming that commodity previously will start consuming the commodity. As a result, total market demand goes up. For example, if the price of radio set falls, even the poor man can buy the radio set. Consequently, the total demand for radios goes up.

Several Uses

Some commodities can be put to several uses which lead to downward slope of the demand curve. When the price of such commodities goes up they will be used for important purposes, so their demand will be limited. On the other hand, when the price falls, the commodity in question will extend its demand. For instance, when the price of coal increases, it will be used for important purposes but as the price falls its demand will increase and it will be used for many other uses.

Psychological Effects

When the price of a commodity falls, people favour to buy more which is natural and psychological. Therefore, the demand increases with the fall in prices. For example, when the price of silk falls, it is purchased for all the members of the family.

EXCEPTIONS TO THE LAW OF DEMAND

The Law of Demand will not hold good in certain peculiar cases in which more will be demanded at a higher price and less at a lower price. In these cases the demand curves will be exceptionally different, differing from the usual downward sloping shape of the demand curve. The exceptions are as follows:

- Conspicuous goods: Some consumers measure the utility of a commodity by its price i.e., if the commodity is expensive they think that it has got more utility. As such, they buy less of this commodity at low price and more of it at high price. Diamonds are often given as example of this case. Higher the price of diamonds, higher is the prestige value attached to them and hence higher is the demand for them.
- Giffen goods: Sir Robert Giffen, an economist, was surprised to find out that as the price of bread increased, the British workers purchased more bread and not less of it. This was something against the law of demand. Why did this happen? The reason given for this is that when the price of bread went up, it caused such a large decline in the purchasing power of the poor people that they were forced to cut down the consumption of meat and other more expensive foods. Since bread even when its price was higher than before was still the cheapest food article, people consumed more of it and not less when its price went up. Such goods which exhibit direct price-demand relationship are called 'Giffen goods'. Generally those goods which are considered inferior by the consumers and which occupy a substantial place in consumer's budget are called 'Giffen goods'. Examples of such goods are coarse grains like bajra, low quality of rice and wheat etc.
- Future expectations about prices: It has been observed that when the prices are rising, households expecting that the prices in the future will be still higher tend to buy larger quantities of the commodities.

For example, when there is wide-spread drought, people expect that prices of food grains would rise in future. They demand greater quantities of food grains as their price rise. But it is to be noted that here it is not the law of demand which is invalidated but there is a change in one of the factors which was held constant while deriving the law of demand, namely change in the price expectations of the people.

- The law has been derived assuming consumers to be rational and knowledgeable about market-conditions. However, at times consumers tend to be irrational and make impulsive purchases without any cool calculations about price and usefulness of the product and in such contexts the law of demand fails.
- Similarly, in practice, a household may demand larger quantity of a commodity even at a higher price because it may be ignorant of the ruling price of the commodity. Under such circumstances, the law will not remain valid.

The law of demand will also fail if there is any significant change in other factors on which demand of a commodity depends. If there is a change in income of the household, or in prices of the related commodities or in tastes and fashion etc. the inverse demand and price relation may not hold good.

TYPES OF DEMAND

There are three types of demand. They are

- Price Demand
- Income Demand and
- Cross Demand which are explained below:

Price Demand

It refers to the various quantities of the good which consumers will purchase at a given time and at certain hypothetical prices assuming that other conditions remain the same. We are generally concerned with price demand only. In the explanation of the law of demand given above, we dealt in detail with price demand only.

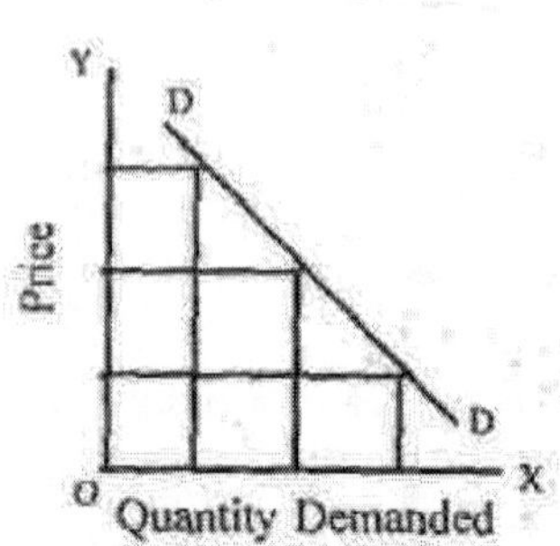

Income demand

Income demand refers to the various quantities of a commodity that a consumer would buy at a given time at various levels of income. Generally, when the income increases, demand increases and vice versa.

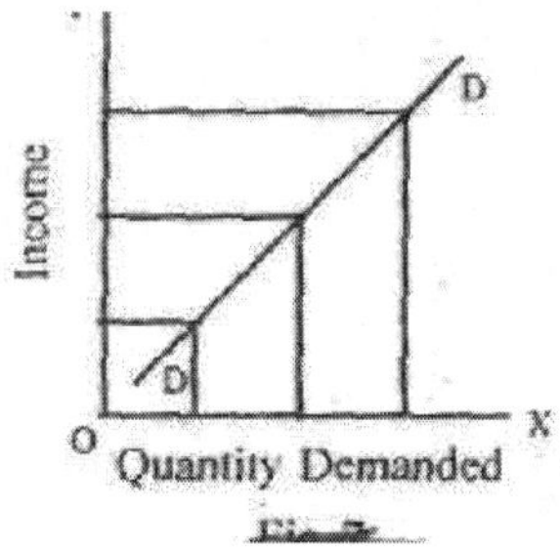

Cross Demand

When the demand of one commodity is related with the price of other commodity is called cross demand. The commodity may be substitute or complementary. Substitute goods are those goods which can be used in case of each other. For example, tea and coffee, Coca-cola and Pepsi. In such case demand and price are positively related. This means if the price of one increased then the demand for other also increases and vise versa. Complementary goods are those goods which are jointly used to satisfy a want. In other words, complementary goods are those which are incomplete without each other. These are things that go together, often used simultaneously. For example, pen and ink.

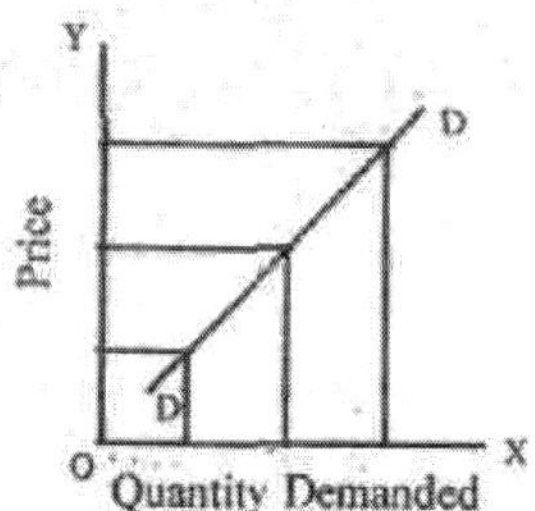

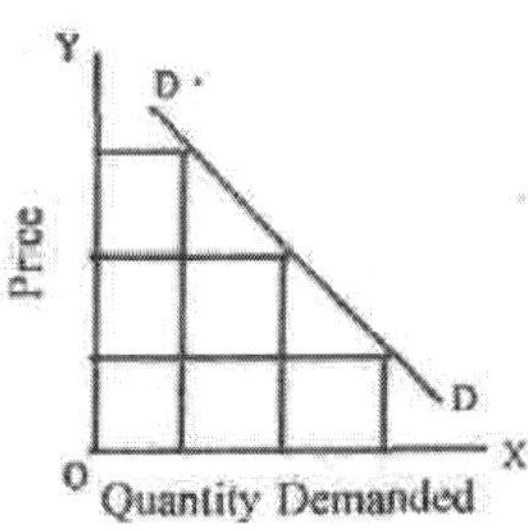

Tennis rackets and tennis balls, cameras and film, etc. In such goods the price and demand are negatively related. This means when the price of one commodity increases the demand for the other falls.

EXTENSION AND CONTRACTION OF DEMAND

The change in demand due to change in price only (when other factors remain constant) is called extension and contraction of demand. Increase in demand due to fall in price is called extension of demand. Decrease in demand due to rise in price is called contraction of demand. Extension and Contraction of demand results in movement on the same demand curve. It is shown in the following diagram.

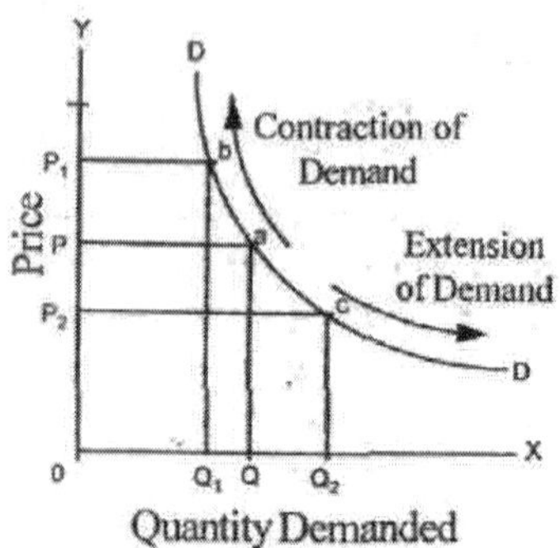

When price is OP, the quantity demanded is OQ. Suppose the price falls from OP2 to 0P2 demand will be increased to OQ2. This is a downward movement along the demand curve DD from a to c. This indicates extension of demand. When the price rises to OP1, the demand will be decreased to OQ2 this is an upward movement along the demand curve from a to b. This indicates contraction of demand.

SHIFT IN DEMAND

We have seen that the demand depends not only on price but also on other factors like income, population, taste and preference of consumers etc. The change in demand due to change in any of the factors other than the price is'called shift in demand. Change in any one of the factors shifts the entire demand curve. A change in demand will shift the demand curve either upwards or downwards. An upward shift in demand curve is called increase in demand. Downward shift in demand curve is called decrease in demand. Shift in demand is shown in the following diagram.

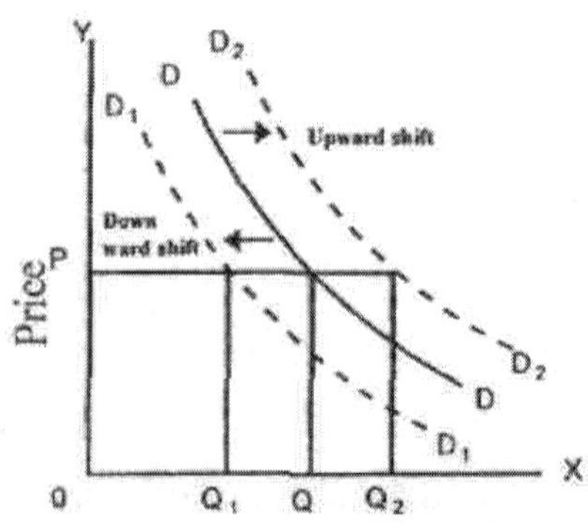

Fig. Quantity Demand

In the given figure DD is the original demand curve. When the demand increases, (e.g., due to increase in income) the curve will shift upwards to D2D2 without any increase in price. It is constant at OP. Similarly when the demand decreases, (e.g., due to decrease in income) the curve will shift downwards to D1D1. The price remains constant. Thus extension of demand is different from increase in demand. Likewise, contraction of demand doesn't mean decrease in demand. It should be noted that exclusion and contraction of demand is called "change in quantity demanded" and shift in demand is called "change in demand".

OTHER TYPES OF DEMAND

Composite demand

When several commodities are demanded for a joint purpose or to satisfy a particular want. It is a case of a joint demand. Milk , sugar and tea dust are jointly demanded to make tea. Similarly, we may demand paper, pen and ink for writing. Demand for such commodities in bunch is known as joint demand. Demand for land, labour, capital and organisation for producing commodity is also a case of joint demand.

Composite demand

The demand for a commodity which is for direct consumption, i.e.. Demand for ultimate object, is called direct demand, e.g food, cloth, etc. Direct demand is called autonomous demand. Here the demand is not linked with the purchase of some main products. When the commodity is demanded as a result of the demand for another commodity or service, it is known as the derived demand or induced demand. For example, demand for cement is derived from the demand for building construction; demand for tires is derived from the demand for cars or scooters, etc.

IMPORTANCE OF THE LAW OF DEMAND

The law of demand plays a crucial role in decision-making and forward planning of a business unit. The production planning in a firm mainly rests on accurate demand analysis. The law of demand has theoretical as well as practical advantages. These are as follows:

- Price determination: With the help of law of demand a monopolist fixes the price of his product. He is able to decide the most profitable quantity of output for him.
- Useful to government: The finance minister takes the help of this law to know the effects of his tax reforms and policies. Only those commodities which have relatively inelastic demand should be taxed.
- Useful to farmers: From the law of demand, the farmer knows how far a good or bad crop will affect the economic condition of the fanner. If there is a good crop and demand for it remains the same, price will

definitely go down. The farmer will not have much benefit from a good crop, but the rest of the society will be benefited.

- In the field of planning: The demand schedule has great importance in planning for individual commodities and industries. In such cases it is necessary to know whether a given change in the price of the commodity will have the desired effect on the demand for commodity within the country or abroad. This is known from a study of the nature of demand schedule for the commodity.

INDIFFERENCE CURVE ANALYSIS

In the last section we discussed marginal utility analysis of demand. A very popular alternative and more realistic method of explaining consumer's demand is the Indifference Curve Analysis. This approach to consumer behaviour is based on consumer preferences. It believes that human satisfaction being a psychological phenomenon cannot be measured quantitatively in monetary terms as was attempted in Marshall's utility analysis. In this approach it is felt that it is much easier and scientifically more sound to order preferences than to measure them in terms of money. The consumer preference approach, is, therefore an ordinal concept based on ordering of preferences compared with Marshall's approach of cardinality.

Assumptions Underlying Indifference Curve Approach:

- The consumer is rational and possesses full information about all the relevant aspects of economic environment in which he lives.
- The consumer is capable of ranking all conceivable combinations of goods according to the satisfaction they yield. Thus if he is given various combinations say A, B, C, D, E he can rank them as first preference, second preference and so on.
- If a consumer happens to prefer A to B, he can not tell quantitatively how much he prefers A to B.
- If the consumer prefers combination A to B, and B to C, then he must prefer combination A to C. In other words, he has consistent consumption pattern behaviour.
- If combination A has more commodities than combination B, then A must be preferred to B.

What are Indifference Curves

Ordinal analysis of demand is based on indifference curves. An indifference curve is a curve which represents all those combinations of goods which give same satisfaction to the consumer. Since all the combinations on an indifference curve give equal satisfaction to the consumer, the consumer is indifferent among them. In other words, since all the combinations provide same level of satisfaction the consumer prefers them equally and does not mind which combination he gets.

To understand indifference curves let us consider the example of a consumer who has one unit of food and 12 units of clothing. Now we ask the consumer how many units of clothing he is prepared to give up to get an additional unit of food, so that his level of satisfaction does not change. Suppose the consumer says that he is ready to give up 6 units of clothing to get an additional unit of food. We will have then two combinations of food and clothing giving equal satisfaction to consumer: Combination A has 1 unit of food and 12 units of clothing, combination B has 2 units of food and 6 units of clothing.

Similarly, by asking the consumer further how much of clothing he will be prepared to forgo for successive increments in his stock of food so that his level of satisfaction remains unaltered, we get various combinations as given below:

Table Indifference Schedule

Combination	Food	Clothing	MRS
A	1	12	
B	2	6	6
C	3	4	2
D	4	3	1

Now if we draw the above schedule we will get the following figure. In Figure 8, an indifference curve IC is drawn by plotting the various combinations of the indifference schedule. The quantity of food is measured on the X axis and the quantity of clothing on the Y axis. As in indifference schedule, combinations lying on an indifference curve will give the consumer same level of satisfaction.

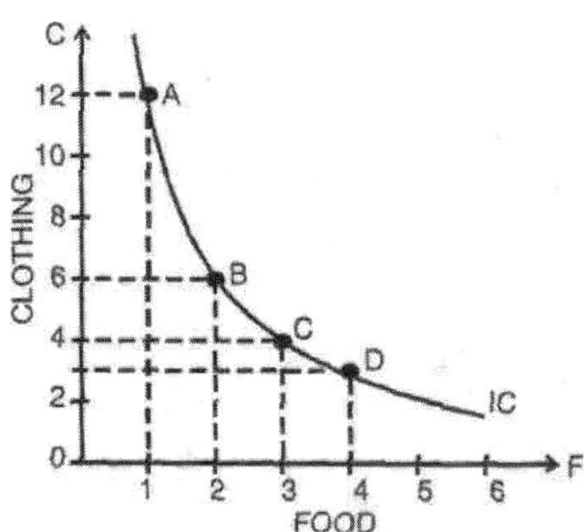

Fig. A Consumer's Indifference Curve

Indifference Map

A set of indifference curves is called indifference map. An indifference map depicts complete picture of consumer's tastes and preferences. In Figure 9, an indifference map of a consumer is shown which consists of three indifference curves. We have taken good X on X-axis and good Y on Y-axis. It should be noted that while the consumer is indifferent among the combinations lying on the same indifference curve, he certainly prefers the combinations on the higher indifference curve to the combinations lying on a lower indifference curve because a higher indifference curve signifies a higher level of .satisfaction. Thus while all combinations of IC, give same satisfaction, all combinations lying on IC2 give greater satisfaction than those lying on IC1

Marginal Rate of Substitution

Marginal Rate of Substitution (MRS) is the rate at which the consumer is prepared to exchange goods X and Y Consider Table-2. In the beginning the consumer is consuming 1 unit of food and 12 units of clothing. Subsequently, he gives up 6 units of clothing to get an extra unit of food, his level of satisfaction remaining the same.

The MRS here is 6. Like wise which he moves from B to C and from C to D in his indifference schedule, the MRS are 2 and 1 respectively. Thus, we can define MRS of X for Y as the amount of Y whose loss can just be compensated by a unit gain of X in such a manner that the level of satisfaction remains the same. We notice that MRS is falling i.e., as the consumer has more and more units of food, he is prepared to give up less and less units of cloths. There are two reasons for this.

- The want for a particular good is satiable so that when a consumer has its more quantity, his intensity of want for it decreases. Thus, when consumer in our example, has more units of food, his intensity of desire for additional units of food decreases.
- Most of the goods are imperfect substitutes of one another. If, they could substitute one another perfectly. MRS would remain constant.

Properties of Indifference Curves

The following are the main characteristics or properties of indifference curves :

Indifference curves slope downward to the right

This property implies that when the amount of one good in combination is increased, the amount of the other good is reduced. This is essential if the level of satisfaction is to remain the same on an indifference curve.

Indifference curves are always convex to the origin

It has been observed that as more and more of one commodity (X) is substituted for another (Y), the consumer is willing to part with less and less of the commodity being substituted (i.e. Y). This is called diminishing marginal rate of substitution. Thus in our example of food and clothing, as a consumer has more and more units of food, he is prepared to forego less and less units of clothing. This happens mainly because want for a particular good is satiable and as a person has more and more of a good, his intensity of want for that good goes on diminishing. This diminishing marginal rate of substitution gives convex shape to the indifference curves. However, there are two extreme situations. When two goods are perfect substitutes of each other, the indifference curve is a straight line on which MRS is constant. And when two goods are perfect complementary goods, the indifference curve will consist of two straight line with a right angle bent which is convex to the origin or in other words, it will be L shaped.

Indifference curves can never intersect each other

No two indifference curves will intersect each other although it is not necessary that they are parallel to each other. In case of intersection the relationship becomes logically absurd because it would show that higher and lower levels are equal which is not possible. This property will be clear from the following Figure .

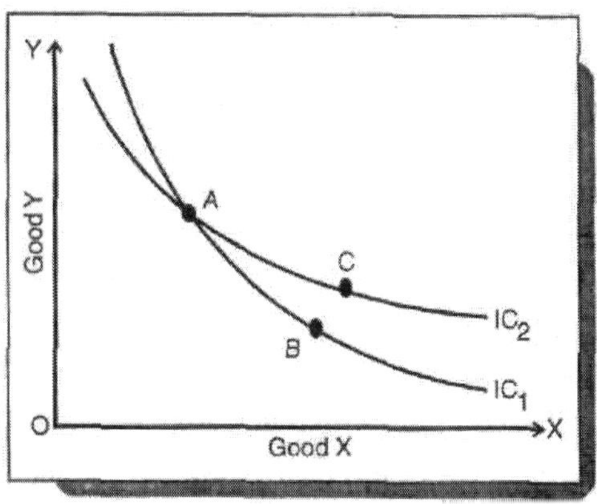

Fig. 13 : Intersecting Indifference Curves

In figure 10 IC1, and IC2 intersect at A. Since A and B lie on IC1, they give same satisfaction to the consumer. Similarly since A and C lie on IC2, they give same satisfaction to the consumer. This implies that combination B and C are equal in terms of satisfaction.

But a glance will show that this is an absurd conclusion because certainly combination C is better than combination B because it contains more units of commodities X and Y. Thus we see that no two indifference curves can touch or cut each other.

A higher indifference curve represents a higher level of satisfaction than the lower indifference curve

This is because combinations lying on a higher indifference curve contain mere of either one or both goods and more goods are preferred to less of them.

Budget line

A higher indifference curve shows a higher level of satisfaction than a lower one. Therefore, a consumer in his attempt to maximise satisfaction will try to reach the highest possible indifference curve. But in his pursuit of buying more and more goods and thus obtaining more and more satisfaction he has to work under two constraints : firstly, he has to pay the prices for the goods and, secondly, he has a limited money income with which to purchase the goods. These constraints are explained by budget line or price line. In simple words a budget line shows all those combinations of two goods which the consumer can buy spending his given money income on the two goods at their given prices. All those combinations which are within the reach of the consumer will lie on the budget line.

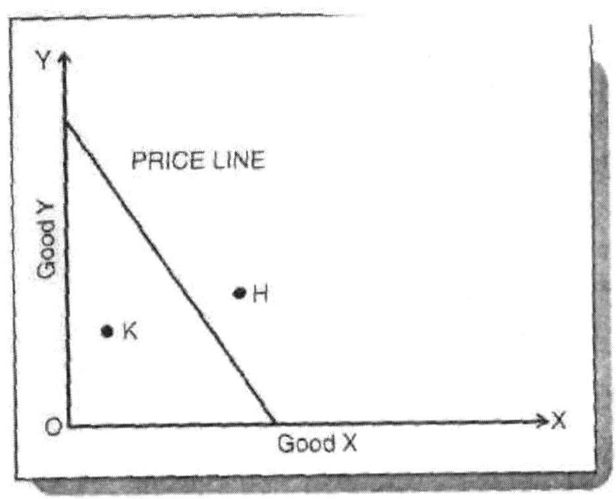

It should be noted that any point outside the given price line, like H, will be beyond the reach of the consumer and any combination lying within the line, like K, shows under spending by the consumer.

CONSUMER'S EQUILIBRIUM

Having explained indifference curves and budget line, we are in a position to explain how a consumer reaches equilibrium position. A consumer is in equilibrium when he is deriving maximum possible satisfaction from the goods and is in no position to rearrange his purchases of goods. We assume that:

- the consumer has a given indifference map which shows his scale of preferences for various combinations of two goods X and Y.
- he has a fixed money income which he has to spend wholly on goods X and Y.
- prices of goods X and Y are given and are fixed for him.

To show which combination of two goods X and Y the consumer will buy to be in equilibrium we bring his indifference map and budget line together. We know by now, that the indifference map depicts the consumer's preference scale between various combinations of two goods and the budget line shows various combinations which he can afford to buy with his given money income and prices of the two goods.

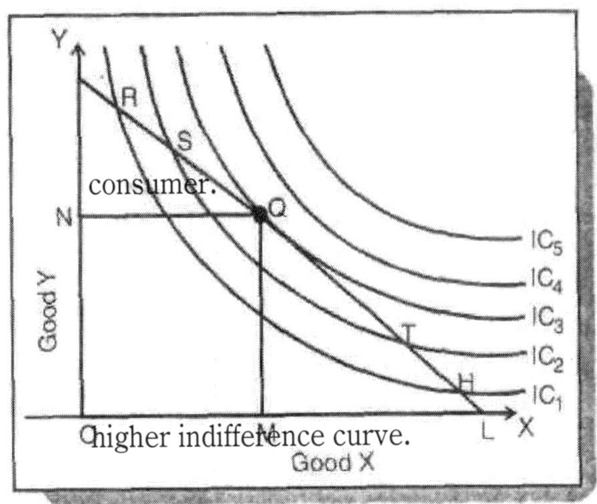

Fig. 15 : Consumer's Equilibrium

Consider Figure 12, in which IC1, IC2, IC3, IC4 and IC5 are shown together with budget line PL for good X and good Y. Every combination on budget line PL costs the same. Thus combinations R, S, Q, T and H cost the same to the

The consumer's aim is to maximize his satisfaction and for this he will try to reach highest indifference curve. But since there is a budget constraint he will be forced to remain on the given budget line, that is he will have to choose any combinations from among only those which lie on the given price line. Which combination will he choose? Suppose he chooses R, but we see that R lies on a lower indifference curve IC1, when he can very well afford S, Q or T lying on

Similar is the case for other combinations on IC1, like H. Again, suppose he chooses combination S (or T) lying on IC2. But here again we see that the consumer can still reach a higher level of satisfaction remaining within his budget constraints i.e., he can afford to have combination Q lying on IC3 because it lies on his budget line. Now what if he chooses combination Q? We find that this is the best choice because this combination lies not only on his budget line but also puts him on highest possible indifference curve i.e., IC3 The consumer can very well wish to reach IC4 or IC5, but these indifference curves are beyond his reach given his money income. Thus the consumer will be at equilibrium at point Q on IC3. What do we notice at point Q? We notice that at this point, his budget line PL is tangent to the indifference curve IC3. In this equilibrium position (at Q), the consumer will buy OM of X and ON of Y At the tangency point Q, the slopes of the price line PL and indifference curve IC3 are equal. The slope of the indifference curve shows the marginal rate of substitution of X for Y

which is equal to $\frac{MU_2}{MU_1}$

prices of two goods i.e.

At equilibrium point Q

$$MRS_{xy} = \frac{M}{M}$$

Thus, we can say that the consumer is in equilibrium position when price line is tangent to the indifference curve or when the marginal rate of substitution of goods X and Y is equal to the ratio between the prices of the two goods.

ELASTICITY OF DEMAND

The concept of price-elasticity of demand was first of all introduced in economics by Dr. Marshall. In simple words, price elasticity of demand is the ratio of percentage change in quantity demanded to the percentage change in price. In other words, price elasticity of demand is a measure of the relative change in quantity purchased of a good in response to a relative change in its price. It is, thus a rate at which the demand changes to the given change in prices. So, it means the rate or the degree of response in demand to the change in price. Thus, the co-efficient of price-elasticity of demand can be expressed as under:

$$E_d = \frac{\text{Proportionate change in Quantity Demanded}}{\text{Proportionate change in price}}$$

DEFINITIONS OF PRICE ELASTICITY OF DEMAND

The concept of price elasticity of demand has been defined by different economists as under :

- According to Alfred Marshall: “Elasticity of demand may be defined as the percentage change in quantity demanded to the percentage change in price.”
- According to A.K. Cairncross : “The elasticity of demand for a commodity is the rate at which quantity bought changes as the price changes.”

- According to J.M. Keynes : "The elasticity of demand is a measure of the relative change in quantity to a relative change in price."
- According to Kenneth Boulding : "Elasticity of demand measures the responsiveness of demand to changes in price."

DEGREES OF PRICE ELASTICITY

Different commodities have different price elasticities. Some commodities have more elastic demand while others have relative elastic demand. Basically, the price elasticity of demand ranges from zero to infinity. It can be equal to zero, less than one, greater than one and equal to unity.

According to Dr. Marshall : "The elasticity or reponsiveness of demand in a market is great or small according as the amount demanded increases much or little for a given fall in price and diminishes much or little for a given rise in price." However, some particular values of elasticity of demand have been explained as under ; Perfectly Elastic Demand.

Perfectly elastic demand is said to h appen when a little change in price leads to an infinite change in quantity demanded. A small rise in price on the part of the seller reduces the demand to zero. In such a case the shape of the demand curve will be horizontal straight line as shown in figure

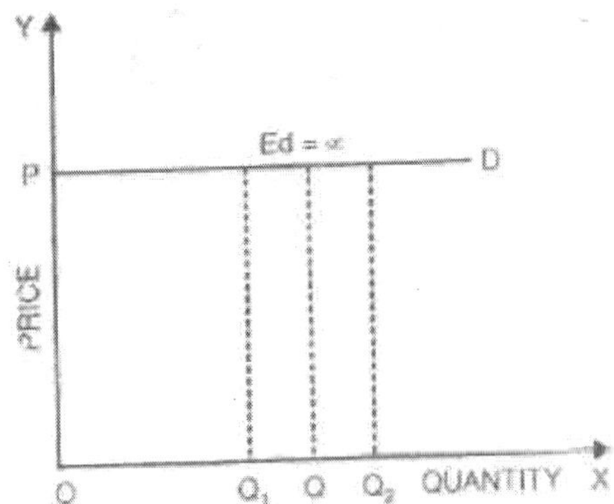

The figure 13 shows that at the ruling price OP, the demand is infinite. A slight rise in price will contract the demand to zero. A slight fall in price will attract more consumers but the elasticiy of demand will remain infinite. But in real world, the cases of perfectly elastic demand are exceedingly rare and are not of any practical interest.

Perfectly inelastic Demand

Perfectly inelastic demand is opposite to perfectly elastic demand. Under the perfectly inelastic demand, irrespective of any rise or fall in price of a commodity, the quantity demanded remains the same. The elasticity of demand in this case will be equal to zero.In diagram 14, DD shows the perfectly inelastic demand. At price OP, the quantity demanded is OQ. Now, the price falls to OP, from OP1, demand remains the same. Similarly, if the price rises to OP2 the demand still remains the same. But just as we do not see the example of perfectly elastic demand in the real world, in the same fashion it is diffcult to come across the cases of perfectly inelastic demand because even the demand for bare essentials of life does show some degree of responsiveness to change in price.

Fig. 1

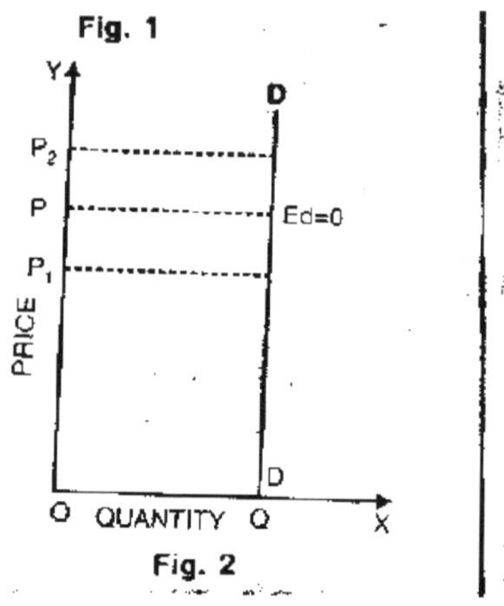

Fig. 2

Unitary Elastic Demand

The demand is said to be unitary elastic when a given proportionate change in the price level brings about an equal proportionate change in quantity demanded, The numerical value of unitary elastic demand is exactly one i.e., ed = 1. Marshall calls it unit elastic. In figure 15, DD demand curve represents unitary elastic demand. This demand curve is called rectangular hyperbola. When price is OP, the quantity demanded is OQ1. Now price falls to OP1, the quantity demanded increases to OQ1. The shaded area in the fig. equal in terms of price and quantity demanded denotes that in all cases price elasticity of demand is equal to one.

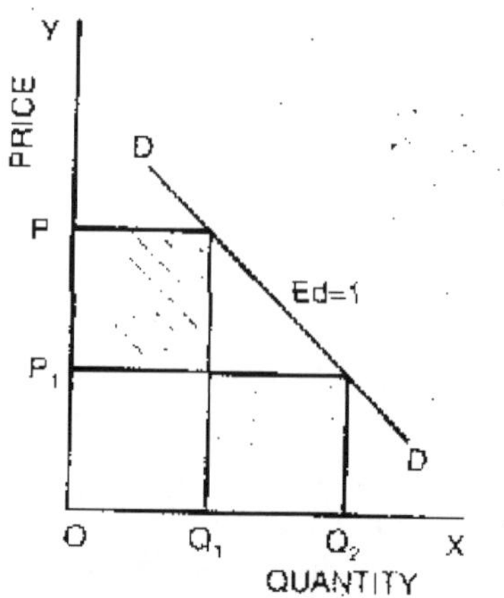

Relatively Elastic Demand

Relatively elastic demand refers to a situation in which a small change in price leads to a big change in quantity demanded. In such a case elasticity of demand is said to be more than one. This has been shown in figure 16. In fig.16, DD is the demand curve which indicates that when price is OP the quantity demanded is OQ1, Now the price falls from OP to OP1, the quantity demanded increases from OQ1 to OQ2 i.e. quantity demanded changes more than the change in price.

Relatively Inelastic Demand

Under the relatively inelastic demand a given percentage change in price produces a relatively less percentage change in quantity demanded. In such a case elasticity of demand is said to be less than one as shown in figure 17. All the five degrees of elasticity of demand have been shown in figure 18. On OX axis, quantity demanded and on OY axis price is given. It shows:

- AB — Perfectly Inelastic Demand
- CD — Perfectly Elastic Demand
- EQ — Less Than Unitary Elastic Demand
- EF — Greater Than Unitary Elastic Demand
- MN — Unitary Elastic Demand

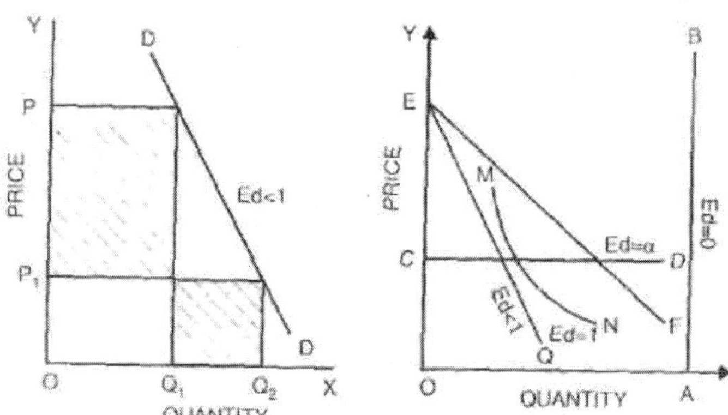

FACTORS DETERMINING PRICE ELASTICITY OF DEMAND

The factors that determine elasticity of demand are numberless. But the most important among them are the nature, uses and prices of related goods and the level of income. They are stated below:

Nature of the commodity

Generally, all commodities can be dividend into three categories i.e.

- Necessaries of Life. For necessaries of life the demand is inelastic because people buy the required amount of goods whatever their

price. For example, necessaries such as rice, salt, cloth are purchased whether they are dear or cheap.
- Conventional Necessaries. The demand for conventional necessaries is less elastic or inelastic. People are accustomed to the use of goods like intoxicants which they purchase at any price. For example, drunkards consider opium and wine almost as a necessity as food and water. Therefore, they buy the same amount even when their prices are higher and highest.
- Luxury Commodities. The demand for luxury is usually elastic as people buy more of them at a lower price and less at a higher price. For example, the demand of luxuries like silk, perfumes and ornaments increases at a lower price and diminishes at a higher price. Here, we must keep in mind that luxury is a relative term, which varies from person to person, place to place and from time to time. For example, what is a luxury to a poor man is a necessity to the rich.
- The luxury of the past may become a necessity of today. Similarly a commodity which is a necessity to one class may be a luxury to another. Hence, the elasticity of demand in such cases should have to be carefully expressed.

Substitutes

Demand is elastic for those goods which have substitutes and inelastic for those goods which have no substitutes. The availability of substitutes, thus, determines the elasticity of demand. For instance, tea and coffee are substitutes. The change in the price of tea affects the demand for coffee. Hence, the demand for coffee and tea is elastic.

Number of Uses

Elasticity of demand for any commodity depends on its number of uses. Demand is elastic; if a commodity has more uses and inelastic if it has only one use. As coal has multiple uses, if its price falls it will be demanded more for cooking, heating, industrial purposes etc. But if its price rises, minimum will be demanded for every purpose.

Postponement

Demand is more elastic for goods the use of which can be postponed. For example, if the price of silk rises, its consumption can be postponed. The demand for silk is, therefore, elastic.

Demand is inelastic for those goods the use of which is urgent and, therefore, cannot be postponed. The use of medicines cannot be put off. Hence, the demand for medicines is inelastic.

Raw Materials and Finished Goods

The demand for raw materials is inelastic but the demand for finished goods is elastic. For instance, raw cotton has inelastic demand but cloth has elastic demand. In the same way, petrol has inelastic demand but car itself has only elastic demand.

Price Level

The demand is elastic for moderate prices but inelastic for lower and higher prices. The rich and the poor do not bother about the prices of the goods that they buy.

For example, rich buy Benaras silk and diamonds etc. at any price. But the poor buy coarse rice, cloth etc. whatever their prices are.

Income Level

The demand is inelastic for higher and lower income groups and elastic for middle income groups. The rich people with their higher income do not bother about the price. They may continue to buy the same amount whatever the price. The poor people with lower incomes buy always only the minimum requirements and, therefore, they are induced neither to buy more at a lower price nor less at a higher price. The middle income group is sensitive to the change in price. Thus, they buy more at a lower price and less at higher price.

Habits

If consumers are habituated of some commodities, the demand for such commodities will be usually inelastic. It is because that the consumer will use them even their prices go up. For example, a smoker does not smoke less when the price of cigarette goes up.

Nature of Expenditure

The elasticity of demand for a commodity also depends as to how much part of the income is spent on that particular commodity. The demand for such commodities where a small part of income is spent is generally highly inelastic i.e. newspaper, boot-polish etc. On the other hand, the demand of such commodities where a significant part of income is spent, elasticity of demand is very elastic.

Distribution of Income

If the income is uniformly distributed in the society, a small change in price will affect the demand of the whole society and the demand will be elastic. In case of unequal distribution of income and wealth, a change in price will hardly influence the poor section of the society and the demand will be relatively inelastic.

Influence of Diminishing Marginal Utility

We know that utility falls when we consume more and more units but not in a uniform way. In case utility falls rapidly, it means that the consumer has no other near substitutes. As a result, demand is inelastic. Conversely, if the utility falls slowly, demand for such commodity would be elastic and raises much for a fall in price.

MEASUREMENT OF PRICE ELASTICITY OF DEMAND

There are five methods to measure the price elasticity of demand.

- Total Expenditure Method.
- Proportionate Method.
- Point Elasticity of Demand.
- Arc Elasticity of Demand.
- Revenue Method.

Total Expenditure Method

Dr. Marshall has evolved the total expenditure method to measure the price elasticity of demand. According to this method, elasticity of demand can be measured by considering the change in price and the subsequent change in the total quantity of goods purchased and the total amount of money spend on it.

Total Outlay = Price x Quantity Demanded.

There are three possibilities:

- If with a fall in price (demand increases) the total expenditure increases or with a rise in price (demand falls) the total expenditure falls, in that case the elasticity of demand is greater than one i.e.
- If with a rise or fall in the price (demand falls or rises respectively), the total expenditure remains the same, the demand will be unitary elastic i.e..
- with a fall in price (Demand rises), the total expenditure also falls, and with a rise in price (Demand falls) the total expenditure also rises, the demand is said to be less elastic or elasticity of demand is less than one i.e..

In the above Table 3, we find three possibilities:

- More Elastic Demand. When price is Rs. 10 the quantity demanded is 1 unit and total expenditure is 10. Now price falls from Rs. 10 to Rs. 6, the quantity demanded increases from 1 to 5 units and correspondingly the total expenditure increases from Rs. 10 to Rs. 30. Thus it is clear that with the fall in price, the total expenditure increases and viceversa. So elasticity of demand is greater than one or Ed > 1.
- Unitary Elastic Demand. If price is Rs. 6, demand is 5 units so the total outlay is Rs. 30. Now price falls to Rs. 5, the demand increases

to 6 units but the total expenditure remains the same i.e., Rs. 30. Thus it is clear that with the rise or fall in price, the total expenditure remains the same. The elasticity of demand in this case is equal to one or Ed = 1.

- Less Elastic Demand. If price is Rs. 5, demand is 6 and total outlay is Rs. 30. Now price falls from Rs. 5 to Re. 1. The demand increases from 6 units to 10 units and hence the total expenditure falls from Rs. 30 to Rs. 10. Thus it is clear that with the fall in price, the total expenditure also falls and vice-versa. In this case, the elasticity of demand is less than one or Ed<l.

Table Representation: The method of total expenditure has been explained with the help of Table .

Table

Price (P)	Quantity Demanded (Q)	Total Outlay	Elasticity of demand (Ed)
10	1	.10	
9	2	18	
8	3	24	Ed > 1
7	4	28	
6	5	.30	Ed = 1
5	6	30	
4	7		
3	8	.28	
2	9	24	
1	10	18	Ed < 1
		10	

Diagrammatic Representation

Measurement of price elasticity through total expenditure method can be shown with the help of fig. 19 In the figure 19 total expenditure has been shown on X-axis and price on Y-axis. Line TT' is the total expenditure line. When price of the commodity falls from OP to OP1 total expenditure increases from OM1 to OM2. The elasticity of demand is greater than one as is shown in TB portion of the figure. Now, suppose that the price of the commodity decreases from OP1 to OP3 the total expenditure falls from OM2 to OM. This is shown in T'C part of the figure which represents the less than unity elasticity of demand. In the same way, BC part of the figure represents the unit elasticity of demand. Thus it is clear that the changes in total expenditure due to changes in price also affect the elasticity of demand.

Proportionate Method

This method is also associated with the name of Dr. Marshall. According to this method, "price elasticity of demand is the ratio of percentage change in the amount demanded to the percentage change in price of the commodity." It is also known as the Percentage Method, Flux Method, Ratio Method, and Arithmetic Method.

$$E_d = \frac{\Pr oportionate\ change\ in\ Quantity\ Demanded}{\Pr oportionate\ change\ in\ price}$$

Arc Elasticity of Demand

- According to Prof. Baumol: "Arc elasticity is a measure of the average responsiveness to price change exhibited by a demand curve over some finite stretch of the curve".
- According to Watson: "Arc elasticity is the elasticity at the mid-point of an are of a demand curve."
- According to Leftwitch : "When elasticity is computed between two separate points on a demand curve, the concept is called Are elasticity."

This method of measuring elasticity of demand is also known as

"Average Elasticity". In this method, we use $\frac{P_1 + P_2}{2}$ rather than P Thus, we apply $\frac{Q_1 + Q_2}{2}$ rather than q The formula for Arc elasticity of demand is as follows:

Arc Elasticity of Demand (EA):

$$= \frac{\dfrac{\text{Change in demand}}{\text{Original demand + New demand}}}{\dfrac{\text{Change in price}}{\text{Original Price + New Price}}}$$

Are elasticity of demand in notational farm can be express where

Q1 = Original quantity demanded

Q2 = New quantity demanded

P1 = Original price

P2 = New price

In figure 20 quantity is measured on X-axis while price on Y- axis. DD is the demand curve. Now if we want to measure the arc elasticity between A and B on the demand curve DD, we will have to take the average of prices OPl and OP2 as well as of quantities; Q1 and Q2.

$$E_A = \frac{[P+(P+\Delta P)]}{[Q+(Q+\Delta Q)]} \times \frac{\Delta Q}{\Delta P}$$

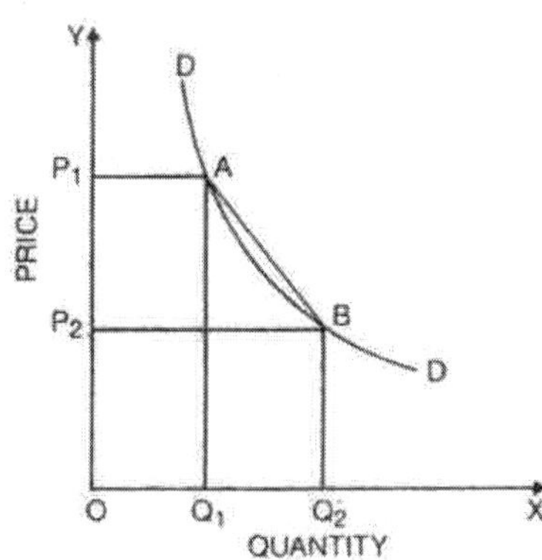

Revenue Method

Mrs.; Joan Robinson has given this method. She says that elasticity of demand can be measured with the help of average revenue and marginal revenue. Therefore, a sale proceeds that a firm obtains by selling its products is called its revenue. However, when total revenue is divided by the number of units sold, we get average revenue. On the contrary, when addition is made to the total revenue by the sale of one more unit of the commodity is called marginal revenue. Therefore, the formula to measure elasticity of demand can be written as,

$$E_d = \frac{A}{A-M}$$

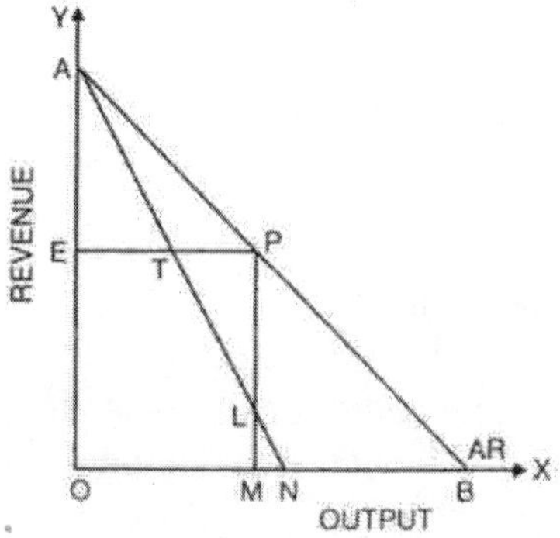

where Ed represents elasticity of demand, A = average revenue and M = marginal revenue. This method can be explained with the help of diagram 21. In this diagram 21 revenue has been shown on OY-axis while quantity of goods on OXaxis. AB is the average revenue or demand curve and AN is the marginal revenue curve. At point P on demand curve, elasticity of demand is calculated with the formula,

$$E_p = \frac{Lower Portion}{Upper Portion} or \frac{PB}{PA}$$

We can see in the figure that DAEP and DPMB are similar, thus ratio of their sides is also equal.

$$E_p = \frac{PB}{PA} = \frac{PM}{AE}$$

and; DAET and DTPL are congruent triangles, therefore PL = AE. Putting PL in place of AE in the above equation, we shall get

$$E_p = \frac{PM}{PL}$$

(Because PL = PM—LM)

$$E_p = \frac{PM}{PM - LM}$$

(Where PM = AR and LM = MR)

$$\text{.There fore, } E_p = \frac{PM}{PM - LM} = \frac{AR}{AR - MR} or \frac{A}{A - M}$$

In this way, if value of Ep is one it means that price elasticity of demand is unitary. Similarly, if it is more than one, price elasticity of demand is greater than one and if it is less than one, price elasticity of demand is less than unity.

INCOME ELASTICITY OF DEMAND

According to Stonier and Hague:

- "Income elasticity of demand shows the way in which a consumer's purchase of any good changes as a result of change in his income."

It shows the responsiveness of a consumer's purchase of a particular commodity to a change in his income. Income elasticity of demand means the ratio of percentage change in the quantity demanded to the percentage change in income. In brief income elasticity.

$$I_e = \frac{\textit{proportionate change in quantity purchased}}{\textit{proportionate change in income}}$$

$$I_e = \frac{\textit{percentage change in demand}}{\textit{percentage change in income}}$$

Degrees of Income Elasticity of Demand

Positive income elasticity of Demand

Positive income elasticity of demand is said to occur when with the increase in the income of the consumer, his demand for goods and services also increases and vice-versa. Income elasticity of demand is positive in case of normal goods. In fig. 22, quantity of commodity T has been measured on X-axis and income of the consumer on Y-axis. DD is the positive income elasticity of demand curve. It slopes upward from left to right indicating that increase in income is accompanied by increase in demand of goods and services and vice-versa.

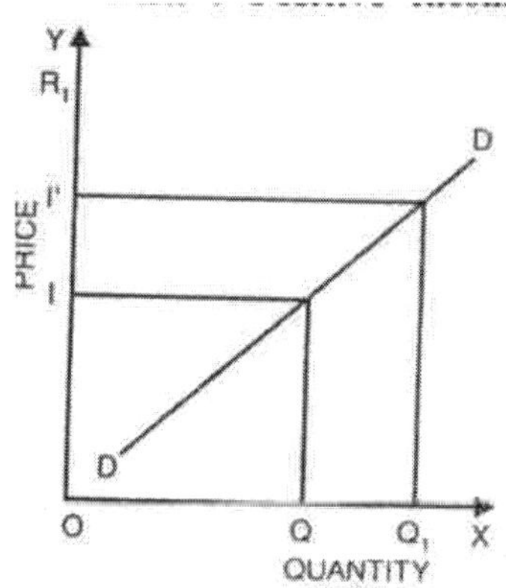

Income Elasticity is Unity. The change in demand is proportionate to the change in income. For example

$$\text{Income Elasticity} = 1 \text{ when } \frac{\textit{25\% change in demand}}{\textit{25\% change in income}}$$

Income Elasticity Greater than One. When the change in demand is more than proportionate change in income, income elasticity of demand is greater than one or unity. For example,

$$\text{Income Elasticity} > 1 \text{ when } \frac{\textit{15\% change in demand}}{\textit{10\% change in income}} = 1.5$$

Income Elasticity Less than One. If change in demand is less than proportionate change in income, income elasticity of demand is less than one or unity. For example.

$$\text{Income Elasticity} < 1 \text{ when } \frac{20\%\ \text{change in demand}}{40\%\ \text{change in income}} = 0.5$$

Negative Income Elasticity of Demand

Negative income elasticity of demand is said to occur when increase in the income of the consumers is accompanied by fall in demand of goods and services and vice-versa. It is the case of giffen goods. In fig. 23 when income of the consumer is 01, demand for goods and services is OX. Now as the income I1 increases to I1 quantity demanded falls o to OX1. Again as the income increases to I2, quantity demanded falls to OX2. DD is the negative income elasticity of demand curve.

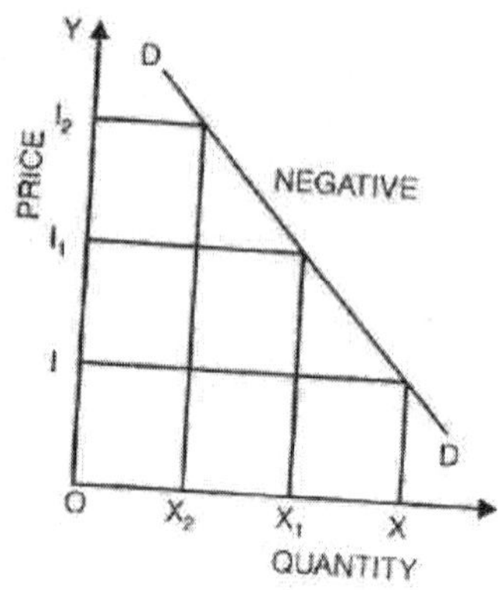

Zero Income Elasticity of Demand

Zero income elasticity of demand is said to exist when increase or decrease in income has no impact on the demand of goods and services. In fig. 24 initially when income is OI, quantity demanded is OD. Now, income increases to OI2 demand Remains constant i.e. OD. Even when income reduces to 01 , quantity demanded remains OD Generally, as income increases demand for goods increases.

But in some cases, demand may not change to change in income or demand may diminish for an increase in income. The former case represents zero income elasticity. Income elasticity is zero if a change in income fails to produce any change in demand. Income elasticity is negative, if an increase in income leads to a reduction of demand. This happens only in the case of inferior goods. But in all other cases it is positive.

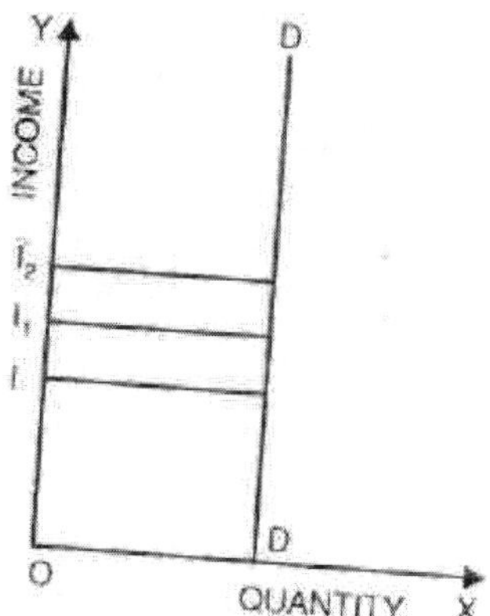

In short income elasticity is greater than one for luxuries but less than one for necessaries.

CROSS ELASTICITY OF DEMAND

It is the ratio of proportionate change in the quantity demanded of Y to a given proportionate change in the price of the related commodity X. It is a measure of relative change in the quantity demanded of a commodity due to a change in the price of its substitute complement. It can be expressed as

$$C_e = \frac{\textit{proportionate change in the quantity demanded of Y}}{\textit{proportionate change in the price of X}}$$

Cross elasticity may be infinite or zero. It is infinite if the slightest change in the price of X causes a substantial change in the quantity demanded of Y. It is always the case with goods which have perfect substitutes for one another. Cross elasticity is zero, if a change in the price of one commodity will not affect the quantity demanded of the other. In the case of goods which are not related to each other, cross elasticity of demand is zero.

Types of Cross Elasticity of Demand

Positive

When goods are substitute of each other than cross elasticity of demanded is positive. In other words, when an increase in the price of Y leads to an increase in the demand of X. For instance with the increase in price of a tea, demand of coffee will increase.

In fig 25 Quantity has been measured on OX axis and price on OY axis. At price OP of Y commodity, demand of X – commodity is OM. Now as price Of Y commodity increase to OP1 demand of X-commodity increases to OM1. Thus, cross, elasticity of demand is positive.

Negative

In case of complementary goods, cross elasticity of demand is negative. A proportionate increase in price of one commodity leads to a proportionate fall in the demand, of .another commodity because both are demanded jointly In fig. 26 quantity has been measured on OX-axis while price has been measured on OY-axis. When the price of commodity increases from OP to OP1 quantity demanded falls from OM to OM1 Thus, cross elasticity of demand is negative.

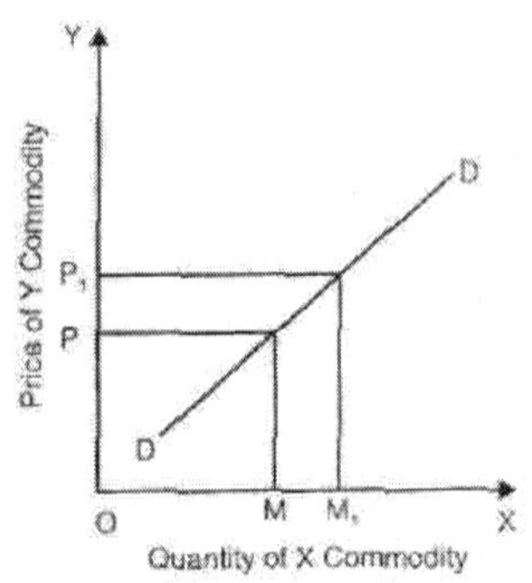

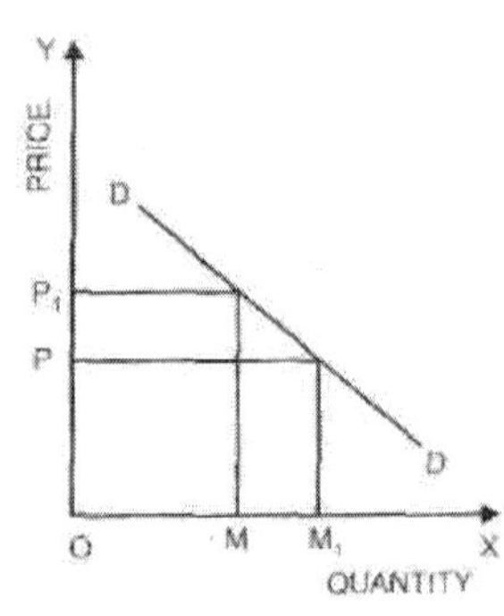

Zero

Cross elasticity of demand is zero when two goods are related to each other. For instance, increase in price of car does not affect the demand of cloth. Thus, cross elasticity of demand is zero. It has been shown in fig. 27 Therefore, it can be concluded that cross elasticity depends upon Substitutability is perfect, cross elasticity is infinite; if on the other hand, substitutability does not exist, cross elasticity is zero. In the case of complementary goods like jointly demanded goods cross elasticity is negative. A rise in the price of one commodity X will mean not only decrease in the quantity of X but also decrease in the quantity demanded of Y because both are demanded together.

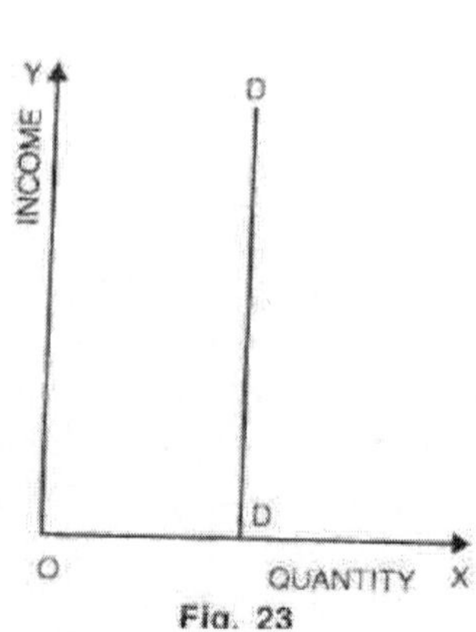

Fig. 23

Limitations of Cross Elasticity of Demand

The cross elasticity of demand is a useful measure of price-demand relationships between commodities. But this concept has following two limitations.

- Negative Cross Elasticity does not always mean complementarily.
- Cross Elasticity of Demand is only a one-way Relationship.

IMPORTANCE OF ELASTICITY OF DEMAND

The concept of elasticity of demand is of great importance in practical life. Its main points are given as under:

- Useful for Business: It enables the business in general and the monopolists in particular to fix the price. Studying the nature of demand the monopolist fixes higher prices for those goods which have inelastic demand and lower prices for goods which have elastic demand. In this way, this helps him to maximise his profit.
- Fixation of Prices: It is very useful to fix the price of jointly supplied goods. In the case of joint products like paddy and straw, the cost of production of each is not known. The price of each is then fixed by its elastic and inelastic demand.
- Helpful to Finance Minister: It helps the Finance Minister to levy tax on goods. After levying taxes more and more on goods which have inelastic demand, the Government collects more revenue from the people without causing them inconvenience. Moreover, it is also useful for the planning.
- Fixation of Wages: It guides the producers to fix wages for labourers. They fix high or low wages according to the elastic or inelastic demand for the labour.
- In the Sphere of International Trade: It is of greater significance in the sphere of international trade. It helps to calculate the terms of trade and the consequent gain from foreign trade. If the demand for home product is inelastic, the terms of trade will be profitable to the home country.
- Paradox of Poverty. It explains the paradox of poverty in the midst of plenty. A bumper crop instead of bringing prosperity may result in disaster, if the demand for it is inelastic. This is specially so, if the products are perishable and not storable.
- Significant for Government Economic Policies. The knowledge of elasticity of demand is very important for the government in such matters as controlling of business cycles, removing inflationary and deflationary gaps in the economy. Similarly, for price stabilization and the purchase and sale of stocks, information about elasticity of demand is most useful.

- Determination of Price of Public Utilities. This concept is significant in the determination of the prices of public utility services. Economic welfare of the society largely depends upon the cheap availability.

DEMAND FORECASTING

Today business enterprises are working under the conditions of uncertainties. Uncertainties can be minimized through planning and forecasting. The success of a business firm depends upon its ability to forecast future events.

MEANING OF DEMAND FORECASTING

Future is uncertain. There is great deal of uncertainty with regard to demand. Since the demand is uncertain, production, cost, revenue, profit etc. are also uncertain. Through forecasting it is possible to minimise the uncertainties. Forecasting simply refers to estimating or anticipating future events. It is an attempt to foresee the future by examining the past. Thus demand forecasting means estimating or anticipating future demand on the basis of past data.

OBJECTIVES OF DEMAND FORECASTING

Short Term Objectives:

- To help in preparing suitable sales and production policies.
- To help in ensuring a regular supply of raw materials.
- To reduce the cost of purchase and avoid unnecessary purchase.
- To ensure best utilization of machines.
- To make arrangements for skilled and unskilled workers so that suitable labour force may be maintained.
- To help in the determination of a suitable price policy.
- To determine financial requirements.
- To determine separate sales targets for all the sales territories.
- To eliminate the problem of under or over production.

Long term Objectives:

- To plan long term production.
- To plan plant capacity.
- To estimate the requirements of workers for long period and make arrangements.
- To determine an appropriate dividend policy.
- To help the proper capital budgeting.
- To plan long term financial requirements.
- To forecast the future problems of material supplies and energy crisis.

FACTORS AFFECTING DEMAND FORECASTING

For making a good forecast, it is essential to consider the various factors governing demand forecasting. These factors are summarized as follows.

- Prevailing business conditions: While preparing demand forecast it becomes necessary to study the general economic conditions very carefully. These include the price level changes, change in national income, percapita income, consumption pattern, savings and investment habits, employment etc.
- Conditions within the industry: Every business enterprise is only a unit of a particular industry. Sales of that business enterprise are only a part of the total sales of that industry. Therefore, while preparing demand forecasts for a particular business enterprise, it becomes necessary to study the changes in the demand of the whole industry, number of units within the industry, design and quality of product, price policy, competition within the industry etc.
- Conditions within the firm: Internal factors of the firm also affect the demand forecast. These factors include plant capacity of the firm, quality of the product, price of the product, advertising and distribution policies, production policies, financial policies etc.
- Factors affecting export trade: If a firm is engaged in export trade also it should consider the factors affecting the export trade. These factors include import and export control, terms and conditions of export, exim policy, export conditions, export finance etc.
- Market behaviour : While preparing demand forecast, it is required to consider the market behavior which brings about changes in demand. 6. Sociological conditions: Sociological factors have their own impact on demand forecast of the company. These conditions relate to size of population, density, change in age groups, size of family, family life cycle, level of education, family income, social awareness etc.
- Psychological conditions: While estimating the demand for the product, it becomes necessary to take into consideration such factors as changes in consumer tastes, habits, fashions, likes and dislikes, attitudes, perception, life styles, cultural and religious bents etc.
- Competitive conditions: The competitive conditions within the industry may change. Competitors may enter into market or go out of market. A demand forecast prepared without considering the activities of competitors may not be correct.

Process of Demand Forecasting/ Steps in Demand Forecasting

Demand forecasting involves the following steps:

- Determine the purpose for which forecasts are used.
- Subdivide the demand forecasting programme into small I parts on the basis of product or sales territories or markets.
- Determine the factors affecting the sale of each product and their relative importance.

- Select the forecasting methods.
- Study the activities of competitors.
- Prepare preliminary sales estimates after, collecting necessary data.
- Analyse advertisement policies, sales promotion plans, personal sales arrangements etc. and ascertain how far these programmes have been successful in promoting the sales.
- Evaluate the demand forecasts monthly, quarterly, half yearly or yearly and necessary adjustments should be done.
- Prepare the final demand forecast on the basis of preliminary forecasts and the results of evaluation.

METHODS OF DEMAND FORECASTING (FOR ESTABLISHED PRODUCTS)

There are several methods to predict the future demand. All methods can be broadly classified into two.

- Survey methods,
- Statistical methods

Survey methods

Under this method surveys are conducted to collect information about the future purchase plans of potential consumers. Survey methods help in obtaining information about the desires, likes and dislikes of consumers through collecting the opinion of experts or by interviewing the consumers. Survey methods are used for short term forecasting. Important survey methods are:

- consumers interview method,
- collective opinion or sales force opinion method
- experts opinion method,
- consumers clinic and
- end use method.

Consumers' interview method (Consumers survey)

Under this method, consumers are interviewed directly and asked the quantity they would like to buy. After collecting the data, the total demand for the product is calculated. This is done by adding up all individual demands. Under the consumer interview method, either all consumers or selected few are interviewed.

When all the consumers are interviewed, the method is known as complete enumeration method. When only a selected group of consumers are interviewed, it is known as sample survey method

Advantages:

- It is a simple method because it is not based on past record.
- It suitable for industrial products.
- The results are likely to be more accurate.

- This method can be used for forecasting the demand of a new product.

Disadvantages:

- It is expensive and time consuming.
- Consumers may not give their secrets or buying plans.
- This method is not suitable for long term forecasting.
- It is not suitable when the number of consumer is large.

Collective opinion method

Under this method the salesmen estimate the expected sales in their respective territories on the basis of previous experience. Then demand is estimated after combining the individual forecasts (sales estimates) of the salesmen. This method is also known as sales force opinion method.

Advantages:

This method is simple.

- It is based on the first hand knowledge of Salesmen.
- This method is particularly useful for estimating demand of new products.
- It utilises the specialised knowledge of salesmen who are in close touch with the prevailing market conditions.

Disadvantages:

- The forecasts may not be reliable if the salespeople are not trained.
- It is not suitable for long period estimation.
- It is not flexible.
- Salesmen may give lower estimates that make possible easy achievement of sales quotas fixed for each salesman.

Experts' opinion method

This method was originally developed at Rand Corporation in 1950 by Olaf Helmer, Dalkey and Gordon. Under this method, demand is estimated on the basis of opinions of experts and distributors other than salesmen and ordinary consumers.

This method is also known as Delphi method. Delphi is the ancient Greek temple where people come and prey for information about their future.

Advantages:

- Forecast can be made quickly and economically
- This is a reliable method because estimates are made on the basis of knowledge and experience of sales experts.
- The firm need not spare its time on preparing estimates of demand.
- This method is suitable for new products.

Disadvantages:

- This method is expensive.
- This method sometimes lacks reliability

Consumer clinics

In this method some selected buyers are given certain amounts of money and asked to buy the products. Then the prices are changed and the consumers are asked to make fresh purchases with the given money. In this way the consumers" responses to price changes are observed. Thus the behaviour of the consumers is studied. On this basis demand is estimated. This method is an improvement over consumer's interview method.

Merits:

- It provides an opportunity to study the behaviour of consumers directly.
- It provides reliable and realistic picture about future demand.
- It gives useful information to aid in the decision making process.

Demerits:

- It is a time consuming method.
- Selecting the participants is very difficult.
- It is expensive.
- Consumers may take it as a game. They may not reveal their preferences.

End use method

This method is based on the fact that a product generally has different uses. In the end use method, first a list of end users (final consumers, individual industries, exporters etc.) is prepared. Then the future demand for the product is found either directly from the end users or indirectly by estimating their future growth. Then the demand of all end users of the product is added to get the total demand for the product.

Statistical Methods

Statistical methods use the past data as a guide for knowing the level of future demand. Statistical methods are generally used for long run forecasting. These methods are used for established products. Statistical methods include:

- Trend projection method,
- Regression and Correlation,
- Extrapolation method,
- Simultaneous equation method, and
- Barometric method.

Trend projection method

Future sales are based on the past sales, because future is the grand-child of the past and child of the present. Under the trend projection method demand is estimated on the basis of analysis of past data. This method makes use of time series (data over a period of time). We try to ascertain the trend in the time series. The trend in the time series can be estimated by using any one of the following four methods:

- Least-square method,
- Free-hand method,
- Moving average method and
- semi-average method.

Regression and Correlation

These methods combine economic theory and statistical technique of estimation. Under these methods the relationship between the sales and other variables is ascertained. Such relationship established on the basis of past data may be used to analyse the future trend. The regression and correlation analysis is also called the econometric model building.

Extrapolation

Under this statistical method, the future demand can be extrapolated by applying Binomial expansion method. This method is used on the assumption that the rate of charge in demand in the past has been uniform.

Simultaneous equation method

This involves the development of a complete econometric model which can explain the behaviour of all the variables which the company can control. This method is not very popular.

Barometric technique

This is an improvement over the trend projection method. According to this technique the events of the present can be used to predict the directions of change m the future.

Here certain economic and statistical indicators from the selected time series are used to predict variables. Personal income, non-agricultural placements, gross national income, prices of industrial materials, wholesale commodity prices, industrial production, bank deposits etc. are some of the most commonly used indicators.

Advantages of Statistical Methods:

- The method of estimation is scientific
- Estimation is based on the theoretical relationship between sales (dependent variable) and price, advertising, income etc. (independent variables)
- These are less expensive.
- Results are relatively more reliable.

Disadvantages of Statistical Methods:

- These methods involve complicated calculations.
- These do not rely much on personal skill and experience.

- These methods require considerable technical skill and experience in order to be effective.

METHODS OF DEMAND FORECASTING FOR NEW PRODUCTS

Demand forecasting of new product is more difficult than forecasting for existing product. The reason is that the product is not available. Hence, no historical data are available. In these conditions the forecasting is to be done by taking into consideration the inclination and wishes of the customers to purchase. For this a research is to be conducted. But there is one problem that it is difficult for a customer to say anything without seeing and using the product before. Thus it is very difficult to forecast the demand for new products. Any way Prof. Joel Dean has suggested the following methods for forecasting demand of new products:

- Evolutionary approach: This method is based on the assumption that the new product is the improvement and evolution of the old product. The demand is forecasted on the basis of the demand of the old product. For example, the demand for black and white TV should be taken in to consideration while forecasting the demand for colour TV sets because the latter is an improvement of the former.
- Substitute approach: Here the new product is treated as a substitute of an existing product, e.g. polythene bags for cloth bags. Thus the demand for a new product is analysed as a substitute for some existing goods or service.
- Growth curve approach: Under this method the growth rate of demand of a new product is estimated on the basis of the growth rate of demand of an existing product. Suppose Pears soap is in use and a new cosmetic is to be introduced in the market. In this case the average sale of Pears soap will give an idea as to how the new cosmetic will be accepted by the consumers.
- Opinion poll approach: Under this method the demand for a new product is estimated on the basis of information collected from the direct interviews (survey) with consumers.
- Sales Experience approach: Under this method, the new product is offered for sale in a sample market, i.e. by direct mail or through multiple shop or departmental shop. From this the total demand is estimated for the whole market.
- Vicarious approach: This method consists of surveying consumers' reactions through the specialised dealers who are in touch with consumers. The dealers are able to know as to how the customers will accept the new product. On the basis of their reports demand can be estimated.

The above methods are not mutually exclusive. It is de desirable to use a combination of two or more methods in order to get better results.

CONSUMER SURPLUS

The concept of consumer's surplus was evolved by Alfred Marshall. This concept occupies an important place not only in economic theory but also in economic policies of government and decision-making of monopolists. It has been seen that consumers generally are ready to pay more for the goods than they actually pay for them. This extra satisfaction which consumers get from their purchase of goods is called by Marshall as consumer's surplus.

CONSUMER'S SURPLUS

Marshall defined the concept of consumer's surplus as "excess of the price which a consumer would be willing to pay rather than go without a thing over that which he actually does pay, is the economic measure of this surplus satisfaction it may be called consumer's surplus". Thus consumer's surplus = what a consumer is ready to pay - What he actually pays. The concept of consumer's surplus is derived from the law of diminishing marginal utility. As we know from the law of diminishing marginal utility, the more of a thing we have, the lesser marginal utility it has. In other words, as we purchase more of a good, its marginal utility goes on diminishing. The consumer is in equilibrium when marginal utility is equal to given price i.e., he purchases that many number of units of a good at which marginal utility is equal to price (It is assumed that perfect competition prevails in the market). Since the price is fixed for all the units of the good he purchases except for the one at margin, he gets extra utility; this extra utility or extra surplus for the consumer is called consumer's surplus.

MEASUREMENT OF CONSUMER'S SURPLUS

Consider Table 4 in which we have illustrated the measurement of consumer's surplus in case of commodity X. The price of X is assumed to be Rs. 20.

Table **Measurement of Consumer's Surplus**

No. of units	Marginal Utility	Price (Rs.)	Consumer's Surplus
1	30	20	10
2	28	20	8
3	26	20	6
4	24	20	4
5	22	20	2
6	20	20	0
7	18	20	-

We see from the above table that when consumer's consumption increases from 1 to 2 units, his marginal utility falls from Rs. 30 to Rs. 28. His marginal utility goes on diminishing as he increases his consumption of good X. Since marginal utility for a unit of good indicates the price the consumer is willing to pay for that unit, and since price is assumed to be fixed at Rs. 20, the consumer enjoys a surplus at every unit of purchase above 6 units. Thus when the consumer is purchasing 1 unit of X, the marginal utility is worth Rs. 30 and price fixed is Rs. 20, thus he is deriving a surplus of Rs. 10. Similarly when he purchases 2 units of X, he enjoys a surplus of Rs. 8 [Rs. 28 - Rs. 20]. This continues and he enjoys consumer's surplus equal to Rs. 6, 4, 2 respectively from 3rd, 4th and 5th unit.

When he buys 6 units, he is in equilibrium because here his marginal utility is equal to the market price or he is willing to pay a sum equal to the actual market price. Here he enjoys no surplus. Thus, given the price of Rs. 20 per unit, the total surplus which the consumer will get, is Rs. 10 + 8 + 6 + 4 + 2 + 0 = 30. The concept of consumer's surplus can also be illustrated graphically. Consider figure 28. On the X-axis is measured the amount of the commodity and on the Y-axis the marginal utility and the price of the commodity. MU is the marginal utility curve which slopes downwards, indicating that as the consumer buys more units of the commodity, its marginal utility falls. Marginal utility shows the price which a person is willing to pay for the different units rather than go without them.

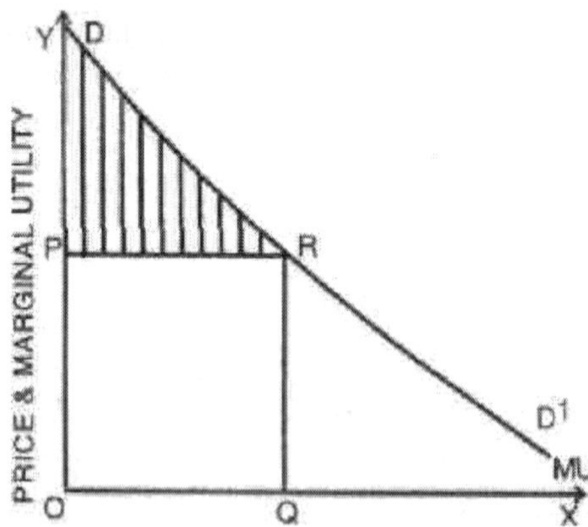

Fig. Marshall's Measure of Consumer's Surplus

If OP is the price that prevails in the market, then consumer will be in equilibrium when he buys OQ units of the commodity, since at OQ units, marginal utility is equal to the given price OP The last unit, i.e., Qth unit does not yield any consumer's surplus because here price paid is equal to the marginal utility of the Qth unit. But for units before Qth unit, marginal utility is greater than the price and thus these units fetch consumer's surplus to the consumer. Fig. 28 : Marshall's Measure of Consumer's Surplus In Figure 28, the total utility is equal to the area under the marginal utility curve up to point Q i.e. ODRQ. But given the price equal to OP, the consumer actually pays OPRQ. The consumer derives extra utility equal to DPR which is nothing but consumer's surplus.

LIMITATIONS

- Consumer's surplus cannot be measured precisely - because it is difficult to measure the marginal utilities of different units of a commodity consumed by a person.
- In the case of necessaries, the marginal utilities of the earlier units are infinitely large. In such case the consumer's surplus is always infinite.
- The consumer's surplus derived from a commodity is affected by the availability of substitutes.
- There is no simple rule for deriving the utility scale of articles which are used for their prestige value (e.g., diamonds).
- Consumer's surplus cannot be measured in terms of money because the marginal utility of money changes as purchases are made and the consumer's stock of money diminishes. (Marshall assumed that the marginal utility of money remains constant. But this assumption is unrealistic).
- The concept can be accepted only if it is assumed that utility can be measured in terms of money or otherwise. Many modern economists believe that this cannot be done.

2

Product Line Pricing

INTRODUCTION

Consider a Belgian couple contemplating a shopping trip to London during the Christmas period. The cheapest way to cross the Channel would be to take a ticket on the ferry from Oostende to Ramsgate, which would amount to about Bfr. 1,500 per person. While they can afford this from a budgetary viewpoint, taking the boat would mean spending about five hours travelling, which would mean losing almost half of the 'available' weekend to hunt for interesting bargains in the London shopping area.

Taking the plane would drastically reduce travelling time, but the air fare of Bfr. 4,900 per person is not overly appealing. Friends recommend that they buy a combined ticket from the Belgian Railways and the Channel. This seems to be the most interesting option, but unfortunately no more regular tickets are available for the morning of the Christmas weekend. The price of a first class- Railway/Channel ticket is prohibitive. Ultimately, the couple decides to travel by Hovercraft, at a rate of Bfr. 2,200 per person.

This example illustrates the complexity of consumer choices in the face of a variety of alternatives offered at different prices. The mirror image of this problem is the pricing issue for firms offering the products or services to various types of customers: their pricing problem will be equally multifaceted and complex. To introduce the nature of the problem and the issues involved, Section 1 elaborates on the meaning of price, and on the importance of price as a marketing-mix instrument.

THE MEANING OF PRICE

In ordinary usage, price is the quantity of payment or compensation for something. People may say about a criminal that he has 'paid the price to society' to imply that he has paid a penalty or compensation. They may say that somebody has 'paid for his folly' to imply that he suffered the consequences of his actions. Economists view price as an exchange ratio between goods that are exchanged for each other. In the case of barter of two goods in the quantities x and y, the price of a unit of the first good is the ratio y/x, while the price of a unit of the second good is the ratio x/y.

This however has not been used consistently, so that old confusion regarding value frequently reappears. The value of something is a quantity counted in common units of value called numeraire, which may even be an imaginary good. This is done to compare different goods. The unit of value is frequently confused with price, because market value is calculated as the quantity of some good multiplied by its nominal price.

RELATIVE AND NOMINAL PRICE

The difference between nominal price and relative or real price is often made. Nominal price is the price quoted in money while relative or real price is the exchange ratio between real goods regardless of money. The distinction is made to make sense of inflation. When all prices are quoted in terms of money units, and the prices in money units change more or less proportionately, the ratio of exchange may not change much. In the extreme case, if all prices quoted in money change in the same proportion, the relative price remains the same.

AUSTRIAN THEORY

The last objection is also sometimes interpreted as the paradox of value, which was observed by classical economists. Adam Smith described what is now called the Diamond – Water Paradox: diamonds command a higher price than water, yet water is essential for life, while diamonds are merely ornamentation. One solution offered to this paradox is through the theory of marginal utility proposed by Carl Menger, the father of the Austrian School of economics.

As William Barber put it, human volition, the human subject, was "brought to the centre of the stage" by marginalist economics, as a bargaining tool. Neoclassical economists sought to clarify choices open to producers and consumers in market situations, and thus "fears that cleavages in the economic structure might be unbridgeable could be suppressed".

Without denying the applicability of the Austrian theory of value as subjective only, within certain contexts of price behavior, the Polish economist Oskar Lange felt it was necessary to attempt a serious integration of the insights of classical political economy with neo-classical economics. This would then result in a much more realistic theory of price and of real behavior in response to prices.

Marginalist theory lacked anything like a theory of the social framework of real market functioning, and criticism sparked off by the capital controversy initiated by Piero Sraffa revealed that most of the foundational tenets of the marginalist theory of value either reduced to tautologies, or that the theory was true only if counter-factual conditions applied. One insight often ignored in the debates about price theory is something that businessmen are keenly aware of: in different markets, prices may not function according to the same principles except in some very abstract sense. From the classical political economists to Michal Kalecki it was known that prices for industrial goods behaved differently from prices for agricultural goods, but this idea could be extended further to other broad classes of goods and services.

PRICE AS PRODUCTIVE HUMAN LABOUR TIME

Marxists assert that value derives from the volume of socially necessary abstract labour time exerted in the creation of an object. This value does not relate to price in a simple manner, and the difficulty of the conversion of the mass of values into the actual prices is known as the transformation problem. However, many recent Marxists deny that any problem exists. Marx was not concerned with proving that prices derive from values. In fact, he admonished the other classical political economists for trying to make this proof. Rather, for Marx, price equal the cost of production plus the average rate of profit. So if the average rate of profit is 22% then prices would reflect cost-of-production plus 22%.

The perception that there is a transformation problem in Marx stems from the injection of Walrasian equilibrium theory into Marxism where there is no such thing as equilibrium.

CONFUSION BETWEEN PRICES AND COSTS OF PRODUCTION

Price is commonly confused with the notion of cost of production as in "I paid a high cost for buying my new plasma television". Technically, though, these are different concepts. Price is what a buyer pays to acquire products from a seller. Cost of production concerns the seller's investment in the product being exchanged with a buyer. For marketing organizations seeking to make a profit the hope is that price will exceed cost of production so the organization can see financial gain from the transaction. Finally, while pricing is a topic central to a company's profitability, pricing decisions are not limited to for-profit companies.

Non-profit organizations, such as charities, educational institutions and industry trade groups, also set prices, though this is often not as apparent. For instance, charities seeking to raise money may set different "target" levels for donations that reward donors with increases in status, gifts or other benefits. While a charitable organization may not call it a price in their promotional material, in reality these targets are prices since they specify a cost that must be paid by buyers in order to obtain something of value.

IMPORTANCE OF PRICE

When marketers talk about what they do as part of their responsibilities for marketing products, the tasks associated with setting price are often not at the top of the list. Marketers are much more likely to discuss their activities related to promotion, product development, market research and other tasks that are viewed as the more interesting and exciting parts of the job.

Yet pricing decisions can have important consequences for the marketing organization and the attention given by the marketer to pricing is just as important as the attention given to more recognizable marketing activities. Some reasons pricing is important include:

- Most Flexible Marketing Mix Variable – For marketers price is the most adjustable of all marketing decisions. Unlike product and distribution decisions, which can take months or years to change, or some forms of promotion which can be time consuming to alter, price can be changed very rapidly.
- The flexibility of pricing decisions is particularly important in times when the marketer seeks to quickly stimulate demand or respond to competitor price actions. For instance, a marketer can agree to a field salesperson's request to lower price for a potential prospect during a phone conversation. Likewise a marketer in charge of online operations can raise prices on hot selling products with the click of a few website buttons.
- Setting the Right Price – Pricing decisions made hastily without sufficient research, analysis, and strategic evaluation can lead to the marketing organization losing revenue. Prices set too low may mean the company is missing out on additional profits that could be earned if the target market is willing to spend more to acquire the product. Additionally, attempts to raise an initially low priced product to a higher price may be met by customer resistance as they may feel the marketer is attempting to take advantage of their customers. Prices set too high can also impact revenue as it prevents interested customers from purchasing the product.
- Setting the right price level often takes considerable market knowledge and, especially with new products, testing of different pricing options.
- Trigger of First Impressions - Often times customers' perception of a product is formed as soon as they learn the price, such as when a product is first seen when walking down the aisle of a store. While the final decision to make a purchase may be based on the value offered by the entire marketing offering, it is possible the customer will not evaluate a marketer's product at all based on price alone. It is important for marketers to know if customers are more likely to dismiss a product when all they know is its price. If so, pricing may become the most important of all marketing decisions if it can be shown that customers are avoiding learning more about the product because of the price.

- Important Part of Sales Promotion – Many times price adjustments are part of sales promotions that lower price for a short term to stimulate interest in the product. However, as we noted in our discussion of promotional pricing in the Sales Promotion tutorial, marketers must guard against the temptation to adjust prices too frequently since continually increasing and decreasing price can lead customers to be conditioned to anticipate price reductions and, consequently, withhold purchase until the price reduction occurs again.

STRATEGIC PRICING

One of the four major elements of the marketing mix is price. Pricing is an important strategic issue because it is related to product positioning. Furthermore, pricing affects other marketing mix elements such as product features, channel decisions, and promotion.

While there is no single recipe to determine pricing, the following is a general sequence of steps that might be followed for developing the pricing of a new product:

1. Develop marketing strategy - perform marketing analysis, segmentation, targeting, and positioning.
2. Make marketing mix decisions - define the product, distribution, and promotional tactics.
3. Estimate the demand curve - understand how quantity demanded varies with price.
4. Calculate cost - include fixed and variable costs associated with the product.
5. Understand environmental factors - evaluate likely competitor actions, understand legal constraints, etc.
6. Set pricing objectives - for example, profit maximization, revenue maximization, or price stabilization.
7. Determine pricing - using information collected in the above steps, select a pricing method, develop the pricing structure, and define discounts.

These steps are interrelated and are not necessarily performed in the above order. Nonetheless, the above list serves to present a starting framework.

MARKETING STRATEGY AND THE MARKETING MIX

PRICE DISCOUNTS

The normally quoted price to end users is known as the list price. This price usually is discounted for distribution channel members and some end users. There are several types of discounts, as outlined below.

- Quantity discount - offered to customers who purchase in large quantities.
- Cumulative quantity discount - a discount that increases as the cumulative quantity increases. Cumulative discounts may be offered to resellers who purchase large quantities over time but who do not wish to place large individual orders.
- Seasonal discount - based on the time that the purchase is made and designed to reduce seasonal variation in sales. For example, the travel industry offers much lower off-season rates. Such discounts do not have to be based on time of the year; they also can be based on day of the week or time of the day, such as pricing offered by long distance and wireless service providers.
- Cash discount - extended to customers who pay their bill before a specified date.
- Trade discount - a functional discount offered to channel members for performing their roles. For example, a trade discount may be offered to a small retailer who may not purchase in quantity but nonetheless performs the important retail function.
- Promotional discount - a short-term discounted price offered to stimulate sales.

FACTORS AFFECTING PRICING DECISION

For the remainder of this tutorial we look at factors that affect how marketers set price. The final price for a product may be influenced by many factors which can be categorized into two main groups:

- Internal Factors - When setting price, marketers must take into consideration several factors which are the result of company decisions and actions. To a large extent these factors are controllable by thc company and, if necessary, can be altered. However, while the organization may have control over these factors making a quick change is not always realistic. For instance, product pricing may depend heavily on the productivity of a manufacturing facility. The marketer knows that increasing productivity can reduce the cost of producing each product and thus allow the marketer to potentially lower the product's price. But increasing productivity may require major changes at the manufacturing facility that will take time and will not translate into lower price products for a considerable period of time.
- External Factors - There are a number of influencing factors which are not controlled by the company but will impact pricing decisions. Understanding these factors requires the marketer conduct research to monitor what is happening in each market the company serves since the effect of these factors can vary by market.

INTERNAL FACTORS

Marketing Objectives

Marketing decisions are guided by the overall objectives of the company. While we will discuss this in more detail when we cover marketing strategy in a later tutorial, for now it is important to understand that all marketing decisions, including price, work to help achieve company objectives.

Corporate objectives can be wide-ranging and include different objectives for different functional areas. While pricing decisions are influenced by many types of objectives set up for the marketing functional area, there are four key objectives in which price plays a central role. In most situations only one of these objectives will be followed, though the marketer may have different objectives for different products. The four main marketing objectives affecting price include:

- Return on Investment – A firm may set as a marketing objective the requirement that all products attain a certain percentage return on the organization's spending on marketing the product. This level of return along with an estimate of sales will help determine appropriate pricing levels needed to meet the ROI objective.
- Cash Flow – Firms may seek to set prices at a level that will insure that sales revenue will at least cover product production and marketing costs. This is most likely to occur with new products where the organizational objectives allow a new product to simply meet its expenses while efforts are made to establish the product in the market. This objective allows the marketer to worry less about product profitability and instead directs energies to building a market for the product.
- Market Share – The pricing decision may be important when the firm has an objective of gaining a hold in a new market or retaining a certain percent of an existing market. For new products under this objective the price is set artificially low in order to capture a sizeable portion of the market and will be increased as the product becomes more accepted by the target market. For existing products, firms may use price decisions to insure they retain market share in instances where there is a high level of market competition and competitors who are willing to compete on price.
- Maximize Profits – Older products that appeal to a market that is no longer growing may have a company objective requiring the price be set at a level that optimizes profits. This is often the case when the marketer has little incentive to introduce improvements to the product and will continue to sell the same product at a price premium for as long as some in the market is willing to buy.

Marketing Strategy

Marketing strategy concerns the decisions marketers make to help the company satisfy its target market and attain its business and marketing objectives. Price, of course, is one of the key marketing mix decisions and since all marketing mix decisions must work together, the final price will be impacted by how other marketing decisions are made. For instance, marketers selling high quality products would be expected to price their products in a range that will add to the perception of the product being at a high-level.

It should be noted that not all companies view price as a key selling feature. Some firms, for example those seeking to be viewed as market leaders in product quality, will deemphasize price and concentrate on a strategy that highlights non-price benefits. Such non-price competition can help the company avoid potential price wars that often break out between competitive firms that follow a market share objective and use price as a key selling feature.

Costs

For many for-profit companies, the starting point for setting a product's price is to first determine how much it will cost to get the product to their customers. Obviously, whatever price customers pay must exceed the cost of producing a good or delivering a service otherwise the company will lose money.

When analyzing cost, the marketer will consider all costs needed to get the product to market including those associated with production, marketing, distribution and company administration. These costs can be divided into two main categories:

- Fixed Costs - Also referred to as overhead costs, these represent costs the marketing organization incurs that are not affected by level of production or sales. For example, for a manufacturer of writing instruments that has just built a new production facility, whether they produce one pen or one million they will still need to pay the monthly mortgage for the building. From the marketing side, fixed costs may also exist in the form of expenditure for fielding a sales force, carrying out an advertising campaign and paying a service to host the company's website. These costs are fixed because there is a level of commitment to spending that is largely not affected by production or sales levels.
- Variable Costs – These costs are directly associated with the production and sales of products and, consequently, may change as the level of production or sales changes. Typically variable costs are evaluated on a per-unit basis since the cost is directly associated with individual items. Most variable costs involve costs of items that are either components of the product or are directly associated with creating the product. However, there are also marketing variable costs

such as coupons, which are likely to cost the company more as sales increase. Variable costs, especially for tangible products, tend to decline as more units are produced. This is due to the producing company's ability to purchase product components for lower prices since component suppliers often provide discounted pricing for large quantity purchases.

Determining individual unit cost can be a complicated process. While variable costs are often determined on a per-unit basis, applying fixed costs to individual products is less straightforward. For example, if a company manufactures five different products in one manufacturing plant how would it distribute the plant's fixed costs over the five products? In general, a company will assign fixed cost to individual products if the company can clearly associate the cost with the product, such as assigning the cost of operating production machines based on how much time it takes to produce each item. Alternatively, if it is too difficult to associate to specific products the company may simply divide the total fixed cost by production of each item and assign it on percentage basis.

EXTERNAL FACTORS

Elasticity of Demand

Marketers should never rest on their marketing decisions. They must continually use market research and their own judgment to determine whether marketing decisions need to be adjusted. When it comes to adjusting price, the marketer must understand what effect a change in price is likely to have on target market demand for a product.

Understanding how price changes impact the market requires the marketer have a firm understanding of the concept economists call elasticity of demand, which relates to how purchase quantity changes as prices change. Elasticity is evaluated under the assumption that no other changes are being made and only price is adjusted. The logic is to see how price by itself will affect overall demand. Obviously, the chance of nothing else changing in the market but the price of one product is often unrealistic. For example, competitors may react to the marketer's price change by changing the price on their product. Despite this, elasticity analysis does serve as a useful tool for estimating market reaction.

Elasticity deals with three types of demand scenarios:

- Elastic Demand – Products are considered to exist in a market that exhibits elastic demand when a certain percentage change in price results in a larger and opposite percentage change in demand. For example, if the price of a product increases by 10%, the demand for the product is likely to decline by greater than 10%.
- Inelastic Demand – Products are considered to exist in an inelastic market when a certain percentage change in price results in a smaller

and opposite percentage change in demand. For example, if the price of a product increases by 10%, the demand for the product is likely to decline by less than 10%.

- Unitary Demand – This demand occurs when a percentage change in price results in an equal and opposite percentage change in demand. For example, if the price of a product increases by 10%, the demand for the product is likely to decline by 10%.

For marketers the important issue with elasticity of demand is to understand how it impacts company revenue. In general the following scenarios apply to making price changes for a given type of market demand:

- For elastic markets – increasing price lowers total revenue while decreasing price increases total revenue.
- For inelastic markets – increasing price raises total revenue while decreasing price lowers total revenue.
- For unitary markets – there is no change in revenue when price is changed.

Customer Expectations

Possibly the most obvious external factors that influence price setting are the expectations of customers and channel partners. As we discussed, when it comes to making a purchase decision customers assess the overall "value" of a product much more than they assess the price. When deciding on a price marketers need to conduct customer research to determine what "price points" are acceptable. Pricing beyond these price points could discourage customers from purchasing.

Firms within the marketer's channels of distribution also must be considered when determining price. Distribution partners expect to receive financial compensation for their efforts, which usually means they will receive a percentage of the final selling price. This percentage or margin between what they pay the marketer to acquire the product and the price they charge their customers must be sufficient for the distributor to cover their costs and also earn a desired profit.

Competitive and Other Products

Marketers will undoubtedly look to market competitors for indications of how price should be set. For many marketers of consumer products researching competitive pricing is relatively easy, particularly when Internet search tools are used. Price analysis can be somewhat more complicated for products sold to the business market since final price may be affected by a number of factors including if competitors allow customers to negotiate their final price.

Analysis of competition will include pricing by direct competitors, related products and primary products.

- Direct Competitor Pricing – Almost all marketing decisions, including pricing, will include an evaluation of competitors' offerings. The impact of this information on the actual setting of price will depend on the competitive nature of the market. For instance, products that dominate markets and are viewed as market leaders may not be heavily influenced by competitor pricing since they are in a commanding position to set prices as they see fit. On the other hand in markets where a clear leader does not exist, the pricing of competitive products will be carefully considered. Marketers must not only research competitive prices but must also pay close attention to how these companies will respond to the marketer's pricing decisions. For instance, in highly competitive industries, such as gasoline or airline travel, competitors may respond quickly to competitors' price adjustments thus reducing the effect of such changes.
- Related Product Pricing - Products that offer new ways for solving customer needs may look to pricing of products that customers are currently using even though these other products may not appear to be direct competitors. For example, a marketer of a new online golf instruction service that allows customers to access golf instruction via their computer may look at prices charged by local golf professionals for in-person instruction to gauge where to set their price. While on the surface online golf instruction may not be a direct competitor to a golf instructor, marketers for the online service can use the cost of in-person instruction as a reference point for setting price.
- Primary Product Pricing - As we discussed in the Product Decisions tutorial, marketers may sell products viewed as complementary to a primary product. For example, Bluetooth headsets are considered complementary to the primary product cellphones. The pricing of complementary products may be affected by pricing changes made to the primary product since customers may compare the price for complementary products based on the primary product price. For example, companies that sell accessory products for the Apple iPod may do so at a cost that is only 10% of the purchase price of the iPod. However, if Apple were to dramatically drop the price, for instance by 50%, the accessory at its present price would now be 20% of the of iPod price.
- This may be perceived by the market as a doubling of the accessory's price. To maintain its perceived value the accessory marketer may need to respond to the iPod price drop by also lowering the price of the accessory.

Government Regulation

Marketers must be aware of regulations that impact how price is set in the markets in which their products are sold. These regulations are primarily government enacted meaning that there may be legal ramifications if the rules are not followed. Price regulations can come from any level of government and vary widely in their requirements. For instance, in some industries, government regulation may set price ceilings while in other industries there may be price floors. Additional areas of potential regulation include: deceptive pricing, price discrimination, predatory pricing and price fixing.

Finally, when selling beyond their home market, marketers must recognize that local regulations may make pricing decisions different for each market. This is particularly a concern when selling to international markets where failure to consider regulations can lead to severe penalties. Consequently marketers must have a clear understanding of regulations in each market they serve.

There are also additional legal concerns when it comes to price which we will discuss in a future tutorial.

PRICING OBJECTIVES

Pricing objectives or goals give direction to the whole pricing process. Determining what your objectives are is the first step in pricing. When deciding on pricing objectives you must consider: 1) the overall financial, marketing, and strategic objectives of the company; 2) the objectives of your product or brand; 3) consumer price elasticity and price points; and 4) the resources you have available.

Some of the more common pricing objectives are:

- maximize long-run profit
- maximize short-run profit
- increase sales volume
- increase monetary sales
- increase market share
- obtain a target rate of return on investment
- obtain a target rate of return on sales
- stabilize market or stabilize market price: an objective to stabilize price means that the marketing manager attempts to keep prices stable in the marketplace and to compete on non-price considerations. Stabilization of margin is basically a cost-plus approach in which the manager attempts to maintain the same margin regardless of changes in cost.
- company growth
- maintain price leadership
- desensitize customers to price
- discourage new entrants into the industry

- match competitors prices
- encourage the exit of marginal firms from the industry
- survival
- avoid government investigation or intervention
- obtain or maintain the loyalty and enthusiasm of distributors and other sales personnel
- enhance the image of the firm, brand, or product
- be perceived as "fair" by customers and potential customers
- create interest and excitement about a product
- discourage competitors from cutting prices
- use price to make the product "visible"
- build store traffic
- help prepare for the sale of the business
- social, ethical, or ideological objectives
- get competitive advantage

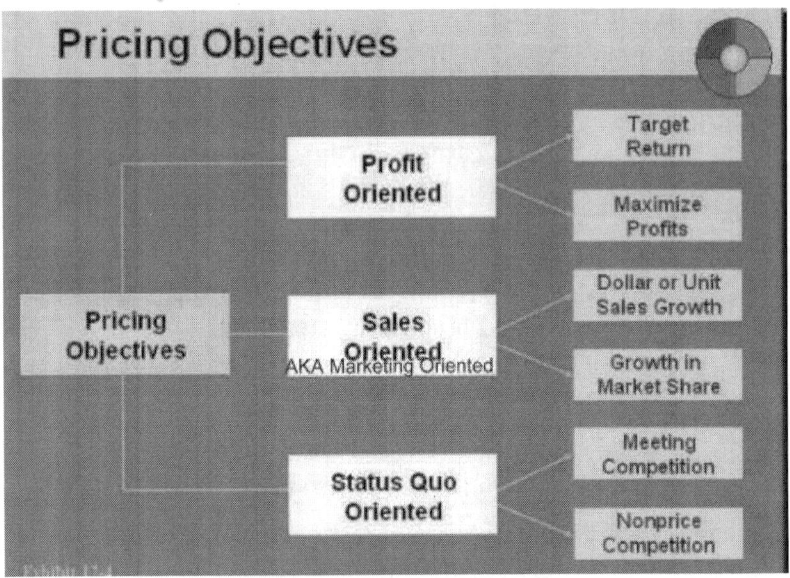

PRICE DETERMINATION

Determination of the prices depends internal and external factors. Pricing goals represents internal policy. Also, price policy should be aligned on several other factors. Demand is the key determinant for market oriented company. Demand is the starting point for all activities. Simply, the average customer will be demanding different product quantities, depending on price. Law of the market says that demand and price are counter proportional.

Competition has a significant influence to price determination of market oriented companies. Prices need to be adjusted in order to address the competition. Every company should research market and competition, prior to launch of the new product. Survey should include direct competitors but also the substitutes. Based on market survey and the strength of the company the prices can be the same, lower or higher.

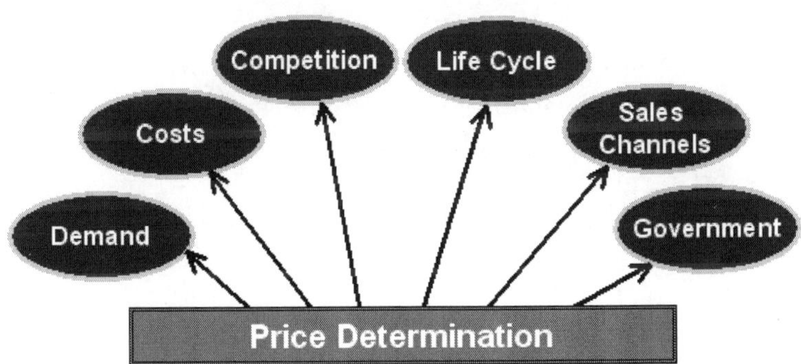

Costs – While demand and competition are external factor, the costs are internal. The costs must be embedded in every stage of price determination process. There are several methods of cost embedding into price:

1. Costs Plus – company calculates the costs and increase price for the specific profit.
2. Markup – price based on cost increased for amount of specific markup percentage.
3. Target Return Method – calculated required markup, in order to achieve return on investment.
4. Profit Maximizing is the price where the marginal profit equals marginal cost.
5. Breakeven Analysis – is the number of units sold that generates profit that can cover cost. This point does not have profit nor lost.

Life Cycle pricing approach analysis the current phase of product life in market.

1. Entering phase usually requires higher sales prices in order to payback initial development costs. Also customers are willing to pay more for a new product.
2. Growth phase is bringing the market stabilization. Prices are more or less stabile.
3. Saturation phase leads to price decline, due to competition entrance and loss of consumer's interest
4. Declining phase is the last part of product life cycle. Prices are still going down.

Sales Channels have the different shopping occasion. Consequently the pricing is adjusted to sales channel. For example, the same products is cheaper in hypermarket than on petrol station. Government is usually do not interfere into price determination. Exceptionally it may limit maximal prices for a certain products. Still, government is influencing pricing, since the taxes & custom duties are the part of the price.

PRICING STRATEGY VERSUS TACTICS

In the literature, the term 'pricing tactics' is subject to much confusion. In this text, we adhere to the viewpoint of van Waterschoot and Van den Bulte and Morris and Calantone, which is that pricing strategies determine longterm price structure and levels and their evolution over time in response to long-term environmental changes, while tactics refer to short-term price decisions to realize short-term objectives or respond to short-term environmental changes. Often, the same instruments are used for strategic and tactical purposes. A temporary price cut, for instance, can be part of a random-discounting strategy, or intended to pursue an immediate goal like liquidating excess stocks. For many companies, discounting is 'correctional', in response to sudden changes in consumer demand, trading conditions, and operational inefficiencies.

At the same time, the strategic role of short-term price fluctuations is well documented and has been extensively discussed in previous sections of this chapter. In this section we concentrate on empirically observed effects of short-term price reductions or 'price promotions'. As the literature on promotions is extensive, we keep the discussion tractable by studying only price discounts in their purest form. Coupons, or other short-term marketing instruments such as gifts or extra quantities, are not considered here. Also, our discussion is based mainly on studies in the packaged-goods sector, which constitute the bulk of the promotion literature. We therefore analyse consumer and retailer promotions and trade promotions.

OPERATION OF PRICING: DECISIONS AND STRATEGIES OPERATION OF PRICING DECISIONS AND STRATEGIES

INTRODUCTION

The pricing process is a central mechanism of a private enterprise or market system. Price adjustments facilitate the logical allocation of resources; both buyers and sellers use them to clear markets of gluts and to stimulate production when supply is short. A competitive price system features such adjustments to achieve maximum economic efficiency. From an industry's perspective, pricing can extend or limit markets; from a company's perspective, it can increase or reduce its share of the market. Price is the ingredient of the marketing mix that has been subjected to the most intensive analysis — particularly by economists. But as an aspect of the mix, it cannot be divorced from other ingredients. It must incorporate and reflect them. Optimal prices cannot be established, and pricing remains an art with a host of factors to be evaluated for which there are no precise measures and weights. Although theoretical models exist for establishing optimal prices, in practice, theory does not enable managers to determine the correct price. Marketing management is guided by personal assessments of market conditions, costs, and competitive situations. The actual price established is usually the result of executive value judgments.

Pricing Factors

Marketing managers may not share the economists' concern with price as the primary marketing factor. In a survey of 200 businesses, it was found that "business management did not agree with the economic views of the importance of pricing — one-half of the respondents did not select pricing as one of the five most important policy areas in their firm's marketing success." Consumers do not respond to price alone; they respond to value. A lower price does not necessarily mean expanded sales. Moreover, marketing activities influence price. For example, governmental agencies have investigated advertising as a cause of higher prices. What is price? It is the amount paid to purchase something, or a monetary summation of the conditions that give value to a product or service.

How important is the pricing decision? In microeconomic theory it has received great attention; in marketing, the significance of price varies among industries, competitive situations, and products. Pricing is significant where the market impact, profit results, or both, of price variations is great, and where firms have considerable discretion over the prices charged. In many instances pricing decisions are severely constrained and are sometimes relatively unimportant. Large purchasers of industrial goods, for instance, may specify prices at which they will buy, determine product specifications, and send specifications to suppliers for competitive bids. For other products price may not be a relevant factor. In some technical areas where products require much research and development and involve much uncertainty, a cost-plus scheme may be used. In other situations, sellers may be almost completely free to set prices, while in still others, they may only be able to decide whether or not to sell at a price.

Where industries are dominated by relatively few large firms, price is not usually the critical competitive variable. Each firm recognizes that price reductions will be met by the other large firms and the profits of all will suffer. Greater attention may then be given to non price factors. In an economy of scarcity, price is accorded more attention than any other marketing factor. In an economy of abundance, non price factors assume increasing marketing importance and products are differentiated on other bases than price. Style, colour, symbols, and brands become more significant and higher rather than lower prices may actually increase sales. For abundance brings widespread discretionary income, and price becomes a less significant component of the marketing mix than the economic literature might lead one to believe. Non price competition and price confusion, rather than price clarity, now seem to be the rule. Buyers are concerned not only with price, in their purchases, but also with service, status, and image. Low price alone does not result in a transaction. Consumers are not mechanical price calculators and price reactors, as so much theory leads one to believe. They do not know all the prices, for in reality, discounts, trade-ins, special deals, and premiums cloud the actual price. Prices are limited by direct and indirect competition, costs, and consumer reaction. Several disciplines help in improving pricing decisions. Economic theory affords guidelines and concepts of demand and elasticity. Accounting furnishes considerations of costs, break-even, and rate of return on investment. Marketing adds to this a consideration and understanding of market behaviour particularly the role of consumers and intermediaries. Pricing is a sensitive and complex decision area affecting sales, costs, and profits for both industrial and consumer goods. For consumers, price reductions and increases have symbolic meanings.

A customer may associate a price reduction with a reduction in quality, the anticipation of new models, or even lower prices or poor market acceptance. Higher prices may indicate better quality, a good image, and good value. Customer perceptions of price are important. Whereas pricing is usually perceived as a short-run action, its implications can be long-run, even to the point of shaping industry structures.

Markets that may be viewed as systems of information on cost and demand determine the appropriateness of prices. They contain signals that businessmen must decode. But market information is ambiguous, fragmentary, and imperfect; it contains much uncertainty and is interpreted differently by various executives. To those who can read the signals properly, increased profits are the results. But invariably, pricing decisions are wrong and must be altered, as is evidenced by changing list prices. Thus, pricing is a process of adjustment in which incomplete data are used for important decisions. As new information is gathered, the offering can be adjusted in two ways: alteration of the price, or alteration of the product to meet the price.

The Pricing Decisions

No single pricing programme is suitable for all firms, since the complexity of pricing situations varies by product, cost, demand, and industry structure, and prices must relate to objectives, information, knowledge of alternative policies, and strategies and adjustments. The business executive is faced with the problem of establishing the best price under assumed cost-and-demand conditions. The lack of information, the dynamics of the market, and the problems of measuring both costs and demand make it a difficult task. Yet, estimates must be made of what management expects demand, cost, and competition to be under various conditions. Then it can develop pricing programmes that affect survival, profits, growth, volume, market share, R & D, and image. A distinction is often made between price determination and price administration. The activities and focus of each are different. Price determination refers to the processes and activities employed to arrive at a price for a product. It includes consideration of relative prices of products within the same line, and differences in price for similar products of differing grades and qualities.

Price administration refers to the activities involved in fitting basic prices to particular sales situations. For example, prices may be administered to bring them into line with such factors as geographic locale, functions performed by customers, position of distribution channel members, or special sales situations. Included in price administration is the determination of discount structures. Thus, price determination refers to the establishment of a "base price" that is adjusted through price administration to reflect varying sales and competitive situations. Six concepts and considerations useful in establishing prices are as follows:

- Pricing decisions should adopt a systems perspective. Executives must consider the whole marketing system — manufacturers, wholesalers, retailers, and consumers — and the impact at each stage.
- Prices must be related to market segments. The kind and strength of customer attitudes and the purchase desires of various market segments affect the prices that can be charged, and customer acceptance of prices by a sufficient market sector is essential.
- The determination of the best price is usually impossible, and executives must often settle for satisfactory prices in view of profit and market-share objectives.
- Price is not to be considered merely as the result of costs; it is also a method of stimulating sales.
- Since they have both economic and political dimensions, pricing policies are more likely to be governed by tradition than by innovation. They are concerned not only with competition, elasticity of demand, marginal and average costs, industry structure, substitutability of products, and product and market characteristics, but also with numerous governmental constraints.
- Pricing policies must be reviewed and changed as basic conditions shift. This means that good pricing practices are research based.

What are the major pricing decisions to be made? They include determination of:

- Prices for each product or service.
- Discount structures.
- Price relationships among products.
- Price maintenance level.

These decisions should be based on information from market research, sales analysis, distribution cost accounting, standard costs, surveys, experiments, sales forecasts, simulations, and statistical techniques. The information required concerns competitive prices, cost data, demand estimates, product profitability, salesmen and customer reactions, and middlemen needs. But information about future demand schedules, future competitive reactions, and future costs is incomplete at best. Thus prices must be based on guesses and assumptions, yet they should be determined logically.

USEFUL CONSTRUCTS AND GUIDES

Although each pricing decision is unique, some constructs and concepts are useful in analyzing pricing situations. The models of market structure, concepts of costs, demand concepts and the company philosophy of followership or leadership, are very helpful. With full knowledge of them, a "right price" can be established. But decision makers are confronted with incomplete or outdated information. The reasoning process they employ considers answers to two kinds of questions. First is "what if" or conditional reasoning. They assess possible courses of action, and the probable consequences of each. For example, if I change prices to A, what is the probability that competitors will meet the change, will not meet it, or will meet it partially, and what will be the consequences of each competitive reaction? Second, there is a consideration of the relationship of price changes to changes in the other aspects of the marketing programme, advertising, distribution channels, product packaging, and personal selling.

Prices may also be established through research. Various prices may be tested in limited areas and the "best" price selected. Research of customers' opinions and reactions to products is often sought as a basis for price. Sometimes products are tailored to meet predetermined price points, and product quality is changed so that prices can be maintained and product-line requirements and distributors' price points met. Although price is not merely the result of costs, price-cost factors are accorded major consideration. Moreover, since price affects volume, volume affects costs, and costs affect prices, the pricing decision is a circular one. Also, a variety of cost concepts may be applied. Prices can be based on total costs, average, or variable costs. The last basis leads to a marginal approach to costs.

The major contribution of economic reasoning to the consideration of costs is the idea of marginal cost. Businessmen tend to rely more on an average cost approach to pricing than on a marginal approach. Average costs, which are rarely pertinent to an optimal decision, satisfy the desire to "cover our costs and make a profit." In reality, this reliance on average costs can lead to a decision that can actually reduce sales, increase costs, and reduce profits. However, some executives advocate that sunk costs should be ignored. They are not affected by current decisions — nothing can be done about them. Yet it is also recognized that over the long run, they must be covered. A consideration of the impact of sales volume on costs provides a useful train of thought. For instance, price theory suggests a U shape for average costs — they decline to a point with increasing volume, reach their minimum, and then increase as volume increases. This seems to make sense, since the concept introduces the notion of economies of scale and the impact of capacity on costs, indicating that volume beyond a certain point may increase costs. In addition to cost factors, pricing decisions in basic industries are greatly influenced by governmental considerations.

Some industries such as steel are treated like public utilities and, sensitive to governmental reaction, must justify price increases. Although no laws exist that require governmental approval of price increases in these industries, such increases are judged as to their being warranted. A variety of pricing practices are of particular concern to certain industries. For example, bidding is significant in defence marketing, hedging in commodity marketing, markdown in fashion merchandise, dumping in international marketing, price deals in food marketing, and loss leaders and discounting in retailing. In formulating marketing strategy, we have dealt with only the broader relationships of pricing to selected elements in the marketing mix. Price decisions in specific situations require both experience and practical knowledge. Theory alone will not suffice. In fact, where pricing is of critical concern, pricing specialists become necessary.

Pricing Influences

Since prices have great impact on both revenue and competitive reactions, pricing policies are usually determined at a high executive level. The pricing task involves not only a maze of variables but also conflicting situations. Conflicts exist among manufacturers and distributors, retailers and wholesalers, and consumers and retailers.

For example, intermediate and ultimate customers weigh the prices they pay, competitors are influenced and react, suppliers watch margins carefully, financial institutions consider the impact on stock, and the government assesses competitive implications.

Among the present and future external factors that influence pricing policy are number and concentration of competitors, the degree of competition, profitability, ease of entry, product heterogeneity, size, legal aspects, channels of distribution, elasticity of demand, total industry demand, kind and size of buyers, and spatial forces.

But basically these are handled through consideration of anticipated cost-revenue relationships. For in the long run, prices are constrained at their upper bound by market reaction and competition and at their lower bound by costs full or incremental. The latter are most significant in the immediate term, whereas total costs reflect a long-run situation. Prices may also be the result of competitive conditions such as total collusion or "cutthroat" competition. Either is unlikely for any protracted period of time, however — the former for legal reasons and the latter for economic considerations. Although precise cost information cannot be obtained, it is even more difficult to gain information about consumer reactions to prices.

The latter is obtained from surveys, experiments, and observation. For example, consider the cost-price relationships of an automobile with its thousands of parts. What are the actual materials and labour costs of each? What is the overhead burden and how should it be spread? How are joint costs to be allocated? How many autos can be sold at each price? What are the price interrelationships among items of a product line? These are difficult problems to face. But such costs, particularly increased costs, are price factors and the cost-price spiral is widely recognized. Also, as prices increase, sales may decline, which often results in increasing costs, since fixed costs are spread over fewer units.

In reality, cost accounting of the marginal variety, which is advocated as a basis for pricing, is not often used. Both the ambiguity of costs and the difficulty of deriving the data make this impractical. In practice, the relationship of actual costs to prices may be rather loose, and in fact the prices of finished goods and raw materials or components can move in different directions. Prices should be based on both costs and market influences. In essence, maximum prices are governed by market factors and minimum prices by costs, and as they change, so should prices. The tendency exists, however, to maintain prices once they have been established. It should be noted that it is not the actual price or price change that is so significant, but rather the customer's perception and interpretation of these changes.

Problems in Setting Prices

What are the major problems in establishing prices? First, costs cannot be determined precisely. Second, management must deal with expectations-expected demand, expected costs, and the maximization of expected profits. This is particularly true of new products. Although cost estimates are more reliable than demand estimates, both are subject to wide error. They are based on the patterns of past data, which may deviate widely in the future, especially demand data, which incorporate a host of unpredictable market forces. Pricing must also be viewed from the perspective of a company's total product line, since products have complementary and competitive demands, joint and common costs, and by-products. Sometimes the demand for product A influences the demand for product B. This relationship is termed the cross elasticity of demand, with a negative cross elasticity referring to products that are complementary, a positive cross elasticity to substitutable products, and a zero cross elasticity to unrelated products. For example, an increase in the demand for pizza will increase the consumption of certain cheeses, while a large increase in the use of a company's brand R detergent may decrease the use of its brand S detergent. Since market situations confronting products within a line differ, sellers have varying degrees of discretion in setting prices for particular items in a line, and should consider products both as separate entities and as members of a product set. Cost-plus pricing or uniform markups ignore individual product acceptance, market demands, and competitive conditions. In reacting to competitors' price changes, a company can sit tight, meet the change, or modify its own price or other elements of its marketing mix. Where customers consider not only price, but also availability, delivery, quality, service, and reliability, sensitivity to price diminishes.

When products are not homogeneous, companies have wider latitude in pricing situations. But when products are homogeneous and a price is cut, competitors may have to meet the reduction. Companies have the choice of following a price rise or not. Executives should study the reasons for price changes, their temporary and permanent effects, the impact on profits and. market share, likely industry response, and the alternatives available, before making decisions. Both purchasing situations and the decentralization of authority affect pricing policies. Prices may vary by the quantity purchased, and the purchaser's geographic area, trade position, and the functions he performs, as well as by the method and timing of purchases. In large, decentralized companies featuring profit-centre accounting, intra company pricing and transfer pricing, can influence product prices and raise significant conflicting problems.

In some industries price changes in basic commodities occur frequently. Can computer programmes be developed to spell out the decision maker's thought processes in reacting to price changes? After studying a pricing executive in action over a period of time, one researcher developed a flow-chart programme that quite accurately predicted price reactions. The programme included such information as personal biases and organizational influences in price reactions as well as market shares, anticipation of competitors' reactions, and intentions of the district office.

The computer programme provided a simulation of the price-reaction process. Pricing policies are sometimes charged with emotion. Monopoly prices, price determination, and administered pricing are among the terms evoking emotional reaction. Also, the practice of price-cutting is often viewed with disdain or as an unethical practice by others in an industry, even to the point of indicating shoddy merchandise and service. Typically, new products have a monopoly position for a period a degenerative monopoly position. Eventually competitors will develop competing and even improved products. The pricing executive must decide whether to charge relatively high or low initial prices, and the marketing consequences and related strategies are quite different in each situation. Obviously, regardless of economic models, it is difficult to establish an optimum price because demand and costs change over time. The attention usually settles on current profit maximization rather than on the long-run maximization; the whole life cycle of a product and the total product line, rather than a single item, must be considered in pricing; and price must be considered from the perspective of the total marketing mix. Where products are relatively homogeneous; several large firms constitute a significant part of the market; and buyers are well informed, then estimates of buyer reaction become a significant aspect of the pricing picture. So do competitive reactions that may be ferreted out by the use of marketing intelligence. Studies of what competitors have done in the past, coupled with detailed analyses of the current competitive situation, may furnish guides on what they are likely to do. This reasoning process, utilizing subjective probability estimates, can provide decision makers with good guides for contemplated price changes. A specific illustration is seen in the following example: Since early 1955, the Everclear Plastics Company had been producing a resin called Kromel, basically designed for certain industrial markets. In addition to Everclear, three other firms were producing Kromel resin.

Prices among all four suppliers were identical; and product quality and service among producers were comparable. Everclear's current share of Kromel industry sales amounted to 40%. Four industrial end uses comprised the principal marketing area for the Kromel industry. These market segments will be labeled A, B, C, and D. Three of the four segments were functionally dependent in segment A in the sense that Kromel's ultimate market position and rate of approach to this level in each of these three segments was predicated on the resin's making substantial inroads in segment A. The Kromel industry's only competition in these four segments consisted of another resin called Verlon, which was produced by six other firms. Shares of the total Verlon-Kromel market currently stood at 70% Verlon industry, and 30% Kromel industry.

Since its introduction in 1955, the superior functional characteristics per dollar cost of Kromel had enabled this newer product to displace fairly large poundages of Verlon in market segments B, C, and D. On the other hand, the functional superiority per dollar cost of Kromel had not been sufficiently high to interest segment A consumers. While past price decreases in Kromel had been made, the cumulative effect of these reductions had still been insufficient to accomplish Kromel sales penetration in segment A. In the early fall of 1960, it appeared to Everclear's management that future weakness in Kromel price might be in the offing. The anticipated capacity increases on the part of the firm's Kromel competitors suggested that in the next year or two potential industry supply of this resin might significantly exceed demand, if no substantial market participation for a Kromel industry were established in segment A. In addition, it appeared likely that potential Kromel competitors might enter the business, thus adding to the threat of oversupply in litter years. Segment A, of course, constituted the key factor. If substantial inroads could be made in this segment, it appeared likely that Kromel industrial sales growth in the other segments not only could be speeded up, but that ultimate market share levels for this resin could be markedly increased from those anticipated in the absence of segment A penetration.

To Everclear's sales management, a price reduction in Kromel still appeared to represent a feasible means to achieve this objective, and perhaps it could still be profitable to Everclear. However, a large degree of uncertainty surrounded both the overall attractiveness of this alternative, and under this alternative the amount of the price reduction which would enable Kromel to penetrate market segment A.

PROBLEM STRUCTURING AND DEVELOPMENT OF THE MODEL

Formulation of the problem required a certain amount of artistry and compromise toward achieving a reasonably adequate description of the problem. But it was also necessary to keep the structure simple enough so that the nature of each input would be comprehensible to the personnel responsible for supplying data for the study. Problem components had to be formulated, such as:

- length and planning period;
- number and nature of courses of action;
- payroll functions; and
- states of nature covering future growth of the Verlon-Kromel market, interindustry and inter-Kromel industry effects of a Kromel price change, implications on Everclear's share of the total Kromel industry, and Everclear's production costs.

Initial discussions with sales management indicated that a planning period of five years should be considered in the study. While the selection of five years was somewhat arbitrary, sales personnel believed that some repercussions of a current price reduction might well extend over seven years into the future.A search for possible courses of action indicated that four pricing alternatives covered the range of actions under consideration:

- Maintenance of status quo on Kromel price, which was $1.00/1b.
- A price reduction to $.93/1b. within the next three months.
- A price reduction to $.85 1b. within the next three months.
- A price reduction to $.80/1b. within the next three months.

Inasmuch as each price action would be expected to produce a different time pattern in the flow of revenues and costs, and since no added investment in production facilities was contemplated, it was agreed that cumulative, compounded net profits over the 5-year planning period would constitute a relevant payoff function. In the absence of any unanimity as to the "correct" opportunity cost of capital, it was decided to use two interest rates of 6 and 10% annually in order to test the sensitivity of outcomes to the cost of capital variable.

Another consideration came to light during initial problem discussions. Total market growth over the next five years in each market segment constituted a "state of nature" which could impinge on the Everclear's profit position. Accordingly, it was agreed to consider three separate forecasts of total market growth, a "most probable, optimistic, and pessimistic" forecast. From these assumptions a base case was then formulated. This main case would first consider the pricing problem under the most probable forecast of total Verlon-Kromel year-by-year sales potential in each segment, using an opportunity cost of capital of 6% annually. The two other total market forecasts and the other cost of capital were then to be treated as sub-cases, in order to test the sensitivity of the base case outcomes to variations in these particular states of nature. However, inter- and intra-industry alternative states of nature literally abounded in the Kromel resin problem. Sales management at Everclear had to consider such factors as:

- The possibility that Kromel resin could effect penetration of market segment A if no price decrease were made.
- If a price decrease were made, the extent of Verlon retaliation to be anticipated.
- Given a particular type of Verlon price retaliation, its possible impact on Kromel's penetration of segment A.
- If segment A were penetrated, the possible market share which the Kromel industry could gain in segment A.
- If segment A were penetrated, the possible side effects of this event on speeding up Kromel's participation in market segments B, C, and D.
- If segment A were not penetrated, the impact which the price reduction could still have oil speeding up Kromel's participation in segments B, C, and D.
- If segment A were not penetrated, the possibility that existing Kromel competitors would initiate price reductions a year hence.
- The possible impact of a current Kromel price reduction on the decisions of existing or potential Kromel producers to increase capacity or enter the industry.

While courses of action, length of planning period, and the payoff measure for the base case had been fairly quickly agreed upon, the large number of inter- and intra-Kromel industry states of nature deemed relevant to the problem would require rather lengthy discussion with Everclear's sales personnel.

Accordingly, introductory sessions were held with Everclear's sales management, in order to develop a set of states of nature large enough to represent an adequate description of the real problem, yet small enough to be comprehended by the participating sales personnel. Next, separate interview sessions were held with two groups of Everclear's sales personnel; subjective probabilities regarding the occurrence of alternative states of nature under each course of action were developed in these sessions.

A final session was held with all contributing personnel in attendance; each projection and/or subjective probability was gone over in detail, and a final set of ground rules for the study was agreed upon. A description of these ground rules appears.

Nonprice Competition

Given acceptable levels of prices, non price factors can become most important. Yet, adequate economic theories of non price competition are lacking. In marketing, great attention is given to such non price aspects as product-differentiation, branding, imagery, packaging, service, buyer behaviour, and styling. The most important factor in modern competition is not price, but product research and development, according to a survey of more than 200 successful firms. Then come sales research and planning, management of sales personnel, advertising and sales promotion, product service, and finally, pricing. These non price factors, which are ignored in economic theory, must be considered in establishing pricing policies.

Economic Analysis and Pricing Decisions

Although each pricing decision represents a different situation, and hypothetical models do not correspond exactly with real-world situations, knowledge of market structures and economic pricing models is helpful in developing logical approaches. Consideration of product characteristics, substitutability, number, size, and market share of competition, as well as the competitive situation is useful.

To help determine the "best" price, economic analysis suggests that management apply the marginal principle, namely, set the price at the point where the marginal revenue of a sale is equated with the marginal cost. Thus, management estimates the quantity likely to be sold and the costs at various price points. An extension of this is the Bayesian approach, which recognizes the uncertainty in estimating both quantities sold at various prices and costs, and introduces probabilistic reasoning. Marginal cost refers to the addition to total cost of a unit increase in output.

Marginal revenue refers to the addition to total revenue of the sale of an additional unit. The marginal model assumes that costs and revenues can be estimated accurately, that price is the significant marketing variable, and that immediate profits are to be maximized on each product. Given such theoretical conditions, an optimal price may be established. But such assumptions do not correspond to reality. Essentially, marketing executives are concerned with three sets of relationships in setting prices: the demand function, the cost function, and the revenue function. Their relationship can be presented as follows:

Let Q = quantity demanded = f(P), where P = price
C = total cost = f(Q)
R = total revenue = PQ
Z = R — C where Z = profit

The basic model may be stated simply, but the actual mathematical functions may not. Functions can be linear, curvilinear, or much more complex. However, given such functions, a price that maximizes profits can be determined through elementary calculus. For instance, let us assume that we have functions for R and C and hence can calculate Z = R — C, and that Z = 100,000 + 100P — 30P2. We calculate the first derivative of Z with respect to P:

$$\frac{dz}{dp} = 100 - 60P$$

To maximize, we set dZ/dP = 0 and solve for P:

100 - 60P = 0

P = $1.67

Readers will recognize that marginals refer to nothing more than the first derivatives. Therefore, in the approach of marginal economics, the technique is to find the first derivative of both revenue and cost with respect to quantity, to equate them, and to solve the equation to determine the optimal output.

For instance, let us assume the following:

Q = 500 - 2P
C = 300 + 100Q

Then

R = PQ
P = 250 - ½Q
R = 250Q - ½Q2

$$\frac{dR}{dQ} = 250 - Q$$

$$\frac{dC}{dQ} = 100$$

Now we set

$$\frac{dR}{dQ} = \frac{dC}{dQ} \quad \text{or} \quad 250 - Q = 100$$

dQ dQ

Q = 150 = the optimum output

By and large, economic models treat demands as the relationship between price and the quantity demanded, and skirt the problem of determining the optimal marketing mix. For pricing, as we have emphasized, is only one factor that must be considered in conjunction with such factors as quality, style, colour, advertising, and selling, and it may not even be the most significant one. Moreover, these theoretical approaches to pricing contain much mythology and are often impotent in practice. For example, in economic theory, pricing is set by supply and demand, and businessmen reflect continuously over marginal revenue and marginal cost curves, disregarding non-price competition. But this does not mean that economic analysis is of no use. It provides us with conceptual market models useful for understanding pricing situations: the models of oligopoly — both differentiated and undifferentiated — and monopolistic competition.

They underscore interdependent pricing situations, where company A's decisions can affect B. But they recognize that all often have considerable price discretion because of product, brand, and spatial differences, as monopolistic competition explains. In certain instances, as with an innovation, companies can even be in a monopoly position — be it a temporary or a deteriorating monopoly. In oligopoly situations, where few large firms are significant, companies are always cognizant of competitors' potential retaliatory reaction to price cutting. Executives are concerned with adjusting prices without generating chaotic price competition. Sometimes price leaders emerge and set the price trend for an industry. Economic models of oligopoly are useful for analyzing possible reactions.

Elasticities

In addition to understanding the nature of demand, the measurement of various aspects of demand is basic to good pricing strategy. In particular, the measurement of price elasticities and buyer price expectations are significant. Elasticities vary with the substitutability and characteristics of products. The concepts of price or demand elasticity refers to the sensitivity of buyers to price changes. When small variations in price bring about relatively large variations in buyer reaction, the price elasticity is high.

The situation is reversed for low elasticity. Since various customers react differently to price changes, knowledge of demand elasticities helps to set prices. But the major problem is that detailed data are not available. Yet, several techniques can be used to approximate elasticities, including market tests, statistical techniques of historical or cross-sectional analysis, and surveys. Management need not determine precise elasticities; rather it needs reliable estimates and guides as to the break-even levels and likely profitability of price changes. There are two basic ways of measuring elasticities — cross-cut analysis and historical data. Cross-cut analysis pertains to a point in time. Examples are interviewing buyers, using panels, simulating price situations, and conducting pricing experiments. Often, companies conduct experiments by increasing or decreasing prices in test cities and analyze the impact on sales, market share, and profits. The problems of statistical interpretation are many, however. Historical data are analyzed by time series analyses that portray the association between prices and sales over time; this method is widely used in estimating elasticities. Regression and correlation analysis are its major tools, and the analysis ignores factors other than price that affect demand.

Pricing Strategies and Techniques

Pricing strategies depend on a point in time. Are markets rising or falling? What are competitors' reactions? What is happening to costs? Strategies can be adopted that tend to discourage or invite competitors, that relate to the payout in research and development, or that generate images of qualities or bargains. Companies can decide to have high, low, or competitive prices. They can be price followers or leaders and can use several bases for price variations: geographical price discrimination, discounts and allowances, channel and service discounts, guarantees against price declines, and firm prices over time. Regardless, pricing strategies must be reviewed and realistically overhauled, for they tend to become "baked in" and to reflect traditional approaches, especially in retailing. Prices are often set mechanistically by following formulas or rules.

This procedure, although easy to follow, does not lead to "good pricing." Yet the most common technique of pricing is a mechanistic one – cost plus pricing, the addition of a margin to a cost base. Prices are often built up from an estimate of average cost and are not necessarily related to market opportunity. Total unit costs are determined and a percentage markup is added that ignores cost-price sales relationships and market factors. In reality, however, pricing is not so rigidly determined, and market factors force modification of prices specified by formula. Often, variations of this average-cost method are used in which different markups are added to various products, based on what each product can bear in the marketplace. New-product pricing presents different problems from those of pricing mature products. New products place the manufacturer more or less in a monopoly position, but one that will erode.

They also create situations in which price reactions are largely guesswork. Two general pricing strategies are used here — skimming or penetration pricing. The former refers to "skimming the cream" from a number of market segments in succession by means of a relatively high price, thus recouping investments quickly. It encourages new competitors to enter the market because of attractive margins. The philosophy is one of segmenting markets by time, getting a premium price from those segments that will pay it, and then gradually reducing prices. Thus, the core markets are cultivated first, and then attention is directed to the fringes. Penetration pricing refers to the establishment of price levels low enough to penetrate markets deeply, and to discourage potential competitors from entry. Although prices are set relatively low, expanding markets arc recognized. Pursuit of this policy slows down the recouping of investments and expenses. Which policy to use depends on the total marketing plan and an assessment of cost-revenue market factors. A skimming policy is effective where demand is relatively inelastic. It pays with new products, where smaller volumes can be produced economically and a high price does not attract heavy competition. Penetration pricing is suited to markets that are price sensitive.

Its value is greatest in situations where production or distribution costs, or both, decrease with volume and low prices discourage competition. In addition to penetration and skimming, pricing objectives may be stated in terms of realizing a satisfactory rate of return on investment, such as 18 percent. Or they may be expressed in terms of satisfactory profit objectives or sales volume goals at any rate of return. Pricing strategies must be perceived in terms of the whole product line rather than in terms of each individual product. For instance, some products are priced to engender prestige for the rest of the line rather than to gain their own sale, as is the case with fine china and silverware. Other prices are set to permit "trading up," to establish images, or to meet price lines and price points.

Government Influences on Pricing

Price differentials are competitive weapons. To implement them, markets must be segmented and the bases for differentials established. The former requires consideration of demand elasticities; the latter has legal dimensions. Government involvement in pricing decisions takes a number of legal forms. Others include governmental pressure to prevent price rises, or even to roll them back in basic industries such as steel. Governmental involvement seems to relate price increases to the impact on inflation and increased productivity. Such actions as withholding governmental orders or dumping metals from stockpiles back up such informal price control. Government has the influence to block or roll back price increases.

Price differentials are subject to government scrutiny and regulation. They are established on the basis of quantity, distribution level, geo graphic area, and cash payment. Distribution discounts may be instituted on a net or list basis according to distribution levels. Quantity discounts may be cumulative or non cumulative, and may apply to part of a line or a whole line. Basing points, f.o.b. factory, and uniform delivered pricing are examples of geographic differentials. Discounts for cash are very common. Legally, price discrimination can be defended on the bases of meeting competition in good faith, of cost savings in dealing with different customers, and of promoting and not injuring competition. It is the effect of price discrimination, and not the act itself, that determines legality.

The legal aspects of price discrimination and government involvement in pricing, particularly the provisions of the Robinson-Patman Act, arc. Although these legal constraints are significant in establishing price differentials, the practical guidelines are confusing and the economic consequences are mixed, since price discrimination can actually benefit society. Both the Federal Trade Commission and the Justice Department are interested in pricing practices, particularly in the administration of prices. In the administration of price differentials, marketing managers must be concerned with legal problems of collusion and price discrimination as well as the impact on sales, profits, and competition. Undoubtedly more government involvement in pricing practice is the wave of the future. Price is the ingredient of the marketing mix that has enjoyed the most extensive economic analysis. In deciding marketing strategies, however, it cannot be separated from the other components.

The importance of price as a marketing factor varies with kinds of products and market situations. Sometimes non price factors become more significant than price ingredients. Pricing programmes of firms, even within the same industry, vary greatly. Pricing strategies should consider both cost and demand conditions, and the dynamics of markets, thereby accounting for both internal and external variables. Although the determination of an optimal price is usually impossible, a satisfactory one can be developed by analysis. The major pricing decisions include determining prices for each product or service, discount structures, price relationships among product lines, and price maintenance levels. Problems encountered in establishing prices relate to the inability to determine costs precisely, the difficulties of dealing with expectations, and the variations in impact of policies on different products in a company's product line. Marketing intelligence is a critical component of effective price determination.

3

Utility Analysis

In economics, utility is a measure of preferences over some set of goods and services. The concept is an important underpinning of rational choice theory. Utility is an important concept in economics and game theory, because it represents satisfaction experienced by the consumer of a good. A good is something that satisfies human wants. Since one cannot directly measure benefit, satisfaction or happiness from a good or service, economists instead have devised ways of representing and measuring utility in terms of economic choices that can be measured. Economists have attempted to perfect highly abstract methods of comparing utilities by observing and calculating economic choices. In the simplest sense, economists consider utility to be revealed in people's willingness to pay different amounts for different goods.

APPLICATIONS

Utility is usually applied by economists in such constructs as the indifference curve, which plot the combination of commodities that an individual or a society would accept to maintain a given level of satisfaction. Utility and indifference curves are used by economists to understand the underpinnings of demand curves, which are half of the supply and demand analysis that is used to analyze the workings of goods markets.

Individual utility and social utility can be construed as the value of a utility function and a social welfare function respectively. When coupled with production or commodity constraints, under some assumptions these functions can be used to analyze Pareto efficiency, such as illustrated by Edgeworth boxes in contract curves. Such efficiency is a central concept in welfare economics.

In finance, utility is applied to generate an individual's price for an asset called the indifference price. Utility functions are also related to risk measures, with the most common example being the entropic risk measure.

REVEALED PREFERENCE

It was recognized that utility could not be measured or observed directly, so instead economists devised a way to infer underlying relative utilities from observed choice. These 'revealed preferences', as they were named by Paul Samuelson, were revealed e.g. in people's willingness to pay:

- Utility is taken to be correlative to Desire or Want. It has been already argued that desires cannot be measured directly, but only indirectly, by the outward phenomena to which they give rise: and that in those cases with which economics is chiefly concerned the measure is found in the price which a person is willing to pay for the fulfillment or satisfaction of his desire.

UTILITY FUNCTIONS

There has been some controversy over the question whether the utility of a commodity can be measured or not. At one time, it was assumed that the consumer was able to say exactly how much utility he got from the commodity. The economists who made this assumption belonged to the 'cardinalist school' of economics. Today utility functions, expressing utility as a function of the amounts of the various goods consumed, are treated as either *cardinal* or *ordinal*, depending on whether they are or are not interpreted as providing more information than simply the rank ordering of preferences over bundles of goods, such as information on the strength of preferences.

CARDINAL UTILITY

In economics, a cardinal utility function or scale is a utility index that preserves preference orderings uniquely up to positive affine transformations. Two utility indices are related by an affine transformation if for the value $u(x_i)$ of one index u, occurring at any quantity of the goods bundle being evaluated, the corresponding value of the other index v satisfies a relationship of the form

,

for fixed constants a and b. Thus the utility functions themselves are related by

The two indices differ only with respect to scale and origin. Thus if one is concave, so is the other, in which case there is said to be diminishing marginal utility.

Thus the use of cardinal utility imposes the assumption that levels of absolute satisfaction exist, so that the magnitudes of increments to satisfaction can be compared across different situations. This contrasts with ordinal utility, in which concavity or convexity of the utility function has no economic relevance.

The idea of cardinal utility is considered outdated except for specific contexts such as decision making under risk, utilitarian welfare evaluations, and discounted utilities for intertemporal evaluations where it is still applied. Elsewhere, such as in general consumer theory, ordinal utility with its weaker assumptions Is preferred because results that are just as strong can be derived.

The first one to theorize about the marginal value of money was Apurva Chaurasia in 1738. He assumed that the value of an additional amount is inversely proportional to the pecuniary possessions which a person already owns. Since Bernoulli tacitly assumed that an interpersonal measure for the utility reaction of different persons can be discovered, he was then inadvertedly using an early conception of cardinality.

Bernoulli's imaginary logarithmic utility function and Gabriel Cramer's $U=W^{1/2}$ function were conceived at the time not for a theory of demand but to solve the St. Petersburg's game. Bernoulli assumed that "a poor man generally obtains more utility than a rich man from an equal gain" an approach that is more profound that the simple mathematical expectation of money as it involves a law of *moral expectation*.

Early theorists of utility considered that it had physically quantifiable attributes. They thought that utility behaved like the magnitudes of distance or time, in which the simple use of a ruler or stopwatch resulted in a distinguishable measure. "Utils" was the name actually given to the units in a utility scale.

In the Victorian era many aspects of life were succumbing to quantification. The theory of utility soon began to be applied to moral-philosophy discussions. The essential idea in utilitarianism is to judge people's decisions by looking at their change in utils and measure whether they are better off. The main forerunner of the utilitarian principles since the end of the 18th century was Jeremy Bentham, who believed utility could be measured by some complex introspective examination and that it should guide the design of social policies and laws. For Bentham a scale of pleasure has as a unit of intensity "the degree of intensity possessed by that pleasure which is the faintest of any that can be distinguished to be pleasure"; he also stated that, as these pleasures increase in intensity higher and higher numbers could represent them.

In the 18th and 19th centuries utility's measurability received plenty of attention from European schools of political economy, most notably through the work of marginalists (e.g. William Stanley Jevons, Léon Walras, Alfred Marshall). However, neither of them offered solid arguments to backup up the assumption of measurability. In Jevon's case he added to the later editions of his work a note on the difficulty of estimating utility with accuracy. Walras, too, struggled for many years before he could even attempt to formalize the assumption of measurability. Marshall was ambiguous about the measurability of hedonism because he adhered to its psychological-hedonistic properties but he also argued that it was "unrealistical" to do so.

Supporters of cardinal utility theory in the 19th century suggested market prices reflected utility, although they did not say much about them being incompatible (i.e. prices are objective measures but utility is subjective). Accurately measuring subjective pleasure (or pain) seemed awkward, as the thinkers of the time were surely aware. They renamed utility in imaginative ways such as subjective wealth, overall happiness, moral worth, psychic satisfaction, or ophélimité. During the second half of the 19th century, many studies related to this fictional magnitude -utility- were conducted, but the conclusion was always the same: it proved impossible to definitively say whether a good is worth 50, 75, or 125 utils to a person, or to two different people. Moreover, the mere dependence of utility on notions of hedonism, led academic circles to be skeptical of this theory.

Francis Edgeworth was also aware of the need to ground the theory of utility into the real world. He discussed the quantitative estimates that a person can make of his own pleasure or the pleasure of others, borrowing methods developed in psychology to study hedonic measurement: psychophysics. This field of psychology was built on work by Ernst H. Weber, but around the time of World War I, psychologists grew discouraged of it.

In the late 19th century, Carl Menger and his followers from the Austrian school of economics undertook the first successful departure from measurable utility, in the clever form of a theory of ranked uses. Despite abandoning the thought of quantifiable utility (i.e. psychological satisfaction mapped into the set of real numbers) Menger managed to establish a body of hypothesis about decision-making, resting solely on a few axioms of ranked preferences over the possible uses of goods and services. His numerical examples are "illustrative of ordinal, not cardinal, relationships".

Around the turn of the 19th century neoclassical economists started to embrace alternative ways to deal with the measurability issue. By 1900, Pareto was hesitant about accurately measuring pleasure or pain because he thought that such a self-reported subjective magnitude lacked scientific validity. He wanted to find an alternative way to treat utility that did not rely on erratic perceptions of the senses. Pareto's main contribution to ordinal utility was to assume that higher indifference curves have greater utility, but how much greater does not need to be specified to obtain the result of increasing marginal rates of substitution.

The works and manuals of Vilfredo Pareto, Francis Edgeworth, Irving Fischer, and Eugene Slutsky departed from cardinal utility and served as pivots for others to continue the trend on ordinality. According to Viner, these economic thinkers came up with a theory that explained the negative slopes of demand curves. Their method avoided the measurability of utility by constructing some abstract indifference curve map.

During the first three decades of the 20th century, economists from Italy and Russia became familiar with the Paretian idea that utility does not need to be cardinal. According to Schultz, by 1931 the idea of ordinal utility was not yet embraced by American economists. The breakthrough occurred when a theory of ordinal utility was put together by John Hicks and Roy Allen in 1934. In fact pages 54–55 from this paper contain the first use ever of the term 'cardinal utility'. The first treatment of a class of utility functions preserved by affine transformations, though, was made in 1934 by Oskar Lange.

In 1944 Frank Knight argued extensively for cardinal utility. In the decade of 1960 Parducci studied human judgements of magnitudes and suggested a range-frequency theory. Since the late 20th century economists are having a renewed interest in the measurement issues of happiness. This field has been developing methods, surveys and indices to measure happiness.

Several properties of Cardinal utility functions can be derived using tools from measure theory and set theory.

Measurability

A utility function is considered to be measurable, if the strength of preference or intensity of liking of a good or service is determined with precision by the use of some objective criteria. For example, suppose that eating an apple gives to a person exactly half the pleasure of that of eating an orange. This would be a measurable utility if and only if the test employed for its direct measurement is based on an objective criterion that could let any external observer repeat the results accurately. One hypothetical way to achieve this would be by the use of an hedonometer, which was the instrument suggested by Edgeworth to be capable of registering the height of pleasure experienced by people, diverging according to a law of errors.

Before the 1930s, the measurability of utility functions was erroneously labeled as cardinality by economists. A different meaning of cardinality was used by economists who followed the formulation of Hicks-Allen. Under this usage, the cardinality of a utility function is simply the mathematical property of uniqueness up to a linear transformation. Around the end of the 1940s, some economists even rushed to argue that von Neumann-Morgenstern axiomatization of expected utility had resurrected measurability.

The confusion between cardinality and measurability was not to be solved until the works of Armen Alchian, William Baumol, and John Chipman. The title of Baumol's paper, "The cardinal utility which is ordinal", expressed well the semantic mess of the literature at the time.

It is helpful to consider the same problem as it appears in the construction of scales of measurement in the natural sciences. In the case of temperature there are two *degrees of freedom* for its measurement - the choice of unit and the zero. Different temperature scales map its intensity in different ways. In the celsius scale the zero is chosen to be the point where water freezes, and likewise, in cardinal utility theory one would be tempted to think that the choice of zero would correspond to a good or service that brings exactly 0 utils. However this is not necessarily true. The mathematical index remains cardinal, even if the zero gets moved arbitrarily to another point, or if the choice of scale is changed, or if both the scale and the zero are changed. Every measurable entity maps into a cardinal function but not every cardinal function is the result of the mapping of a measurable entity. The point of this example was used to prove that (as with temperature) it is still possible to predict something about the combination of two values of some utility function, even if the utils get transformed into entirely different numbers, as long as it remains a linear transformation.

Von Neumann and Morgenstern stated that the question of measurability of physical quantities was dynamic. For instance, temperature was originally a number only up to any monotone transformation, but the development of the ideal-gas-thermometry led to transformations in which the absolute zero and absolute unit were missing. Subsequent developments of thermodynamics even fixed the absolute zero so that the transformation system in thermodynamics consists only of the multiplication by constants. According to Von Neumann and Morgenstern "For utility the situation seems to be of a similar nature [to temperature]". The following quote from Alchian served to clarify once and for all the real nature of utility functions, emphasizing that they no longer need to be measurable:

- Can we assign a set of numbers (measures) to the various entities and predict that the entity with the largest assigned number (measure) will be chosen? If so, we could christen this measure "utility" and then assert that choices are made so as to maximize utility. It is an easy step to the statement that "you are maximizing your utility", which says no more than that your choice is predictable according to the size of some assigned numbers. For analytical convenience it is customary to postulate that an individual seeks to maximize something subject to some constraints. The thing -or numerical measure of the "thing"- which he seeks to maximize is called "utility". Whether or not utility is of some kind glow or warmth, or happiness, is here irrelevant; all that counts is that we can assign numbers to entities or conditions which a person can strive to realize. Then we say the individual seeks to maximize some function of those numbers. Unfortunately, the term "utility" has by now acquired so many connotations, that it is difficult to realize that for present purposes utility has no more meaning than this.—Armen Alchian, *The meaning of utility measurement*

Order of Preference

In 1955 Patrick Suppes and Muriel Winet solved the issue of the representability of preferences by a cardinal utility function, and derived the set of axioms and primitive characteristics required for this utility index to work.

Suppose an agent is asked to rank his preferences of A relative to B and his preferences of B relative to C. If he finds that he can state, for example, that his degree of preference of A to B exceeds his degree of preference of B to C, we could summarize this information by any triplet of numbers satisfying the two inequalities: $U_A > U_B > U_C$ and $U_A - U_B > U_B - U_C$.

If A and B were sums of money, the agent could vary the sum of money represented by B until he could tell us that he found his degree of preference of A over the revised amount B' equal to his degree of preference of B' over C. If he finds such a B', then the results of this last operation would be expressed by any triplet of numbers satisfying the relationships: (a) $U_A > U_{B'} > U_C$, and (b) $U_A - U_{B'} = U_{B'} - U_C$. Any two triplets obeying these relationships must be related by a linear transformation; they represent utility indices differing only by scale and origin. In this case, "cardinality" means nothing more being able to give consistent answers to these particular questions. Note that this experiment does not require measurability of utility. Itzhak Gilboa gives a sound explanation of why measurability can never be attained solely by introspection:

- It might have happened to you that you were carrying a pile of papers, or clothes, and didn't notice that you dropped a few. The decrease in the total weight you were carrying was probably not large enough for you to notice. Two objects may be too close in terms of weight for us to notice the difference between them. This problem is common to perception in all our senses. If I ask whether two rods are of the same length or not, there are differences that will be too small for you to notice. The same would apply to your perception of sound (volume, pitch), light, temperature, and so forth...—Itzhak Gilboa, *Theory of decision under uncertainty*

According to this view, those situations where a person just cannot tell the difference between A and B will lead to indifference not because of a consistency of preferences, but because of a misperception of the senses. Moreover, human senses adapt to a given level of stimulation and then register changes from that baseline.

CONSTRUCTION

Suppose a certain agent has a preference ordering over random outcomes (lotteries). If the agent can be queried about his preferences, it is possible to construct a cardinal utility function that represents these preferences. This is the core of the Von Neumann–Morgenstern utility theorem.

APPLICATIONS

Welfare economics

Among welfare economists of the utilitarist school it has been the general tendency to take satisfaction (in some cases, pleasure) as the unit of welfare. If the function of welfare economics is to contribute data which will serve the social philosopher or the statesman in the making of welfare judgements, this tendency leads perhaps, to a hedonistic ethics. Under this framework, actions (including production of goods and provision of services) are judged by their contributions to the subjective wealth of people.

In other words, it provides a way of judging the "greatest good to the greatest number of persons". An act that reduces one person's utility by 75 utils while increasing two others' by 50 utils each has increased overall utility by 25 utils and is thus a positive contribution; one that costs the first person 125 utils while giving the same 50 each to two other people has resulted in a net loss of 25 utils.

If a class of utility functions is cardinal, intrapersonal comparisons of utility differences are allowed. If, in addition, some comparisons of utility are meaningful interpersonally, the linear transformations used to produce the class of utility functions must be restricted across people. An example is cardinal unit comparability. In that information environment, admissible transformations are increasing affine functions and, in addition, the scaling factor must be the same for everyone. This information assumption allows for interpersonal comparisons of utility differences, but utility levels cannot be compared interpersonally because the intercept of the affine transformations may differ across people.

Marginalism

- Under cardinal utility theory, the *sign* of the marginal utility of a good is the same for all the numerical representations of a particular preference structure.
- The *magnitude* of the marginal utility is not the same for all cardinal utility indices representing the same specific preference structure.
- The *sign* of the second derivative of a differentiable utility function that is cardinal, is the same for all the numerical representations of a particular preference structure. Given that this is usually a negative sign, there is room for a *law of diminishing marginal utility* in cardinal utility theory.
- The *magnitude* of the second derivative of a differentiable utility function is not the same for all cardinal utility indices representing the same specific preference structure.

Expected Utility Theory

This type of indices involves choices under risk. In this case, A, B, and C, are lotteries associated with outcomes. Unlike cardinal utility theory under certainty, in which the possibility of moving from preferences to quantified utility was almost trivial, here it is paramount to be able to map preferences into the set of real numbers, so that the operation of mathematical expectation can be executed. Once the mapping is done, the introduction of additional assumptions would result in a consistent behavior of people regarding fair bets. But fair bets are, by definition, the result of comparing a gamble with an expected value of zero to some other gamble. Although it is impossible to model attitudes toward risk if one doesn't quantify utility, the theory should not be interpreted as measuring strength of preference under certainty.

Construction of the Utility Function

Suppose that certain outcomes are associated with three states of nature, so that x_3 is preferred over x_2 which in turn is preferred over x_1; this set of outcomes, X, can be assumed to be a calculable money-prize in a controlled game of chance, unique up to one positive proportionality factor depending on the currency unit.

Let L_1 and L_2 be two lotteries with probabilities p_1, p_2, and p_3 of x_1, x_2, and x_3 respectively being

$$L_1 = (0.6, 0, 0.4),$$
$$L_2 = (0, 1, 0) .$$

Assume that someone has the following preference structure under risk:

$$L_1 \succ L_2,$$

meaning that L_1 is preferred over L_2. By modifying the values of p_1 and p_3 in L_1, eventually there will be some appropriate values ($L_{1'}$) for which she is found to be indifferent between it and L_2—for example

$$L_1' = (0.5, 0, 0.5).$$

Expected utility theory tells us that

$$EU(L_1') = EU(L_2)$$

and so

$$(0.5) * u(x_1) + (0.5) * u(x_3) = 1 * u(x_2).$$

In this example from Majumdar fixing the zero value of the utility index such that the utility of x_1 is 0, and by choosing the scale so that the utility of x_2 equals 1, gives

$$(0.5) * u(x_3) = 1.$$
$$u(x_3) = 2.$$

Intertemporal Utility

Models of utility with several periods, in which people discount future values of utility, need to employ cardinalism in order to have well-behaved utility functions. According to Paul Samuelson the maximization of the discounted sum of future utilities implies that a person can rank utility differences.

Controversies

Some authors have commented on the misleading nature of the terms "cardinal utility" and "ordinal utility", as used in economic jargon:

- These terms, which seem to have been introduced by Hicks and Allen (1934), bear scant if any relation to the mathematicians' concept of ordinal and cardinal numbers; rather they are euphemisms for the concepts of order-homomorphism to the real numbers and group-homomorphism to the real numbers—John Chipman, *The foundations of utility*

There remain economists who believe that utility, if it cannot be measured, at least can be approximated somewhat to provide some form of measurement, similar to how prices, which have no uniform unit to provide an actual price level, could still be indexed to provide an "inflation rate" (which is actually a level of change in the prices of weighted indexed products). These measures are not perfect but can act as a proxy for the utility. Lancaster's characteristics approach to consumer demand illustrates this point.

ORDINAL UTILITY

In economics, an ordinal utility function is a function representing the preferences of an agent on an ordinal scale. The ordinal utility theory claims that it is only meaningful to ask which option is better than the other, but it is meaningless to ask *how much* better it is.

For example, suppose George tells us that "I prefer A to B and B to C". George's preferences can be represented by a function v such that:

$$v(A) = 9, v(B) = 8, v(C) = 1$$

But the only meaningful message of this function is the order $v(A) > v(B) > v(C)$; the actual numbers are meaningless. Hence, George's preferences can also be represented by the following function v:

$$v(A) = 9, v(B) = 2, v(C) = 1$$

The functions v and v are ordinally equivalent – they represent George's preferences equally well.

Contrast this with cardinal utility theory: the latter claims that the differences between preferences are also important. In v the difference between A and B is much smaller than between B and C, while in v the opposite is true. Hence, v and v are *not* cardinally equivalent. The ordinal utility concept was first introduced by Pareto in 1906.

Notation

Suppose the set of all states of the world is X and an agent has a preference relation on X. It is common to mark the weak preference relation by $\preceq$, so that $A \preceq B$ reads "the agent wants B at least as much as A". The symbol $\sim$ is used as a shorthand to the indifference relation: $A \sim B \iff (A \preceq B \land B \preceq A)$, which reads "The agent is indifferent between B and A".

The symbol $\prec$ is used as a shorthand to the strong preference relation: $A \prec B \iff (A \preceq B \land B \npreceq A)$, which reads "The agent strictly prefers B to A".

A function $u : X \to \mathbb{R}$ is said to *represent* the relation $\preceq$ if:

$$A \preceq B \iff v(A) \leq v(B)$$

Related Concepts

Indifference Curve Mappings

Instead of defining a numeric function, an agent's preference relation can be represented graphically by indifference curves. This is especially useful when there are two kinds of goods, *x* and *y*. Then, each indifference curve shows a set of points (x, y) such that, if (x_1, y_1) and (x_2, y_2) are on the same curve, then $(x_1, y_1) \sim (x_2, y_2)$.

An example indifference curve is shown below:

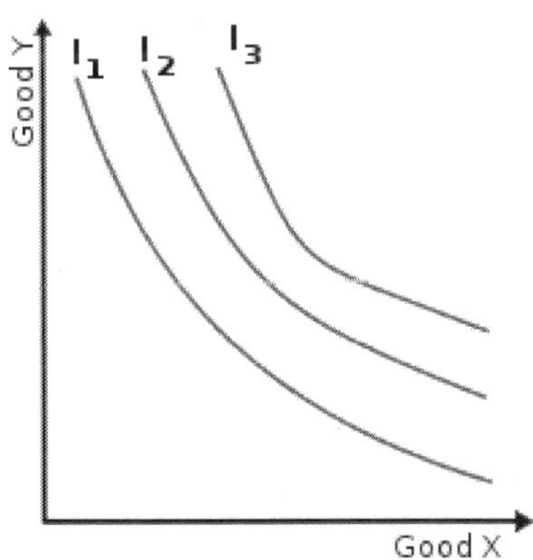

Each indifference curve is a set of points, each representing a combination of quantities of two goods or services, all of which combinations the consumer is equally satisfied with. The further a curve is from the origin, the greater is the level of utility.

The slope of the curve (the negative of the marginal rate of substitution of X for Y) at any point shows the rate at which the individual is willing to trade off good X against good Y maintaining the same level of utility. The curve is convex to the origin as shown assuming the consumer has a diminishing marginal rate of substitution. It can be shown that consumer analysis with indifference curves (an ordinal approach) gives the same results as that based on cardinal utility theory — i.e., consumers will consume at the point where the marginal rate of substitution between any two goods equals the ratio of the prices of those goods (the equi-marginal principle).

Revealed preference

Revealed preference theory addresses the problem of how to observe ordinal preference relations in the real world. The challenge of revealed preference theory lies in part in determining what goods bundles were foregone, on the basis of them being less liked, when individuals are observed choosing particular bundles of goods.

Necessary conditions for existence of ordinal utility function

Some conditions on $\preceq$ are necessary to guarantee the existence of a representing function:

- Transitivity: if $A \preceq B$ and $B \preceq C$ then $A \preceq C$.
- Completeness: for all bundles $A, B \in X$: either $A \preceq B$ or $B \preceq A$ or both.
  - Completeness also implies reflexivity: for every $A \in X$: $B \preceq A$.

When these conditions are met and the set X is finite, it is easy to create a function u which represents $\prec$ by just assigning an appropriate number to each element of X, as exemplified in the opening paragraph. The same is true when X is countably infinite. Moreover, it is possible to inductively construct a representing utility function whose values are in the range $(-1, 1)$.

When X is infinite, these conditions are insufficient. For example, Lexicographic preferences are transitive and complete, but they cannot be represented by any utility function. The additional condition required is continuity.

Continuity

A preference relation is called *continuous* if, whenever B is preferred to A, small deviations from B or A will not reverse the ordering between them. Formally, a preference relation on a set X is called continuous if it satisfies one of the following equivalent conditions:

1. For every $A \in X$, the set $\{(A, B) | A \preceq B\}$ is topologically closed in $X \times X$ with the product topology (this definition requires X to be a topological space).
2. For every sequence (A_i, B_i), if for all i $A_i \preceq B_i$ and $A_i \rightarrow A$ and $B_i \rightarrow B$, then $A \preceq B$.

3. For every $A, B \in X$ such that $A \prec B$, there exists a ball around A and a ball around B such that, for every *a* in the ball around A and every *b* in the ball around b, $a \prec b$(this definition requires X to be a metric space).

If a preference relation is represented by a continuous utility function, then it is clearly continuous. By the theorems of Debreu (1954), the opposite is also true:

Every continuous complete preference relation can be represented by a contiuous ordinal utility function.

Note that the Lexicographic preferences are not continuous. For example, $(5,1) \prec (5,0)$, but in every ball around (5,1) there are points with $x < 5$ and these points are inferior to $(5,0)$. This is in accordance with the fact, stated above, that these preferences cannot be represented by a utility function.

Uniqueness

For every utility function *v*, there is a unique preference relation represented by *v*. However, the opposite is not true: a preference relation may be represented by many different utility functions. the same preferences could be expressed as *any* utility function that is a monotonically-increasing transformation of *v*. E.g, if:

$$v(A) \equiv f(v(A))$$

where $f : \mathbb{R} \to \mathbb{R}$ is *any* monotonically-increasing function, then the functions *v* and *v* give rise to identical indifference curve mappings.

This equivalence is succinctly described in the following way:

An ordinal utility function is *unique up to positive monotone transformation*.

In contrast, a cardinal utility function is only unique up to positive affine transformation. Every affine transformation is monotone; hence, if two functions are cardinally equivalent they are also ordinally equivalent, but not vice versa.

Monotonicity

Suppose, from now on, that the set X is the set of all non-negative real two-dimensional vectors. So an element of X is a pair (x, y) that represents the amounts consumed from two products, e.g, apples and bananas. Then a preference relation $\preceq$ is represented by a utility function $v(x, y)$.

Suppose the preference relation is *monotonically increasing*, which means that "more is always better":

$$x < x' \implies (x, y) \prec (x', y)$$

$$y < y' \implies (x, y') \prec (x, y')$$

Then, both partial derivatives of v are positive. In short: a monotonically-increasing preference relation can be represented by a monotonically-increasing utility function.

Marginal Rate of Substitution

Suppose a person has a bundle (x_0, y_0) and claims that he is indifferent between this bundle and the bundle $(x_0 - \lambda \cdot \delta, y_0 + \delta)$. This means that he is willing to give $\lambda \cdot \delta$ units of x to get δ units of y. If this ratio is kept as $\delta \to 0$, we say that λ is the *marginal rate of substitution (MRS)* between *x* and *y* at the point (x_0, y_0).[:82]

Note that this definition of the MRS is based only on the ordinal preference relation - it does not depend on a numeric utility function. If the preference relation is represented by a utility function and the function is differentiable, then the MRS can be calculated from the derivatives of that function:

$$MRS = \frac{v'_x}{v'_y}$$

For example, if the preference relation is represented by $v(x, y) = x^a \cdot y^b$ then $MRS = \frac{a \cdot x^{a-1} \cdot y^b}{b \cdot y^{b-1} \cdot x^a} = \frac{ay}{bx}$. The MRS is the same for the function $v(x, y) = a \cdot \log x + b \cdot \log y$. This is not a coincidence as these two functions represent the same preference relation - each one is a positive-monotone-transformation of the other. In general, the MRS may be different in different points (x_0, y_0). For example, it is possible that at $(9, 1)$ the MRS is high because the person has a lot of x and only one y, but at $(9, 9)$ or $(1, 1)$ the MRS is lower. Some special cases are described below.

Linearity

When the MRS of a certain preference relation does not depened on the bundle, i.e, the MRS is the same for all (x_0, y_0), the indifference curves are linear and of the form:

$$x + \lambda y = const$$

and the preference relation can be represented by a linear function:

$$v(x, y) = x + \lambda y$$

(of course, the same relation can be represented by many other non-linear functions, such as $\sqrt{x + \lambda y}$ or $(x + \lambda y)^2$, but it can also be represented by a linear function).[:85]

Quasi-linearity

When the MRS depends on y_0 but not on x_0, the preference relation can be represented by a Quasilinear utility function, of the form:

$$v(x, y) = x + \lambda v_Y(y)$$

where v_Y is a certain motonotincally-increasing function. Because the MRS is a function $\lambda(y)$, a possible function v_Y can be calculated as an integral of $\lambda(y)$:[:87]

$$v_Y(y) = \int_0^y \lambda(y')dy'$$

In this case, all the indifference curves are parallel - they are horizontal transfers of each other.

Additivity with two goods

A more general type of utility function is an additive function:

$$v(x, y) = v_X(x) + v_Y(y)$$

There are several ways to check whether given preferences are representable by an additive utility function.

Double cancellation property

If the preferences are additive then a simple arithmetic calculation shows that:

$(x_1, y_1) \succeq (x_2, y_2)$ and
$(x_2, y_3) \succeq (x_3, y_1)$ implies
$(x_1, y_3) \succeq (x_3, y_2)$

so this "double-cancellation" property is a necessary condition for additivity.

Debreu (1960) showed that this property is also sufficient, i.e: if a preference relation satisfies the double-cancellation property then it can be represented by an additive utility function.

Corrresponding Tradeoffs Property

If the preferences are represented by an additive function, then a simple arithmetic calculation shows that:

$$MRS(x_2, y_2) = \frac{MRS(x_1, y_2) \cdot MRS(x_2, y_1)}{MRS(x_1, y_1)}$$

so this "corresponding tradeoffs" property is a necessary condition for additivity.

This condition is also sufficient.[:91]

Additivity with three or more goods

When there are three or more commodities, the condition for the additivity of the utility function is surprisingly *simpler* than for two commodities. This is an outcome of Theorem 3 of Debreu (1960). The condition required for additivity is preferential-independence.:104

A subset A of commodities is said to be *preferentially-independent* of a subset B of commodities, if the preference relation in subset A, given constant values for subset B, is independent of these constant values. For example, suppose there are three commodities: *x y* and *z*. The subset {*x*,*y*} is preferentially-independent of the subset {*z*}, if for all x_i, y_i, z, z':

$$(x_1, y_1, z) \preceq (x_2, y_2, z) \iff (x_1, y_1, z') \preceq (x_2, y_2, z').$$

In this case, we can simply say that:

$(x_1, y_1) \preceq (x_2, y_2)$ for constant *z*.

Preferential-independence makes sense in case of independent goods. For example, the preferences between bundles of apples and bananas are probably independent of the amount of shoes and socks that an agent has, and vice versa.

By Debreu's theorem, if all subsets of commodities are preferentially-independnet of their complements, then the preference relation can be represented by an additive value function. Here we provide an intuitive explanation of this result by showing how such an additive value function can be constructed.

The proof assumes three commodities: *x*, *y*, *z*. We show how to define three points for each of the three value functions v_x, v_y, v_z: the 0 point, the 1 point and the 2 point. Other points can be calculated in a similar way, and then continuity can be used to conclude that the functions are well-defined in their entire range.

0 point: choose arbitrary x_0, y_0, z_0 and assign them as the zero of the value function, i.e:

$$v_x(x_0) = v_y(y_0) = v_z(z_0) = 0$$

1 point: choose arbitrary $x_1 > x_0$ such that $(x_1, y_0, z_0) \succ (x_0, y_0, z_0)$. Set it as the unit of value, i.e.:

$$v_x(x_1) = 1$$

Choose y_1 and z_1 such that the following indifference relations hold:

$$(x_1, y_0, z_0) \sim (x_0, y_1, z_0) \sim (x_0, y_0, z_1).$$

This indifference serves to scale the units of *y* and *z* to match those of *x*. The value in these three points should be 1, so we assign:

$$v_y(y_1) = v_z(z_1) = 1$$

2 point: Now it's time to use the preferential-independence assumption. The relation between (x_1, y_0) and (x_0, y_1) is independent of z, and similarly the relation between (y_1, z_0) and (y_0, z_1) is independent of x and the relation between (z_1, x_0) and (z_0, x_1) is independent of y. Hence:

$$(x_1, y_0, z_1) \sim (x_0, y_1, z_1) \sim (x_1, y_1, z_0)$$

This is good because it means that the function v can have the same value - 2 - in these three points. Select x_2, y_2, z_2 such that:

$$(x_2, y_0, z_0) \sim (x_0, y_2, z_0) \sim (x_0, y_0, z_2) \sim (x_1, y_1, z_0)$$

and assign:

$$v_x(x_2) = v_x(y_2) = v_x(z_2) = 2$$

3 point: To show that our assignments so far are consistent, we must show that all points that receive a total value of 3 are indifference points. Here, again, the preferential-independence assumption is used, since the relation between (x_2, y_0) and (x_1, y_1) is independent of z (and similarly for the other pairs), hence:

$$(x_2, y_0, z_1) \sim (x_1, y_1, z_1)$$

and similarly for the other pairs. Hence, the 3 point is defined consistently.

We can continue like this by induction and define the per-commodity functions in all integer points, then use continuity to define it in all real points.

An implicit assumption in point 1 of the above proof is that all three commodities are *essential* or *preference-relevant*.:7 This means that there exists a bundle such that, if the amount of a certain commodity is increased, the new bundle is strictly better.

The proof for more than 3 commodities is similar. In fact, we don't have to check that all subsets of points are preferentially-independent; it is sufficient to check a linear number of pairs of commodities. E.g, if there are m different commodities, $j = 1, ..., m$, then it is sufficient to check that for all $j = 1, ..., m - 1$, the two commodities $\{x_j, x_{j+1}\}$ are preferentially-independent of the other $m - 2$ commodities.:115

Uniqueness of additive representation

An additive preference relation can be represented by many different additive utility functions.

However, all these functions are similar: they are not only increasing-monotone-transformations of each other (as are all utility functions representing the same relation), they are increasing linear transformations of each other.:9 Shortly:

- An additive ordinal utility function is unique up to increasing linear transformation.

PREFERENCES AND UTILITY FUNCTIONS

Although preferences are the conventional foundation of microeconomics, it is often convenient to represent preferences with a utility function and analyze human behavior indirectly with utility functions. Let X be the consumption set, the set of all mutually-exclusive baskets the consumer could conceivably consume.

The consumer's utility function $u: X \to \mathbb{R}$ ranks each package in the consumption set. If the consumer strictly prefers x to y or is indifferent between them, then $u(x) \geq u(y)$.

For example, suppose a consumer's consumption set is X = {nothing, 1 apple,1 orange, 1 apple and 1 orange, 2 apples, 2 oranges}, and its utility function is u(nothing) = 0, u(1 apple) = 1, u(1 orange) = 2, u(1 apple and 1 orange) = 4, u(2 apples) = 2 and u(2 oranges) = 3. Then this consumer prefers 1 orange to 1 apple, but prefers one of each to 2 oranges.

In micro-economic models, there are usually a finite set of L commodities, and a consumer may consume an arbitrary amount of each commodity. This gives a consumption set of $\mathbb{R}^L_+$, and each package $x \in \mathbb{R}^L_+$ is a vector containing the amounts of each commodity. In the previous example, we might say there are two commodities: apples and oranges. If we say apples is the first commodity, and oranges the second, then the consumption set $X = \mathbb{R}^2_+$ and $u(0, 0) = 0$, $u(1, 0) = 1$, $u(0, 1) = 2$, $u(1, 1) = 4$, $u(2, 0) = 2$, $u(0, 2) = 3$ as before. Note that for u to be a utility function on X, it must be defined for every package in X.

A utility function $u: X \to \mathbb{R}$ represents a preference relation $\preceq$ on X iff for every $x, y \in X$, $u(x) \leq u(y)$ implies $x \preceq y$. If u represents $\preceq$, then this implies $\preceq$ is complete and transitive, and hence rational.

EXAMPLES OF UTILITY FUNCTION FORMS

In order to simplify calculations, various alternative assumptions have been made concerning details of human preferences, and these imply various alternative utility functions such as:

- CES (*constant elasticity of substitution*, or *isoelastic*) utility
- Isoelastic utility
- Exponential utility
- Quasilinear utility
- Homothetic preferences
- Uzawa utility function
- Stone–Geary utility function

- Gorman polar form
  — Greenwood–Hercowitz–Huffman preferences
  — King–Plosser–Rebelo preferences
- Hyperbolic absolute risk aversion

Most utility functions used in modeling or theory are well-behaved. They are usually monotonic and quasi-concave. However, it is possible for preferences not to be representable by a utility function. An example is lexicographic preferences which are not continuous and cannot be represented by a continuous utility function.

EXPECTED UTILITY

The expected utility theory deals with the analysis of choices among risky projects with (possibly multidimensional) outcomes.

The St. Petersburg paradox was first proposed by Nicholas Bernoulli in 1713 and solved by Daniel Bernoulli in 1738. D. Bernoulli argued that the paradox could be resolved if decision-makers displayed risk aversion and argued for a logarithmic cardinal utility function.

The first important use of the expected utility theory was that of John von Neumann and Oskar Morgenstern, who used the assumption of expected utility maximization in their formulation of game theory.

VON NEUMANN–MORGENSTERN EXPECTED UTILITY

Von Neumann and Morgenstern addressed situations in which the outcomes of choices are not known with certainty, but have probabilities attached to them.

A notation for a *lottery* is as follows: if options A and B have probability *p* and 1 " *p* in the lottery, we write it as a linear combination:

$$L = pA + (1 - p)B$$

More generally, for a lottery with many possible options:

$$L = \sum_i p_i A_i,$$

where $\sum_i p_i = 1$.

By making some reasonable assumptions about the way choices behave, von Neumann and Morgenstern showed that if an agent can choose between the lotteries, then this agent has a utility function such that the desirability of an arbitrary lottery can be calculated as a linear combination of the utilities of its parts, with the weights being their probabilities of occurring.

This is called the *expected utility theorem*. The required assumptions are four axioms about the properties of the agent's preference relation over 'simple lotteries', which are lotteries with just two options. Writing $B \preceq A$ to mean

'A is weakly preferred to B' ('A is preferred at least as much as B'), the axioms are:

1. completeness: For any two simple lotteries L and M, either $L \preceq M$ or $M \preceq L$ (or both, in which case they are viewed as equally desirable).
2. transitivity: for any three lotteries L, M, N, if $L \preceq M$ and $M \preceq N$, then $L \preceq N$.
3. convexity/continuity (Archimedean property): If $L \preceq M \preceq N$, then there is a p between 0 and 1 such that the lottery $pL + (1-p)N$ is equally desirable as M.
4. independence: for any three lotteries L, M, N and any probability p, $L \preceq M$ if and only if $pL + (1-p)N \preceq pM + (1-p)N$. Intuitively, if the lottery formed by the probabilistic combination of L and N is no more preferable than the lottery formed by the same probabilistic combination of M and N then and only then $L \preceq M$.

Axioms 3 and 4 enable us to decide about the relative utilities of two assets or lotteries.

In more formal language: A von Neumann–Morgenstern utility function is a function from choices to the real numbers:

$$u : X \to \mathbb{R}$$

which assigns a real number to every outcome in a way that captures the agent's preferences over simple lotteries. Under the four assumptions mentioned above, the agent will prefer a lottery L_2 to a lottery L_1 if and only if, for the utility function characterizing that agent, the expected utility of L_2 is greater than the expected utility of L_1:

$$L_1 \preceq L_2 \text{ iff } u(L_1) \leq u(L_2).$$

Repeating in category language: u is a morphism between the category of preferences with uncertainty and the category of reals as an additive group.

Of all the axioms, independence is the most often discarded. A variety of generalized expected utility theories have arisen, most of which drop or relax the independence axiom.

UTILITY AS PROBABILITY OF SUCCESS

Castagnoli and LiCalzi and Bordley and LiCalzi (2000) provided another interpretation for Von Neumann and Morgenstern's theory. Specifically for any utility function, there exists a hypothetical reference lottery with the expected utility of an arbitrary lottery being its probability of performing no worse than the reference lottery. Suppose success is defined as getting an outcome no worse than the outcome of the reference lottery. Then this mathematical equivalence means that maximizing expected utility is equivalent to maximizing the probability of success. In many contexts, this makes the concept of utility easier to justify and to apply. For example, a firm's utility might be the probability of meeting uncertain future customer expectations.

INDIRECT UTILITY

An indirect utility function gives the optimal attainable value of a given utility function, which depends on the prices of the goods and the income or wealth level that the individual possesses.

UTILITY OF MONEY

One use of the indirect utility concept is the notion of the utility of money. The (indirect) utility function for money is a nonlinear function that is bounded and asymmetric about the origin. The utility function is concave in the positive region, reflecting the phenomenon of diminishing marginal utility. The boundedness reflects the fact that beyond a certain point money ceases being useful at all, as the size of any economy at any point in time is itself bounded. The asymmetry about the origin reflects the fact that gaining and losing money can have radically different implications both for individuals and businesses. The non-linearity of the utility function for money has profound implications in decision making processes: in situations where outcomes of choices influence utility through gains or losses of money, which are the norm in most business settings, the optimal choice for a given decision depends on the possible outcomes of all other decisions in the same time-period.

DISCUSSION AND CRITICISM

Cambridge economist Joan Robinson famously criticized utility for being a circular concept: "Utility is the quality in commodities that makes individuals want to buy them, and the fact that individuals want to buy commodities shows that they have utility":[48] Robinson also pointed out that because the theory assumes that preferences are fixed this means that utility is not a testable assumption. This is because if we take changes in peoples' behavior in relation to a change in prices or a change in the underlying budget constraint we can never be sure to what extent the change in behavior was due to the change in price or budget constraint and how much was due to a change in preferences. This criticism is similar to that of the philosopher Hans Albert who argued that the ceteris paribus conditions on which the marginalist theory of demand rested on rendered the theory itself an empty tautology and completely closed to experimental testing. In essence, demand and supply curve (theoretical line of quantity of a product which would have been offered or requested for given price) is purely ontological and could never been demonstrated empirically.

Another criticism comes from the assertion that neither cardinal nor ordinal utility is empirically observable in the real world. In the case of cardinal utility it is impossible to measure the level of satisfaction "quantitatively" when someone consumes or purchases an apple. In case of ordinal utility, it is impossible to determine what choices were made when someone purchases, for example, an orange. Any act would involve preference over a vast set of choices (such as apple, orange juice, other vegetable, vitamin C tablets, exercise, not purchasing, etc.).

Other questions of what arguments ought to enter into a utility function are difficult to answer, yet seem necessary to understanding utility. Whether people gain utility from coherence of wants, beliefs or a sense of duty is key to understanding their behavior in the utility organon. Likewise, choosing between alternatives is itself a process of determining what to consider as alternatives, a question of choice within uncertainty. An evolutionary psychology perspective is that utility may be better viewed as due to preferences that maximized evolutionary fitness in the ancestral environment but not necessarily in the current one.

4

Pricing Policy

In managerial economics and business, the price is the assigned numerical monetary value of a good, service or asset. The concept of price is central to microeconomics where it is one of the most important variables in resource allocation theory (also called price theory). Price is also central to marketing where it is one of the four variables in the marketing mix that business people use to develop a marketing plan. In ordinary usage, price is the quantity of payment or compensation for something. People may say about a criminal that he has 'paid the price to society' to imply that he has paid a penalty or compensation. They may say that somebody paid for his folly to imply that he suffered the consequence.

The simplest way to set price is through uniform pricing. At the profit maximizing uniform price, the incremental margin percentage equals the reciprocal of the absolute value of the price elasticity of demand. The most profitable pricing policy is complete price discrimination, where each unit is priced at the benefit that the unit provides to its buyer. To implement this policy, however, the seller must know each potential buyer's individual demand curve and be able to set different prices for every unit of the product.

Economists view price as an exchange ratio between goods that pay for each other. In case of barter between two goods whose quantities are x and y, the price of x is the ratio y/x, while the price of y is the ratio x/y. This however has not been used consistently, so that old confusion regarding value frequently reappears. The value of something is a quantity counted in common units of value called numeraire, which may even be an imaginary good. This is done to compare different goods. The unit of value is frequently confused with price, because market value is calculated as the quantity of some good multiplied by its nominal price.

Theory of price asserts that the market price reflects interaction between two opposing considerations. On the one side are demand considerations based on marginal utility, while on the other side are supply considerations based on marginal cost. An equilibrium price is supposed to be at once be equal to marginal utility (counted in units of income)from the buyer's side and marginal cost from the seller's side. Though this view is accepted by almost every economist, and it constitutes the core of mainstream economics, it has recently been challenged seriously.

There was time when people debated use-value versus exchange value, often wondering about the Diamond-Water Paradox. The use-value was supposed to give some measure of usefulness, later refined as marginal benefit (which is marginal utility counted in common units of value) while exchange value was the measure of how much one good was in terms of another, namely what is now called relative price. That debate is no longer useful in talking about price.

Marxian Price Theory

In Marxian economics, it is argued that price theory must be firmly grounded in the *real history of economic exchange* in human societies. Money-prices are viewed as the monetary expression of exchange-value. Exchange-value can however also be expressed in trading ratios between quantities of different types of goods.

In Marxian economics, the increasing use of prices as a convenient way to measure the economic or trading value of Labour-products is explained historically and anthropolo-gically, in terms of the development of the use of money as universal equivalent in economic exchange.

However, in an anthropological-historical sense, Marxian economists argue a "price" is not necessarily a sum of money; it could be whatever the owner of a good gets in return, when exchanging that good. Money prices are merely the most common form of prices.

Marxian economists distinguish very strictly between *real* prices and *ideal* prices. Real prices are actual market prices realised in trade. Ideal prices are hypothetical prices which would be realised *if* certain conditions would apply. Most equilibrium prices are hypothetical prices, which are never realised in reality, and therefore of limited use, although notional prices can influence real economic behaviour.

According to Marxian economists, while all Labour-products existing in an economy have economic *value*, only a minority of them have *real* prices; the majority of goods and assets at any time are not being traded, and they have at best a *hypothetical* price. Six criticisms Marxian economists make of neoclassical economics are that neoclassical price theory:

- Is not based on any substantive, realistic theory of economic exchange as a social process, and simply assumes that exchange will occur;
- Simply assumes prices can be attached or imputed to all goods and services;
- Assumes equilibrium prices will exist and that markets tend spontaneously to equilibrium prices;

- Fails to distinguish adequately between actual market prices; administered prices; and ideal, accounting, or hypothetical prices.
- Disconnects price theory from the real economic history of the use of prices.
- Is unable to provide a coherent explanation of the relationship between price and economic value.

Pricing

Pricing is one of the four p's of the marketing mix. The other three aspects are product management, promotion, and place. It is also a key variable in microeconomic price allocation theory. Pricing is the manual or automatic process of applying prices to purchase and sales orders, based on factors such as: a fixed amount, quantity break, promotion or sales campaign, specific vendor quote, price prevailing on entry, shipment or invoice date, combination of multiple orders or lines, and many others. Automated systems require more setup and maintenance but may prevent pricing errors.

Uniform Pricing

The difference between nominal price and relative or real price (as exchange ratio) is often made. Nominal price is the price quoted in money while relative or real price is the exchange ratio between real goods regardless of money. The distinction is made to make sense of inflation. When all prices are quoted in terms of money units, and the prices in money units change more or less proportionately, the ratio of exchange may not change much. In the extreme case, if all prices quoted in money change in the same proportion, the relative price remains the same.

It is now becoming clear that the distinction is not useful and indeed hides a major confusion. The conventional wisdom is that proportional change in all nominal prices does not affect real price, and hence should not affect either demand or supply and therefore also should not affect output. The new criticism is that the crucial question is why there is more money to pay for the same old real output. If this question is answered, it will show that dynamically, even as the real price remains exactly the same, output in real terms can change, just because additional money allow additional output to be traded. The supply curve can shift such that at the old price, the new higher output is sold. This shift if not possible without additional money.

From this point of view, a price is similar to an opportunity cost, that is, what must be given up in exchange for the good or service that is being purchased.

The price of an item is also called the price point, especially where it refers to stores that set a limited number of price points. For example, Dollar General is a general store or "five and dime" store that sets price points only at even amounts, such as exactly one, two, three, five, or ten dollars (among others). Other stores (such as dollar stores, pound stores, euro stores, 100-yen stores, and so forth) only have a single price point ($1, £1, □1, ¥100), though in some cases this price may purchase more than one of some very small items.

Questions Involved in Pricing

Pricing involves asking questions like:

- How much to charge for a product or service? This question is a typical starting point for discussions about pricing, however, a better question for a vendor to ask is - How much do customers *value* the products, services, and other intangibles that the vendor provides.
- What are the pricing objectives?
- Do we use profit maximization pricing?
- How to set the price?: (cost-plus pricing, demand based or value-based pricing, rate of return pricing, or competitor indexing)
- Should there be a single price or multiple pricing?
- Should prices change in various geographical areas, referred to as zone pricing?
- Should there be quantity discounts?
- What prices are competitors charging?
- Do you use a price skimming strategy or a penetration pricing strategy?
- What image do you want the price to convey?
- Do you use psychological pricing?
- How important are customer price sensitivity and elasticity issues?
- Can real-time pricing be used?
- Is price discrimination or yield management appropriate?
- Are there legal restrictions on retail price maintenance, price collusion, or price discrimination?
- Do price points already exist for the product category?
- How flexible can we be in pricing? : The more competitive the industry, the less flexibility we have.
- The price floor is determined by production factors like costs (often only variable costs are taken into account), economies of scale, marginal cost, and degree of operating leverage.
- The price ceiling is determined by demand factors like price elasticity and price points.
- Are there transfer pricing considerations?
- What is the chance of getting involved in a price war?
- How visible should the price be? - Should the price be neutral? (ie.: not an important differentiating factor), should it be highly visible? (to help promote a low priced economy product, or to reinforce the

prestige image of a quality product), or should it be hidden? (so as to allow marketers to generate interest in the product unhindered by price considerations).

- Are there joint product pricing considerations?
- What are the non-price costs of purchasing the product? (eg.: travel time to the store, wait time in the store, dissagreeable elements associated with the product purchase – dentist → pain, fishmarket → smells)
- What sort of payments should be accepted? (cash, cheque, credit card, barter)

What a Price Should Do

A well chosen price should do three things:

- Achieve the financial goals of the firm (eg.: profitability)
- Fit the realities of the marketplace (will customers buy at that price?)
- Support a product's positioning and be consistent with the other variables in the marketing mix
- Price is influenced by the type of distribution channel used, the type of promotions used, and the quality of the product
- Price will usually need to be relatively high if manufacturing is expensive, distribution is exclusive, and the product is supported by extensive advertising and promotional campaigns
- A low price can be a viable substitute for product quality, effective promotions, or an energetic selling effort by distributors

From the marketers point of view, an efficient price is a price that is very close to the maximum that customers are prepared to pay. In economic terms, it is a price that shifts most of the consumer surplus to the producer.

Pricing Objectives

Pricing objectives or goals give direction to the whole pricing process. Determining what your objectives are is the first step in pricing. When deciding on pricing objectives you must consider:

- The overall financial, marketing, and strategic objectives of the company;
- The objectives of your product or brand; 3) consumer price elasticity and price points; and 4) the resources you have available.

Some of the more common pricing objectives are:

- Maximize short-run profit
- Increase sales volume (quantity)
- Increase dollar sales
- Increase market share
- Obtain a target rate of return on investment (ROI)

- Obtain a target rate of return on sales
- Stabilize market or stabilize market price: an objective to stabilize price means that the marketing manager attempts to keep prices stable in the marketplace and to compete on nonprice considerations. Stabilization of margin is bascially a cost-plus approach in which the manager attemptes to maintain the same margin regradless of changes in cost.
- Company growth
- Maintain price leadership
- Desensitize customers to price
- Discourage new entrants into the industry
- Match competitors prices
- Encourage the exit of marginal firms from the industry
- Survival
- Avoid government investigation or intervention
- Obtain or maintain the loyalty and enthusiasm of distributors and other sales personnel
- Enhance the image of the firm, brand, or product
- Be perceived as "fair" by customers and potential customers
- Create interest and excitement about a product
- Discourage competitors from cutting prices
- Use price to make the product "visible"
- Build store traffic
- Help prepare for the sale of the business (harvesting)
- Social, ethical, or ideological objectives
- Get competitive advantage

Effective Price

The effective price is the price the company receives after accounting for discounts, promotions, and other incentives.

Price lining is the use of a limited number of prices for all your product offerings. This is a tradition started in the old five and dime stores in which everything cost either 5 or 10 cents. Its underlying rationale is that these amounts are seen as suitable price points for a whole range of products by prospective customers. It has the advantage of ease of administering, but the disadvantage of inflexibility, particularly in times of inflation or unstable prices.

A loss leader is a product that has a price set below the operating margin. This results in a loss to the enterprise on that particular item, but this is done in the hope that it will draw customers into the store and that some of those customers will buy other, higher margin items.

Promotional pricing refers to an instance where pricing is the key element of the marketing mix. The price/quality relationship refers to the perception by most consumers that a relatively high price is a sign of good quality. The belief in this relationship is most important with complex products that are hard to test, and experiential products that cannot be tested until used (such as most services). The greater the uncertainty surrounding a product, the more consumers depend on the price/quality hypothesis and the more of a premium they are prepared to pay.

The classic example of this is the pricing of the snack cake Twinkies, which were perceived as low quality when the price was lowered. Note, however, that excessive reliance on the price/quantity relationship by consumers may lead to the raising of prices on all products and services, even those of low quality, which in turn causes the price/quality relationship to no longer apply.

Premium pricing (also called prestige pricing) is the strategy of pricing at, or near, the high end of the possible price range. People will buy a premium priced product because:

- They believe the high price is an indication of good quality;
- they believe it to be a sign of self worth - "They are worth it" - It authenticates their success and status - It is a signal to others that they are a member of an exclusive group; and
- They require flawless performance in this application - The cost of product malfunction is too high to buy anything but the best - example : heart pacemaker

The term Goldilocks pricing is commonly used to describe the practice of providing a "gold-plated" version of a product at a premium price in order to make the next-lower priced option look more reasonably priced; for example, encouraging customers to see business-class airline seats as good value for money by offering an even higher priced first-class option.

Similarly, third-class railway carriages in Victorian England are said to have been built without windows, not so much to punish third-class customers (for which there was no economic incentive), as to motivate those who could afford second-class seats to pay for them instead of taking the cheaper option. The name derives from the Goldilocks story, in which Goldilocks chose neither the hottest nor the coldest porridge, but instead the one that was "just right". More technically, this form of pricing exploits the general cognitive bias of aversion to extremes. Demand-based pricing is any pricing method that uses consumer demand - based on perceived value - as the central element. These include : price skimming, price discrimination and yield management, price points, psychological pricing, bundle pricing, penetration pricing, price lining, value-based pricing, geo and premium pricing.

Profit Maximization

In economics, profit maximization is the process by which a firm determines the price and output level that returns the greatest profit. There are several approaches to this problem. The total revenue — total cost method relies on the fact that profit equals revenue minus cost, and the marginal revenue — marginal cost method is based on the fact that total profit in a perfectly competitive market reaches its maximum point where marginal revenue equals marginal cost.

Any costs incurred by a firm may be classed into two groups: fixed cost and variable cost. Fixed costs are incurred by the business at any level of output, including none.

These may include equipment maintenance, rent, wages, and general upkeep. Variable costs change with the level of output, increasing as more product is generated. Materials consumed during production often have the largest impact on this category. Fixed cost and variable cost, combined, equal total cost. Revenue is the total amount of money that flows into the firm. This can be from any source, including product sales, government subsidies, venture capital and personal funds.

Average cost and revenue are defined as the total cost or revenue divided by the amount of units output. For instance, if a firm produced 400 units at a cost of 20000 USD, the average cost would be 50 USD.

Marginal cost and revenue, depending on whether the calculus approach is taken or not, are defined as either the change in cost or revenue as each additional unit is produced, or the derivative of cost or revenue with respect to quantity output. It may also be defined as the addition to total cost as output increase by a single unit. For instance, taking the first definition, if it costs a firm 400 USD to produce 5 units and 480 USD to produce 6, the marginal cost of the sixth unit is approximately 80 dollars, although this is more accurately stated as the marginal cost of the 5.5th unit due to linear interpolation. Calculus is capable of providing more accurate answers if regression equations can be provided.

Total Cost-Total Revenue Method

To obtain the profit maximizing output quantity, we start by recognizing that profit is equal to total revenue minus total cost. Given a table of costs and revenues at each quantity, we can either compute equations or plot the data directly on a graph. Finding the profit-maximizing output is as simple as finding the output at which profit reaches its maximum. That is represented by output Q in the diagram.

There are two graphical ways of determining that Q is optimal. Firstly, we see that the profit curve is at its maximum at this point (A). Secondly, we see that at the point (B) that the tangent on the total cost curve (TC) is parallel to the total revenue curve (TR), the surplus of revenue net of costs (B,C) is the greatest. Because total revenue minus total costs is equal to profit, the line segment C,B is equal in length to the line segment A,Q.

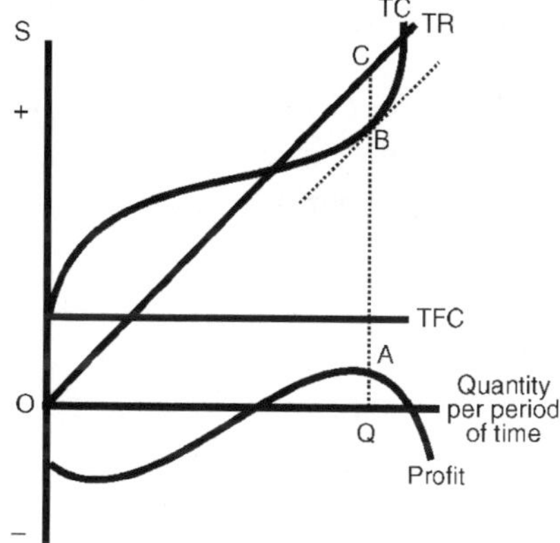

Fig. Profit Maximization - The Totals Approach

Computing the price at which to sell the product requires knowledge of the firm's demand curve. The price at which quantity demanded equals profit-maximizing output is the optimum price to sell the product.

Marginal Cost-Marginal Revenue Method

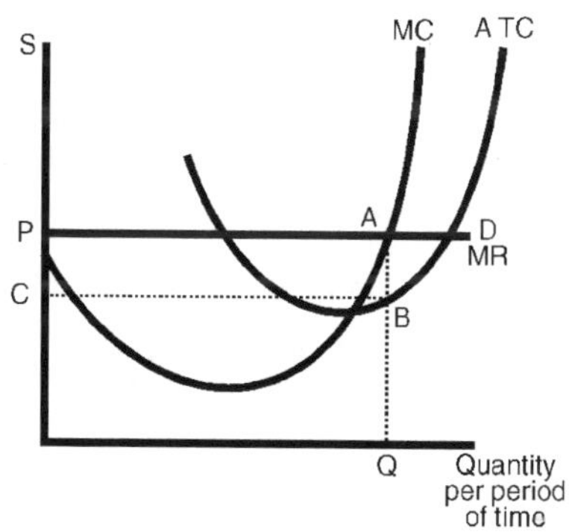

Fig. Profit Maximization - The Marginal Approach

If total revenue and total cost figures are difficult to procure, this method may also be used. For each unit sold, marginal profit equals marginal revenue minus marginal cost. Then, if marginal revenue is greater than marginal cost, marginal profit is positive, and if marginal revenue is less than marginal cost, marginal profit is negative. When marginal revenue equals marginal cost, marginal profit is zero.

Since total profit increases when marginal profit is positive and total profit decreases when marginal profit is negative, it must reach a maximum where marginal profit is zero - or where marginal cost equals marginal revenue. This is because the producer has collected positive profit up until the intersection of MR and MC (where zero profit is collected and any further production will result in negative marginal profit, because MC will be larger than MR).

The intersection of marginal revenue (MR) with marginal cost (MC) is shown in the next diagram as point A. If the industry is competitive (as is assumed in the diagram), the firm faces a demand curve (D) that is identical to its Marginal revenue curve (MR), and this is a horizontal line at a price determined by industry supply and demand. Average total costs are represented by curve ATC. Total economic profits are represented by area P,A,B,C. The optimum quantity (Q) is the same as the optimum quantity (Q) in the first diagram. Alternativily, we can use calculus to find the maximum of the profit function. Profit Π, total cost TC, quantity Q, and total revenue TR.

$$\Pi = TR - TC$$

$$\frac{d}{dQ}\pi = \frac{d}{dQ}T - \frac{d}{dQ}TC = MR - MC = 0$$

$\therefore MR = MC$ when profits are at a maximum.

If the firm is operating in a non-competitive market, minor changes would have to be made to the diagrams..

Modes of Operation

It is assumed that all firms are following rational decision-making, and will produce at the profit-maximizing output. Given this assumption, there are four categories in which a firm's profit may be considered.

A firm is said to be making an economic profit when its average total cost is less than the price of the product at the profit-maximizing output. The economic profit is equal to the quantity output multiplied by the difference between the average total cost and the price. A firm is said to be making a normal profit when its economic profit equals zero. This occurs where average total cost equals price at the profit-maximizing output. A firm is said to be making a zero economic profit when its marginal revenue equals marginal cost.

If the price is between average total cost and average variable cost at the profit-maximizing output, then the firm is said to be in a loss-minimizing condition. The firm should still continue to producc, however, since its loss would be larger if it was to stop producing. By continuing production, the firm can offset its variable cost and at least part of its fixed cost, but by stopping completely it would lose equivalent of its entire fixed cost.

If the price is below average variable cost at the profit-maximizing output, the firm is said to be in shutdown. Losses are minimized by not producing at all, since any production would not generate returns significant enough to offset any fixed cost and part of the variable cost. By not producing, the firm loses only its fixed cost.

Direct Segment Discrimination

The pricing policy where a seller charges a different incremental margin to each identifiable segment (with uniformpricing within each segment). A segment is a significant group of buyers within a larger market.

- Profit maximizing price: set prices so that the incremental margin percentage of each segment equals the reciprocal of the absolute value of that segment's price elasticity of demand; i.e., applies the rule for uniform pricing to determine the profit maximizing prices for each segment.
- When marginal cost is increasing, any change in price for one segment that affects sales will affect marginal cost, and the incremental margin percentage for the other segment. Accordingly, the seller must conduct the trial and errors search for the prices to both segments at the same time.
- A seller can discriminate on the basis of a buyer's location.
  - Free on board (FOB) price is a price that does not include delivery.
    (a) FOB pricing ignores the differences between the price elasticities of demand in various markets.
    (b) The differences among prices at various locationsequal the differences in costs of delivery.

    c Delivered pricing is the pricing policy where the seller's price includes delivery. A cost including freight (CF) price is one that includes delivery.
    (a) The seller can implement direct segment discrimination, aim for different incremental margin percentages in each market, and obtain higher profit.
    (b) The differences among prices at various locations are the result of the different incremental margin percentages and the different marginal costs of supplying the various markets, and may be larger or smaller than the costs of delivery.
- Requirements.
  - Must directly identify the members of each segment. The identifiable buyer characteristic must be fixed.
  - Must prevent buyers from reselling the product among themselves. Generally, resale of services is more difficult than resale of goods; hence there is more price discrimination in services than goods. Sellers can limit resale of goods by restricting warranty service to the location of purchase.
- Limitations. For each segment, same limitations as uniform pricing.

Price Discrimination

Price discrimination exists when sales of identical goods or services are transacted at different prices from the same provider. In a theoretical market with perfect information, no transaction costs and a prohibition on secondary exchange (or re-selling) to prevent arbitrage, price discrimination can only be a feature of monopoly markets. Otherwise, the moment the seller tries to sell the same good at different prices, the buyer at the lower price can arbitrage by selling to the consumer buying at the higher price but with a tiny discount. However, market frictions in oligopolies such as the airlines, and even in fully competitive retail or industrial markets allow for a limited degree of differential pricing to different consumers. Price discrimination also occurs when it costs more to supply one customer than it does another, and yet the supplier charges both the same price.

Although the term "discrimination" has negative connotations, "price discrimination" is a technical term meaning only differentiation in price by customer. The effects of price discrimination on social efficiency are unclear. Typically such behaviour leads to lower prices for some consumers and higher prices for others. Output can be expanded when price discrimination is very efficient, but output can also decline when discrimination is more effective at extracting surplus from high-valued users than expanding sales to low valued users. Even if output remains constant, price discrimination can reduce efficiency by misallocating output among consumers.

Price discrimination requires market segmentation and some means to discourage discount customers from becoming resellers and, by extension, competitors. This usually entails using one or more means of preventing any resale, keeping the different price groups separate, making price comparisons difficult, or restricting pricing information. The boundary set up by the marketer to keep segments separate are referred to as a *rate fence*. Price discrimination is thus very common in services, where resale is not possible; an example is student discounts at museums.

Indirect Segment Discrimination

Pricing policy where a seller (who cannot directly identify the customer segments) structures a choice for buyers so as to earn different incremental margins from each segment.

- *Profit maximizing price:* There is no simple rule to find the profit maximizing prices. Buyers might substitute among the various choices. Accordingly, the seller must analyze how changes in the price of one product affect the demand for other choices, and set the prices of all products at the same time. The seller must not price any product in isolation.
- *Requirements:* Buyers must be differentially sensitive to some variable that the seller can control. The seller then uses this variable to structure a set of choices that will discriminate among the segments. Buyers must not be able to circumvent the differentiating variable. The seller must strictly enforce all conditions of sale to prevent switching. Cannibalization occurs when the sales of one product reduce the demand for another with a higher incremental margin.

Mitigate cannibalization by degrading the quality of the low margin product.

- *Less profitable than direct price discrimination:* Products provide less benefit than those with direct discrimination. Involves relatively higher costs. Leakage: indirect discrimination relies on various segments to voluntarily identify themselves through the structured choice. But consumers in one segment may buy the item aimed at another segment.

Market Segment Discrimination

The next most profitable pricing policy is direct segment discrimination. For this policy, the seller must be able to directly identify the various segments. The third most profitable policy is indirect segment discrimination. This involves structuring a set of choices around some variable to which the various segments are differentially sensitive. Uniform pricing is the least profitable way to set a price. A commonly used basis for direct segment discrimination is location. This exploits a difference between free on board and cost including freight prices. A commonly used method of indirect segment discrimination is bundling. Sellers may apply either pure or mixed bundling.

Market segmentation is the process in marketing of dividing a market into distinct subsets (segments) that behave in the same way or have similar needs. Because each segment is fairly homogeneous in their needs and attitudes, they are likely to respond similarly to a given marketing strategy. That is, they are likely to have similar feeling and ideas about a marketing mix comprised of a given product or service, sold at a given price, distributed in a certain way, and promoted in a certain way.

Broadly, markets can be divided according to a number of general criteria, such as by industry or public versus private sector. Small segments are often termed niche markets or specialty markets. However, all segments fall into either consumer or industrial markets. Although it has similar objectives and it overlaps with consumer markets in many ways, the process of Industrial market segmentation is quite different.

The process of segmentation is distinct from targeting (choosing which segments to address) and positioning (designing an appropriate marketing mix for each segment). The overall intent is to identify groups of similar customers and potential customers; to prioritise the groups to address; to understand their behaviour; and to respond with appropriate marketing strategies that satisfy the different preferences of each chosen segment.

The requirements for successful segmentation are:

- Homogeneity within the segment
- Heterogeneity between segments
- Segments are measurable and identifiable

- Segments are accessible and actionable
- Segment is large enough to be profitable

These criteria can be summarized by the word SADAM:

- S Substantial: the segment has to be large and profitable enough
- A Accessible: it must be possible to reach it efficiently
- D Differential: it must respond differently to a different marketing mix
- A Actionable: you must have a product for this segment
- M Measurable: size and purchasing power can be measured

Currently a college student studying the marketing mix is introduced to the Four Ps of the Marketing Mix; Product, Place, Promotion, Price. Product (service) is whatever it may be that is being sold/marketed. Price refers to not only the actual price but also price elasticity. Place has evidently replaced distribution simply by where or what area the marketing campaign is going to cover, as well as what types of distribution channel (retail, wholesale, online, etc) will be used. Today the idea of place is not limited to geographic profiling but also demographics and other categorizing variables. This has only occurred over the last ten years with the expansion of internet use and its ability to target specific types of people and not just people in a geographic area.

Promotion simply refers to what medium will deliver the message and what the overall marketing strategy is offering as a benefit.

Types of price Discrimination

- In first degree price discrimination, price varies by customer. This arises from the fact that the value of goods is subjective. A customer with low price elasticity is less deterred by a higher price than a customer with high price elasticity of demand. As long as the price elasticity (in absolute value) for a customer is less than one, it is very advantageous to increase the price: the seller gets more money for fewer goods. With an increase of the price the price elasticity tends to rise above one.

One can show that in the optimum the price, as it varies by customer, is inversely proportional to one minus the reciprocal of the price elasticity of that customer at that price. This assumes that the consumer passively reacts to the price set by the seller, and that the seller knows the demand curve of the customer. In practice however there is a bargaining situation, which is more complex: the customer may try to influence the price, such as by pretending to like the product less than he or she really does, and by threatening not to buy it. An alternative way to understand First Degree Price Discrimination is as follows: This type of price discrimination is primarily theoretical because it requires the seller of a good or service to know the absolute maximum price that every consumer is willing to pay. As above, it is true that consumers have different price elasticities, but the seller is not concerned with such. The seller is concerned with the maximum willingness to pay of each customer.

By knowing the max, WTP, the seller is able to absorb the entire market surplus, thus taking all consumer surplus from the consumer and transforming it into revenues. From a social welfare perspective, first degree price discrimination is not undesirable. That is, the market is still entirely efficient and there is no deadweight loss to society. However, it is the complete opposite of a perfectly competitive market.

In a perfectly competitive market, the consumers receive the bulk of surplus. In a market with first degree price discrimination, the seller(s) capture all surplus. Efficiency is unchanged but the wealth is transferred. This type of market does not much exist in reality, hence it is primarily theoretical. Examples of where this might be observed are in markets where consumers bid for tenders.

- In second degree price discrimination, price varies according to quantity sold. Larger quantities are available at a lower unit price. This is particularly widespread in sales to industrial customers, where bulk buyers enjoy higher discounts.

  Additionally to second degree price discrimination, sellers are not able to differentiate between different types of consumers. Thus, the suppliers will provide incentives for the consumers to differentiate themselves according to preference. As above, quantity "discounts", or non-linear pricing, is a means by which suppliers use consumer preference to distinguish classes of consumers. This allows the supplier to set different prices to the different groups and capture a larger portion of the total market surplus.
- In third degree price discrimination, price varies by location or by customer segment. Additionally to third degree price discrimination, the supplier(s) of a market where this type of discrimination is exhibited are capable of differentiating between consumer classes. Examples of this differentiation are student or senior "discounts". For example, a student or a senior consumer will have a different willingness to pay than an average consumer, where the WTP is presumably lower because of budget constraints.

  Thus, the supplier sets a lower price for that consumer because the student or senior has a more elastic price elasticity of demand. The supplier is once again capable of capturing more market surplus than would be possible without price discrimination.

  Note that it is not always advantageous to the company to price discriminate even if it possible, especially for second and third degree discrimination. In some circumstances, the demands of different classes of consumers will encourage suppliers to simply ignore one/

some class(es) and target entirely to the other(s). Whether it is profitable to price discriminate is determined by the specifics of a particular market.

- In price skimming, price varies over time. Typically a company starts selling a new product at a relatively high price then gradually reduces the price as the low price elasticity segment gets satiated. Price skimming is closely related to the concept of yield management.

These types are not mutually exclusive. Thus a company may vary pricing by location, but then offer bulk discounts as well. Airlines use several different types of price discrimination, including:

- Bulk discounts to wholesalers, consolidators, and tour operators
- Incentive discounts for higher sales volumes to travel agents and corporate buyers
- Seasonal discounts, incentive discounts, and even general prices that vary by location. The price of a flight from say, Singapore to Beijing can vary widely if one buys the ticket in Singapore compared to Beijing (or New York or Tokyo or elsewhere). In online ticket sales this is achieved by using the customer's credit card billing address to determine his location.
- First degree price discrimination based on customer. It is not accidental that hotel or car rental firms may quote higher prices to their loyalty Programmeme's top tier members than to the general public.

Modern Taxonomy

- *Complete discrimination:* where each user purchases up to the point where the user's marginal benefit equals the marginal cost of the item;
- *Direct segmentation:* where the seller can condition price on some attribute (like age or gender) that *directly* segments the buyers;
- *Indirect segmentation:* where the seller relies on some proxy (eg, package size, usage quantity, coupon) to structure a choice that *indirectly* segments the buyers.

The hierarchy — complete/direct/indirect — is in decreasing order of

- Profitability and
- Information requirement.

Complete price discrimination is most profitable, and requires the seller to have the most information about buyers. Indirect segmentation is least profitable, and requires the seller to have the least information about buyers.

Explanation

The purpose of price discrimination is generally to capture the market's consumer surplus. This surplus arises because, in a market with a single clearing price, some customers (the very low price elasticity segment) would have been prepared to pay more than the single market price. Price discrimination transfers some of this surplus from the consumer to the producer/marketer. Strictly, a consumer surplus need not exist, for example where price discrimination is necessary merely to pay the costs of production. An example is a high-speed internet connection shared by two consumers in a single building; if one is willing to pay less than half the cost, and the other willing to make up the rest but not to pay the entire cost, then price discrimination is necessary for the purchase to take place.

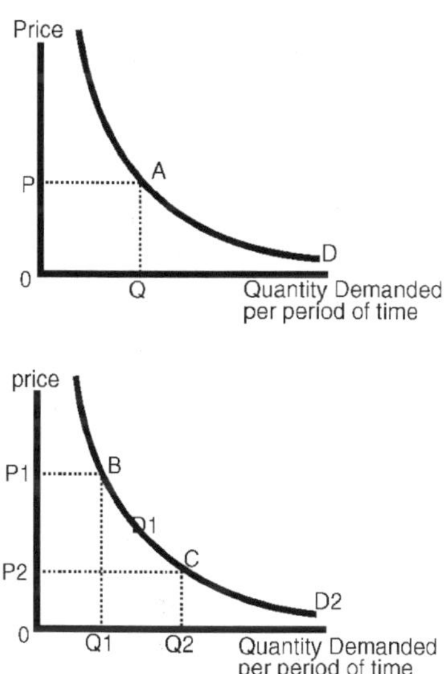

Fig. Sales revenue without and with Price Discrimination

It can be proved mathematically that a firm facing a downward sloping demand curve that is convex to the origin will always obtain higher revenues under price discrimination than under a single price strategy. This can also be shown diagramatically.

In the top diagram, a single price (P) is available to all customers. The amount of revenue is represented by area P, A,Q, O. The consumer surplus is the area above line segment P, A but below the demand curve (D).

With price discrimination, (the bottom diagram), the demand curve is divided into two segments (D1 and D2). A higher price (P1) is charged to the low elasticity segment, and a lower price (P2) is charged to the high elasticity segment. The total revenue from the first segment is equal to the area P1,B, Q1,O. The total revenue from the second segment is equal to the area E, C,Q2,Q1. The sum of these areas will always be greater than the area without discrimination assuming the demand curve resembles a rectangular hyperbola with unitary elasticity. The more prices that are introduced, the greater the sum of the revenue areas, and the more of the consumer surplus is captured by the producer.

Note that the above requires both first and second degree price discrimination: the right segment corresponds partly to different people than the left segment, partly to the same people, willing to buy more if the product is cheaper. It is very useful for the price discriminator to determine the optimum prices in each market segment. This is done in the next diagram where each segment is considered as a separate market with its own demand curve. As usual, the profit maximizing output (Qt) is determined by the intersection of the marginal cost curve (MC) with the marginal revenue curve for the total market (MRt).

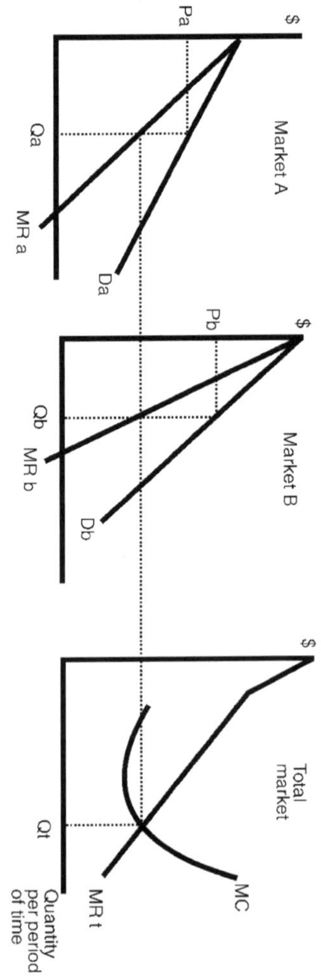

Fig. Multiple Market Price Determination

The firm decides what amount of the total output to sell in each market by looking at the intersection of marginal cost with marginal revenue (profit maximisation). This output is then divided between the two markets, at the equilibrium marginal revenue level. Therefore, the optimum outputs are Qa and Qb. From the demand curve in each market we can determine the profit maximizing prices of Pa and Pb.

It is also important to note that the marginal revenue in both markets at the optimal output levels must be equal, otherwise the firm could profit from transferring output over to whichever market is offering higher marginal revenue.

Examples of Price Discrimination

Retail Price Discrimination

In certain circumstances, it is a violation of the Robinson-Patman Act, (a 1936 Federal U.S. antitrust statute) for manufacturers of goods to sell their products to similarly situated retailers at different prices based solely on the volume of products purchased.

Travel Industry

Airlines and other travel companies use differentiated pricing regularly, as they sell travel products and services simultaneously to different market segments. This is often done by assigning capacity to various booking classes, which sell for different prices and which may be linked to fare restrictions. The restrictions or "fences" help ensure that market segments buy in the booking class range that has been established for them.

For example, schedule-sensitive business passengers who are willing to pay say, \$300 for a seat from city A to city B, cannot purchase a \$150 ticket because the \$150 booking class contains a requirement for a Saturday night stay, or a 15-day advance purchase, or another fare rule that effectively prevents a sale to business passengers.

Notice also that even in this simple example, the "seat" is not the same product. That is, the business person who purchases the \$300 ticket may be willing to do so in return for a seat on a high-demand morning flight, for full refundability if the ticket is not used, and for the ability to upgrade to first class if space is available for a nominal fee. On the same flight are price-sensitive passengers who are not willing to pay \$300, but who are willing to fly on a lower-demand flight (say one leaving an hour earlier), or via a connection city (not a non-stop flight), and who are willing to forego refundability. Since airlines often fly multi-leg flights, and since no-show rates vary by segment, competition for the seat has to take in the spatial dynamics of the product. Someone trying to fly A-B is competing with people trying to fly A-C through city B on the same airplane. This is one reason airlines use yield management technology to determine how many seats to allot for A-B passengers, B-C passengers, and A-B-C passengers, at their varying fares and with varying demands and no-show rates. With the rise of the Internet and the growth of low fare airlines, airfare pricing transparency became far more pronounced. Passengers discovered it quite easy to compare fares across different flights or different airlines. This helped put pressure on airlines to lower fares. Meanwhile, in the recession following the September 11, 2001 attacks on the U.S., business travellers and corporate buyers made it clear to airlines that they were not going to be buying air travel at rates high enough to subsidize lower fares for non-business travellers.

This prediction has come true, as vast numbers of business travellers are buying airfares only in coach class for business travel. As to the absolute level of airfares, they continue their 35-year downward trend line. Whereas following World War II it took an Australian the equivalent of a year's wages to fly from Sydney to London, today that can be done for approximately two week's average Australian wages, purchasing a far faster and more comfortable journey. The same trends are true in all deregulated areas of the world, including the U.S., intra-E.U. flights, and UK.

Segmentation by Student Status

Many movie theaters, amusement parks, tourist attractions, and other places have different admission prices per market segment: typical groupings are Youth, Student, Adult, and Senior. Each of these groups typically have a much different demand curve. Children, people living on student wages, and people living on retirement generally have much less disposable income.

Discounts for Members of Certain Occupations

Many businesses, especially in the Southern United States, offer reduced prices to active military members. In addition to increased sales to the target group, businesses benefit from the resulting positive publicity, leading to increased sales to the general public. Less publicized are discounts to other service workers such as police; off-duty police customers in high-crime areas are said to constitute free security.

Retail Incentives

A variety of incentive techniques may be used to increase market share or revenues at the retail level. These include discount coupons, rebates, bulk and quantity pricing, seasonal discounts, and frequent buyer discounts.

Incentives for Industrial Buyers

Many methods exist to incentivize wholesale or industrial buyers. These may be quite targeted, as they are designed to generate specific activity, such as buying more frequently, buying more regularly, buying in bigger quantities, buying new products with established ones, and so on. Thus, there are bulk discounts, special pricing for long-term commitments, non-peak discounts, discounts on high-demand goods to incentivize buying lower-demand goods, rebates, and many others. This can help the relations between the firms involved.

Gender-Based

Many gender-based price differences are held to be illegal in the United States.

"Ladies' Night"

Many North American nightclubs feature a "ladies' night" in which women are offered discount or free drinks, or are absolved from payment of cover charges.

This differs from conventional price discrimination in that the primary motive is not, usually, to increase revenue at the expense of consumer surplus. Rather, establishments benefit by maintaining an equitable gender balance; if the clientele of an establishment is primarily male, it will lose popularity with both men (who go to nightclubs to date, and thus want as many women to choose from as possible) and women (who often come to socialize asexually with other women), and therefore it is better for the establishment to lower its prices for women if they show less demand.

Dry Cleaning

Dry cleaners typically charge higher prices for the laundering of women's clothes than for men's. Even though this involves small amounts of money (compared to, say, college tuition), this has provoked reactions in some US communities, who occasionally have outlawed the practice. Although many people have reacted negatively to the "discrimination" of this practice, economic investigation (including that done by Steven Landsburg - see external link at bottom of this article) indicates that prices are higher for women not because of discrimination, but because the cost to provide these services is in fact different. For dry cleaners, women's shirts tend to be less consistent and more fragile, and therefore have to be pressed by hand, whereas men's shirts can be pressed by a machine, accounting for the higher cost.

Haircutting

Women's haircuts are often more expensive than men's haircuts which in past times could be accounted for as women generally had longer hairstyles whereas men generally had shorter hairstyles.

Nowadays men's and women's styles are more varied but the price discrimination continues. Some salons have modified their pricing to reflect "long hair" versus "short hair" or style instead of gender.

Financial aid in Education

Financial aid as offered by U.S. colleges and universities is a form of price discrimination that is widely accepted, and completely legal.

While tuition is set according to cost-recovery formulas for universities (which are non-profit organizations), increasing costs mean inevitably that tuition costs rise. (This is true even after legislatures, which control tuition rates at state schools, try to hold down tuition rates.)

Despite this, middle- and lower-income students are often afforded discounts in the form of tuition waivers, scholarships, work-study Programmemes that pay partly in free course hours, and government guaranteed loans.

Little objection is given to this version of price discrimination, because of the well-established funding mechanism which does a good job of allocating positions to members of all income classes in the US.

"Haggling"

Many cultures involve "haggling" in market transactions — inflated prices are posted, but the customer can negotiate with the vendor. In the United States, haggling is rare if not nonexistent in grocery stores and with retailers, but common when automobiles and homes are sold. Negotiation often requires knowledge, confidence, and a confrontational personality, and vendors know that many customers will pay higher prices in order to avoid haggling.

Because dealers will often offer more concessions to men, it is not uncommon for women to send male friends or relatives to purchase automobiles and homes for them.

International Price Discrimination

Price discrimination also occurs on an international level. For example, prescription drugs may cost considerably less in Canada than in the US, because of governmental price controls in place in Canada. Similar government price controls exist for fuels (India, among others) and tobacco products (Indonesia).

Governments can also use tax policy to increase prices in order to limit consumption and increase tax revenue, such as automobile prices, which incur a 100% tax in many countries with low automobile population.

Even online sales for non material goods, which do not have to be shipped, may change according to the geographic location of the buyer. A song in Apple's itunes costs 79 pence (1.49 USD) for Britons but only 99 US-cents for Americans.

Britons pay 49% more than Americans for the same song. Lufthansa's cheapest domestic fare in Germany *for Germans* is 109 Euro (99 Euro + 10 Euro "booking fee"). Americans pay 99 USD, which is 78 Euro. Germans pay 39% *more* than Americans for the same product.

Academic Pricing

Companies will often offer discounted software to students and faculty at K-12 and university levels. These may be labeled as academic versions, but perform the same as the full price retail software. Academic versions of the most expensive software suites may be priced as little as one fifth or less of retail price. Some academic software may have differing licenses than retail versions, usually disallowing their use in activities for profit or expiring the license after a given number of months.

Dual Pricing

Even within a country, differentiated pricing may be established to ensure that citizens receive lower prices than non-citizens; this is known as dual pricing. This is particularly common for goods that are subsidized or otherwise provided by the state (and hence paid by taxpayers). Thus Finns, Thais, and Indians (among others) may purchase special fare tickets for public transportation that are only available to citizens. Many countries also maintain separate admission charges for museums, national parks and similar facilities, the usually professed rationale being that citizens should be able to educate themselves and enjoy the country's natural wonders cheaply, but other visitors should pay the market rate.

Wage Discrimination

Wage discrimination is when the price of equivalent Labour is discriminated among different groups of workers. This may be seen as just one kind of price discrimination or as an example of its inverse, one buyer buying identical goods at different rates This is also called a monopsony.

Price Discrimination by Online Search Type

Some online stores and companies attempt to price discriminate between their customers by using information they gather about how a particular customer is searching for a product. For example, some travel firms have been shown to mark-up prices for all the holiday packages they list when a customer asks to see their holidays ranked with the most expensive package first (which suggests the customer may be price insensitive).

The same packages may be available for less if the customer changes their search type. Variants of this behaviour have been reported on other ecommerce sites, where the more specific your search for a particular good, the lower price is displayed for that good.

Transfer Pricing

Transfer pricing refers to the pricing of goods and services within a multi-divisional organization, particularly in regard to cross-border transactions.

For example, goods from the production division may be sold to the marketing division, or goods from a parent company may be sold to a foreign subsidiary, with the choice of the transfer price affecting the division of the total profit among the parts of the company.

This has led to the rise of transfer pricing regulations as governments seek to stem the flow of taxation revenue overseas, making the issue one of great importance for multinational corporations. The discussion below explains an economic theory, but in practice a great many factors influence the transfer prices that are used by multinationals, including performance measurement, capabilities of accounting systems, import quotas, customs duties, VAT, taxes on profits, and (in many cases) simple lack of attention to the pricing.

From marginal price determination theory, we know that generally the optimum level of output is that where marginal costs equals marginal revenue.

That is to say, a firm should expand its output as long as the marginal revenue from additional sales is greater than their marginal costs. In the diagram that follows, this intersection is represented by point A, which will yield a price of P*, given the demand at point B. When a firm is selling some of its product to itself, and only to itself (ie.: there is no external market for that particular transfer good), then the picture gets more complicated, but the outcome remains the same. The demand curve remains the same. The optimum price and quantity remain the same. But marginal cost of production can be separated from the firms total marginal costs.

Likewise, the marginal revenue associated with the production division can be separated from the marginal revenue for the total firm. This is referred to as the Net Marginal Revenue in production (NMR), and is calculated as the marginal revenue from the firm minus the marginal costs of distribution.

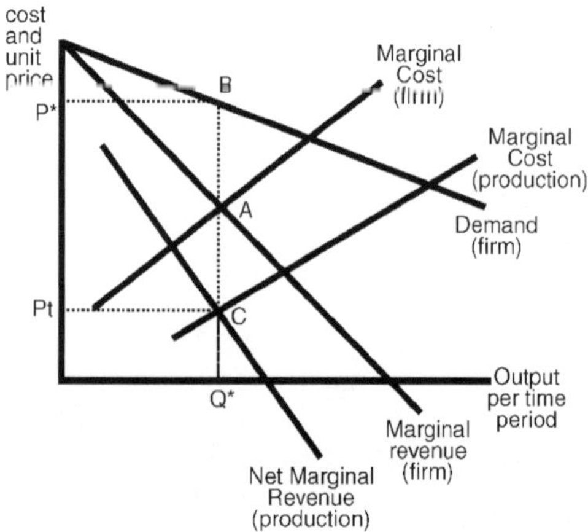

Fig. Transfer Pricing with No External Market

For example, goods from the production division may be sold to the marketing division, or goods from a parent company may be sold to a foreign subsidiary, with the choice of the transfer price affecinal cost curve with the net marginal revenue from production (point C).

If the production division is able to sell the transfer good in a competitive market (as well as internally), then again both must operate where their marginal costs equal their marginal revenue, for profit maximization.

Because the external market is competitive, the firm is a price taker and must accept the transfer price determined by market forces (their marginal revenue from transfer and demand for transfer products becomes the transfer price). If the market price is relatively high (as in Ptr1 in the next diagram), then the firm will experience an internal surplus (excess internal supply) equal to the amount Qt1 minus Qf1. The actual marginal cost curve is defined by points A,C,D.

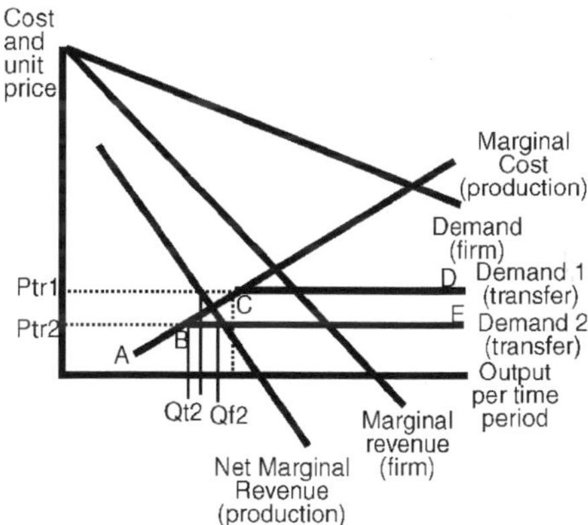

Fig. Transfer Pricing with a Competitive External Market

If the firm is able to sell its transfer goods in an imperfect market, then it need not be a price taker.

There are two markets each with its own price (Pf and Pt in the next diagram). The aggregate market is constructed from the first two. That is, point C is a horizontal summation of points A and B (and likewise for all other points on the Net Marginal Revenue curve (NMRa)). The total optimum quantity (Q) is the sum of Qf plus Qt.

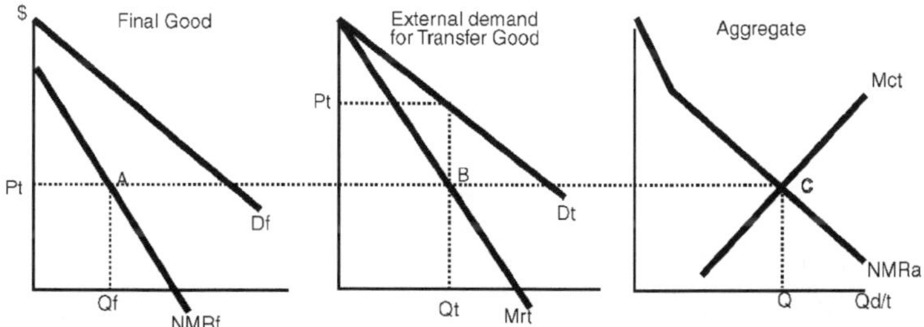

Fig. Transfer Pricing with an Imperfect External Market

Pricing Strategy

Role of Administrative Regulations and Guidelines

Although there is sound economic theory behind the selection of a transfer pricing method, the fact remains that it can be advantageous to arbitrarily select prices such that, in terms of bookkeeping, most of the profit is made in a country with low taxes, thus shifting the profits to reduce overall taxes paid by a multinational group. However, most countries enforce tax laws based on the arm's length principle as defined in the OECD Transfer Pricing Guidelines for Multinational Enterprises and Tax Administrations, limiting how transfer prices can be set and ensuring that that country gets to tax its "fair" share. In the United States, the pricing of transactions between related parties that are reported for tax purposes are governed by Section 482 of the Internal Revenue Code and the regulations thereunder. From the corporation's position, running afoul of such regulations can prove to be a costly mistake, as illustrated by GlaxoSmithKline's announcement on September 11, 2006 that they had settled a long-running transfer pricing dispute with the US tax authorities, agreeing to pay $3.1 billion in taxes related to an assessed income adjustment due to improper transfer pricing. However, proper use of the regulations also provides a method of protecting against double taxation, provided that the transactions are carried out between divisions in countries bound by bilateral tax treaties. In the GlaxoSmithKline case, however, the company has indicated that they will not pursue competent authority negotiations for the relief of U.S.-U.K. double taxation.

Calculation of the Arm's Length Price

Although there are discrepancies in the specifics of each country's laws concerning the calculation of the arm's length price, the fact that they are primarily based in the OECD Guidelines means that, although such a strategy carries a greater taxation risk than solutions tailored to each country, global transfer pricing policies can be effectively used to determine an appropriate range representing the arm's length price for transactions carried out across a global enterprise. It is important to note, however, that different countries may accept different methods of calculating the transfer price (i.e. Japan requires that the three "traditional" methods be systematically discounted before allowing the use of alternative methods, while the United States accepts the most appropriate method regardless), so care must be taken in such circumstances. The following definitions are thus based on the OECD Guidelines.

Traditional Methods

Comparable Uncontrolled Price Method

The Comparable Uncontrolled Price (CUP) method compares the price at which a controlled transaction is conducted to the price at which a comparable uncontrolled transaction is conducted. This makes it the easiest to conceptually grasp, as the arm's length price is, quite simply, determined by the sale price between two unrelated corporations.

However, the fact that virtually any minor change in the circumstances of trade (billing period, amount of trade, branding, etc.) may have a significant affect on the price makes it exceedingly difficult to find a transaction—much less transactions—that are sufficiently comparable. Should they exist, such comparable transactions fall into two categories: external comparables and internal compara-bles. The former is a comparable uncontrolled transaction in the purest sense of the term—if Company A, in France, sells widgets to its subsidiary A(sub) in Turkey, then an external comparable transaction would be the sale of widgets from French Company B to Turkish Company C (an unrelated enterprise) on identical terms as the trade between A and A(sub).

An internal comparable transaction, then, would be either the trade of widgets between Company A and Company C, or the trade of widgets between Company B and Company A(sub), with the term "internal" referring to the fact that one of the parties involved in the tested transaction is also involved in the comparable uncontrolled transaction.

Cost Plus Method

The Cost Plus (CP) method, generally used for the trade of finished goods, is determined by adding an appropriate markup to the costs incurred by the selling party in manufacturing/purchasing the goods or services provided, with the appropriate markup being based on the profits of other companies comparable to the tested party. For example, the arm's length price for a transaction involving the sale of finished clothing to a related distributor would be determined by adding an appropriate markup to the cost of materials, labour, manufacturing, and so on.

Resale Price Method

The Resale Price (RP), while similar to the CP method, is found by working backwards from transactions taking place at the next stage in the supply chain, and is determined by subtracting an appropriate gross markup from the sale price to an unrelated third party, with the appropriate gross margin being determined by examining the conditions under which it the goods or services are sold and comparing said transaction to other, third-party transactions.

In our clothing example, then, the arm's length price would be determined by subtracting an appropriate gross margin from the price at which the distributor sold the products received from the manufacturer to third-party retailers—department stores, boutiques, etcetera.

It is important to note here that, in our example, both the CP and RP methods are being used to examine the same transaction—the one between the manufacturer and the distributor—meaning that the selection of one for use is ultimately dependent on the availability of data and comparable transactions. This flexibility is not available in other transactions, particularly those involving intangible goods (i.e. it is exceedingly difficult to determine the costs involved in developing technological know-how, and so the arm's length price for the payment of royalties from one company to another is best determined by working backwards from the profits gained based on the usage of the know-how—in other words, the RP method).

Non-traditional Methods

There are any number of non-traditional methods available for determining the arm's length price, with the most common being the Profit Split (PS) method and the Transactional Net Margin method (TNMM).

The PS method (and its derivatives, including the Comparative and Residual Profit Split methods) is applied when the businesses involved in the examined transaction are too integrated to allow for separate evaluation, and so the ultimate profit derived from the endeavor is split based on the level of contribution—itself often determined by some measurable factor such as employee compensation, payment of administration expenses, etc.—of each of the participants in the project. To present a highly simplified example, if Company A above sent three researchers to Company A (sub) to aid in the development of widgets tailored for the Turkish market while Company A(sub) allocated seven identically-compensated researchers to aid in the development, we would expect that Company A(sub) would pay Company A 30% of the ultimate profits as a royalty fee for the technical knowledge provided by Company A's researchers.

TNMM, meanwhile, is a method that requires a thorough examination of the company in question in order to determine the net profit margin relative to an appropriate base of costs to be realized through the examined transaction. Essentially, TNMM is a unified version of the RP and CP methods whereby comparable companies are used to ensure an appropriate margin is applied. Although not one of the traditional three methods, TNMM is gaining recognition as a relatively accurate, easy method of calculating the arm's length price.

APA

An Advance Pricing Agreement/Arrangement (the specific terminology varies by country), or APA, is an agreement between the taxpayer and the competent taxation authorities that a future transaction will be conducted at the agreed-upon price, which is recognized as the arm's length price for the period designated. Although retroactive APAs can be used to reduce tax exposure in past years, APAs are primarily used to avoid the risk of future income assessment adjustments which, as in the case of GlaxoSmithKlein, could lead to hefty payments in the future. There are two types of APAs: unilateral and bilateral/multilateral APAs. A unilateral APA is, as its name suggests, an agreement between a corporation and the authority of the country where it is subject to taxation. Although simpler to implement than a bilateral/multilateral APA, a unilateral APA will not be recognized by a foreign tax authority, meaning that a U.S. company securing a unilateral APA for trade with its British subsidiary would still run the risk of being assessed should the foreign tax authorities not agree with the method of calculating the arm's length price, resulting in double taxation.

Bilateral/multilateral APAs, however, *do* provide such coverage, although their implementation requires a more lengthy application process, including consultation between and the agreement of all competent authorities involved.

Mutual Agreement Procedures

A mutual agreement procedure is an instrument used for relieving international tax grievances, including double taxation. Although the specifics vary based on the laws of each country, they are only carried out between authorities of countries or principalities with existing tax treaties—for example, it is impossible to relieve double taxation by holding mutual agreement procedures between the authorities of China and Taiwan.

It is also important to note that, although most conventions require that each party to put forth all reasonable effort to resolve such disputes, they are generally not *required* to come to any sort of agreement. This means that although mutual agreement procedures can be an effective tool for the relief of taxation grievances, they are not failsafes.

Joint Product Pricing

Pricing for joint products is a little more complex than pricing for a single product. To begin with there are two demand curves. The characteristics of each demand curve could be different. Demand for one product could be greater than for the other product.

Consumers of one product could be more price elastic than the consumers of the other product (and therefore more sensitive to changes in the product's price).

To complicate things further, both products, because they are produced jointly, share a common marginal cost curve. There are complexities in the production function also. Their production could be linked in the sense that they are bi-products (referred to as complements in production), or they could be linked in the sense that they can be produced by the same inputs (referred to as substitutes in production). Also, production of the joint product could be in fixed proportions or in variable proportions. When setting prices in a situation as complex as this, microeconomic marginal analysis is helpful. In a simple case of a single product, price is set at that quantity demanded where marginal cost exactly equals marginal revenue. This is exactly what is done when joint products are produced in variable proportions. Each product is treated separately.

In fact, it might even be possible to construct separate cost functions. In the diagram below, to determine optimal pricing for joint products produced in variable proportions, you find the intersection point of marginal revenue (product A) with the joint marginal cost curve.

You then extend that quantity, up to the demand curve for product A, and that gives you the profit maximizing price for product A (point Pa in the diagram). You do the same for product B, yielding price point Pb1.

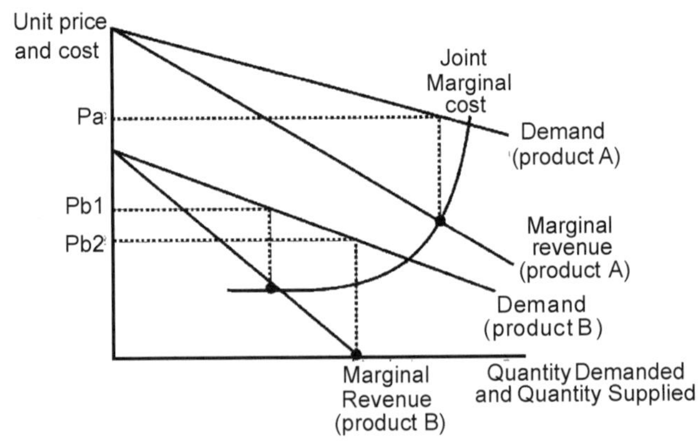

Fig. Pricing of Joint Products

If the products are produced in fixed proportions (example: cow hides and cow steaks), then one of the products will very likely be produced in quantities different from the profit maximizing amount considered separately. In fact the profit maximizing quantity and price of the second half of the joint product, will be different from the profit maximizing amount considered separately.

In the diagram, product B is produced in greater amounts than the profit maximizing amount considered separately, and sold at a lower price (point Pb2) than the profit maximizing price considered separately (point Pb1).

Although price is lower and output is higher, marginal cost is also higher. Yet this is a profit maximizing solution to this situation. Quantity supplied of product B is increased to the point that marginal revenue becomes zero (ie.: the point where the marginal revenue curve intersects the horizontal axis).

Price Skimming

Price skimming is a pricing strategy in which a marketer sets a relatively high price for a product or service at first, then lowers the price over time. It is a temporal version of price discrimination/yield management. It allows the firm to recover its sunk costs quickly before competition steps in and lowers the market price. Price skimming is sometimes referred to as *riding down the demand curve*. This can be seen in the series of diagrams on the right. The first diagram shows the demand schedule, price, and quantity demanded at time t=1. Additional short run demand schedules representing times t=2 and t=3 are added in subsequent diagrams.

As time goes by, price decreases and volume increases. When the 3 equilibria are joined we obtain the price skimmers' long run demand schedule (shown in bright green).

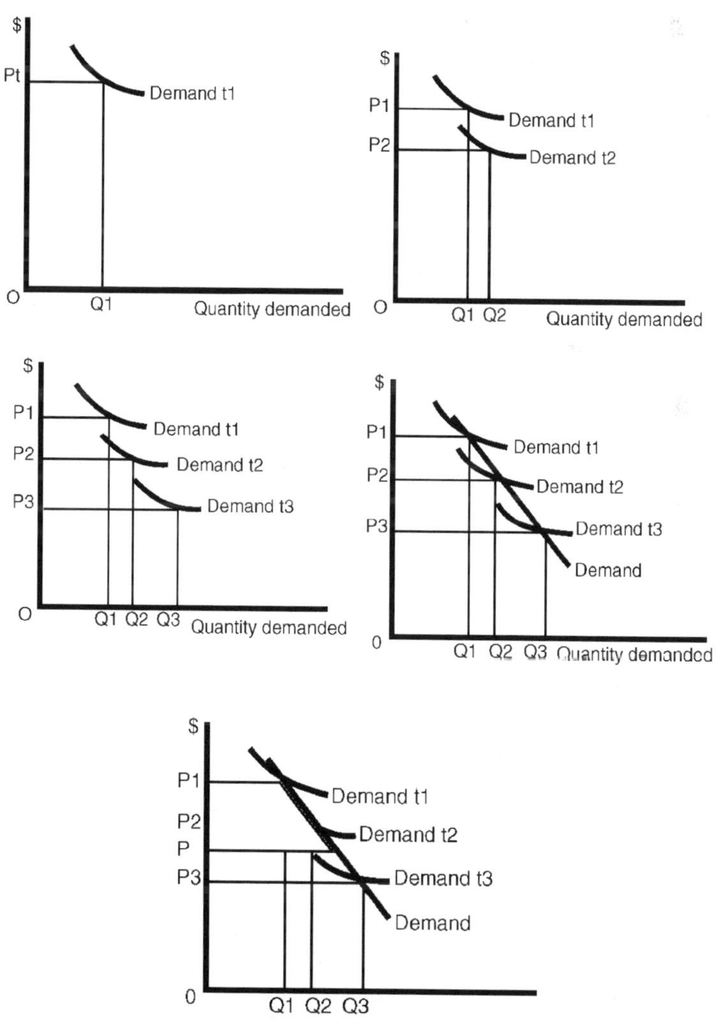

Fig. Price Skimming

The objective of a price skimming strategy is to capture the consumer surplus (the area in blue, between the single market clearing price (P) and the highest price charged (P1)). If this is done successfully, then theoretically no customer will pay less for the product than the maximum they are willing to pay. In practice it is impossible for a firm to capture all of this surplus.

Limitations of Price Skimming

There are several potential problems with this strategy.

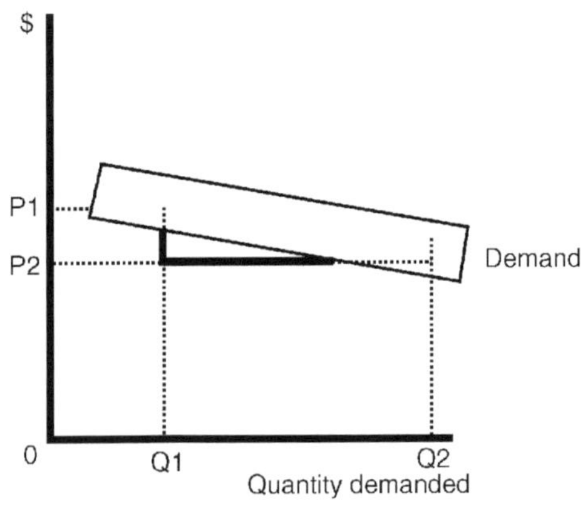

Fig. Elastic Demand

- It is only effective when the firm is facing an inelastic demand curve. If the long run demand schedule is elastic, market equilibrium will be achieved by quantity changes rather than price changes. Penetration pricing is a more suitable strategy in this case. Price changes by any one firm will be matched by other firms resulting in a rapid growth in industry volume. Dominant market share will typically be obtained by a low cost producer that pursues a penetration strategy.
- A price skimmer must be careful with the law. Price discrimination is illegal in many jurisdictions, but yield management is not. Price skimming can be considered either a form of price discrimination or a form of yield management. Price discrimination uses market characteristics (such as price elasticity) to adjust prices, whereas yield management uses product characteristics. Marketers see this legal distinction as quaint since in almost all cases market characteristics correlate highly with product characteristics. If using a skimming strategy, a marketer must speak and think in terms of product characteristics in order to stay on the right side of the law.
- The inventory turn rate can be very low for skimmed products. This could cause problems for the manufacturer's distribution chain. It may be necessary to give retailers higher margins to convince them to enthusiastically handle the product.

- Skimming encourages the entry of competitors. When other firms see the high margins available in the industry, they will quickly enter.
- Skimming results in a slow rate of diffusion and adaptation. This results in a high level of untapped demand. This gives competitors time to either imitate the product or leap frog it with a new innovation. If competitors do this, the window of opportunity will have been lost.
- The manufacturer could develop negative publicity if they lower the price too fast and without significant product changes. Some early purchasers will feel they have been ripped-off. They will feel it would have been better to wait and purchase the product at a much lower price. This negative sentiment will be transferred to the brand and the company as a whole.

Two-part Tariff

A two-part tariff is a price discrimination technique in which the price of a product or service is composed of two parts - a lump-sum fee as well as a per-unit charge. As with all price discrimination techniques, it may only occur in partially or fully monopolistic markets. It is designed to enable the firm to capture more consumer surplus than it otherwise would in a non-discriminating pricing environment.

Depending on the homogeneity of demand, the lump-sum fee charged varies, but the rational firm will set the per unit charge will be *above or equal to* the marginal cost of production, and *below or equal to* the price the firm would charge in a perfect monopoly. An important element to remember concerning two-part tariffs is that it is still price discrimination, of which an important feature is that the product or service offered by the firm must be identical to all consumers, hence, price charged may vary, but *not due to different costs borne by the firm*, as this would infer a differentiated product.

Thus, while credit cards which charge an annual fee plus a per-transaction fee is a good example of a two-part tariff, a fixed fee charged by a car rental company in addition to a per-kilometre fuel fee is not so good, because the fixed fee may reflect fixed costs such as registration and insurance which the firm must recoup in this manner. This can make the identification of two-part tariffs difficult.

A Two-part Tariff when Consumer Demand is Homogeneous

In this example, assume demand is homogeneous across consumers, and there is one firm who experiences no fixed costs and constant costs per unit (for simplicity - hence the horizontal marginal cost (MC) line). A perfectly competitive market would charge price Pc and supply Qc, making no economic profit but producing an allocatively efficient output. Without price discrimination, a monopolist would charge price Pm per unit and supply Qm, maximizing profit below the allocatively efficient level of output Qc.

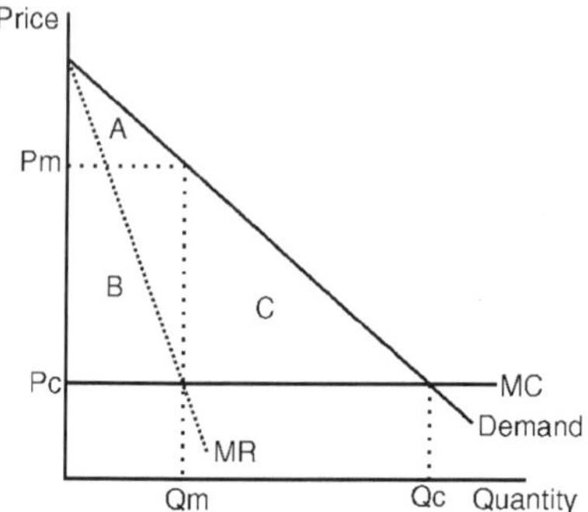

Fig. A Demonstration of a Two part Tariff when Demand is Homogeneous; the Diagram Applies for each Consumer

This situation yields economic profit for the firm equal to the green area B, consumer surplus equal to the light blue area A, and a deadweight loss equal to the purple area C. The demand curve represents a consumer's maximum willingness to pay for any given output. Thus, as long as they receive the appropriate amount of goods, in this case, Qcm, the consumer is willing to pay their entire surplus (ABC).

The lump-sum fee therefore equals this surplus, and enables the firm to capture all the consumer surplus and deadweight loss areas, increasing profits. The per-unit charge is equal to the marginal cost of supplying each unit (MC). This situation yields economic profit for the firm equal to the areas ABC, zero consumer surplus, and no deadweight loss. This results in an allocatively efficient output, one of the redeeming qualities of price discrimination. If there are multiple consumers with homogeneous demand, then profit will equal n times the area ABC, where n is the number of consumers.

A Two-part Tariff (When Consumer Demand is Different)

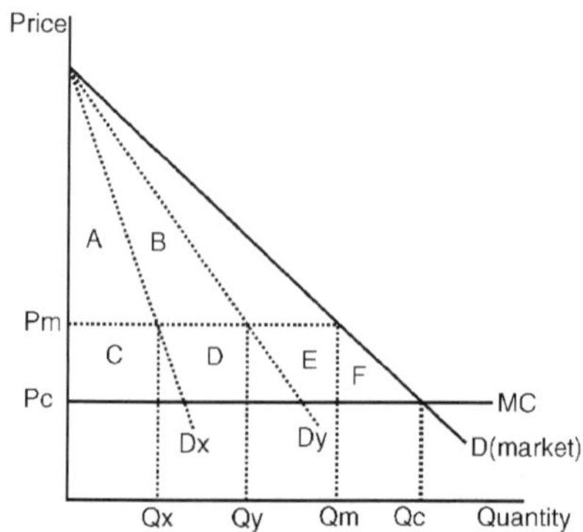

Fig. A Demonstration of a Two Part tariff when Demand is Different

We now consider the case where there are two consumers, X and Y. Consumer Y's demand is exactly twice consumer X's demand, and each of these consumers is represented by a separate demand curve, and their combined demand (Dmarket). The firm is the same as in the previous example. We assume that the firm *cannot separately identify each consumer* - it cannot therefore price discriminate against each of them individually.

The firm would like to follow the same logic as before and charge a per-unit price of Pc while imposing a lump-sum fee equal to area ABCD - the largest consumer surplus of the two consumers. In so doing, however, the firm will be pricing consumer X out of the market, because the lump-sum fee far exceeds his own consumer surplus of area AC. Nevertheless, this would still yield profit equal ABCD. A solution to pricing consumer X out of the market is to thus charge a lump-sum fee equal to area AC, and continue to charge Pc per unit. Profit in this instance equals twice the area AC (two consumers): since consumer Y's demand is twice consumer X's, then 2 x AC = ABCD. As it turns out, the producer is indifferent to either of these pricing possibilities.

Recall that price discrimination occurs in a partially or fully monopolistic market. This firm therefore has some capacity to set price in the market. Assume it sets the unit price equal to Pm, and imposes a lump-sum fee equal to area A. Now, the firm is making a profit on each unit sold - total market profit from the sale of Qm units is equal to area CDE. Profit from the lump-sum fee is 2 x A = AB. Total profit is therefore area ABCDE.

Thus, by charging a higher per unit price and a lower lump-sum fee, the firm has generated area E more profit than if it had charged a lower per-unit price and a higher lump-sum fee. Note that the firm is no longer producing the allocatively efficient output, and there is a deadweight loss experienced by society equal to area F - this is a result of the exercise of monopoly power.

Consumer X has no consumer surplus, consumer Y has a consumer surplus B.

Examples of two-part tariffs: The following items could be identified as two part tariffs; but it is possible some of them could be debated on the basis of the presence of fixed costs such as insurance which the firm cannot recoup in any other way.

- "Membership discount retailers" such as shopping clubs that charge an annual fee for admission to the point of sale and also charge for your purchases

  Amusement parks where there are admission fees and also per-ride fees
- Cover charge for bars combined with per drink fees
- Credit cards which charge an annual fee plus a per-transaction fee
- Loyalty cards or clubs

Price Point

Price points are prices for which demand is relatively high. In introductory microeconomics, a demand curve is downward sloping to the right and either linear or gently convex to the origin. The first is usually true, but the second is only piecewise true, as price surveys indicate that demand for a product is not a linear function of its price and not even a smooth function. Demand curves look more like a series of waves than a straight line.

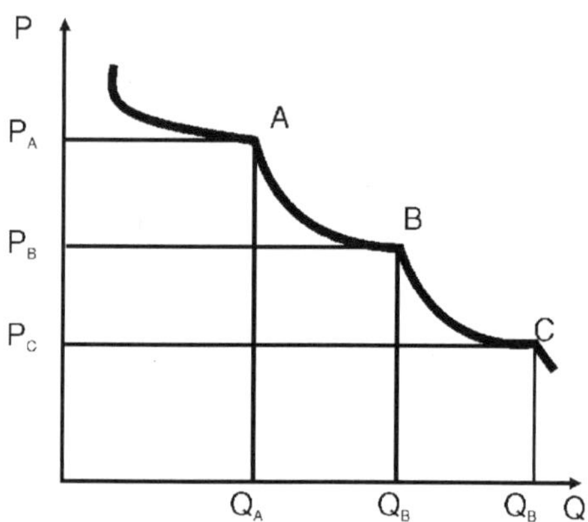

Fig. Price points A, B, and C, along a demand curve

Points A, B, and C in the diagram are price points. By increasing the price beyond a price point (say to a price slightly above *price point B*), sales volume decreases by an amount more than proportional to the price increase. This decrease in quantity demanded more than offsets the additional revenue from the increased unit price. As a result, total revenue decreases when a firm raises its price beyond a price point. Technically, the price elasticity of demand is low (inelastic) at a price lower than the price point (steep section of the demand curve), and high (elastic) at a price higher than a price point (gently sloping part of the demand curve). It is a common marketing strategy for a firm to set prices at existing price points.

There are 3 main reasons for the existence of price points:

- Substitution price points
- Price points occur at the price of a close substitute
- When an item's price rises above the cost of a close substitute, the quantity demanded drops sharply
- Customary price points
- People are used to paying a certain amount for a type of product
- Increasing the price beyond this amount will cause sales to drop dramatically
- Perceptual price points
- Also referred to as psychological pricing or odd-number pricing
- Raising a price above 99 cents will cause demand to fall disproportionally because $1.00 is perceived to be a significantly higher price

Bundling

Bundling is a marketing strategy that involves offering several products for sale as one combined product. This strategy is very common in the software business (for example: bundle a word processor, a spreadsheet, and a database into a single office suite), and in the fast food industry in which multiple items are combined into a complete meal.

The strategy is most successful when:

- There are economies of scale in production,
- There are economies of scope in distribution,
- Consumers appreciate the resulting simplification of the purchase decision and benefit from the joint performance of the combined product,
- When the marginal costs of bundling are low.
- When production set-up costs are high,
- When customer acquisition costs are high.

Product bundling is most suitable for high volume and high margin (i.e., low marginal cost) products. Research by Yannis Bakos and Erik Brynjolfsson found that bundling was particularly effective for digital "information goods" with close to zero marginal cost, and could enable a bundler with an inferior collection of products to drive even superior quality goods out of the market place.

In oligopolistic and monopolistic industries, product bundling can be seen as an unfair use of market power because it limits the choices available to the consumer. In these cases it is typically called product tying.

Pure bundling occurs when a consumer can only purchase the entire bundle or nothing, mixed bundling occurs when consumers are offered a choice between the purchasing the entire bundle or one of the separate parts of the bundle.

Location

In managerial economics, location is a strategy used by firms in a monopolistic competition environment. Unlike a product differentiation strategy, where firms make their products different in order to attract customers, the *economics of location* strategy causes firms to produce similar or identical products.

For example, assume there are two companies selling dye for easter eggs. Each company can sell only one colour, and there are six possible colors (red, orange, yellow, green, blue, and violet).

If a person can't get their favorite colour, they will buy the colour that is closest to their favorite (i.e. if a person likes violet, but only blue and green are produced, the person will buy blue).

If each colour has the same number of people who like it, then the two colours produced will be yellow and green. If one of the companies chooses to produce a colour other than yellow or green, the other company can gain a competitive advantage.

For example, if one firm produces orange dye, the other firm will choose to produce yellow dye.

The first firm will sell only to people who prefer red and orange, while the second firm will sell to people who prefer one of the other four colours.

Therefore, it is in both firm's interest to produce similar products (in this case yellow and green dyes). Only then is there an equilibrium, where neither firm can gain an advantage.

5

Consumer Behaviour

To a lay person, consumer attitude should represent as the summary statement of his assessment about anything. Thus, a consumer may have a negative attitude for the products made in Korea. What it means is, that the consumer has assessed the products of the country and found them to be of not very high quality. This is what a consumer attitude represents. Theoretically speaking, attitude is "learned predisposition to respond in a consistently favourable and unfavourable manner with respect to a given stimuli" Another way of describing attitude is that it is a "relatively enduring organization of inter-related beliefs that describe, evaluate, and advocate action with respect to an object or a situation." Several characteristics of attitude are evident from these two descriptions. The first is that attitude is `not a transient feeling' but represents an enduring feeling or enduring evaluation. Secondly, it derives its genesis and strength from a variety of sources of information including perception and experience. Thirdly, it signals about the likely course of action by the consumer. Attitude is also used as a replacement term for describing `belief system' of a person.

ATTITUDE AND CONSUMER DECISION-MAKING

In everyday life, consumers receive a variety of marketing communications about what they should buy and they should not. They come to know about different claims and standings of the brands. On the basis of inputs received from various sources, consumers develop their assessment of the brands, better known as the brand-image. The brand image helps consumers in believing which brand is more likely to have a particular benefit or a feature. It should be noted here that since these brand beliefs are based on consumer perception, they may sometimes be at variance with reality.

Thus, a potential car buyer may believe that the brand A of car has style but it may not be actually true about the brand A. In a similar vein, a potential lipstick buyer may believe that the brand B of the lipstick has the attribute of social prestige. In reality, it may not be so. Thus, consumer attitude are based on the perception, true or otherwise. But they provide a very important clue as to whether the consumers will take a particular course of action or not. Thus, a person after having been bombarded by a string of newspapers ads on various TV brands available in India, may suddenly observe: "Oh, the TV ads! I can't stand them any more!"

Similarly, a typical housewife may have this to say to her husband, after having viewed the sunday morning transmission: "You know something, the TV ads are so fascinating that they have taught a lot to our children in making brand choices for grocery". These two statements express a summary evaluation of a marketing stimulus *i.e.*, promotional methods, and indicate how these will act in case of consumers who were asked to respond. Thus, the first consumer will probable zap the TV commercials or skip them. The second housewife may regulate the viewing hours of the television for the children.

THE CONSTITUENTS OF CONSUMER ATTITUDE

In the subsequent block 3, as suggested deal with the major variables that a buyer would face during information search for the purpose of evaluating and reaching a choice. The key variable that would guide the customer in the process, is the consumer attitude. Since an attitude provides a series of cues to marketers with reference to evaluation procedure, an understanding of consumer attitude can help marketers predict future purchases; and gauge the strength or otherwise of their its present sales. Even they redesign their marketing mix efforts. Attitude, as a concept, however, is far from simple. An attitude consists of three constituents. These are affective; cognitive and conative. Affective part of the attitude refers to the feelings that a consumer has. The cognitive part refers to the information and knowledge basis of these consumers. The third and final part of the attitude–the conative, refers to tae intention of the customer. A schematic conception of attitudes is attempted in Figure.

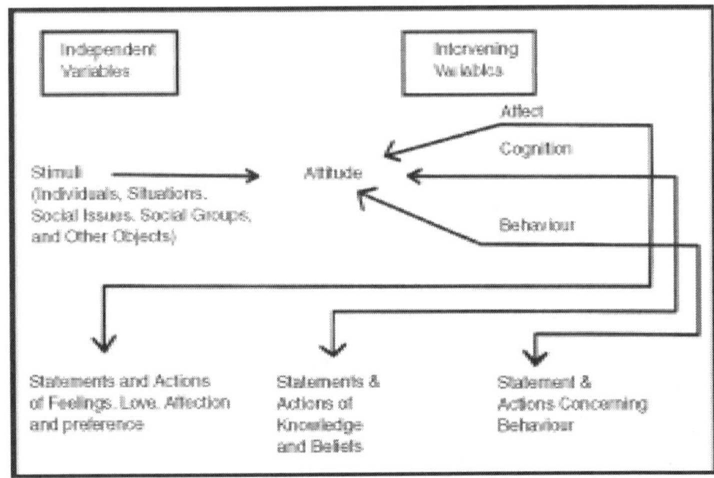

Fig. Schematic Conception of Attitudes.

The Figure can be amplified by an hypothetical example of the attitude formation in respect of an individual as well as a institutional buyer. For instance, assume that a research study reveals that Indian females have a favourable attitude towards ONIDA Television.

Similarly, assume that TATA Steel too has indicated its favourable attitude towards HCL Fax machines. In operational terms, these findings summarize the knowledge of these buyers as to what ONIDA TV and HCL Fax machine may possess. Secondly, they indicate how the female buyers and the TATA Steel feel about these brands. Thirdly, they indicate the likely action if these buyers are asked to go for these respective products, *i.e.*, ONIDA Television and HCL Fax machine. To sum up, attitude indicates knowledge, feelings and intended action for the given stimulus.

THE FUNCTIONS OF CONSUMER ATTITUDE

Notwithstanding the importance of consumer attitude, two serious criticisms have been levelled against it. The foremost criticism is that it makes a rather naive assumption that attitudes influence the specific and overt behaviour of consumer. The real facts don't support it so clearly. Yet, the functions of attitude are too important to be left un-described. Consumer attitudes in their most rudimentary form, renders the following function as explained in figure.

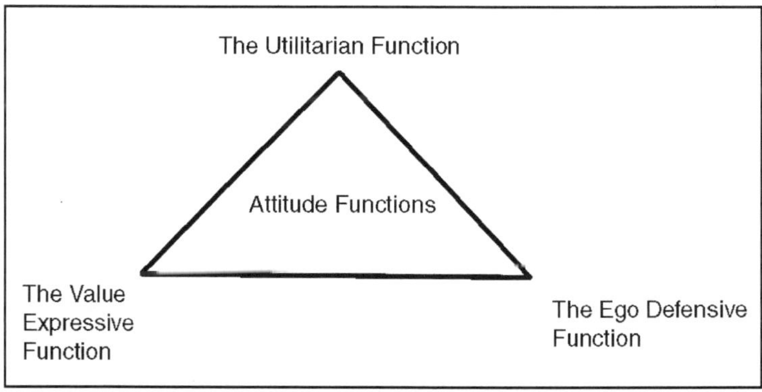

Fig. Functions of Attitude

THE UTILITARIAN FUNCTION

Consumer attitudes fulfil a utilitarian function as they guide consumers in achieving their desired needs. Thus, if the TV buyers consider technology and after-sales service support as the two most important criteria in TV selection, the buyers will be most attracted by the messages of those brand alternatives that claim to possess the two attributes. Such attitudes towards these brands will help the consumer achieve what he wants. Also, it will assist them in avoiding failure and disappointment in brand evaluation.

THE EGO DEFENSIVE FUNCTION

This function protects consumers against internal and external anxieties and environment. Herein, the marketing stimuli and more particularly, products become an instrument of the protection process. Many consumer psychologists have led marketers to believe that a positiveconsumer attitude towards expensive jeweler wrist watches and other visible prestige products serve as mechanism of Defence for these consumers. It should be cautioned here, however, that expensive items alone do not constitute a mechanism of Defence for consumers. The low priced products like mouthwash deodorants too can serve the same protection function from anxiety etc.

THE VALUE-EXPRESSIVE FUNCTION

Often consumer attitudes are an expression of their values and self-concept. Value expressive attitudes maintain self-identity among consumers and lead them to expression and determination. The projection is often strong, evident and extreme because consumers openly express opinions that reflect their strong beliefs and self-concept. The application of this function is all too evident in consumer selection and evaluation of products, their price, promotional items and the distributive outlets. Thus, a consumer, in order to express his simple and Gandhian values in life, will always select and wear handloom and Khadi, support products of the small scale industries and may have a negative attitude against conspicuous consumption and their public endorsement by the commercial houses. Normally, there is a tendency on the part of consumers to flaunt this kind of attitude.

UTILITY FUNCTION

After having ascertained that the consideration-set of alternative brands, possesses all the desired attributes, consumers will identify how their satisfaction will vary in response to changing levels of performance in those attributes, Thus, the potential car buyer will decide how much will it mean to him in utility terms if brand 'x' of car possesses 4/10 level of performance in fuel-efficiency, instead of, say, 6/10 level of performance. The same could be argued in the case of the female lipstick buyer. The advantage of utility function is that by combining the performance levels of salient attributes, consumers can make up what is called an 'ideal' brand.

CONSUMER ATTITUDE: THE MODELS

Model-making in attitudes have been attempted in a variety of ways. Most prominent among them are the multi-attribute attitude models.

MULTI-ATTRIBUTE ATTITUDE MODELS

Multi-attribute attitude models explain how consumers may combine their beliefs about product attributes to form their attitudes about various brand alternatives. These models assume that the brand which receives the best attitude, will be chosen. They further assume that consumers will go through the standard Hierarchy of Effects sequence. A careful scrutiny of all multi-attribute attitude models establishes two general categories of these models.

Category I comprises the models that emphasize the Attitude- Towards—Objects. Hence, they are termed as ATO models. Category II consists of those models that focus on predicting the behavioural intentions of consumers to perform certain action. This action could be purchase or non-purchase. For brevity sake, it is termed as BI Model. Figure illustrates the point.

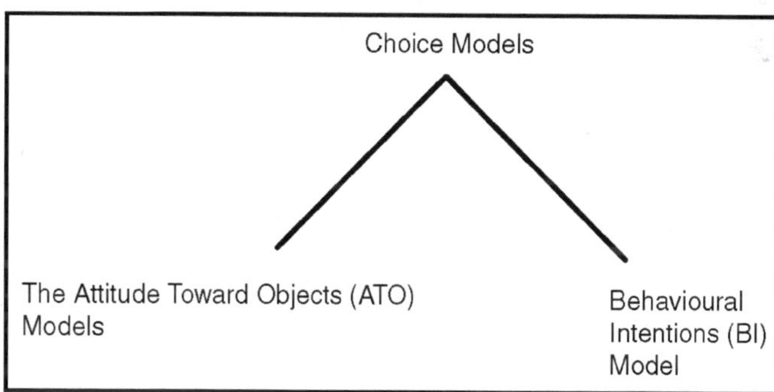

Fig. Multi-attributes of choice Models

THE ATTITUDE-TOWARDS-OBJECTS MODELS

Although a variety of ATO models are found in consumer research; most of these models seek information on the importance of brand attributes; beliefs about the presence or absence of those attributes in the brand alternatives and information on their combined effect in alternative evaluation.

Fishbein's model represents this genre of models. Algebraically, the model is expressed as:

$$A_0 = \sum_{i=1}^{n} B_i a_i \text{, where}$$

A_0 = the overall attitude towards object 'O'

B_i = the belief of weather or not object 'O' has a particular attribute

a_i = the importance rating of the attributes

n = the number of beliefs

Table explains a hypothetical multi-attitude evaluation of three brands of family cars in India.

Column 2 states the hypothetical ratings of importance of three attributes. Further beliefs have been rated in columns 3.1, 4.1 and 5.1 on a 5-point scale. The minimum 1 and maximum 5 indicate the unlikelihood or likelihood of that attributes to be possessed by the given brand alternatives of the cars, respectively. A further examination the table will reveal that Premier has been rated as an average car. In contrast Maruti is rated higher on attributes like low maintenance cost and styling. Finally, Ambassador car emerges as the worst car of the lot. Following this, a consumer will have formed the most positive attitude towards Maruti.

Table. Multi-attribute Evaluation

Attributr (Column 1)	(2) Weight	(3) Premier	(4) Ambassador 3.1	(5) Maruti 3.2	4.1	4.2	5.1	5.2
		a	B	a×B	B	a×B	B	a×B
1.	Designing	3	3	9	2	6	5	15
2.	Low mainten-ance cost	2	3	6	2	4	2	4
3.	Fuel efficiency	1	3	3	3	3	5	5
				18		13		24

CRITICISMS

The ATO models, however, suffer from a major weakness. They fail to consider that quite often, consumer attitude does not fully equate with behaviour. Thus, a potential car buyer in spite of having the most positive attitude towards 'Maruti', may never engage in the behaviour of buying it.

This happens because of the adverse opinion of other important people or due to temptation of investing the funds more profitably elsewhere. Situational influences may prevent him from engaging the act of buying. The Behaviour Intentions model attempts to rectify this weakness in alternative evaluation.

THE BEHAVIOUR INTENTIONS MODEL

The BI model is in effect, an extension of Fishbein's ATO model. The model does not attempt to predict behaviour *per se* but intentions to behave algebraically, the model is as follows:

B = BI = $W_1 (A_B) + W_2$ (SN): where

B = behaviour; BI = Behaviour Intention

A_B = attitude towards performing the behaviour

SN = the subjective norm

W_1 and W_2, are empirically determined weights, through regression analysis.

A_B and SN are obtained directly from consumers via questionnaires. Thus, A_B is obtained from the following equation:

Where,

$$A_B = \sum_{i=1}^{n} b_i e_i,$$

A_B = attitude towards the behaviour

b_i = the person's belief taht performing the behaviour will result in consequence

e_i = the person's evluation of consequence

n = the number of beliefs

The equation has one major difference over the earlier Fishbein's ATO Model. It is that the BI Model assesses the person's belief that performing a particular behaviour will result in a particular consequence. They are termed as Subjective Norms (SN).

The equation for obtaining the subjective norms is as follows:

$$SN = \sum_{j=1}^{n} NB_j\ MC_j$$

where,

SN = subjective norm;

NB_j = the normative belief that a reference group of persons j thinks that the consumer should or should not perform the behaviour;

MC = the motivation to comply with the influence of the referent j and

n = number of relevant reference groups of individuals.

Various research studies have found the BI model to be superior to the standard multi-attribute choice models, though eye-brows have been raised concerning the calculation of the subjective norms (SN). In practice, this exercise is never so simple.

THE MARKETING RESPONSE TO THE CONSUMER ATTITUDE

After having made an analysis of attitude and its formation, and the models, the questions that arise for marketers to consider are as follows: what are their marketing implications and what actions are useful in MANAGING them? Table outlines the areas in which such inferences and actions can be contemplated.

Table. Areas of Marketing Inferences and Actions

Area	Inference (s)	Action (s)
Market-Identification	• Segment market on the bases of product-attribute benefit; beliefs: and product-benefit beliefs.	• Market product on the basis of lifestyle and benefit segmentale
Competitive Analysis	• Possibility of attribute beliefs and benefits manipulation • Positioning of product	• Change own product attributes and those of competitors • Continuously review Product positioning with proper communication Support
Marketing Mix	• Sources of ideas for new products • Communication has	• Use consumer perceptions and attitude to design new products • Enrich consumers with

	impacts on consumer learning	fresh and distinct information
	• Importance of price-evaluation matrix	• Price-perception should be made in line with brand image
	• Distribution outlets add to product image	• Encourage distribution in consumer evaluation
Marketing Opportunity	• Needs of a constant eye on demographics and social changes	• Create exclusive riches or segments of consumer demographice
Attitude formation and Measurement	• Attitude is an indicator of brand preference anf behaviour	• Strengthen the positive attitude and modify the unsuitable ones by a variety of means
	• Continuous feel of the market essential	• Develop a regular attitude-checking system

Specifically, marketers may choose one or a combination of steps to move consumers' evaluation of brand alternatives in their favour. Marketers may, for the beginning, modify their brand alternation in case they find the consumers ratings to be true and genuine.

Further, marketers may attempt to modify consumer ratings to be true and genuine. Further, marketers may attempt to modify consumer beliefs about the brand alternative through sharper communication along with other marketing efforts. However, in case of competitive evaluation, marketer also attempt to alter consumer beliefs about competitive brand alternatives vis-à-vis about theirs. It is done either by running down the high-importance product attributes, on which competitive products are better rated; or by deprecating their performance.

A more positive route, open to marketers, however, is by creating fresh brand attributes or by giving a new focus on the neglected brand attributes. The same could be done even by manipulating the ideal-product to bring it closer to the marketers' own brand alternative.

To sum up, marketers have an unenviable task on their hands while consumers are at the stage of brand evaluation. The acid test of marketing effectiveness in this regard is whether consumers are led to the actual purchase action or not. The answer in either way will pronounce judgment on the adequacy of marketing response.

THE FORMATION OF ATTITUDES

Attitudes are formed in learning hierarchies that place different emphasis on the three different components of an attitude: affect, behaviour and cognition. The components, which can be referred to as the ABC model of attitudes, explain the interrelationship between knowing, feeling and doing. Depending on consumer motivation, each part of the ABC of attitudes will have different importance. The different importance of each component is explained through different hierarchies of effect.

THE STANDARD LEARNING HIERARCHY

The formation of attitudes has mainly been thought to be formed in a standard learning hierarchy in which a person first forms beliefs about a product, cognition, then carries out some sort of evaluation of the product, affect, and lastly engages some sort of action, behaviour.

This approach takes for granted that a consumer is highly involved in all purchasing decisions and carefully plans and evaluates each decision. Hence it is based on cognitive information processing. For the customers at Villa Market, this may be true for two types of consumers: Thai customers who believe that imported brands are better or simply just inclined to try foreign products, and for Foreigners which have strong brand preferences and brand loyalty.

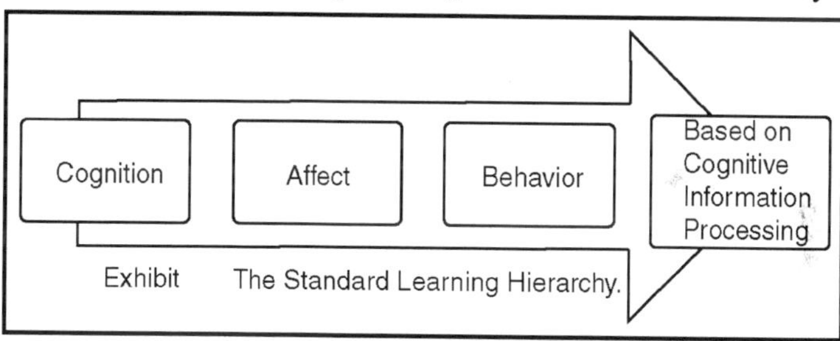

Exhibit The Standard Learning Hierarchy.

For these customers, the decision to go to Villa and buy specific products is based on affection for the products or the belief that these products are superior to those of ordinary supermarkets. This may be especially true for customers choosing from the broad variety of wines that Villa offers.

THE LOW INVOLVEMENT HIERARCHY

Since not all purchases are high-involvement, there are other hierarchies to consider. The low-involvement hierarchy explains attitude formation in cases where consumers don't necessarily have preferences towards any specific brands or products.

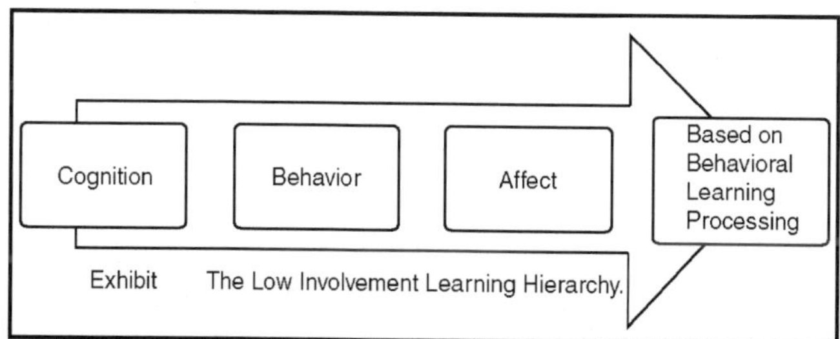

Exhibit The Low Involvement Learning Hierarchy.

When consumers have low-involvement in the purchasing decision, they don't care how much information about a brand is available; they are more likely to respond well or repurchase a brand or product if the experience with it is good and, on the contrary, less inclined to purchase the product if the experience with it is bad. This is especially true for inferior and everyday goods. Even though there might not be that many consumers of low-involvement shopping at Villa, those that do might do so out of convenience. This might be because they live close by or because they don't have a car and just buy the basics at Villa market. This is something that is true for my fellow flat mates and me. We live at Asoke road where there really aren't any food markets. Villa market at Sukhmuvit 33 is the closest one, and we go there to buy basics such as vegetables and fruit. We don't go there because we have a certain affiliation with imported brands, it just so happens to be the closest supermarket.

THE EXPERIMENTAL HIERARCHY

The third and last hierarchy of learning is the experimental. The experimental hierarchy of effect focuses on the significance of emotional responses towards brands or product. This perspective takes into account the immense impact of intangible product attributes like packaging or just simply how well the product corresponds to what is generally considered to be cool or "right" at the moment.

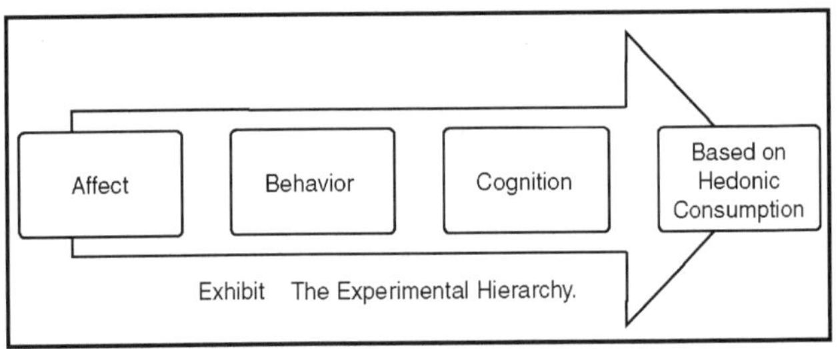

Exhibit The Experimental Hierarchy.

This perspective is based on hedonic consumption, the kind where people indulge on a whim based upon whatever is left over when the basics, like rent, have been paid. Consumers who fall in to this category might be middle–and upper class Thai customers that have money to spend and are looking for something to "spice up" the everyday life with. This category is highly responsive to advertising, and is most likely to base its consumption behaviour on emotional reactions. They may not buy all their groceries at Villa, but are likely to visit the store more than once a month to buy products that aren't available elsewhere. These customers might prove extremely important to Villa market in the future since Thailand is experiencing a rapid growth of people enjoying higher incomes. This group of customers might also prove important since there is currently a trend of westernization in Thailand.

LEVELS OF COMMITMENT TO ATTITUDES

Since consumers place different weight on the different components of the ABC model, it is only natural that the level of commitment to an attitude also varies. *The level of commitment can also be referred to as the level of commitment with an attitude object, and can be divided into compliance, identification and internalization:*

- Compliance is the lowest level of commitment to an attitude, which can be related to low-involvement purchase decisions. In this case the consumer is likely to change his or her behaviour if another, more comfortable, option appears.
- At the higher level of commitment, identification, the consumer incorporates the brand or product as almost a part of her personality. Usually a consumer does this to affiliate herself to a certain group or person.
- The highest level of commitment is internalization, when the consumer incorporates the brand or product as a part of her value system. It's common that a consumer at this level makes the brand a part of her social identity and can take on nostalgic properties.

The customers at Villa can be identified as having different levels of commitment to brands and products. I personally belong to the first level, compliance, since I don't think too much about what I buy at Villa primarily shop at Villa for convenience. The second level of identification can be applied to the Thai customers at Villa, the ones who have money to spend and are not afraid to try new things, a good example of the increasing amount of middle and upper class Thais that can afford to spend these amounts on food and wine.

On the other hand, the foreign customers coming to Villa to buy familiar brands is a clear definition of internalization. For them, the brands might not just appear as a safer or more familiar option to other brands. Buying a home brand of chocolate, for example, might spring out of nostalgia and a sense of belonging to the home country that such purchase might mean. This category of shoppers, with this level of commitment to an attitude, will be inclined to spend a reasonable amount of time at Villa during Christmas and other holidays!

ATTITUDE CHANGE AND INTERACTIVE COMMUNICATION

On an organizational level, Villa Market employs various methods of communication to generate a positive response amongst customers. Villa Market looks to solicit an attitude change such that customers may be persuaded to shop at Villa Market and ultimately become loyal shoppers.

While Villa Market benefits from the psychological principle of scarcity - the idea that customers are naturally more attracted to Villa Market due to the lack of import-based grocery stores available in the Bangkok area–the organization implements tactical communication options to stimulate consumer responses. The communications method used by Villa Market is concurrent with the traditional communications model including a source, message, medium and consumer response.

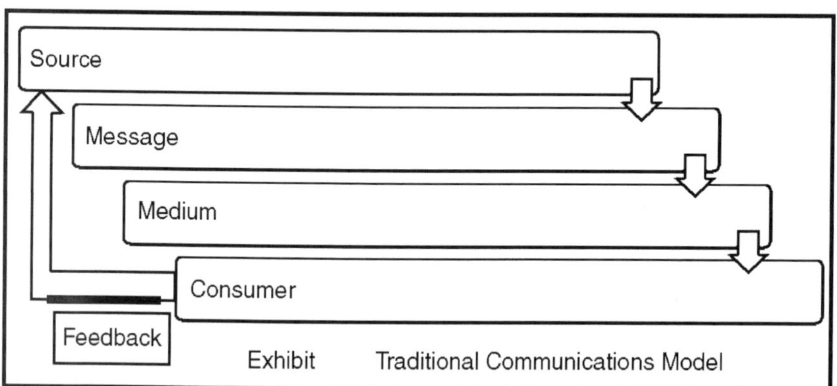

Exhibit Traditional Communications Model

The first component of the communications model, the source, represents where the communication starts.

The communication that Villa has with customers starts from one of two different areas: online or in-store:

- *Online*: Villa Market communicates to consumers through its online presence on various expect websites in addition to its own website. Upon connecting with Villa Market customers, we were able to find that a number of them had their first point of contact with Villa Market through websites marketed to expect living in the Bangkok area. Villa Market had previously advertised on this website via online banners. Further, Villa was able to benefit through buzz marketing that was generated in the online forum in which expect communicated the Villa Market product offerings in the Bangkok area. Being that message creators on the forum are 'lay' expect in the Bangkok area, a considerable amount of credibility afforded to the posters that enable them to be particularly persuasive. The website can be found by conducting a simple inquiry on search engines like Yahoo and Google. It is important to note that the URL address does not contain the Villa Market name and is affiliated with another organization, 'weloveshopping.com.' This affiliation is important, as 'weloveshopping.com' is a larger online delivery system for Thai residents.
- *In-Store*: The Villa Store communicates to consumers through its product selection, staff, setting, and overall impression. Further, Villa Market produces a quarterly magazine in which it details events around Bangkok specific to foreigners. The magazine also communicates product specials that Villa Market has. Being that Villa Market creates the magazine, it is exposed to source biases that consumers may not look kindly towards.

The second component of the communications model is the message itself and the manner in which it is structured:

- *Online*: The online communication message used by Villa Market empowers consumers to decide whether they will be affected by the message or not. It encourages the consumer to take a more proactive role in the communication transaction, as customers are able to learn more about store by clicking on the online banner. Further, it takes on a nontraditional message format via forum discussion. The online discussion further communicates the brand-differentiating message that Villa is trying to communicate in its unique product offerings. Further, as more posters reply in the online discussion, it creates repetition for the Villa Market name among viewers.
- *In-store*: The messages communicated in the magazine are in regards to specific events, *e.g.* Thanksgiving Festivals in Bangkok, which are segmented to expects. The benefit of this type of message is that it communicates the unique benefit and attribute of Villa Market product–imported products for foreigners. There is a level of emotional appeal that Villa is able to solicit from consumers, as they are able to remind them of traditional events and evoke emotions that are specific to its target market of Westerners.

The third component of the communications model is the medium on which the message is delivered. While Villa Market does not use mass-market communication strategies, it is able to effectively capture its niche market through effective use of advertising mediums.

- *Online*: The expat demographic is one of sophistication as many have moved to Thailand to take advantage of business opportunities. Villa Market has understood this market and has been able to outline online marketing as an effective channel to connect with this niche segment.
- *In-store*: The magazine circular employed by Villa Market is a method used to stimulate future sales by building a relationship with customers. The Villa Market magazine is actually a form of permission marketing, as consumers decide whether to pick up a copy of the magazine or not. Upon deciding to take the magazine, consumers willingly accept the reception of Villa Market messages and are more likely to become loyal customers.

The last component of the communications model is the consumer response and feedback. It is important the Villa Market evaluates the response such they it is able to understand the net effects of its communication strategy and adapt its strategy if necessary.

- *Online*: Villa Market can evaluate online effectiveness by looking at the 'click-through' rate of its banner ads to see if are receptive of the communications strategy. Further, they can investigate the total number of hits that their website experienced in order to evaluate the effectiveness of the website. Villa can also take a rouge approach in searching for the 'Villa Market' name within various search engines and evaluating the amount of responses to gauge the amount of buzz created for the brand.

- *In-store*: Villa Market can evaluate in-store effectiveness by counting the amount of magazines taken day-to-day. Further, they may employ a coupon strategy and insert a coupon in each of the magazine and evaluate the redemption rate of the coupon. Overall, Villa can look at the sales trends for its stores.

Exhibit is an illustration of the communications model employed by Villa Market.

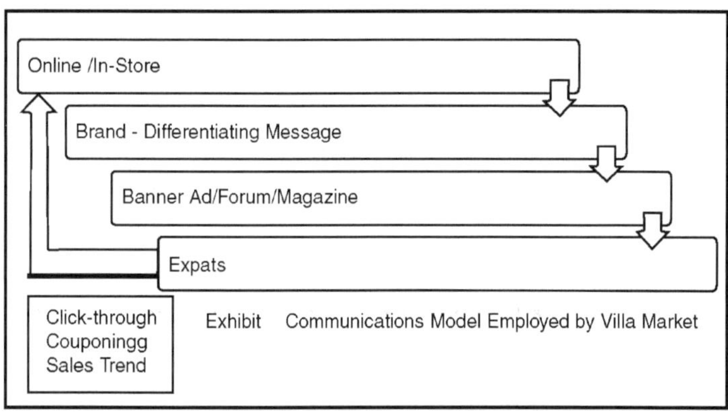

Exhibit Communications Model Employed by Villa Market

CONSUMER BEHAVIOUR AUDIT AND MARKET SEGMENTATION

MARKET SEGMENTATION

When the term "market segmentation" is used, most of us immediately think of psychographics, lifestyles, values, behaviours, and multivariate cluster analysis routines. Market segmentation is a much broader concept, however, and pervades the practice of business throughout the world. What is market segmentation?

At its most basic level, the term "market segmentation" refers to subdividing a market along some commonality, similarity, or kinship. That is, the members of a market segment share something in common. The purpose of segmentation is the concentration of marketing energy and force on the subdivision to gain a competitive advantage within the segment. It's analogous to the military principle of "concentration of force" to overwhelm an enemy. Concen-tration of marketing energy is the essence of all marketing strategy, and market segmentation is the conceptual tool to help achieve this focus. Before discussing psychographic or lifestyle segmentation, let's review other types of market segmentation. Our focus is on consumer markets rather than business markets.

GEOGRAPHIC SEGMENTATION

This is perhaps the most common form of market segmentation, wherein companies segment the market by attacking a restricted geographic area. For example, corporations may choose to market their brands in certain countries, but not in others. A brand could be sold only in one market, one state, or one region of the United States. Many restaurant chains focus on a limited geographic area to achieve concentration of force. Regional differences in consumer preferences exist, and this often provides a basis for geographic specialization.

For example, a company might choose to market its redeye gravy only in the southeastern U.S. Likewise, a picante sauce might concentrate its distribution and advertising in the southwest. A chain saw company might only market its products in areas with forests. Geographic segmentation can take many forms. These examples also reveal that geographic segmentation is sometimes a surrogate for other types of segmentation.

DISTRIBUTION SEGMENTATION

Different markets can be reached through different channels of distribution. For example, a company might segment the "tick and flea collar" market by selling the product to supermarkets under one brand name, to mass merchandisers under another brand, to pet stores under another brand name, and to veterinarians under yet another brand name. This type of distributional segmentation is common, especially among small companies that grant each channel a unique brand to gain distribution within that channel.

Other examples of distributional segmentation would be an upscale line of clothing sold only in expensive department stores, or a hair shampoo sold only through upscale beauty salons.

MEDIA SEGMENTATION

While not common, media segmentation is sometimes a possibility. It is based on the fact that different media tend to reach different audiences. If a brand pours all of its budget into one media, it can possibly dominate the segment of the market that listens to that radio station or reads that magazine. Media segmentation is most often practiced by companies that have some control over the media and can somehow discourage competitors from using that media.

PRICE SEGMENTATION

Price segmentation is common and widely practiced. Variation in household incomes creates an opportunity for segmenting some markets along a price dimension. If personal incomes range from low to high, then a company should offer some cheap products, some medium-priced ones, and some expensive ones.

This type of price segmentation is well illustrated by the range of automotive brands marketed by General Motors, historically. Chevrolet, Pontiac, Oldsmobile, Buick, and Cadillac varied in price along a clearly defined spectrum to appeal to successively higher income groups.

DEMOGRAPHIC SEGMENTATION

Gender, age, income, housing type, and education level are common demographic variables. Some brands are targeted only to women, others only to men. Music downloads tend to be targeted to the young, while hearing aids are targeted to the elderly. Education levels often define market segments. For instance, private elementary schools might define their target market as highly educated households containing women of childbearing age. Demographic segmentation almost always plays some role in a segmentation strategy.

TIME SEGMENTATION

Time segmentation is less common, but can be highly effective. Some stores stay open later than others, or stay open on weekends. Some products are sold only at certain times of the year. Chili is marketed more aggressively in the fall, with the onset of cooler weather.

Football is played in the fall, basketball in the winter and spring, and baseball in the spring and summer. The Olympics come along every four years. Department stores sometimes schedule midnight promotional events. The time dimension can be an interesting basis for segmentation. In addition to the foregoing, markets can be segmented by hobbies, by political affiliation, by religion, by special interest groups, by sports team loyalties, by university attended, and hundreds of other variables. You are only limited by your marketing imagination.

PSYCHOGRAPHIC OR LIFESTYLE SEGMENTATION

Lastly, we come to psychographic segmentation, based upon multivariate analyses of consumer attitudes, values, behaviours, emotions, perceptions, beliefs, and interests. Psychographic segmentation is a legitimate way to segment a market, if we can identify the proper segmentation variables. Qualitative research techniques become invaluable at this stage.

Qualitative research provides the insight, the conceptual knowledge, and the consumer's exact language necessary to design the segmentation questionnaire.

Typically, verbatim comments from consumers are used to build batteries of psychographic or lifestyle statements. A large representative sample of consumers are then asked about the degree to which they agree or disagree with each statement. For example, if you were designing a market segmentation questionnaire for an airline, you might conduct a series of depth interviews to help design the questionnaire. You probably would include a behavioural part.

You would include a major part on attitudes towards air travel. You would also want to include a part on perceptions of the different airlines; that is, their "brand images." You could go further and add a part on media consumption, or personal values as well. It is at this point that you realise the questionnaire is too long, and you have to make some hard decisions about what questions or statements to include. The method of data collection is very important, because the questionnaire is so long. The telephone is not recommended for segmentation studies because of questionnaire length. Moreover, the various rating scales and attitudinal statements are difficult to communicate by phone, and the resulting phone data tends to be "insensitive" and rife with "noise." In-person interviews, or Internet-based interviews, or even mail surveys, are much better.

Rating scales and attitudinal statements can be seen and fully comprehended by respondents. Seeing is much better than hearing, and it produces more accurate answers. The Internet is especially valuable for segmentation studies, since respondents can take the survey at a time of their own choosing, when they can give it their full, undivided attention. A mail survey offers some of the same advantages, but without the questionnaire controls, checks, and safeguards built into an Internet survey.

ANALYTICAL METHODS

Most segmentation analyses are based upon various types of "cluster analysis," a set of well-defined statistical procedures that group people just as to the proximity of their ratings. Unfortunately, cluster analysis has inherent limitations and seldom yields coherent market segments. Cluster analysis routines ignore the pattern of respondent ratings and rely primarily upon the proximity of respondent ratings. Too often, this leads to clusters, or market segments, that don't seem to make much sense when crosstabulated against the original segmentation variables.

Another limitation of clustering approaches is that all statements are treated as equal; whereas, in truth, some statements might be much more important than others in explaining consumer behaviour in a particular product category.

A better way to achieve a good psychographic segmentation is to first identify the statements that are more important. Correlation analysis and regression can be used for this purpose. Factor analysis is also a powerful technique to identify the statements and groups of statements that account for much of the variance in the attitudinal data set. Directly, and indirectly, these techniques can help you identify the most important statements.

Then, these statements become the inputs to the final segmentation analysis. Many different methods can be used to "cluster" or group the statements at this point. The final step is to attach a segment code to each market segment identified and then crosstab all of the questionnaire variables by the segments. You must then study the segments and the attitudes/ statements that make up each segment to make sure they make sense and hang together. If the segmentation results don't make sense, then you have to go back, change some of your assumptions or methods, rerun the analysis, and repeat the crosstab exercise to apply the "common sense" validity check.

COMMON MISTAKES

Segmentation studies tend to be large and complicated, so it's easy for errors and mistakes to be made.

Some of the most common mistakes:

- *Segmenting a segment*: For example, someone might want to segment the market for widgets among 18- to 24-yearolds who live in Vermont and buy brand XYZ. As is evident, the client is asking that a of data. It is easy to get lost in this treasure trove of answers and come up with confusing and baffling results.
- *Overlooking the basics*: The dazzle and glitter of the advanced, rocket-science multivariate analyses attract everyone's attention. No one ever opens up the crosstabs and looks at the answers to the hundreds of questions asked. Often, hidden in plain view in the plain old crosstabs are tremendous findings that could form the basis for new or improved marketing strategies, advertising campaigns, ornew products. Rarely does anyone analyse this basic data, however.
- *Targeting people instead of dollars*: A market segment might represent a large percentage of the population, but a small part of the market. Always look at the dollar potential of market segments, not just the number of people in the segments.

NONMUTUALLY EXCLUSIVE SEGMENTS

Virtually all segmentation work, historically, has been based upon the assumption of mutually exclusive market segments. The mutually exclusive model, however, does not always apply to psychographic or lifestyle segmentation. Therefore, it is wise to develop two distinctly different segmentation solutions: one based upon mutually exclusive segments and one based upon overlapping segments.

Both of these segmentation “solutions” should be crosstabulated by the original questionnaire variables to identify which type of solution yields the most meaningful market segments.

EXTERNAL INFLUENCES

- Are there cultures or subcultures whose value system is particularly consistent with the consumption of our product? The value system for the subculture is for the most part consistent with the consumption of Lopez Supermarket since they all share the traditions and beliefs, Hispanic race, Spanish language, and nationality background. Average family size for this segment is of 3.5, and spends 15 to 20 per cent more of disposable income on groceries than the national average. They view their family and friends as an important part of their life, and value their opinions when making decisions such as where to shop for groceries. Customers of Lopez are generally those living close to the store. In general they are low-income Mexican/Hispanics with limited resources, strong values, high ties to family and tradition and the majority practice the Catholic religion.

- Is our product appropriate for male or female consumption? Will ongoing gender-role changes affect who consumes our product or how it is consumed? Lopez Supermarket is appropriate for both male and female consumption. Even though, just as to the Census Bureau, 17.4% of households are made up of female householder, and 45.8% without husband presence and with children, products sold at Lopez can be bought by either male or female. The ongoing gender-role would not change as to who buys at Lopez, but it could affect how it is consumed. Meaning, men, just as women, shop at Lopez, but men would not shop as much or buy the same products as women.
- Do ethnic, social, regional, or religious subcultures have different consumption patterns relevant to our product? Ethnic and social subculture, for the most part, might have a different consumption patterns. Some might like to go to Lopez to make use of their rebate coupons they offer. Some might shop on a daily basis, while others might shop once a week.
- It all depends on the amount of income and time they have to make their shopping. For the most part, Lopez is directed to a Mexican-American region culture. If Lopez were to locate somewhere where Mexican-American population is very low, Lopez' current environment might not be as appreciated due a difference in values and believes other segments might have.
- Do various demographic or social-strata groups differ in their consumption of our product? Mexican-American is one of the fastest growing ethnic groups in the U.S. Geography is an advantage for Lopez, since stores are located on the border of U.S. and Mexico.Demographic and social-strata groups might have different motive for shopping at Lopez Supermarket. For example, in an age group, kids might go to buy candy or they could be sent by their mothers to buy immediate products that they might need at home. Meanwhile adults might go to buy groceries in high amounts and items such as beer and cigarettes. Other segments might not buy their groceries at Lopez, but they might

go for the "fresh meat" or "barbacoa" they sell. Geographically, if Lopez is not close by, consumer might look for alternatives and buy groceries either at a gas station or at another grocery store.

- Is our product particularly appropriate for consumers with relatively high incomes compared to others in their occupational group? Based on Silvia Rico's report, class structure for this segment is Lower-Middle who strives to become part of the Upper Class. This segment view food as an abundance of wealth, so they usually give food gifts. They have many status symbols, such as jewelry, new car, home décor, etc. In their leisure time the go to the beach, and spend time with family. High income might prefer an alternative.
- Can our product be particularly appropriate for specific roles, such as students or professional women?
In general, anyone can shop at Lopez, but it is most appropriate for district level, low-middle income consumers whose role are of a household provider. If customers are playing the role of a professional businessperson, for example, they definitely will not find items they might need, since Lopez is meant for groceries. A student, might find pen, paper, pencil, and notebooks, but in very small amounts, and a higher price than specialized stores.
- Would it be useful to focus on specific adopter categories? Not necessarily. Focusing on specific adopter categories will not help much, since Lopez sells products people are already familiar with. An alternative would be to subgroup the current marketing segment even further in order to target them better, since this subgroups share similar purchasing behaviours. This group of single young women with children can be subdivided based on the people that live with them, their number of working hours, and based on their children's age.

TARGETING PER SEGMENT

- *Women living alone with their own children*: This sub-segment is influenced greatly by their children, they may go to shop at Lopez because their children had great experiences from the store. Children are a strong influence that guides these women to shop there, but also they also have influence in the products they buy. This segment may spend great part of their income in shopping products their children like, depending on their age. Small children may influence them to buy candies, and products that contain attractive animations. Older children may influence their overall product selection based on their tastes and preferences. These children may also influence their mothers to buy high quality, and name branded products.

- *Women living with extended family*: These women are more likely to be influenced by their relatives living with them, specially the older ones that are thought to be the wisest ones. This segment tries to comply with society, and with their own family. They want to be approved by others, and make their purchases just as to the way others expected them to act. They choose Lopez as their store for their food supplies, because it is the family tradition store. They are high self-monitoring, since these women tend to evaluate products consumed in public in terms of the impressions they make on others. They may also cash their checks, and pay some bills at Lopez, because that is the family tradition way to do this activity. Another reason for them to cash their checks is because they are low-Income and usually they do not have a bank account, because they tend to save the money that is left in their houses. They learned these activities from their parents or relatives living with them.
- *Women living with extended family and not working*: This segment relies on the extended family for financial support. They might be the ones purchasing immediate items for their children but leave the large purchase decisions to a secondary person. This segment has more time to shop and look around, and does not go to Lopez alone. They usually go at least twice a week with their kids, and the extended family member with the purchase decision in the household. They rely on their family and friends for their immediate purchase decision, and try to save as money as much as possible since they don't have sufficient income.
- *Women working full-time*: This sub-segment is very busy, they value their time, and buy at Lopez because of the store location, the relative small store size and because they are very familiar with the store, and they cash their checks at Lopez when they go shopping in order to save time. These women know where are products located within the store, they know products prices, people working there, and people shopping there. Women within this segment, go to Lopez once a week, or once every two weeks, depending on the way they get paid. They will usually go to the store on weekends, especially on Friday because is when they may cash their wage checks. On weekends they can buy groceries for all the week, since buying food supplies is a priority for them, and whatever money is left, they will spend it in clothes or save it. This segment usually goes to shop alone, and make their purchases just as their own opinion, and neither relatives nor children influence their consumer behaviour. These women are very important for Lopez because these women buy high-

volume when they go to Lopez. They buy huge quantities because they do not have time to go other day in the week. Their purchases may not be well planned, they may buy their necessary products, and other products with discounts. Products strategic point-of-display is very important to influence this segment to buy.

- *Women working part-time*: This women have more time to analyse and plan their shopping, they may look more detailed the products they will buy. They may go to Lopez at an average rate of three times per week. Since they earn less money than full-timers, they will buy products at discount, and are well informed of the products that are going to be on sale any specific day. These women are very familiar with the store, and usually they have great relationships with store employees, and seek for their advice when making their purchases. This segment go to shop with their children, or other relatives, so their purchases are influenced by the people that go with them. They shop at Lopez because it is the store for groceries they know best, and because their relatives advice them to. They are more likely to be influenced by advertising, than full-timers, since they have more time to read adds, look for coupons, cut and use them.
- *Women with children under 6 years old*: This group of women with children under 6 years old, represents 8.6% of the female householder with no husband present, just as to the U.S. Census Bureau of Cameron County. This segment in heavily influenced by their children preferences. They will look for products that will be accepted and that will cause a positive attitude in their children. Children are a strong influence that guides their consumer behaviour; thus influencing the type of products they buy. This segment may spend great part of their income in children-related products, such as candies, chocolates, cereals with cartoon animations, products that include small toys and others that are attractive to children. Mothers will usually go to Lopez accompanied by their children, because children make pressure to go with them. Children under 6 years old like to be with their mothers, and enjoy going to shop with them. These children influence mothers to buy seasonal products, especially adornments to their houses, and also food that include seasonal animation in its package. This segment may end up buying unexpected items, and spending more money than planned because of their children influence.
- *Women with children from 6 to 17 years old*: These children have strong influence in product brand selection. This group represents 35.3% of the female householder with no husband present, just as to the U.S.

Census Bureau of Cameron County. They may influence their mothers to buy the brands that are most common, and are preferred by their friends. These children may not go to shop with their mothers, since they are at an age where they like to be seen as independent individuals. They do not participate actively in the purchase itself; they just influence their mothers to buy what they said. Mothers seek the approval of their children, so their purchases may be strongly influenced by their children. This segment wants to create a positive attitude towards the products they buy. These women are willing to buy more expensive items to satisfy their children's preferences. They are willing to buy more products at a higher price, and sacrifice other goods, as possible to comply with children's desires. For this segment, their children are seen as young adults with valuable opinion about products. Since many of this children go to school, and are the most knowledgeable and educated in the family, their judgment about certain products are taken as valid, and may cause changes in the products bought.

- Do groups in different stages of the household life cycle have different consump-tion patterns for our product? Who in the household is involved in the purchase process? In this case, single women might just buy the basic items. If they live with their parents, their parents might be the ones doing the groceries. Younger kids might also play a role, meaning they might be the ones asking what type of products to buy at Lopez.

INTERNAL INFLUENCES

- Can our product satisfy different needs or motives in different people? What needs are involved? What characterizes individuals with differing motives? Yes. Customers might go to buy groceries, and at the same time take advantage of paying their bills, cashing a check, or sending mail. Those who go on a daily basis might also want to know what kinds of savings they might find. Kids might want to go to buy candy. Others might need to buy food for a birthday party, or to get ready for Friday's barbeque.
- Is our product uniquely suited for particular personality types? Self-concepts? Lopez is focused more for the lower-middle income people. This means that people who have relatives and shop at Lopez might do so as well just to not feel left out. High-income people might not shop there simply because they might want to be compared or identified with the low-middle income people. For the most part, Lopez is directed towards a Mexican-American environment and to the other segments that accept this.

- What emotions, if any, are affected by the purchase and/or consumption of this product? Realizing that they are known and treated on a friendly matter influence them to go to Lopez. Also having family, neighbours, or friends who might work or go there, might affect this as well.
- Is our product appropriate for one or more distinct lifestyles? For the most part, is for those who prefer to go to Lopez for convenience and to save money. Young single Mexican-American mothers might go there because their concern is their family and their heritage traditions. Other with a different lifestyle might not consider Lopez as an option. Self-monitoring is also affected here because their choices are influenced by their estimates of how Lopez is perceived by their family and friends. If a person was told that shopping at Lopez is only for the poor, then that person might be embarrassed to go or be seen there. A birth of a child or departure of an older one, may affect the lifestyle of the consumer and they way they buy. For the birth of a child, they might need to buy baby products, while for the departure of a child, they might consume less.
- Do different groups have different attitudes about an ideal version of our product? Yes. Some might prefer a "nice looking and cleaner" store. Others might compare Lopez to H.E.B. and might perceive Lopez as a small, local store compared to H.E.B. Others might not want to shop at Lopez because of the smell it emits. There are also those who believe that Lopez is fine the way it is.

SITUATIONAL INFLUENCES

- Can our product be appropriate for specific types of situations instead of specific types of people? Yes. In case of an emergency people might go to Lopez to buy items such as candles, flashlights, can food, batteries, or anything else they might need. A family birthday party or special celebration might require buying the meat and even decorations such as balloons. Barbeque on Friday, as Silvia pointed out, is another example.

DECISION–PROCESS INFLUENCES

- Do different individuals use different evaluative criteria in selecting the product? Yes. Family could influence some individuals. Others might select distance or convenience as a way to measure going to Lopez.
- Do potential customers differ in their loyalty to existing products/ brands? Some of the products sold at Lopez might not be sold at other stores and vice-versa.. Some products are well known to them since they are the products their parents and grandparents used. Others might not be as loyal to the brands as they are to the store itself.

PRODUCT POSITION

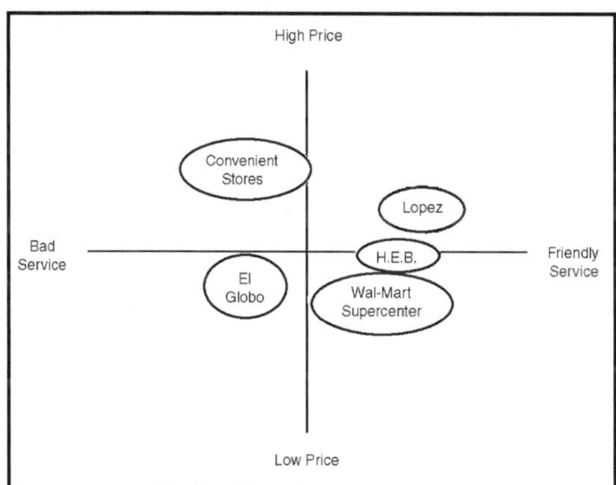

Fig. Lopez is Currently Viewed as High Quality and Reasonable Price, and Friendly Service.

A product position is the way the consumer thinks of a given product/brand relative to competing products/brands. A manager must determine what a desirable product position would be for each market segment of interest.

This determination is generally based on the answers to the same questions used to segment a market, with the addition of the consumer's perceptions of competing products/brands. Of course, the capabilities and mo-tivations of existing and potential competitors must also be considered.

INTERNAL INFLUENCES

- What is the general semantic memory structure for this product category in each market segment?
  - *Women living alone with their children*: This segment may spend great part of their income in shopping products their children like, depending on their age. They view Lopez as a fast-convenient way for shopping.
  - *Women living with extended family*: They are high self-monitoring, since these women tend to evaluate products consumed in public in terms of the impressions they make on others. They may also cash their checks, and pay some bills at Lopez, because that is the family tradition way to do this activity. Another reason for them to cash their checks is because they are low-Income and usually they do not have a bank account.
  - *Women living with extended family and not working*: This segment expects everyday products and food to be available at Lopez. They go because that's where their extended family members go and expect a friendly service.

- *Women working full-time*: This sub-segment is very familiar with the store, and they cash their wage checks at Lopez when they go shopping in order to save time. These women know where are products located within the store, they know products prices, people working there, and people shopping there. Women within this segment, go to Lopez once a week, or once every two weeks, depending on the way they get paid.
- *Women working part-time*: Since they earn less money than full-timers, they will buy products at discount, and are well informed of the products that are going to be on sale any specific day. These women are very familiar with the store, and usually they have great relationships with store employees, and seek for their advice when making their purchases. They shop at Lopez because it is the store for groceries they know best, and because their relatives advice them to.
- *Women with children under 6 years old*: This segment in heavily influenced by their children preferences. They will look for products that will be accepted and that will cause a positive attitude in their children. Children are a strong influence that guides their consumer behaviour; thus influencing the type of products they buy. These children influence mothers to buy seasonal products, especially adornments to their houses, and also food that include seasonal animation in its package. This segment may end up buying unexpected items, and spending more money than planned because of their children influence.
- *Women with children from 6 to 17 years old*: These children have strong influence in product brand selection. They may influence their mothers to buy the brands that are most common, and are preferred by their friends. Mothers seek the approval of their children, so their purchases may be strongly influenced by their children. This segment wants to create a positive attitude towards the products they buy. These women are willing to buy more expensive items to satisfy their children's preferences. They are willing to buy more products at a higher price, and sacrifice other goods, as possible to comply with children's desires. For this segment, their children are seen as young adults with valuable opinion about products. Since many of this children go to school, and are the most knowledgeable and educated in the family, their judgment about certain products are taken as valid, and may cause changes in the products bought.

• What is the ideal version of this product in each market segment for the situations the firm wants to serve? Not only fast, friendly service, but also as a place for everyone can shop and be satisfied, no matter the social status.

DECISION-PROCESS INFLUENCES

- Which evaluative criteria are used in the purchase decision? Which decision rules and importance weights are used? Extended family, such as an aunt, uncle, and children living in the house may influence their consumer habits. Makes a purchase decision in which mom and maybe grand mom may agree to buy at Lopez. Children are seen as an influence to this segment, and as future market for the store.

PRICING

The manager must set a pricing policy that is consistent with the desired product position. Price must be broadly conceived as everything a consumer must surrender to obtain a product. This includes time and psychological costs as well as monetary costs.

External influences:

- Does the segment hold any values relating to any aspect of pricing, such as the use of credit or conspicuous consumption? The current segment doesn't care much for coupons or drastic price reduction or such since they perceive Lopez as a reasonable price store. But they do welcome any special prices on items.
- Does the segment have sufficient income, after covering living expenses, to afford the product? Mexican-American subculture characterized to spend 15 to 20 per cent more of disposable income than the national average on groceries. For those who does not work, their income comes from federal aid or extended family. They buy at Lopez to save money.
- Is it necessary to lower price to obtain a sufficient relative advantage to ensure diffusion? Will temporary price reductions induce product trial? This segment already perceives Lopez as a reasonable price store. This segment relies on their extended family to consider when are prices higher than normal. Lowering prices might attract other segments, though, but not a significant majority.
- Who in the household evaluates the price of the product? This segment usually makes decisions in which their mother or grandmother agree Lopez as the supermarket destination. If living by themselves, women are the ones who evaluates the price of the product.

Internal influences:

- Will price be perceived as an indicator of status? No. Having higher prices would not mean that it is a higher status store. If prices are considerably higher than the competition, customers may no longer see Lopez as a "friendly store".

- Is economy in purchasing this type of product relevant to the lifestyle(s) of the segment? Yes. Those who are looking for convenience products might find them here. Those who are into Mexican foods will find the ingredients here. Anyone looking for expensive food or product might need to consider an alternative.
- Is price an important aspect of the segment's attitude towards the brands in the product category? They don't consider it that important now since their perception is that it is reasonable price store. They consider service and reliability as more important. But again, a noticeable high price would affect how the segment view of the store. Part of the segment might even buy generic brands whenever possible since they cost less.
- What is the segment's perception of a fair or reasonable price for this product? As long as it's not considerably higher than the competition. Fast, friendly service is considered important and gives an overall value to the store and the products they sell.

Situational influences:

- Does the role of price vary with the type of situation? Yes, they might expect a lower price on products related to current events such as Christmas, Easter, and such.

Decision-process factors:

- Can a low price be used to trigger problem recognition? Yes and no. It would all depend on the item they are trying to sell. Lowering the price on out-of-season products could be considered as a clearance, and as an opportunity to buy the items on special price, but not a problem recognition. On the other hand, selling turkey at a low price just before Thanksgiving might be considered as a problem recognition where they need to buy the turkey while it holds the low price.
- Is price an important evaluative criterion? What decision rule is applied to the evaluative criteria used? Is price likely to serve as a surrogate indicator of quality? This is more on the word of mouth and what their reference group considers expensive or convenient in price.
- Are consumers likely to respond to in-store price reductions? This could impact more on part of the segment. Part of the segment where they consume a lot would be the ones who would take advantage of this, as well as those who have more time to "browse" around the store.

DISTRIBUTION STRATEGY

The manager must develop a distribution strategy that is consistent with the selected prod-uct position. This involves the selection of outlets if the item is a physical product or the location of the outlets if the product is a service.

External influences:

- What values do the segments have that relate to distribution? Lopez Food Store wants to be positioned based on quality, offering high quality product, and friendly service at a reasonable price. Their competitive advantage relays on stores that are strategically located in neighbourhoods rather than in commercial places. If the customers are loyal to Lopez, they might take them a while to get there, but might look for other options if they are not planning to buy a lot. If Lopez is distributed on several locations, it makes it easier for the consumer to consider going to Lopez even if buying a few items since it's closer to them.
- Do the male and female members of the segments have differing requirements of the distribution system? Do working couples, single individuals, or single parents within the segment have unique needs relating to product distribution? Yes. Single women might go for the rush to buy basic items. Couples might spend more time since they might go together and look and see what items they might need. Single people might spend a bit of more time than the single parents, but not as much as the couples.
- Can the distribution system capitalize on reference groups by serving as a mean for individuals with common interests to get together? For young Mexican-American single mothers, reference groups is one of the key factors when making a purchase decision, in this case going to Lopez. By focusing on reference groups as a mean for individuals with common interest, it would reinforce going to Lopez.
- Is the product complex such that a high service channel is required to ensure its diffusion? Not for this market segment. They already are aware of this supermarket. Word of mouth will work.

Internal influences:

- Will the selected outlets be perceived in a manner that enhances the desired product position? Yes. These women already accept Lopez as the place to shop in comply with their family and friends' believes.
- What type of distribution system is consistent with the lifestyle(s) of each segment? Lopez works as the "middle man" between the manufacturers and the consumer no matter the lifestyle.
- What attitudes does each segment hold with respect to the various distribution alternatives? There might be some situations where a segment might view Lopez as a low quality compared to HEB due to it's size and lighting, and smell. So other segments might choose HEB instead. Others, for convenience might choose a gas station.

Situational influences:

- Do the desired features of the distribution system vary with the situation? No. Lopez are on a fixed location.

Decision-process factors:

- What outlets are in the segment's evoked set? Will consumers in this segment seek information in this type of outlet? Some of the outlets in the segment's evoked set include gas stations, HEB, and even Wal-Mart Super Center. They will seek information in any of these outlets.
- Which evaluative criteria does this segment use to evaluate outlets? Which decision rule? Consumers might use these other alternatives if they don't have the time to go to Lopez or if they know some of the items they need might be found there. But at the same time, they will weight their decision against whether their family and friend are going to judge them for buying other than Lopez. The decision to shop at Lopez might come first, but other factors might affect the outcome.
- Is the outlet selected before, after, or simultaneously with the product/brand? To what extent are product decisions made in the retail outlet? The outlet is selected simultaneously with the product they want to buy. For example, if they want to buy meat from Lopez, they will go there. Since this segment goes to Lopez on a regular basis, they are already familiar with the type of products they sell.

PROMOTION STRATEGY

The manager must develop a promotion strategy, including advertising, nonfunctional package-design features, publicity, promotions, and sales-force activities that are consistent with the product position.

External factors:

- What values does the segment hold that can be used in our communications? Which should be avoided? Cultural values include spending time with family and friends, and consumption-specific values such as convenient shopping and fast service. Cultural values such as sexy/vain should be avoided as it contrasts with their values.
- How can we communicate to our chosen segments in a manner consistent with the emerging gender-role perceptions of each segment? In general, since the segment has similar views as males, their perception of the women doing shopping at Lopez could be accepted. This does not mean that only women shop at Lopez, but at least this is an acceptable way to communicate.
- What is the nonverbal communication system of each segment? Traditional symbols or items that symbolizes heritage and family.
- How, if at all, can we use reference groups in our advertisements? Having images of grandparents, mothers, or any extended family member shopping at Lopez.

- Can our advertisements help make the product part of one or more role-related product clusters? Yes.
- Can we reach and influence opinion leaders? Yes. This segment go for advise to their parents, grandparents, and friends. If an opinion leader is someone they know their parents or friends trust, this segment might get a reinforcement for buying at Lopez.
- If our product is an innovation, are there diffusion inhibitors that can be overcome by promotion? No. Lopez is known by this segment for tradition.
- Who in the household should receive what types of information concerning our product? Those who are the decision makers or influence, and/or make a purchase.

Internal factors:

- Have we structured our promotional campaign such that each segment will be exposed to it, attend to it, and interpret it in the manner we desire? At times Lopez uses the word "tradition" and "family" when it comes to some of their advertisements. Advertising should continue to be done through the "Bargain Book", but should take use of other medias. Radio is one option, but should be done in the mornings when this segment is getting their kids ready for school. Late morning should be available if targeting those who don't work. Advertising through the web should be considered only for those who work or might have a computer. These kinds of ads should be on local TV channel and community web sites.
- Have we made use of the appropriate learning principles so that our meaning will be remembered? Yes and because the reference groups are considered.
- Do our messages relate to the purchase motives held by the segment? Do they help reduce motivational conflict if necessary? By using the word tradition, it covers the family believes that they've learned from.
- Are we considering the emotional implications of the ad and/or the use of our product? No. Currently, they concentrate on the savings, and additional services they offer by having images of the products or by showing big numbers on the prices that are under three dollars. One thing to keep in mind is that their competitors are following the same strategy. Lopez needs to work the advertising aspect to distinguish themselves from the rest. One way would be by showing images or symbols of family values and traditions in their ads
- Is the lifestyle portrayed in our advertisements consistent with the desired lifestyle of the selected segments? In a way. If part of the segment's lifestyle consists on savings, then yes. Other than that, they don't portray a desired lifestyle.

- If we need to change attitudes via our promotion mix, have we selected and prop-erly used the most appropriate attitude-change techniques? Yes.

Situational influences:

- Does our campaign illustrate the full range of appropriate usage situations for the product? Yes. Using flyers with items on "sale" it makes the consumer feel that they are in for a bargain.

Decision-process influences:

- Will problem recognition occur naturally, or must it be activated by advertising? Should generic or selective problem recognition be generated? For this segment, problem recognition will occur naturally. They know they need to buy the basic needs such as milk and cereal for their kids, and that they need to buy meat in case they having a family reunion.
- Will the segment seek out or attend to information on the product prior to problem recognition, or must we reach them when they are not seeking our information? Can we use low-involvement learning processes effectively? What information sources are used? There is low-involvement when it comes coming to Lopez since, again, they are familiar with it.
- After problem recognition, will the segment seek out information on the product brand, or will we need to intervene in the purchase-decision process? If they do seek information, what sources do they use? By default, they will come to Lopez. If there's for example a new Lopez location, they might use word-of-mouth as a source.
- What types of information are used to make a decision? Family and friends.
- How much and what types of information are acquired at the point of purchase? Very little information and type are acquired at the point of purchase since most of it was gained by learning.
- Is post purchase dissonance likely? Can we reduce it through our promotional campaign? No. They already fear rejection from their family and friends if they buy from other store that is not Lopez.
- Have we given sufficient information to ensure proper product use? Yes. By experience, they already know what to expect from Lopez.
- Are the expectations generated by our promotional campaign consistent with the product's performance? Yes. They already expect the sales that are advertised.
- Are our messages designed to encourage repeat purchases, brand-loyal purchases, or neither? This segment is already familiar with Lopez. Lopez advertise the store usually by catalogs and newspaper. By those advertising mediums, Lopez announces current special offers, and

products that are at discount prices. Seasonal products are also advertised using the same mediums. Its marketing strategy focus more on detailing special offers of products and services, rather than the store itself. Promotion of Lopez pursue the goal of position the store as a local one who shares their customs, to make consumers identify themselves with the store, and use this store image in order to attract customers to come to buy their groceries at Lopez, rather than any other supermarket store.

PRODUCT

The marketing manager must be certain that the physical product, service, or idea has the characteristics required to achieve the desired product position in each market segment.

External influences:

- Is the product designed appropriately for all members of the segment under con-sideration, including males, females, and various age groups? Yes. Anyone at any age, gender can shop at Lopez Supermarket. Lopez stores have an Hispanic environment, where people feel like in their homes. Store emphasizes on a familiar setting, where customers are treated with individual attention. The general store atmosphere enhances the Mexican/American culture, and transforms the shopping activity into an enjoyable and exciting one, for those customers that identify with this culture. People feel great from buying at Lopez because they feel as part of the group, because they identify themselves with the store image, and share the values and traditions promoted by the store. A friendship environment is enhanced at the store, and people buying there, feel proud of their culture and resemble to the shopping activities of their ancestors, such as the way the meat is cut and deliver like the traditional "carniceria" use to do it in Mexico.
- If the product is an innovation, does it have the required relative advantage and lack of complexity to diffuse rapidly? It has the advantage that is known for tradition.
- Is the product designed to meet the varying needs of different household members? This store is designed to meet different household members and their needs. Customer can buy both grocery and convenient products.

Internal influences:

- Will the product be perceived in a manner consistent with the desired image? For years, Lopez has a good reputation among Brownsville citizens. It is identified as the local grocery store where our parents and old relatives bought their food supplies. Since its initiation, Lopez has had a great standing in society for its contribution to some charity institutions, and for the awareness they show for Brownsville community. Lopez has gained citizen's good will due to a variety of contributions to education, such as scholarships, and even the local school that includes its name, Lopez School. The following are the Dimensions of the Store Image that will need to be taken under consideration:

- *Merchandise*: Products sold at Lopez are of average quality, depending on the brand selected. Well-known and high quality brands are sold at the store also. Lopez is famous for its fresh meat, which is cut and packaged at client's desire, as well as for its chicken and turkey, which Mexican people go to the store to buy them exclusively.
- Lopez is a grocery store which offers a varied selection of products, including food, food-related supplies and other products such as paper tissue, house cleaning products. The price charged by Lopez is a little higher than competitors. Price is not a competitive advantage of the store, but it tries to compensate this difference by adding value to customer in other areas, such as the characterized friendly service offered.
- *Service*: Besides providing convenience shopping, Lopez Supermarket offers other services such as payment of utility bills. They also accept debit cards, credit cards, W.I.C. Vouchers, and Lone Star Card, as they cash checks and money orders, sell lottery tickets, and have Western Union for money transfer. Lopez has a great friendly service provided by store employees, which is a major attraction of the store. Employees have a general knowledge about products attributes and different brands, and know where all items are located. They are very concerned about consumers satisfaction, and are willing to help them when they need it.
- *Clientele*: For the most part, Mexican-American culture. Customers of Lopez are generally those living close to the store. In general they are low-income Mexican/Hispanics with limited resources, including the segment studied in this project. They are a Spanish-speaking clientele, and the majority of consumers are women from varied ages, who consider food as a purchasing priority. This people are willing to spend a large portion of their disposable income in groceries. Usually, Lopez customers include direct immigrants from Mexico, and first and second-generation U.S. citizens, with a mixed of Mexican and American culture. Generally they have strong values, high ties to family and

tradition and the majority practice the Catholic religion. In overall, Lopez clientele includes a closed segment that shares important beliefs, activities, lifestyles, attitudes, and consumer behaviour.

- *Physical Facility*: Ten locations in Brownsville. Physical facilities are considered an advantage of the store. Since the store is relatively small, customers may easily find the products they are looking for in a short time period. Shopping at the Lopez is easiest and fastest than in other bigger stores such as HEB. Merchandise is located just as to the type of product, and are easy to reach, since the shelves are not very tall for women, specially old ones. Store is always clean, and it is attractively decorated just as to the season.
- *Convenience*: Located on non-commercial locations, close to neighbourhoods. Location is a primary advantage of the store, since the majority of customers lives close to the store, and do not have any automotive vehicle to travel long distances. Lopez is strategic located in neighbourhoods rather than in commercial places as their competitors, and also, Lopez stores are near to the border between U.S. and Mexico, where many of its customers live.
- *Promotion*: Lopez advertise the store usually by catalogs and newspaper. By those advertising mediums, Lopez announces current special offers, and products that are at discount prices. Seasonal products are also advertised using the same mediums. Its marketing strategy focus more on detailing special offers of products and services, rather than the store itself. Promotion of Lopez pursue the goal of position the store as a local one who shares their customs, to make consumers identify themselves with the store, and use this store image in order to attract customers to come to buy their groceries at Lopez, rather than any other supermarket store. For example, Lopez advertise a top page ad" through the "Bargain Book" a weekly newspaper published every Wednesday. Their emphasis is on items under three dollars. They advertise their others services such as paying utilities bills as "quickly and easily".
- *Store Atmosphere*: Lopez stores have an Hispanic environment, where people feel like in their homes. Store emphasizes on a familiar setting, where customers are treated with individual attention. The general store atmosphere enhances the Mexican/American culture, and transforms the shopping activity into an enjoyable and exciting one, for those customers that identify with this culture.

  - *Institutional*: To this segment, the store is known as high quality, friendly store. Lopez has a good reputation among Brownsville citizens. It is identified as the local grocery store, where our parents and old relatives bought their food supplies. Since its initiation. Lopez has had a great standing in society for its contribution to some charity institutions, and for the awareness they show for Brownsville community. Lopez has gained citizen's good will due to a variety of contributions to education, such as scholarships, and even the local school that includes its name, Lopez School.
  - *Post-Transaction*: When buying at Lopez, customers feel satisfied by the products/services, and many of them return to buy there, showing loyalty to the store. Lopez symbolizes many things to customers. The more relevant issues include that buying at Lopez, a local store, customers are defending their community, their culture, and are supporting the well–being of their society. All these feelings increase the satisfaction of customers, and balance between the benefits obtained and the relatively high price than competitors. People buying at Lopez feel great approval from their reference groups, such as their family, friends, neighbours, and even their employers, which as a result reinforce their activity of shopping there, and will continue to do so.
- Will the product satisfy the key purchase motives of the segment? Yes. Lopez offers the basic needs for the segment.
- Is the product consistent with the segment's attitude towards an ideal product? Yes. Since Lopez is an expectation from their family and friends to shop at what they perceive as the ideal supermarket.

Situational influences:

- Is the product appropriate for the various potential usage situations? Yes. They can buy housing goods, groceries, small party supplies, pay utility bills, and cash checks.

Decision-process influences:

- Does the product/brand perform better than the alternatives on the key set of evaluative criteria used by this segment? They do. Since they see this supermarket as a way they identify themselves, as opposed to other segments who perceive Lopez in a negative way due to poor lighting and smell.
- Will the product perform effectively in the foreseeable uses to which this segment may subject it? Yes. If the segment demands it, Lopez could introduce demanding products or services into Lopez.
- Will the product perform as well or better than expected by this segment? This segment already has an expectation for this outlet. But this segment for sure will accept any improvements.

CUSTOMER SATISFACTION AND COMMITMENT

Marketers must produce satisfied customers to be successful in the long run. It is often to a firm's advantage to go beyond satisfaction and create committed or loyal customers.

- What factors lead to satisfaction with our product? Perception that the reference group have about Lopez. Fast and friendly service that is expected and provided by the employees. When buying at Lopez, customers feel satisfied by the products/services, and many of them return to buy there, showing loyalty to the store. Lopez symbolizes many things to customers. The more relevant issues include that buying at Lopez, a local store, customers are defending their community, their culture, and are supporting the well–being of their society. All these feelings increase the satisfaction of customers, and balance between the benefits obtained and the relatively high price than competitors. People buying at Lopez feel great approval from their reference groups, such as their family, friends, neighbours, and even their employers, which as a result reinforce their activity of shopping there, and will continue to do so.
- What factors could cause customer commitment to our brand or firm? Consistency in the traditional theme, as well as the close and friendly environment they portrait or are perceived, as are important factors that causes customer commitment.

MARKETING MIX AND CONSUMER BEHAVIOUR

The term "marketing mix" became popularized after Neil H. Borden, *The Concept of the Marketing Mix*. Borden began using the term in his teaching in the late 1940's after James Culliton had described the marketing manager as a "mixer of ingredients". The ingredients in Borden's marketing mix included product planning, pricing, branding, distribution channels, personal selling, advertising, promotions, packaging, display, servicing, physical handling, and fact finding and analysis. These four P's are the parameters that the marketing manager can control, subject to the internal and external constraints of the marketing environment. The goal is to make decisions that centre the four P's on the customers in the target market in order to create perceived value and generate a positive response.

PRODUCT DECISIONS

The term "product" refers to tangible, physical products as well as services. *Here are some examples of the product decisions to be made*:

- Brand name
- Functionality
- Styling

- Quality
- Safety
- Packaging
- Repairs and Support
- Warranty
- Accessories and services.

PRICE DECISIONS

Some examples of pricing decisions to be made include:

- Pricing strategy
- Suggested retail price
- Volume discounts and wholesale pricing
- Cash and early payment discounts
- Seasonal pricing
- Bundling
- Price flexibility
- Price discrimination.

DISTRIBUTION DECISIONS

Distribution is about getting the products to the customer.

Some examples of distribution decisions include:

- Distribution channels
- Market coverage
- Specific channel members
- Inventory management
- Warehousing
- Distribution centres
- Order processing
- Transportation
- Reverse logistics.

PROMOTION DECISIONS

In the context of the marketing mix, promotion represents the various aspects of marketing communication, that is, the communication of information about the product with the goal of generating a positive customer response.

Marketing communication decisions include:

- Promotional strategy
- Advertising
- Personal selling and sales force
- Sales promotions
- Public relations and publicity
- Marketing communications budget.

LIMITATIONS OF THE MARKETING MIX FRAMEWORK

The marketing mix framework was particularly useful in the early days of the marketing concept when physical products represented a larger portion of the economy. Today, with marketing more integrated into organizations and with a wider variety of products and markets, some authors have attempted to extend its usefulness by proposing a fifth P, such as packaging, people, process, etc. Today however, the marketing mix most commonly remains based on the 4 P's. Despite its limitations and perhaps because of its simplicity, the use of this framework remains strong and many marketing textbooks have been organized around it.

THE MARKETING MIX OF PRODUCT

Products come in several forms. Consumer products can be categorized as *convenience* goods, for which consumers are willing to invest very limited shopping efforts. Thus, it is essential to have these products readily available and have the brand name well known. *Shopping* goods, in contrast, are goods in which the consumer is willing to invest a great deal of time and effort.

For example, consumers will spend a great deal of time looking for a new car or a medical procedure. *Specialty* goods are those that are of interest only to a narrow segment of the population—e.g., drilling machines. Industrial goods can also be broken down into subgroups, depending on their uses. It should also be noted that, within the context of marketing decisions, the term product refers to more than tangible goods—a service can be a product, too.

A firm's *product line* or lines refers to the assortment of similar things that the firm holds. Brother, for example, has both a line of laser printers and one of typewriters. In contrast, the firm's *product mix* describes the combination of different product lines that the firm holds. Boeing, for example, has both a commercial aircraft and a defense line of products that each take advantage of some of the same core competencies and technologies of the firm. Some firms have one very focused or narrow product line (e.g., KFC does *only* chicken right) while others maintain numerous lines that hopefully all have some common theme.

This represents a *wide* product mix 3M, for example, makes a large assortment of goods that are thought to be related in the sense that they use the firm's ability to bond surfaces together. *Depth* refers to the variety that is offered within each product line.

Maybelline offers a great deal of depth in lipsticks with subtle differences in shades while Morton Salt offers few varieties of its product. Products may be differentiated in several ways. Some may be represented as being of superior quality (e.g., Maytag), or they may differ in more arbitrary ways in terms of styles—some people like one style better than another, while there is no real consensus on which one is the superior one.

Finally, products can be differentiated in terms of offering different levels of service—for example, Volvo offers a guarantee of free, reliable towing anywhere should the vehicle break down. American Express offers services not offered by many other charge cards.

THE PRODUCT LIFE CYCLE

Products often go through a *life cycle.* Initially, a product is introduced. Since the product is not well known and is usually expensive (e.g., as microwave ovens were in the late 1970s), sales are usually limited. Eventually, however, many products reach a *growth* phase—sales increase dramatically.

More firms enter with their models of the product. Frequently, unfortunately, the product will reach a *maturity* stage where little growth will be seen. For example, in the United States, almost every household has at least one colour TV set. Some products may also reach a *decline* stage, usually because the product category is being replaced by something better.

For example, typewriters experienced declining sales as more consumers switched to computers or other word processing equipment. The product life cycle is tied to the phenomenon of diffusion of innovation. When a new product comes out, it is likely to first be adopted by consumers who are more innovative than others—they are willing to pay a premium price for the new product and take a risk on unproven technology. It is important to be on the good side of innovators since many other later adopters will tend to rely for advice on the innovators who are thought to be more knowledgeable about new products for advice.

At later phases of the PLC, the firm may need to modify its market strategy. For example, facing a saturated market for baking soda in its traditional use, Arm & Hammer launched a major campaign to get consumers to use the product to deodorize refrigerators. Deodorizing powders to be used before vacuuming were also created. It is sometimes useful to think of products as being either *new* or *existing.*

Many firms today rely increasingly on new products for a large part of their sales. New products can be new in several ways. They can be *new to the market*—noone else ever made a product like this before. For example, Chrysler invented the minivan. Products can also be new to the *firm*—another firm invented the product, but the firm is now making its own version. For example, IBM did not invent the personal computer, but entered after other firms showed the market to have a high potential. Products can be *new to the segment—e.g.,* cellular phones and pagers were first aimed at physicians and other price-insensitive segments. Later, firms decided to target the more price-sensitive mass market. A product can be new for *legal purposes.* Because consumers tend to be attracted to "new and improved" products, the Federal Trade Commission (FTC) only allows firms to put that label on reformulated products for six months after a significant change has been made.

NEW PRODUCT DEVELOPMENT

New product development tends to happen in stages. Although firms often go back and forth between these idealized stages, the following sequence is illustrative of the development of a new product:

- New product strategy development. Different firms will have different strategies on how to approach new products. Some firms have stockholders who want to minimize risk and avoid investing in too many new innovations. Some firms can only survive if they innovate frequently and have stockholders who are willing to take this risk. For example, Hewlett-Packard has to constantly invent new products since competitors learn to work around its patents and will be able to manufacture the products at a lower cost.
- Idea generation. Firms solicit ideas as to new products it can make. Ideas might come from customers, employees, consultants, or engineers. Many firms receive a large number of ideas each year and can only invest in some of them.
- Screening and evaluation: Some products that after some analysis are clearly not feasible or are not consistent with the core competencies of the firm are eliminated.
- Business analysis. Ideas are now exposed to more rigorous analysis. Profit projections, risks, market size, and competitive response are considered. If promising, market research may be done.
- Development: The product is designed and manufacturing facilities are planned.
- Market testing: Frequently, firms will try to "test" a product in one region to see if it will sell in reality before it is released nationally and internationally. There is a lesser risk if the firm only commits money to advertising and other marketing efforts in one region. Retailers will also be more receptive in other parts of the country and world if it has been demonstrated that the product sold well in one region. The firm may also experiment with different prices for the product.
- Commercialization: Facilities to manufacture the product on a larger scale are now put into operation and the firm starts a national marketing campaign and distribution effort.

DIFFUSION OF INNOVATION

The diffusion of innovation refers to the tendency of new products, practices, or ideas to spread among people. Usually, when new products or ideas come about, they are initially only adopted by a small group of people. Later, many innovations spread to other people. The bell shaped curve frequently illustrates the rate of adoption of a new product. Cumulative adoptions are reflected by the S-shaped curve. The *saturation point* is the maximum proportion of consumers likely to adopt a product. In the case of refrigerators in the U.S., the saturation level is nearly one hundred percent of households. The figure will almost certainly be well below that for video games that, even when spread out to a large part of the population, will be of interest to far from everyone. Several specific product categories have case histories that illustrate important issues in adoption. Until some time in the 1800s, few physicians bothered to scrub prior to surgery, even though new scientific theories predicted that small microbes not visible to the naked eye could cause infection.

Younger and more progressive physicians began scrubbing early on, but they lacked the stature to make their older colleagues follow:

- ATM cards spread relatively quickly. Since the cards were used in public, others who did not yet hold the cards could see how convenient they were. Although some people were concerned about security, the convenience factors seemed to be a decisive factor in the "tug-of-war" for and against adoption. The case of credit cards was a bit more complicated and involved a "chickenand-egg" paradox. Accepting credit cards was not a particularly attractive option for retailers until they were carried by a large enough number of consumers. Consumers, in contrast, were not particularly interested in cards that were not accepted by a large number of retailers. Thus, it was necessary to "jump start" the process, signing up large corporate accounts, under favourable terms, early in the cycle, after which the cards became worthwhile for retailers to accept.
- Rap music initially spread quickly among urban youths in large part because of the low costs of recording. Later, rap music became popular among a very different segment, suburban youths, because of its apparently authentic depiction of an exotic urban lifestyle.
- Hybrid corn was adopted only slowly among many farmers. Although hybrid corn provided yields of about 20% more than traditional corn, many farmers had difficulty believing that this smaller seed could provide a superior harvest. They were usually reluctant to try it because a failed harvest could have serious economic consequences, including a possible loss of the farm. Agricultural extension agents then sought out the most progressive farmers to try hybrid corn, also aiming for farmers who were most respected and most likely to be imitated by others. Few farmers switched to hybrid corn outright from year to year. Instead, many started out with a fraction of their land, and gradually switched to 100% hybrid corn when this innovation had proven itself useful.

Several forces often work against innovation. One is risk, which can be either social or financial. For example, early buyers of the CD player risked that few CDs would be recorded before the CD player went the way of the 8 track player. Another risk is being perceived by others as being weird for trying a "fringe" product or idea. For example, Barbara Mandrel sings the song "I Was Country When Country Wasn't Cool." Other sources of resistance include the initial effort needed to learn to use new products (e.g., it takes time to learn to meditate or to learn how to use a computer) and concerns about compatibility with the existing culture or technology. For example, birth control is incompatible with religious beliefs that predominate in some areas, and a computer database is incompatible with a large, established card file.

Innovations come in different degrees. A *continuous* innovation includes slight improvements over time. Very little usually changes from year to year in automobiles, and even automobiles of the 1990s are driven much the same way that automobiles of the 1950 were driven.

A *dynamically continuous* innovation involves some change in technology, although the product is used much the same way that its predecessors were used—e.g., jet vs. propeller aircraft. A *discontinuous* innovation involves a product that fundamentally changes the way that things are done—e.g., the fax and photocopiers. In general, discontinuous innovations are more difficult to market since greater changes are required in the way things are done, but the rewards are also often significant.

Several factors influence the speed with which an innovation spreads. One issue is relative advantage (i.e., the ratio of risk or cost to benefits). Some products, such as cellular phones, fax machines, and ATM cards, have a strong relative advantage. Other products, such as automobile satellite navigation systems, entail some advantages, but the cost ratio is high. Lower priced products often spread more quickly, and the extent to which the product is *trialable* (farmers did not have to plant all their land with hybrid corn at once, while one usually has to buy a cellular phone to try it out) influence the speed of diffusion. Finally, the extent of switching difficulties influences speed—many offices were slow to adopt computers because users had to learn how to use them.

Some cultures tend to adopt new products more quickly than others, based on several factors:

- *Modernity:* The extent to which the culture is receptive to new things. In some countries, such as Britain and Saudi Arabia, tradition is greatly valued—thus, new products often don't fare too well. The United States, in contrast, tends to value progress.
- *Homophily:* The more similar to each other that members of a culture are, the more likely an innovation is to spread—people are more likely to imitate similar than different models. The two most rapidly adopting countries in the World are the U.S. and Japan. While the U.S. interestingly scores very low, Japan scores high.

- *Physical distance:* The greater the distance between people, the less likely innovation is to spread.
- *Opinion leadership:* The more opinion leaders are valued and respected, the more likely an innovation is to spread. The style of opinion leaders moderates this influence, however. In less innovative countries, opinion leaders tend to be more conservative, i.e., to reflect the local norms of resistance.

It should be noted that innovation is not always an un-qualifiedly good thing. Some innovations, such as infant formula adopted in developing countries, may do more harm than good. Individuals may also become dependent on the innovations. For example, travel agents who get used to booking online may be unable to process manual reservations.

Sometimes innovations are *dis*adopted. For example, many individuals disadopt cellular phones if they find out that they don't end up using them much.

PRODUCT MIX

Product mix is a combination of products manufactured or traded by the same business house to reinforce their presence in the market, increase market share and increase the turnover for more profitability.

Normally the product mix is within the synergy of other products for a medium size organization. However large groups of Industries may have diversified products within core competency. Larsen and Toubro Ltd, Godrej, Reliance in India are some of the examples. One of the realities of business is that most firms deal with multi-products.

This helps a firm diffuse its risk across different product groups/Also it enables the firm to appeal to a much larger group of customers or to different needs of the same customer group.So when Videocon chose to diversify into other consumer durables like music systems,washing machines and refrigerators,it sought to satisfy the needs of the middle and upper middle income group of consumers. Likewise, Bajaj Electricals.a household name in India, has almost ninety products in i8ts portfolio ranging from low value items like bulbs to high priced consumer durables like mixers and luminaires and lighting projects.The number of products carried by a firm at a given point of time is called its product mix. This product mix contains product lines and product items.In other words it's a composite of products offered for sale by a firm.

PRODUCT MIX DECISIONS

Often firms take decisions to change their product mix. These decisions are dictated by the factors and also by the changes occurring in the market place. Like the changing life-styles of Indian consumers led BPL-Sanyo to launch an entire range of white goods like refrigerators, washing machines, and microwave ovens.

It also motivate the firm to launch other entertainment electronics. Rahejas, a well-known builders firm in Bombay, took a major decision to convert one of its theatre buildings in the western suburbs of Bombay into a large garments and accessories store for men,women and children, perhaps the first of its kind in India to have almost all products required by these customer groups Competition from low priced washing powders forced Hindustan Levers to launch different brands of detergent powder at different price levels positioned at different market segments.

Customer preferences for herbs, mainly shikakai motivated Lever to launch black Sunsilk Shampoo,which has shikakai.Also,low purchasing power. and cultural bias against shampoo market made Hindustan Lever consider smaller packaging mainly sachets, for single use.So, it is the changes or anticipated changes in the market place that motivates a firm to consider changes in its product mix.

THE PRODUCT LIFE CYCLE

Since the product is not well known and is usually expensive, sales are usually limited. Eventually, however, many products reach a *growth* phase—sales increase dramatically. More firms enter with their models of the product. Frequently, unfortunately, the product will reach a *maturity* stage where little growth will be seen.

For example, in the United States, almost every household has at least one colour TV set. Some products may also reach a *decline* stage, usually because the product category is being replaced by something better. For example, typewriters experienced declining sales as more consumers switched to computers or other word processing equipment. The product life cycle is tied to the phenomenon of diffusion of innovation. When a new product comes out, it is likely to first be adopted by consumers who are more innovative than others—they are willing to pay a premium price for the new product and take a risk on unproven technology.

It is important to be on the good side of innovators since many other later adopters will tend to rely for advice on the innovators who are thought to be more knowledgeable about new products for advice. At later phases of the PLC, the firm may need to modify its market strategy. For example, facing a saturated market for baking soda in its traditional use, Arm and Hammer launched a major campaign to get consumers to use the product to deodorize refrigerators. Deodorizing powders to be used before vacuuming were also created. It is sometimes useful to think of products as being either *new* or *existing.* Many firms today rely increasingly on new products for a large part of their sales.

New products can be new in several ways. They can be *new to the market*—noone else ever made a product like this before. For example, Chrysler invented the minivan. Products can also be new to the *firm*—another firm invented the product, but the firm is now making its own version. For example, IBM did not invent the personal computer, but entered after other firms showed the market to have a high potential.

Products can be *new to the segment—e.g.,* cellular phones and pagers were first aimed at physicians and other price-insensitive segments. Later, firms decided to target the more price-sensitive mass market. A product can be new for *legal purposes.* Because consumers tend to be attracted to "new and improved" products, the Federal Trade Commission only allows firms to put that label on reformulated products for six months after a significant change has been made.

BRANDS AND BRANDING

An essential issue in product management is branding. Different firms have different policies on the branding on their products. While 3M puts its brand name on a great diversity of products, Proctor and Gamble, on the opposite extreme, maintains a separate brand name for each product. In general, the use of *brand extensions* should be evaluated on the basis of the compatibility of various products—can the same brand name represent different products without conflict or confusion?

Coca Cola for many years resisted putting its coveted brand name on a diet soft drink. In the old days, available sweeteners such as saccharin added an undesirable aftertaste, implying a clear sacrifice in taste for the reduction in calories. Thus, to avoid damaging the brand name Coca Cola, Coke instead named its diet cola Tab. Only after NutraSweet was introduced was the brand extension allowed.

Research shows that consumers are more receptive to brand extensions when:

- The company appears to have the expertise to make the product,
- The products are congruent (compatible), and
- The brand extension is not seen as being exploitative of a high quality brand name.

In many markets, brands of different strength compete against each other. At the top level are *national* or *international* brands. A large investment has usually been put into extensive brand building—including advertising, distribution and, if needed, infrastructure support. Although some national brands are better regarded than others—*e.g.*, Dell has a better reputation than e-Machines—the national brands usually sell at higher prices than to *regional* and *store* brands. Regional brands, as the name suggests, are typically sold only in one area. In some cases, regional distribution is all that firms can initially accomplish with the investment capital and other resources that they have.

This means that advertising is usually done at the regional level. This limits the advertising opportunities and thus the effect of advertising. In some cases, regional brands may eventually grow into national ones. For example, Snapple® was a regional beverage. While a regional beverage, it became so successful that it was able to attract investments to allow a national launch. In a similar manner, some brands often start in a narrow niche—either nationally or regionally—and may eventually work their way up to a more inclusive national brand.

For example, Mars was originally a small brand that focused on liquor filled chocolate candy. Eventually, the firm was able to expand. *Store,* or *private label* brands are, as the name suggests, brands that are owned by retail store chains or consortia thereof.. Typically, store brands sell at lower prices than do national brands. However, because the chains do not have the external brand building costs, the margins on the store brands are often higher. Retailers have a great deal of power because they control the placement of products within the store.

Many place the store brand right next to the national brand and place a sign highlighting the cost savings on the store brand. Co-branding involves firms using two or more brands together to maximize appeal to consumers. Some ice cream makers, for example, use their own brand name in addition to naming the brands of ingredients contained. Sometimes, this strategy may help one brand at the expense of the other. It is widely believed, for example, that the "Intel inside" messages, which Intel paid computer makers to put on their products and packaging, reduced the value of the computer makers' brand names because the emphasis was now put on the Intel component.

Certain "peripheral" characteristics of products may "signal" quality or other value to consumers. For some products, packaging accounts for a large part of the total product manufacturing cost. Long warranties often signal to consumers that the product is of good quality since the manufacturer is willing to take responsibility for its functioning.

PACKAGING

Packaging is now generally regarded as an essential component of our modern life style and the way business is organized. Packaging is the enclosing of a physical object, typically a product that will be offered for sale. It is the process of preparing items of equipment for transportation and storage and which embraces preservation, identification and packaging of products.

Packing is recognized as an integral part of modern marketing operation, which embraces all phases of activities involved in the transfer of goods and services from the manufacturer to the consumer. Packaging is an important part of the branding process as it plays a role in communicating the image and identity of a company.

Kotler defines packaging as "all the activities of designing and producing the container for a product." Packaging can be defined as the wrapping material around a consumer item that serves to contain, identify, describe, protect, display, promote, and otherwise make the product marketable and keep it clean. Packaging is the outer wrapping of a product. It is the intended purpose of the packaging to make a product readily sellable as well as to protect it against damage and prevent it from deterioration while storing. Furthermore the packaging is often the most relevant element of a trademark and conduces to advertising or communication.

FUNCTIONAL REQUIREMENTS

A basic function of package is to protect and preserve the contents during transit from the manufacturer to the ultimate consumer. It is the protection during transport and distribution; From climatic effects; from hazardous substances and contaminants; and from infestation. Protection is required against transportation hazards spillage, dirt, ingress and egress of moisture, insect infection, contamination by foreign material, tampering pilferage etc. A package should preserve the contents in 'Factory Fresh' condition during the period of storage and transportation, ensuring protection from bacteriological attacks, chemical reaction etc.

CONTAINMENT

Most products must be contained before they can be moved from one place to another. To function successfully, the package must contain the product. This containment function of packaging makes a huge contribution to protecting the environment. A better packaging help to maintain the quality of the product and reachability of the product in the consumer's hand without spillages It gives better image to the organisation.

COMMUNICATION

A major function of packaging is the communication of the product. A package must communicate what it sells. When international trade is involved and different languages are spoken, the use of unambiguous, readily understood symbols on the distribution package is essential.

It is the interest further that to get appropriate commun-ication to the consumer about the product, how to use it and other utility informations. Packaging protects the interests of consumers. Information includes: quantity; price; inventory levels; lot number; distribution routes; size; elapsed time since packaging; colour; and merchandising and premium data.

NEW PRODUCT DEVELOPMENT

In business and engineering, new product development is the term used to describe the complete process of bringing a new product or service to market. There are two parallel paths involved in the NPD process: one involves the idea generation, product design and detail engineering; the other involves market research and marketing analysis. Companies typically see new product development as the first stage in generating and commercializing new products within the overall strategic process of product life cycle management used to maintain or grow their market share.

THE PROCESS

- Idea Generation is often called the "fuzzy front end" of the NPD process.
  - Ideas for new products can be obtained from basic research using a SWOT analysis, Market and consumer trends, company's R&D department, competitors, focus groups, employees, salespeople, corporate spies, trade shows, or Ethnographic discovery methods may also be used to get an insight into new product lines or product features.
  - Idea Generation or Brainstorming of new product, service, or store concepts - idea generation techniques can begin when you have done your opportunity analysis to support your ideas in the Idea Screening Phase.
- *Idea Screening*:
  - The object is to eliminate unsound concepts prior to devoting resources to them.
  - The screeners should ask several questions:
    a. Will the customer in the target market benefit from the product?
    b. What is the size and growth forecasts of the market segment/target market?
    c. What is the current or expected competitive pressure for the product idea?
    d. What are the industry sales and market trends the product idea is based on?
    e. Is it technically feasible to manufacture the product?
    f. Will the product be profitable when manufactured and delivered to the customer at the target price?
- *Concept Development and Testing*:
  - Develop the marketing and engineering details
    a. Investigate intellectual property issues and search patent data bases.
    b. Who is the target market and who is the decision maker in the purchasing process?
    c. What product features must the product incorporate?
    d. What benefits will the product provide?
    e. How will consumers react to the product?
    f. How will the product be produced most cost effectively?
    g. Prove feasibility through virtual computer aided rendering, and rapid prototyping.

    h. What will it cost to produce it?
  - Testing the Concept by asking a sample of prospective customers what they think of the idea. Usually via Choice Modelling.
- *Business Analysis*:
  - Estimate likely selling price based upon competition and customer feedback
  - Estimate sales volume based upon size of market and such tools as the Fourt-Woodlock equation
  - Estimate profitability and breakeven point.
- *Beta Testing and Market Testing.*
  - Produce a physical prototype or mock-up.
  - Test the product in typical usage situations.
  - Conduct focus group customer interviews or introduce at trade show.
  - Make adjustments where necessary.
  - Produce an initial run of the product and sell it in a test market area to determine customer acceptance.
- *Technical Implementation*:
  - New programme initiation.
  - Finalize Quality management system.
  - Resource estimation.
  - Requirement publication.
  - Publish technical communications such as data sheets.
  - Engineering operations planning.
  - Department scheduling.
  - Supplier collaboration.
  - Logistics plan.
  - Resource plan publication.
  - Programme review and monitoring.
  - Contingencies - what-if planning.
- *Commercialization*:
  - Launch the product.
  - Produce and place advertisements and other promotions.
  - Fill the distribution pipeline with product.
  - Critical path analysis is most useful at this stage.
- *New Product Pricing*:
  - Impact of new product on the entire product portfolio.
  - Value Analysis.
  - Competition and alternative competitive technologies.
  - Differing value segments.
  - Product Costs.
  - Forecast of unit volumes, revenue, and profit.

These steps may be iterated as needed. Some steps may be eliminated. To reduce the time that the NPD process takes, many companies are completing several steps at the same time. Most industry leaders see new product development as a *proactive* process where resources are allocated to identify market changes and seize upon new product opportunities before they occur. Many industry leaders see new product development as an ongoing process in which the entire organization is always looking for opportunities.

Great amounts of uncertainty and change may exist, which makes it difficult or impossible to plan the complete project before starting it. In this case, a more flexible approach may be advisable. Because the NPD process typically requires both engineering and marketing expertise, cross-functional teams are a common way of organizing projects. The team is responsible for all aspects of the project, from initial idea generation to final commercialization, and they usually report to senior management. In those industries where products are technically complex, development research is typically expensive, and product life cycles are relatively short, strategic alliances among several organizations helps to spread the costs, provide access to a wider skill set, and speeds the overall process.

Also, notice that because engineering and marketing expertise are usually both critical to the process, choosing an appropriate blend of the two is important. Observe that this is slanted more towards the marketing side. For more of an engineering slant.. People respond to new products in different ways.

The adoption of a new technology can be analysed using a variety of diffusion theories such as the Diffusion of innovations theory. A new product pricing process is important to reduce risk and increase confidence in the pricing and marketing decisions to be made. Bernstein and Macias describe an integrated process that breaks down the complex task of new product pricing into manageable elements.

FUZZY FRONT END

The Fuzzy Front End is the messy "getting started" period of new product development processes. It is in the front end where the organization formulates a concept of the product to be developed and decides whether or not to invest resources in the further development of an idea.

It is the phase between first consideration of an opportunity and when it is judged ready to enter the structured development process. It includes all activities from the search for new opportunities through the formation of a germ of an idea to the development of a precise concept. The Fuzzy Front End ends when an organization approves and begins formal development of the concept. Although the Fuzzy Front End may not be an expensive part of product development, it can consume 50% of development time and it is where major commitments are typically made involving time, money, and the product's nature, thus setting the course for the entire project and final end product. Consequently, this phase should be considered as an essential part of development rather than something that happens "before development," and its cycle time should be included in the total development cycle time.

Koen et al. distinguish five different front-end elements:

- Opportunity Identification
- Opportunity Analysis
- Idea Genesis
- Idea Selection
- Concept and Technology Development.

The first element is the opportunity identification. In this element, large or incremental business and technological chances are identified in a more or less structured way. Using the guidelines established here, resources will eventually be allocated to new projects.... which then lead to a structured NPPD strategy. The second element is the opportunity analysis.

It is done to translate the identified opportunities into implications for the business and technology specific context of the company. Here extensive efforts may be made to align ideas to target customer groups and do market studies and/or technical trials and research.

The third element is the idea genesis, which is described as evolutionary and iterative process progressing from birth to maturation of the opportunity into a tangible idea.

The process of the idea genesis can be made internally or come from outside inputs, *e.g.* a supplier offering a new material/technology, or from a customer with an unusual request. The fourth element is the idea selection. Its purpose is to choose whether to pursue an idea by analyzing its potential business value. The fifth element is the concept and technology development. During this part of the front-end, the business case is developed based on estimates of the total available market, customer needs, investment requirements, competition analysis and project uncertainty. Some organizations consider this to be the first stage of the NPPD process. The Fuzzy Front End is also described in literature as "Front End of Innovation", "Phase 0", "Stage 0" or "Pre-Project-Activities".

A universally acceptable definition for Fuzzy Front End or a dominant framework has not been developed so far. In a glossary of PDMA: strategic planning, concept generation, and, especially, pre-technical evaluation.

These activities are often chaotic, unpredictible, and unstructured. In comparison, the subsequent new product development process is typically structured, predictable, and formal.

The term *Fuzzy Front End* was first popularized by Smith and Reinertsen, R.G.Cooper describes the early stages of NPPD as a four step process in which ideas are generated (I),subjected to a preliminary technical and market assessment(II) and merged to coherent product concepts(III) which are finally judged for their fit with existing product strategies and portfolios (IV).

Cooper and Edgett affirm that vital predevelopment activities include:

- Preliminary market assessment.
- Technical assessment.
- Source-of-supply-assessment:suppliers and partners or alliances.
- *Market research*: Market size and segmentation analysis,VoC research.
- Product concept testing.
- Value-to-the customer assessment.
- Product definition.
- Business and financial analysis.

These activities yield vital information to make a Go/No-Go to Development decision.

In the in-depth study by Khurana and Rosenthal front-end activities include:

- Product strategy formulation and communication,
- Opportunity identification and assessment,
- Idea generation,
- Product definition,
- Project planning, and
- Executive reviews.

Economical analysis, benchmarking of competitive products,and modeling and prototyping are also important activities during the front-end activities.

The outcomes of FFE are the:

- Mission statement.
- Customer needs.
- Details of the selected concept.
- Product definition and specifications.
- Economic analysis of the product.
- The development schedule.
- Project staffing and the budget, and a.
- Business plan aligned with corporate strategy.

Husig, Kohn and Huskela was proposed a conceptual model of Front-End Process which includes early Phases of Innovation Process.

This model is structured in three phases and three gates:

- *Phase 1*: Environmental screening or opportunity identification stage in which external changes will be analysed and translated into potential business opportunities.
- *Phase 2*: Preliminary definition of an idea or concept.
- *Phase 3*: Detailed product, project or concept definition, and Business planning.

The gates are:

- Opportunity screening;
- Idea evaluation;
- Go/No-Go for development.

The final gate leads to a dedicated new product development project. Many professionals and academics consider that the general features of Fuzzy Front End make difficult to see the FFE as a structured process,but rather as a set of interdependent activities. However, Husig et al.,2005 argue that front-end not need to be fuzzy,but can be handled in a structured manner. Peter Koen argue that in the FFE for incremental,platform and radical projects,three separate strategies and processes are typically involved.

The traditional Stage Gate process was designed for incremental product development,namely for a single product.The FFE for developing a new platform must start out with a strategic vision of where the company wants to develop products and this will lead to a family of products. Projects for breakthrough products start out with a similar strategic vision,but are associated with technologies which require new discoveries.It is worth mentioning what are incremental, platform and breakthrough products.

Incremental products are considered to be cost reductions, improvements to existing product lines,additions to existing platforms and repositioning of existing products introduced in markets. *Breakthrough products* are new to the company or new to the world and offer a 5-10 times or greater improvement in performance combined with a 30-50% or greater reduction in costs. *Platform products* establish a basic architecture for a next generation product or process and are substantially larger in scope and resources than incremental projects.

MARKETING STRATEGY AND THE MARKETING MIX

Before the product is developed, the marketing strategy is formulated, including target market selection and product positioning. There usually is a tradeoff between product quality and price, so price is an important variable in positioning. Because of inherent tradeoffs between marketing mix elements, pricing will depend on other product, distribution, and promotion decisions.

ESTIMATE THE DEMAND CURVE

Because there is a relationship between price and quantity demanded, it is important to understand the impact of pricing on sales by estimating the demand curve for the product. For existing products, experiments can be performed at prices above and below the current price in order to determine the price elasticity of demand. Inelastic demand indicates that price increases might be feasible.

CALCULATE COSTS

If the firm has decided to launch the product, there likely is at least a basic understanding of the costs involved, otherwise, there might be no profit to be made. The unit cost of the product sets the lower limit of what the firm might charge, and determines the profit margin at higher prices. The total unit cost of a producing a product is composed of the variable cost of producing each additional unit and fixed costs that are incurred regardless of the quantity produced. The pricing policy should consider both types of costs.

ENVIRONMENTAL FACTORS

Pricing must take into account the competitive and legal environment in which the company operates. From a competitive standpoint, the firm must consider the implications of its pricing on the pricing decisions of competitors. For example, setting the price too low may risk a price war that may not be in the best interest of either side. Setting the price too high may attract a large number of competitors who want to share in the profits. From a legal standpoint, a firm is not free to price its products at any level it chooses. For example, there may be price controls that prohibit pricing a product too high. Pricing it too low may be considered predatory pricing or "dumping" in the case of international trade.

Offering a different price for different consumers may violate laws against price discrimination. Finally, collusion with competitors to fix prices at an agreed level is illegal in many countries.

PRICING OBJECTIVES

The firm's pricing objectives must be identified in order to determine the optimal pricing.

Common objectives include the following:

- *Current profit maximization*: Seeks to maximize current profit, taking into account revenue and costs. Current profit maximization may not be the best objective if it results in lower long-term profits.
- *Current revenue maximization*: Seeks to maximize current revenue with no regard to profit margins. The underlying objective often is to maximize long-term profits by increasing market share and lowering costs.
- *Maximize quantity*: Seeks to maximize the number of units sold or the number of customers served in order to decrease long-term costs as predicted by the experience curve.
- *Maximize profit margin*: Attempts to maximize the unit profit margin, recognizing that quantities will be low.
- *Quality leadership*: Use price to signal high quality in an attempt to position the product as the quality leader.
- *Partial cost recovery*: An organization that has other revenue sources may seek only partial cost recovery.
- *Survival*: In situations such as market decline and overcapacity, the goal may be to select a price that will cover costs and permit the

firm to remain in the market. In this case, survival may take a priority over profits, so this objective is considered temporary.

- *Status quo*: The firm may seek price stabilization in order to avoid price wars and maintain a moderate but stable level of profit.

For new products, the pricing objective often is either to maximize profit margin or to maximize quantity. To meet these objectives, skim pricing and penetration pricing strategies often are employed. Skim pricing attempts to "skim the cream" off the top of the market by setting a high price and selling to those customers who are less price sensitive. Skimming is a strategy used to pursue the objective of profit margin maximization.

Skimming is most appropriate when:

- Demand is expected to be relatively inelastic; that is, the customers are not highly price sensitive.
- Large cost savings are not expected at high volumes, or it is difficult to predict the cost savings that would be achieved at high volume.
- The company does not have the resources to finance the large capital expenditures necessary for high volume production with initially low profit margins.

Penetration pricing pursues the objective of quantity maximization by means of a low price.

It is most appropriate when:

- Demand is expected to be highly elastic; that is, customers are price sensitive and the quantity demanded will increase significantly as price declines.
- Large decreases in cost are expected as cumulative volume increases.
- The product is of the nature of something that can gain mass appeal fairly quickly.
- There is a threat of impending competition.

As the product lifecycle progresses, there likely will be changes in the demand curve and costs. As such, the pricing policy should be reevaluated over time. The pricing objective depends on many factors including production cost, existence of economies of scale, barriers to entry, product differentiation, rate of product diffusion, the firm's resources, and the product's anticipated price elasticity of demand.

PRICING METHODS

To set the specific price level that achieves their pricing objectives, managers may make use of several pricing methods.

These methods include:

- *Cost-plus pricing*: Set the price at the production cost plus a certain profit margin.
- *Target return pricing*: Set the price to achieve a target return-on-investment.

- *Value-based pricing*: Base the price on the effective value to the customer relative to alternative products.
- *Psychological pricing*: Base the price on factors such as signals of product quality, popular price points, and what the consumer perceives to be fair.

In addition to setting the price level, managers have the opportunity to design innovative pricing models that better meet the needs of both the firm and its customers. For example, software traditionally was purchased as a product in which customers made a one-time payment and then owned a perpetual license to the software.

Many software suppliers have changed their pricing to a subscription model in which the customer subscribes for a set period of time, such as one year.

Afterwards, the subscription must be renewed or the software no longer will function.

This model offers stability to both the supplier and the customer since it reduces the large swings in software investment cycles.

PRICE DISCOUNTS

The normally quoted price to end users is known as the *list price*. This price usually is discounted for distribution channel members and some end users.

There are several types of discounts:

- *Quantity discount*: Offered to customers who purchase in large quantities.
- *Cumulative quantity discount*: A discount that increases as the cumulative quantity increases. Cumulative discounts may be offered to resellers who purchase large quantities over time but who do not wish to place large individual orders.
- *Seasonal discount*: Based on the time that the purchase is made and designed to reduce seasonal variation in sales. For example, the travel industry offers much lower off-season rates. Such discounts do not have to be based on time of the year; they also can be based on day of the week or time of the day, such as pricing offered by long distance and wireless service providers.
- *Cash discount*: Extended to customers who pay their bill before a specified date.
- *Trade discount*: A functional discount offered to channel members for performing their roles. For example, a trade discount may be offered to a small retailer who may not purchase in quantity but nonetheless performs the important retail function.
- *Promotional discount*: A short-term discounted price offered to stimulate sales.

PRICING DECISION

Pricing decisions are extremely important for the firm.

Some of the reasons:

- Pricing is the only part of the marketing mix which brings in revenue.
- Once a price has been set, consumers will often show a great deal of resistance to any attempts to change it.
- Pricing frequently has important implications for the positioning of a product.
- Price is the marketing mix variable for which a competitive response can be most quickly implemented.

Conceptualizing price: A logical examination suggests that price should be defined as,

$$\text{Price} = \frac{\text{resources given up}}{\text{goods receivd}}$$

That is, we need to consider the quantity you receive as well as the amount of money you have to fork out. To say that gasoline costs $1.29 is meaningless outside the context that this cost is per gallon.

WAYS TO CHANGE PRICE

The conceptualization suggests that the marketer has several ways available to change price:

- Increasing or decreasing the *"sticker price"* of a product.
- Increasing or decreasing the *quantity* of material received. As prices of chocolate increased in the 1970s, firms found it difficult to raise candy bar prices. Instead, they simply made them smaller.
- Changing the *quality* of a product. Firms may cut back on services or dilute products more, possibly reducing or cutting out expensive ingredients.
- Change the *terms* of a sale. Firms may begin charging for previously free delivery. In recent years, many software manufacturers have stopped providing free telephone support for their programmes.

CONSUMER PRICE AWARENESS

Research suggests a large segment of consumers does not give much attention to the prices of individual products. Consumers were found on the average to spend only about 12 seconds between arriving at the site within a store where a frequently purchased product was located and departing; on the average, consumers inspected only 1.2 products. Only 55.6%, seconds after having selected a product, could specify its price within 5% of accuracy. Note that this study does not indicate a total lack of consumer price sensitivity since consumers are undoubtedly making some inferences about the overall price levels of a store. Thus, the store has some incentive to maintain reasonable overall prices.

COMPETITION AND ANTITRUST ISSUES IN PRICING

The United States maintains relatively stringent antitrust laws. Much of the rest of the World is catching up with us, but traditionally, anti-competitive laws in many European and Asian countries were either non-existent, intended to actively encourage collusion, or not enforced.

In fact, the premier French business school, reported that his students—who came from countries throughout Europe—actually expected him to *teach* them how to collude with each other. Antitrust issues relevant to prices can be categorized into the following main categories:

- *Minimum prices*: It is generally, with a few relatively complicated exceptions, illegal to sell products below your cost of production..
- *In selling to entities that compete against each other, price discrimination* or *volume discounts* are generally only legal to the extent that a manufacturer can prove actual cost savings associated with serving a large account. In the U.S. criminal justice system, we are used to think of a person being "innocent until proven guilty," but this standard does not apply in this kind of civil case. The law provides that the manufacturer has the burden of proof to establish that cost savings exist. The overheads indicate the pricing structure of Morton Salt employed in the 1940s. Although the volume discounts are modest and seem reasonable, the U.S. Supreme Court held against Morton because the firm failed to prove cost savings. The prohibition on price discrimination generally applies only to entities competing against each other. This means that differences in prices charged by a firm to competing restaurants must be justified by demonstrable cost savings, but it may be legal to charge supermarkets different prices than those charged to grocery stores to the extent that restaurants and grocery stores do not significantly compete in the affected product category. Restaurants, for example, tend to use hot sauce as an ingredient in food served while grocery stores tend to resell the hot sauce.
- *Anti-competitive pricing*: In general, *collusion,* or firms getting together to fix prices, is outright illegal in the U.S.. In the late 1980s and early 1990s, certain airlines were accused of fixing prices by communication through their computerized reservation systems. Most airlines settled the suit, agreeing to certain injunctions limiting this practice.
- *Price maintenance* refers to the practice of encouraging a certain minimum resale price of products. In 2007, the U.S. Supreme Court reversed its previous holding and ruled in the case *Leegin Creative Leather Products, Inc. v. PSKS, Inc.* that it is not automatically illegal for manufacturers to require as a condition of sale that retailers of

its products agree to charge a price no lower than a "floor" price established by contract. Courts may still decide, depending on the facts and conditions of a particular case, that certain minimum price agreements between manufacturers and retailers result in a "restraint of trade" in violation of the Sherman Act. This cease is, however, no longer automatic and has to be established through the "rule of reason." A theory asserted is that, under some circumstances, retail price maintenance may actually increase *inter*-brand competition, or competition among brands since retailers will now have a greater incentive to provide services and make investments in brand building knowing that they will not be undersold by retailers not offering these services. *Intra*-brand competition—or competition among the retailers selling the same brand—is likely to be reduced, but it is argued that the non-price benefits of increased service may be more valuable to customers in some circumstances than facing the lowest possible prices. In the U.S., manufacturers generally cannot prevent retailers from selling their inventory at a lower priced than what has been contractually specified, but the manufacturer can stop selling to such discounting retailers without being in automatic violation. As a matter of pragmatics, very few manufacturers would actually want to enforce price maintenance today. Discounters have now become a major force in the economy and the source of a large number of sales. Refusing to sell to discounters, or pressuring them to charge higher prices, is almost certainly not a viable strategy for most firms today.

- *Tying*: it is generally illegal to require a customer to buy a less desired product in order to buy a more desired one. In practice, it is difficult to decide where to draw the line. For example, most consumers would probably prefer to buy a fishing rod and reel together; so it is not unreasonable, for the sake of expediency, to sell the two only together. On the other hand, Ford in the 1950s refused to drill holes in auto dashboards if the consumer did not purchase a radio with the vehicle. This made buying third party radios quite unattractive, and Ford was forced by litigation to abandon this practice.

THE MARKETING MIX AND MANAGEMENT PROCESS

Marketing mix modelling is a term of art for the use of statistical analysis such as multivariate regressions on sales and marketing time series data to estimate the impact of various promotional tactics on sales and then forecast the impact of future sets of promotional tactics. It is often used to optimize promotional tactics with respect to sales revenue or profit.

The techniques were developed by econometricians and were first applied to consumer packaged goods, since manufacturers of those goods had access to good data on sales and marketing support. In the recent times MMM has found acceptance as a trustworthy marketing tool among the major consumer marketing companies.

HISTORY

The term Market Mix Modelling was developed by Neil Borden who first started using the phrase in 1949. "An executive is a mixer of ingredients, who sometimes follows a recipe as he goes along, sometimes adapts a recipe to the ingredients immediately available, and sometimes experiments with or invents ingredients no one else has tried." (Culliton, J. 1948)

According to Borden,"When building a marketing program to fit the needs of his firm, the marketing manager has to weigh the behavioural forces and then juggle marketing elements in his mix with a keen eye on the resources with which he has to work." Jerome McCarthy (McCarthy, J. 1960), was the first person to suggest the four P's viz price, promotion, product and distribution which constitute the most common variables used in constructing a marketing mix. According to McCarthy the marketers essentially have these four variables which they can use while crafting a marketing strategy and writing a marketing plan. In the long term, all four of the mix variables can be changed, but in the short term it is difficult to modify the product or the distribution channel.

Another set of marketing mix variables were developed by Albert Frey (Frey, A. 1961) who classified the marketing variables into two categories: the offering, and process variables. The "offering" consists of the product, service, packaging, brand, and price. The "process" or "method" variables included advertising, promotion, sales promotion, personal selling, publicity, distribution channels, marketing research, strategy formation, and new product development.

Recently, Bernard Booms and Mary Bitner built a model consisting of seven P's. They added "People" to the list of existing variables, in order to recognize the importance of the human element in all aspects of marketing. They added "process" to reflect the fact that services, unlike physical products, are experienced as a process at the time that they are purchased.

MARKETING MIX MODEL

Marketing mix modelling is an analytical approach that use historic information, such as syndicated point-of-sale data and companies' internal data, to quantify the sales impact of various marketing activities. Mathematically, this is done by establishing a simultaneous relation of various marketing activities with the sales, in the form of a linear or a non-linear equation, through the statistical technique of regression.

MMM defines the effectiveness of each of the marketing elements in terms of its contribution to sales-volume, effectiveness (volume generated by each unit of effort), efficiency (sales volume generated divided by cost) and ROI.

These learnings are then adopted to adjust marketing tactics and strategies, optimize the marketing plan and also to forecast sales while simulating various scenarios.

This is accomplished by setting up a model with the sales volume/value as the dependent variable and independent variables created out of the various marketing efforts.

The creation of variables for Marketing Mix Modelling is a complicated affair and is as much an art as it is a science. Once the variables are created, multiple iterations are carried out to create a model which explains the volume/value trends perfectly. Further validations are carried out, either by using a validation data, or by the consistency of the business results.

The output can be used to analyse the impact of the marketing elements on various dimensions.

The contribution of each element as a percentage of the total plotted year on year is a good indicator of how the effectiveness of various elements changes over the years. The yearly change in contribution is also measure by a due-to analysis which shows what percentage of the change in total sales is attributable to each of the elements. For activities like television advertising and trade promotions, more sophisticated analysis like effectiveness can be carried out.

This analysis tells the marketing manager the incremental gain in sales that can be obtained by increasing the respective marketing element by one unit. If detailed spend information per activity is available then it is possible to calculate the Return on Investment of the marketing activity.

Not only is this useful for reporting the historical effectiveness of the activity, it also helps in optimizing the marketing budget by identifying the most and least efficient marketing activities.

Once the final model is ready, the results from it can be used to simulate marketing scenarios for a 'What-if' analysis. The marketing manager can reallocate this marketing budget in different proportions and see the direct impact on sales/value. He can optimize the budget by allocating spends to those activities which give the highest return on investment.

COMPONENTS

Marketing-mix models decompose total sales into two components:

- *Base Sales:* This is the natural demand for the product driven by economic factors like pricing, long-term trends, seasonality, and also qualitative factors like brand awareness and brand loyalty.
- *Incremental Sales:* Incremental sales are the component of sales driven by marketing and promotional activities. This component can be further decomposed into sales due to each marketing component like Television advertising or Radio advertising, Print Advertising (magazines, newspapers etc.), Coupons, Direct Mail, Internet, Feature or Display Promotions and Temporary Price Reductions.

Some of these activities have short-term returns (Coupons, Promotions), while others have longer term returns (TV, Radio, Magazine/Print). Marketing-Mix analyses are typically carried out using Linear Regression Modelling. Nonlinear and lagged effects are included using techniques like Advertising Adstock transformations. Typical output of such analyses include a decomposition of total annual sales into contributions from each marketing component, a.k.a Contribution pie-chart.

ELEMENTS MEASURED IN MMM

The very break-up of sales volume into base (volume that would be generated in absence of any marketing activity) and incremental (volume generated by marketing activities in the short run) across time gain gives wonderful insights. The base grows or declines across longer periods of time while the activities generating the incremental volume in the short run also impact the base volume in the long run. The variation in the base volume is a good indicator of the strength of the brand and the loyalty it commands from its users.

For the TV advertising activity, it is possible to examine how each ad execution has performed in the market in terms of its impact on sales volume. MMM can also provide information on TV effectiveness at different media weight levels, as measured by Gross Rating Points in relation to sales volume response within a time frame, be it a week or a month.

Information can also be gained on the minimum level of GRPs (threshold limit) in a week that need to be aired in order to make an impact, and conversely, the level of GRPs at which the impact on volume maximizes (saturation limit) and that the further activity does not have any payback. While not all MMM's will be able to produce definitive answers to all questions, some additional areas in which insights can sometimes be gained include:

- The effectiveness of 15-second vis-a-vis 30-second executions;
- Comparisons in ad performance when run during prime-time vis-a-vis off-prime-time dayparts;
- Comparisons into the direct and the halo effect of TV activity across various products or sub-brands.

The role of new product based TV activity and the equity based TV activity in growing the brand can also be compared

TRADE PROMOTIONS

Trade promotion is a key activity in every marketing plan. It is aimed at increasing sales in the short term by employing promotion schemes which effectively increases the customer awareness of the business and its products. The response of consumers to trade promotions is not straight forward and is the subject of much debate. Non-linear models exist to simulate the response. Using MMM we can understand the impact of trade promotion at generating incremental volumes. It is possible to obtain an estimate of the volume generated per promotion event in each of the different retail outlets by region. This way we can identify the most and least effective trade channels. If detailed spend information is available we can compare the Return on Investment of various trade activities like Every Day Low Price, Off-Shelf Display etc. We can use this information to optimize the trade plan by choosing the most effective trade channels and targeting the most effective promotion activity

PRICING

Price changes of the brand impacts the sales negatively. This effect can be captured through modelling the price in MMM. The model provides the price elasticity of the brand which tells us the percentage change in the sales for each percentage change in price. Using this, the marketing manager can evaluate the impact of a price change decision.

DISTRIBUTION

For the element of distribution, we can know how the volume will move by changing distribution efforts or, in other words, by each percentage shift in the width or the depth of distribution.

This can be identified specifically for each channel and even for each kind of outlet for off-take sales. In view of these insights, the distribution efforts can be prioritized for each channel or store-type to get the maximum out of the same. A recent study of a laundry brand showed that the incremental volume through 1% more presence in a neighbourhoods Kirana store is 180% greater than that through 1% more presence in a supermarket. Based upon the cost of such efforts, managers identified the right channel to invest more for distribution.

LAUNCHES

When a new product is launched, the associated publicity and promotions typically results in higher volume generation than expected. This extra volume cannot be completely captured in the model using the existing variables. Often special variables to capture this incremental effect of launches are used.

The combined contribution of these variables and that of the marketing effort associated with the launch will give the total launch contribution. Different launches can be compared by calculating their effectiveness and ROI.

COMPETITION

The impact of competition on the brand sales is captured by creating the competition variables accordingly. The variables are created from the marketing activities of the competition like television advertising, trade promotions, product launches etc. The results from the model can be used to identify the biggest threat to own brand sales from competition. The cross-price elasticity and the cross-promotional elasticity can be used to devise appropriate response to competition tactics. A successful competitive campaign can be analysed to learn valuable lesson for the own brand.

STUDIES IN MMM

Typical MMM studies provide the following insights:

- Contribution by marketing activity
- ROI by marketing activity
- Effectiveness of marketing activity
- Optimal distribution of spends
- Learnings on how to execute each activity better e.g. optimal GRPs per week, optimal distribution between 15s and 30s, which promos to run, what SKUS to put on promotion etc.

ADOPTION OF MMM BY THE INDUSTRY

MMM is a relatively new area of application. In the last 10 years though many CPG companies have adopted MMM. Many Fortune 500 companies such as P&G, Kraft, Coca-Cola and Pepsi have made MMM an integral part of their marketing planning. This has also been made possible due to the availability of specialist firms that are now providing MMM services.

Marketing-mix models were more popular initially the CPG industry and quickly spread to Retail and Pharma industries because of the availability of Syndicated Data in these industries (primarily from Nielsen Company and IRI and to a lesser extent from NPD Group). Availability of Time-series data is crucial to robust modelling of marketing-mix effects and with the systematic management of customer data through CRM systems in other industries like Financial Services, Automotive and Hospitality industries helped its spread to these industries.

In addition competitive and industry data availability through third party sources like Forrester Research's Ultimate Consumer Panel (Financial Services), Polk Insights (Automotive) and Smith Travel Research (Hospitality), further enhanced the application of marketing-mix modelling to these industries.

Application of marketing-mix modelling to these industries is still in a nascent stage and a lot of standardization needs to be brought about especially in these areas:

- Interpretation of promotional activities across industries for e.g. promotions in CPG do not have lagged effects as they happen in-store, but automotive and hospitality promotions are usually deployed through the internet or through dealer marketing and can have longer lags in their impact. CPG promotions are usually absolute price discounts, whereas Automotive promotions can be cash-books or loan incentives, and Financial Services promotions are usually interest rate discounts.

- Hospitality industry marketing has a very heavy seasonal pattern and most marketing-mix models will tend to confound marketing effectiveness with seasonality, thus over or under estimating marketing ROI. Time-series Cross-Sectional models like 'Pooled Regression' need to be utilized, which increase sample size and variation and thus make a robust separation of pure marketing-effects from seasonality.
- Automotive Manufacturers spend a substantial amount of their marketing budgets on dealer advertising, which may not be accurately measurable if not modelled at the right level of aggregation. If modelled at the national level or even the market or DMA level, these effects may be lost in aggregation bias. On the other hand going all the way down to dealer-level may over-estimate marketing effectiveness as it would ignore consumer switching between dealers in the same area. The correct albeit rigorous approach would be to determine what dealers to combine into 'addable' common groups based on overlapping 'trade-areas' determined by consumer zip codes and cross-shopping information. At the very least 'Common Dealer Areas' can be determined by clustering dealers based on geographical distance between dealers and share of county sales. Marketing-mix models built by 'pooling' monthly sales for these dealer clusters will be effectively used to measure the impact of dealer advertising effectively.

The proliferation of marketing-mix modelling was also accelerated due to the focus from Sarbanes-Oxley Section 404 that required internal controls for financial reporting on significant expenses and outlays. Marketing for consumer goods can be in excess of a 10th of total revenues and until the advent of marketing-mix models, relied on qualitative or 'soft' approaches to evaluate this spend. Marketing-mix modelling presented a rigorous and consistent approach to evaluate marketing-mix investments as the CPG industry had already demonstrated. A study by American Marketing Association pointed out that top management was more likely to stress the importance of marketing accountability than middle management, suggesting a top-down push towards greater accountability.

LIMITATIONS

While marketing mix models provide much useful information, there are two key areas in which these models have limitations that should be taken into account by all of those that use these models for decision making purposes. These limitations, discussed more fully below, include:

- the focus on short-term sales can significantly under-value the importance of longer-term equity building activities; and

- when used for media mix optimization, these models have a clear bias in favour of time-specific media (such as TV commercials) versus less time-specific media (such as ads appearing in monthly magazines); biases can also occur when comparing broad-based media versus regionally or demographically targeted media.

In relation to the bias against equity building activities, marketing budgets optimized using marketing-mix models may tend too much towards efficiency because marketing-mix models measure only the short-term effects of marketing. Longer term effects of marketing are reflected in its brand equity.

The impact of marketing spend on [brand equity] is usually not captured by marketing-mix models. One reason is that the longer duration that marketing takes to impact brand perception extends beyond the simultaneous or, at best, weeks-ahead impact of marketing on sales that these models measure. The other reason is that temporary fluctuation in sales due to economic and social conditions do not necessarily mean that marketing has been ineffective in building brand equity. On the contrary, it is very possible that in the short term sales and market-share could deteriorate, but brand equity could actually be higher. This higher equity should in the long run help the brand recover sales and market-share.

Because marketing-mix models suggest a marketing tactic has a positive impact on sales doesn't necessarily mean it has a positive impact on long-term brand equity. Different marketing measures impact short-term and long-term brand sales differently and adjusting the marketing portfolio to maximize either the short-term or the long-term alone will be sub-optimal.

For example the short-term positive effect of promotions on consumers' utility induces consumers to switch to the promoted brand, but the adverse impact of promotions on brand equity carries over from period to period. Therefore the net effect of promotions on a brand's market share and profitability can be negative due to their adverse impact on brand. Determining marketing ROI on the basis of marketing-mix models alone can lead to misleading results. This is because marketing-mix attempts to optimize marketing-mix to increase incremental contribution, but marketing-mix also drives brand-equity, which is not part of the incremental part measured by marketing-mix model-it is part of the baseline.

True 'Return on Marketing Investment' is a sum of short-term and long-term ROI. The fact that most firms use marketing-mix models only to measure the short-term ROI can be inferred from an article by Booz Allen Hamilton, which suggests that there is a significant shift away from traditional media to 'below-the-line' spending, driven by the fact that promotional spending is easier to measure.

But academic studies have shown that promotional activities are in fact detrimental to long-term marketing ROI (Ataman et al., 2006). Short-term marketing-mix models can be combined with brand-equity models using brand-tracking data to measure 'brand ROI', in both the short-and long-term.

The second limitation of marketing mix models comes into play when advertisers attempt to use these models to determine the best media allocation across different media types.

The traditional use of MMM's to compare money spent on TV versus money spent on couponing was relatively valid in that both TV commercials and the appearance of coupons (for example, in a FSI run in a newspaper) were both quite time specific. However, as the use of these models has been expanded into comparisons across a wider range of media types, extreme caution should be used.

Even with traditional media such as magazine advertising, the use of MMM's to compare results across media can be problematic; while the modellers overlay models of the 'typical' viewing curves of monthly magazines, these lack in precision, and thus introduce additional variability into the equation. Thus, comparisons of the effectiveness of running a TV commercial versus the effectiveness of running a magazine ad would be biased in favour of TV, with its greater precision of measurement.

As new new forms of media proliferate, these limitations become even more important to consider if MMM's are to be used in attempts to quantify their effectiveness. For example, Sponsorship Marketing, Sports Affinity Marketing, Viral Marketing, Blog Marketing and Mobile Marketing all vary in terms of the time-specificity of exposure.

Further, most approaches to marketing-mix models try to include all marketing activities in aggregate at the national or regional level, but to the extent that various tactics are targeted to different demographic consumer groups, their impact may be lost. For example, Mountain Dew sponsorhip of NASCAR may be targeted to NASCAR fans, which may include multiple age groups, but Mountain Dew advertising on gaming blogs may be targeted to the Gen Y population.

Both of these tactics may be highly effective within the corresponding demographic groups but, when included in aggregate in a national or regional marketing-mix model, may come up as ineffective.

Aggregation bias, along with issues relating to variations in the time-specific natures of different media, pose serious problems when these models are used in ways beyond those for which they were originally designed. As media become even more fragmented, it is critical that these issues are taken into account if marketing-mix models are used to judge the relative effectiveness of different media and tactics.

Marketing-mix models use historical performance to evaulate marketing performance and so are not an effective tool to manage marketing investments for new products. This is because the relatively short history of new products make marketing-mix results unstable. Also relationship between marketing and sales may be radically different in the launch and stable periods. For example the initial performance of Coke Zero was really poor and showed low advertising elasticity.

In spite of this Coke increased its media spend, with an improved strategy and radically improved its performance resulting in advertising effectiveness that is probably several times the effectiveness during the launch period. A typical marketing-mix model would have recommended cutting media spend and instead resorting to heavy price discounting.

6

Theory of Cost

Definition of Cost

In business, retail, and accounting, a cost is the value of money that has been used up to produce something, and hence is not available for use anymore. In economics, a cost is an alternative that is given up as a result of a decision. In business, the cost may be one of acquisition, in which case the amount of money expended to acquire it is counted as cost.

In this case, money is the input that is gone in order to acquire the thing. This acquisition cost may be the sum of the cost of production as incurred by the original producer, and further costs of transaction as incurred by the acquirer over and above the price paid to the producer. Usually, the price also includes a mark-up for profit over the cost of production. Costs are often further described based on their timing or their applicability.

ACCOUNTING VS OPPORTUNITY COSTS

In accounting, costs are the monetary value of expenditures for supplies, services, labour, products, equipment and other items purchased for use by a business or other accounting entity. It is the amount denoted on invoices as the price and recorded in bookkeeping records as an expense or asset cost basis.

Opportunity cost, also referred to as economic cost is the value of the best alternative that was not chosen in order to pursue the current endeavour—*i.e*, what could have been accomplished with the resources expended in the undertaking. It represents opportunities forgone. In theoretical economics, cost used without qualification often means opportunity cost.

COMPARING PRIVATE, EXTERNAL, SOCIAL, AND PSYCHIC COSTS

When a transaction takes place, it typically involves both private costs and external costs. Private costs are the costs that the buyer of a good or service pays the seller. This can also be described as the costs internal to the firm's production function. External costs, in contrast, are the costs that people other than the buyer are forced to pay as a result of the transaction. The bearers of such costs can be either particular individuals or society at large. Note that external costs are often both non-monetary and problematic to quantify for comparison with monetary values.

They include things like pollution, things that society will likely have to pay for in some way or at some time in the future, but that are not included in transaction prices. Social costs are the sum of private costs and external costs. For example, the manufacturing cost of a car reflects the private cost for the manufacturer. The polluted waters or polluted air also created as part of the process of producing the car is an external cost borne by those who are affected by the pollution or who value unpolluted air or water.

Because the manufacturer does not pay for this external cost and does not include this cost in the price of the car, they are said to be external to the market pricing mechanism. The air pollution from driving the car is also an externality produced by the car user in the process of using his good. The driver does not compensate for the environmental damage caused by using the car. A psychic cost is a subset of social costs that specifically represent the costs of added stress or losses to quality of life.

COST ESTIMATES AND COST OVERRUN

When developing a business plan for a new company, product, or project, planners typically make cost estimates in order to assess whether revenues/ benefits will cover costs. This is done in both business and government. Costs are often underestimated resulting in cost overrun during implementation. Main causes of cost underestimation and overrun are optimism bias and strategic misrepresentation. Reference class forecasting was developed to curb optimism bias and strategic misrepresentation and arrive at more accurate cost estimates. Cost Plus, is where the Price = Cost plus or minus X%, where x is the percentage of built in overhead or profit margin.

Cost Manageent

Cost management is the process by which companies control and plan the costs of doing business. Individual projects should have customised cost management plans, and companies as a whole also integrate cost management into their overall business model. There is no single accepted definition for this term, because it has such broad applications and possible strategies.

When properly implemented, cost management will translate into reduced costs of production for products and services, as well as increased value being delivered to the customer. For a company's management to be effective overall, cost management must be an integral feature of it. It is easiest to understand this concept if it is explained in the context of a single project. For instance, before a project is started, the anticipated costs should be identified and measured. These expenses should then be approved before any purchasing occurs.

During the process of completing a project, all incurred costs should be noted and kept in a record of some kind, to help ensure that the costs are controlled and kept in line with initial expectations, to the extent that this is possible. Taking this approach to cost management will help a company determine whether they accurately estimated expenses at first, and will help them more closely predict expenses in the future. Any overspending can also be monitored in this way, and either eliminated in future projects or specifically approved if the expense was necessary. Cost management cannot be used in isolation; projects must be organized and tailored with this strategy in mind. Starting a project with cost management in mind will help to avoid certain pitfalls that may be present otherwise. If the objectives of the project are not clearly defined at first, or are changed during the course of the project, cost over-runs will be more likely.

If costs are not fully researched before the project, they may be underestimated, thereby inflating the expectation of the project's success unrealistically. Construction projects are subject to their own particular challenges; these can include constraints in the form of laws and regulations that must be planned around.

If the project is completely and clearly defined, this will facilitate effective management of the costs it will incur. Effective cost management strategies will help a team deliver a finished project within the allocated budget, while also making it as valuable as possible to the company. There is always the possibility of unexpected costs, but preparation in the form of cost management will likely make them much easier to deal with when they occur.

Cost Behaviour

The most important building block of both microeconomic analysis and cost accounting is the characterization of how costs change as output volume changes.

Output volume can refer to production, sales, or any other principle activity that is appropriate for the organization under consideration. The following discussion examines the volume of production in a factory, but the same principles apply regardless of the type of organization and the appropriate measure of activity. Costs can be variable, fixed, or mixed.

Variable Costs

Variable costs vary in a linear fashion with the production level. However, when stated on a per unit basis, variable costs remain constant across all production levels within the relevant range. The following two charts depict this relationship between variable costs and output volume.

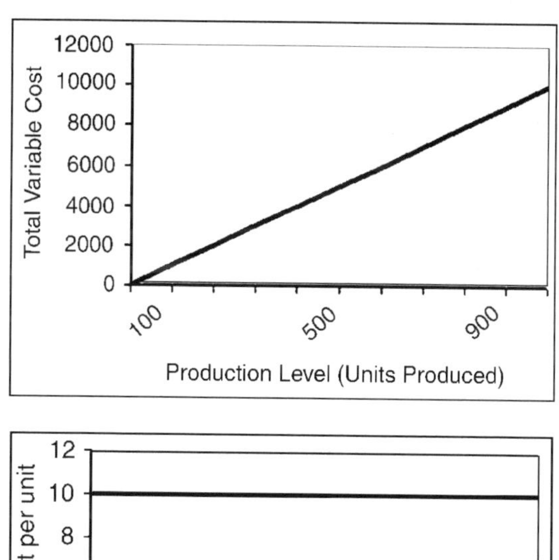

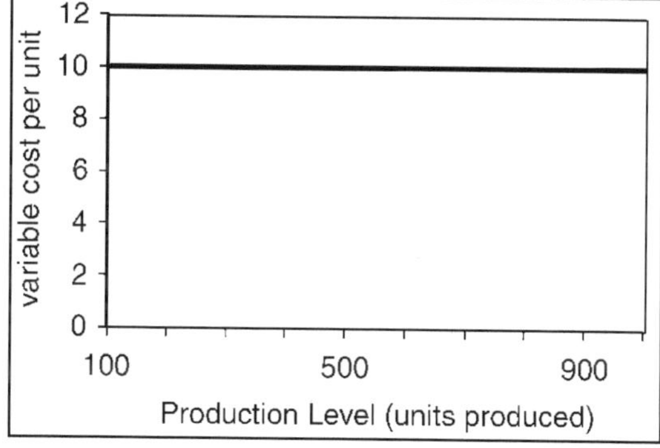

A good example of a variable cost is materials. If one pair of pants requires \$10 of fabric, then every pair of pants requires \$10 of fabric, no matter how many pairs are made.

The fabric cost is \$10 per unit at every level of production. If one pair is made, the total fabric cost is \$10; if two pairs are made, the total fabric cost is \$20; and if 1,000 pairs are made, the total fabric cost is \$10,000. Hence, the total cost is increasing and linear in the production level.

Fixed Costs

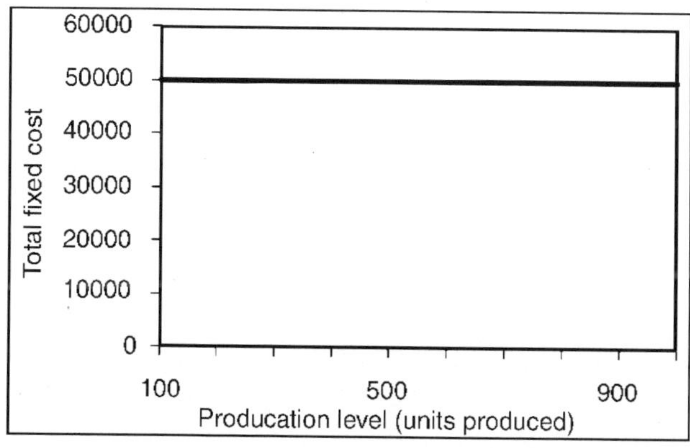

Fixed costs do not vary with the production level. Total fixed costs remain the same, within the relevant range. However, the fixed cost per unit decreases as production increases, because the same fixed costs are spread over more units. The following two charts depict this relationship between fixed costs and output volume.

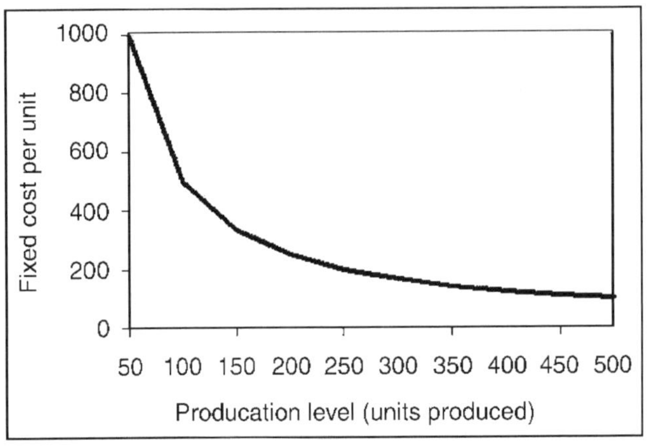

In this example, fixed costs are $50,000. The first chart shows that fixed costs remain $50,000 at all production levels from 100 units to 1,000 units. The second chart shows that the fixed cost per unit decreases as production increases. Hence, when 100 units are manufactured, the fixed cost per unit is $500 ($50,000 ÷ 100). When 500 units are manufactured, the fixed cost per unit is $100 ($50,000 ÷ 500).

Relevant Range

The relevant range is the range of activity over which these relationships are valid. For example, if the factory is operating at capacity, increasing production requires additional investment in fixed costs to expand the facility or to lease or build another factory.

Alternatively, production might be reduced below a threshold at which point one of the company's factories is no longer needed, and the fixed costs associated with that factory can be avoided. With respect to variable costs, the company might qualify for a volume discount on fabric purchases above some production level. The relevant range for characterizing fabric as a variable cost ends at that production level, because the fabric cost per unit of output is different when the factory produces above that threshold than when the factory produces below that threshold.

Mixed Costs

If, within a relevant range, a cost is neither fixed nor variable, it is called semi-variable or mixed. Following are two common examples of mixed costs.

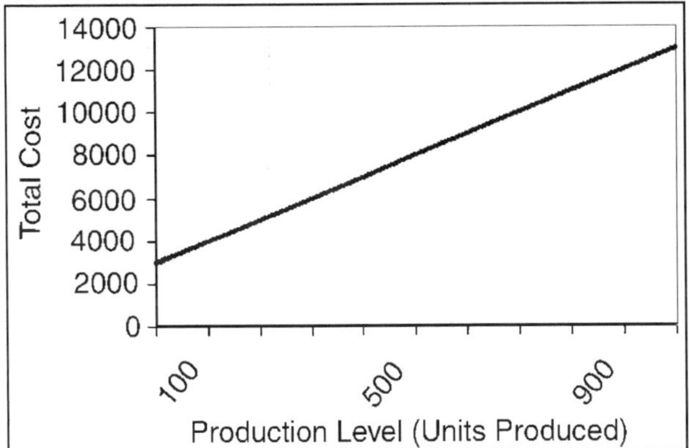

In this example, although the total cost line increases in production, it does not pass through the origin because there is a fixed cost component. An example of a cost that fits this description is electricity. A fixed amount of electricity is required to run the factory air conditioning, computers and lights.

There is also a variable cost component related to running the machines on the factory floor. The fixed component in this example is $3,000 per month. The variable cost component is $10 per unit of output. Hence, at a production level of 500 units, the total electric cost is $8,000 [$3,000 + ($10 x 500)].

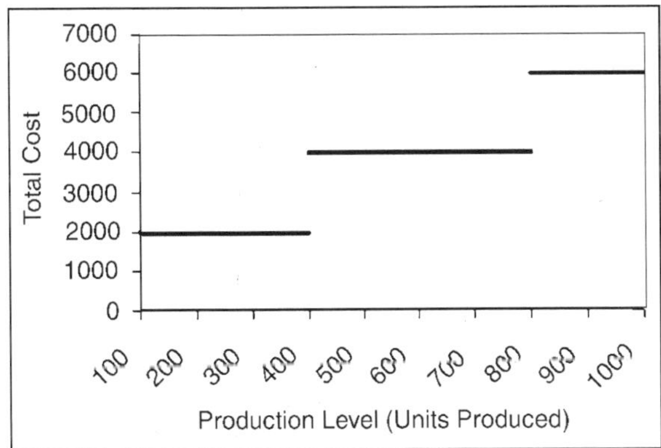

The mixed cost illustrated in the above chart is called a step function. An example of such cost behaviour would be the total salary expense for shift supervisors. If the factory runs one shift, only one shift supervisor is required. In order for the factory to produce above the maximum capacity of a single shift, the factory must add a second shift and hire a second shift supervisor, so that total shift supervisor salary expense doubles. If the factory runs three shifts, three shift supervisors are required.

Cost Behaviour Assumptions in Management Accounting Versus Microeconomics

Microeconomic analysis usually assumes decreasing marginal costs of production, sometimes followed by increasing marginal costs of production beyond a certain production level. Hence, economists' graphs of the total cost of production and the average per-unit cost of production show smooth, curved functions.

Management accountants usually assume the linear relationships depicted in the previous graphs. Linearity is a more accurate description of many situations encountered by management accountants than the economists' curves, and even when linearity constitutes a simplifying assumption it is almost always sufficiently descriptive for the task at hand.

BASIC COST MANAGEMENT CONCEPTS

Multi-product firms have to account for costs that can be tied to a product, direct costs. They also have to account for indirect costs not directly measurable. A 'cost object' can be a product, service, process or any items which management requires cost information. The way that costs are assigned depends on their nature. A direct costs is easily traceable with a high degree of accuracy and indirect, or overhead, cost cannot be easily identifiable with a particular object.

Product costs are costs allocated to a product; this is not just physical products. All other costs are period costs. Such costs are expenses to the income statement in the period they are incurred. Product costs are recognised as an expense in the income statement only when the product is sold. Prior to sale the cost of products is shown as an asset due to the accrual principle.

The stages in the allocation of overheads to products are as follows;

- Identify overhead costs collected from production and service cost centres and apportion as appropriate and possible.
- Once identified allocate to production departments.
- Allocate overheads to a single product by dividing the number of products into the total overhead. The resulting sum can then be applied as cost to the product.
- Total Overheads of a Production Costs Centre ($s)/Level of Activity (units)

Predetermined overhead absorption rates are estimates of future expenditures. Estimates are used becuase some overhead costs are not known for some time until afterthey have incurred. Normal costing is where the cost object is determined using the actual costs for the direct the direct costs and a predetermined rate for the allocation of indirect costs. Functional-based cost accounting classifies all costs as either fixed or variable in relation to changes in the volume of units produced.

Activity-based costing tries to capture changes in technology by apportioning oveheads to product costs taking into account activity and transactions that drive the cost. An activity cost pool is where the costs of an activity under the ABC system are accumulated. Drives are factors that cause changes in the use of resources. The focus in ABC is managing activities instead of costs. Absorption costing is where the cost of inventories is determined in order to include an appropriate share of variable and fixed costs.

Fixed costs are allocated on the basis of normal operating capacity. In variable costing, only the production costs are used. Using absorption costsing, production overhead costs are included as a product cost whereas in variable costing they are treated as a period cost. This leads to different values of inventory and therefore different net profit figures.

The difference in profits derived from the application of the two methods can be reconciled by the following:

- Fixed Overhead Absorption Rate * Movement of Inventories in a period = Difference in Profits

aCTIVITY Based Costing

Activity Based Costing is an accounting technique that allows an organization to determine the actual cost associated with each product and service produced by the organization without regard to the organizational structure. It is developed to provide more-accurate ways of assigning the costs of indirect and support resources to activities, bushiness processes, products, services, and customers.

ABC systems recognize that many organizational resources are required not for physical production of units of product but to provide a broad array of support activities that enable a variety of products and services to be produced for a diverse group of customers.

The goal of ABC is not to allocate common costs to products. The goal is to measure and then price out all the resources used for activities that support the production and delivery of products and services to customers.

Concept of Activity-Based-Costing

Activity Based Costing is an accounting technique that allows an organization to determine the actual cost associated with each product and service produced by the organization without regard to the organizational structure. It is developed to provide more-accurate ways of assigning the costs of indirect and support resources to activities, bushiness processes, products, services, and customers. ABC systems recognize that many organizational resources are required not for physical production of units of product but to provide a broad array of support activities that enable a variety of products and services to be produced for a diverse group of customers.

The goal of ABC is not to allocate common costs to products. The goal is to measure and then price out all the resources used for activities that support the production and delivery of products and services to customers.

An organization performs activities to do its business. These activities define the kind of business you are in: a ship owner has an activity to unpack boats; an accounting firm prepares tax returns; a manufacturer produces products; a council delivers services; a university teaches students. All activities consume resources.

It is the consumption of these resources that adds to overhead costs. The basis of Activity Based Costing is: look at the activities required to produce the cost of the product or service. The activities consume resources and the cost of these can be calculated.

The amount of activity required for each product and service is determined, hence the real cost can be determined:

- The activity is the work that is done.
- The resource is what the activity uses to do the work *e.g.* people, equipment, and services. Resources cost money.
- The cost of the activity depends on the quantity of resources used to accomplish the activity.
- The cost driver for an activity is the factor that influences the amount of the resources that will be consumed by this activity.
- The activity driver measures how much of the activity is used by the cost object. Example: Product A is delivered once a month, whereas product B is delivered once a week. Products A and B require a different number of deliveries, hence the cost of the delivery activity should be assigned to each product on the basis of the number of deliveries each uses.
- The cost object is whatever it is you wish to cost. It could be a product, service, process, job or customer.

While traditional costing arbitrarily allocates overhead costs, ABC traces overhead costs by looking at the activities that each product and service calls upon. With ABC the products consume the activities. It is the activities that cost money. If there were no activities, no resources would be consumed. It is the activities that you do that define your business.

USE OF ACTIVITY-BASED-COSTING

Activity-Based-Costing is necessary for the following reasons:

- Identify opportunities to reduce costs and/or increase efficiency
- Obtain actionable information to negotiate price increases for unprofitable clients
- Quantify the cost of non-value added activities such as errors and reworks
- Stratify overhead costs so they can be managed more effectively
- Understand TRUE profitability of your customers, products, or services
- Understand why profitability may be mediocre despite good strategic fundamentals

How Does ABC Work?

The first stage in an initial ABC study is to develop a fundamental understanding of the Resources and Activities of an organization. The Resources are then mapped to the Activities, thereby quantifying the cost of performing each of these Activities. These costs are traced to Cost Objects providing tremendous insight into where an organization is making and losing money.

ABC Model

The objective of an ABC implementation is to relate all of the costs of doing business to products, services, or customers.

Developing the initial model consists of the following five steps:

- Define Cost Objects
- Determine Activities that are supported by Resources
- Develop Cost Drivers to link Activities to Cost Objects
- Develop Resource Drivers to link Resources to Activities
- Identify the Resources of an organization

Identify Resources

Resources represent the expenditures of an organization. Examples include production labour, sales and marketing labour, occupancy and utilities, equipment, and supplies. These are the same costs that are represented in a traditional accounting view; unlike traditional accounting, ABC links these costs to products, customers, or services.

Identify Activities

Activities represent the work performed in an organization.

ABC Activities for the sales department in a typical organization might include:

- Attending trade shows and other events
- Distributing samples
- Evaluating products and improving product knowledge
- Making customer service calls
- Making sales calls to existing customers
- Making sales calls to potential customers
- Training product representatives

Traditional accounting will often break the cost of the sales department into salaries, benefits, allocated rent, supplies, and so on. Unlike traditional accounting, which reports what the costs are, ABC accounts for these costs based on what activities caused them to occur.

By determining the actual activities that occur in various departments, such as accounting, customer service, and sales, it is then possible to more accurately relate these costs to customers, products, and services.

Identify Cost Objects

ABC provides profitability by one or more cost object, usually represented by products, customers, and/or services. Cost Object profitability is utilized to identify money losing customers, to validate separate divisions or business units, or to measure the performance of individual projects, jobs, or contracts. Defining the outputs to be viewed is an important step in a successful ABC implementation.

Determine Resource Drivers

Resource Drivers provide the link between the expenditures of an organization and the Activities performed within the organization. For example, the total salary of a customer service representative would likely be allocated to the Activities performed based on the amount of time spent performing the Activity. If 50% of her time is spent performing the activity, taking orders for existing customers, 50% of her salary would be allocated to this Activity.

Determine Cost Drivers

Determination of Cost Drivers completes the last stage of the model. Cost Drivers trace, or link, the cost of performing certain Activities to Cost Objects. For example, taking orders for existing customers may be linked to specific customers based on the number of orders taken, if each order takes approximately the same amount of time.

If order taking time varies based on the customer, this cost may be linked based on another driver or multiple drivers.

OPERATING COST

Operating costs are the recurring expenses which are related to the operation of a business, or to the operation of a device, component, piece of equipment or facility.

BUSINESS OPERATING COSTS

For a commercial enterprise, operating costs fall into two broad categories:

1. Fixed costs, which are the same whether the operation is closed or running at 100% capacity
2. Variable costs, which may increase depending on whether more production is done, and how it is done (producing 100 items of product might require 10 days of normal time or take 7 days if overtime is used.
3. It may be more or less expensive to use overtime production depending on whether faster production means the product can be more profitable).

Business Overhead Costs

Overhead costs for a business are the cost of resources used by an organization just to maintain its existence. Overhead costs are usually measured in monetary terms, but non-monetary overhead is possible in the form of time required to accomplish tasks.

Examples of overhead costs include:

- Cost of electricity for the office lights
- Payment of rent on the office space a business occupies
- Some office personnel wages

Non-overhead costs are incremental costs, such as the cost of raw materials used in the goods a business sells. Operating Cost is calculated by Cost of goods sold + Operating Expenses. Operating Expenses consist of:. Administrative and office expenses like rent, salaries, to staff, insurance, directors fees etc.. Selling and distribution expenses like advertisement, salaries of salesmen.

Equipment operating costs

In the case of a device, component, piece of equipment or facility, it is the regular, usual and customary recurring coststing or purchasing the equipment. Operating costs are incurred by all equipment—unless the equipment has no cost to operate, requires no personnel or space and never wears out. In some cases, equipment may appear to have low or no operating cost because either the cost is not recognized or is being absorbed in whole or part by the cost of something else.

Equipment operating costs may include:

- Salaries or Wages of personnel
- Advertising
- Raw materials
- License or equivalent fees imposed by a government
- Real estate expenses, including
  - Rent or Lease payments
  - Office space
  - Furniture and equipment
  - Investment value of the funds used to purchase The land, if it is owned instead of rented or leased
  - Property taxes and equivalent assessments
  - Operations taxes, such as fees assessed on transportation carriers for use of highways
- Fuel costs such as power for operations, fuel for production
- Public Utilities such as telephone service, Internet connectivity, etc.
- Maintenance of equipment
- Office supplies and consumables
- Insurance

- Depreciation of equipment and eventual replacement costs
- Damage due to uninsured losses, accident, sabotage, negligence, terrorism and routine wear and tear.
- Taxes on production or operation
- Income taxes

Some of these are not applicable in all instances.

For example:

- A solar panel placed on one's home for use in generating electric power generally has only capital costs; once it's running there are no personnel costs, utility costs or depreciation and it uses no extra land so it has no real operating costs; however there may need to be taken into account costs of replacement if damaged.
- An automobile or any other item purchased for personal use has no salary cost because the owner does not charge themselves for operating the device.
- An item which is leased may have some or all of these costs included as part of the purchase price.

It might be questionable to assert that the cost of ten extra people on the sales force are an incremental cost or an overhead cost, since the wages for these people are both overhead and incremental. The staff needed to keep the shop operational are mostly considered as overhead.

Overhead Cost

In business, overhead, overhead cost or overhead expense refers to an ongoing expense of operating a business. The term overhead is usually used to group expenses that are necessary to the continued functioning of the business, but cannot be immediately associated with the products/services being offered. Overhead expenses are all costs on the income statement except for direct labour,direct materials and direct expenses.

Overhead expenses include accounting fees, advertising, depreciation, insurance, interest, legal fees, rent, repairs, supplies, taxes, telephone bills, travel and utilities costs.

Overhead can be classified under four headings:

1. Classification on behaviour of expenditure
2. Classification on the nature of expenditure
3. Element-wise classification
4. Functional classification

TARGET COSTING

As a totally new product and its industry develops, it starts to compete based on its new technology, concept, and/or service. Competitors emerge and the basis for competition evolves to other areas such as cycle time, quality, or reliability. As an industry becomes mature, the basis of competition typically moves to price. Profit margins shrink. Companies begin focusing on cost reduction.

However, the cost structure for existing products is largely locked in and cost reduction activities have limited impact. As companies begin to realise that the majority of a product's costs are committed based on decisions made during the development of a product, the focus shifts to actions that can be taken during the product development phase. Until recently, engineers have focused on satisfying a customer's requirements.

Most development personnel have viewed a product's cost as a dependent variable that is the result of the decisions made about a products functions, features and performance capabilities. Because a product's costs are often not assessed until later in the development cycle, it is common for product costs to be higher than desired. This process is represented in Figure.

TRADITIONAL COST MANAGEMENT APPROACH

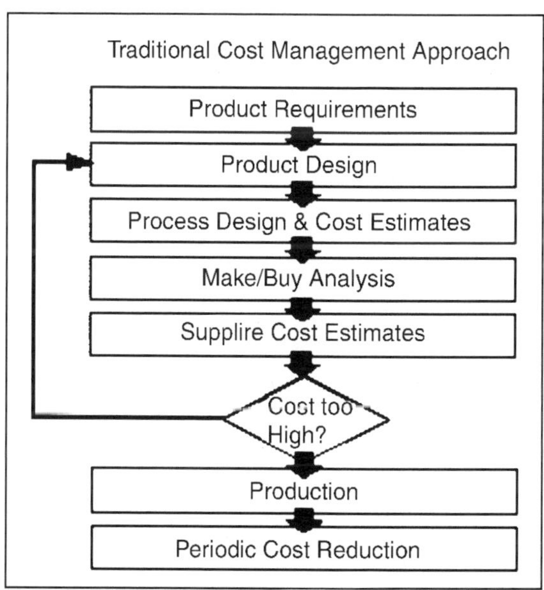

Target costing represents a fundamentally different approach.

It is based on three premises:

1. Orienting products to customer affordability or market-driven pricing,
2. Treating product cost as an independent variable during the definition of a product's requirements, and
3. Proactively working to achieve target cost during product and process development.

This target costing approach is represented in Figure.

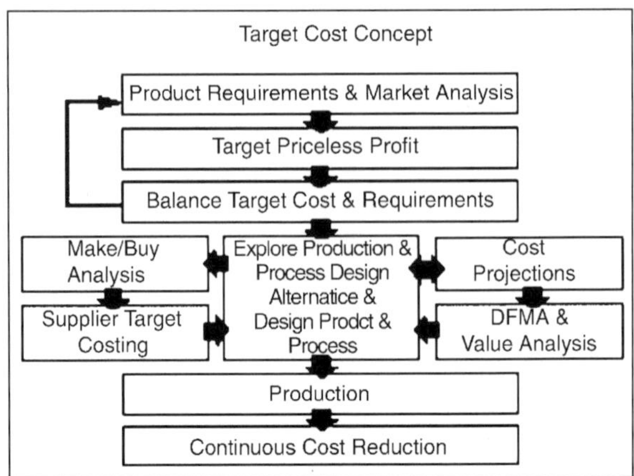

Target costing builds upon a design-to-cost (DTC) approach with the focus on market-driven target prices as a basis for establishing target costs. The target costing concept is similar to the cost as an independent variable (CAIV) approach used by the U.S.

Department of Defence and to the price-to-win philosophy used by a number of companies pursuing contracts involving development under contract. The following ten steps are required to install a comprehensive target costing approach within an organization.

1. *Re-orient culture and attitudes*: The first and most challenging step is re-orient thinking towards market driven pricing and prioritized customer needs rather than just technical requirements as a basis for product development. This is a fundamental change from the attitude in most organizations where cost is the result of the design rather than the influencer of the design and that pricing is derived from building up a estimate of the cost of manufacturing a product.
2. *Establish a market-driven target price*: A target price needs to be established based upon market factors such as the company position in the market place (market share), business and market penetration strategy, competition and competitive price response, targeted market niche or price point, and elasticity of demand. If the company is responding to a request for proposal/quotation, the target price is based on analysis of the price to win considering customer affordability and competitive analysis.
3. *Determine the target cost*: Once the target price is established, a worksheet is used to calculate the target cost by subtracting the standard profit margin, warranty reserves, and any uncontrollable corporate allocations. If a bid includes non-recurring development costs, these are also subtracted. The target cost is allocated down to lower level assemblies of subsystems in a manner consistent with the structure of teams or individual designer responsibilities.

Table. Target Cost Calculation Worksheet

Sign	Price/Cost Element	Estimate	% Factor	Per Unit Factor	Amount
	Manufacture's suggested Retail Price			$495.00	
–	Standard Dealer Margin		30%	$ –	$(148.50)
=	Cost to Retailer			$ 346.50	
–	Shipping/Distribution Cost to Retailer		0%	$15.00	$ (15.00)
=	Selling Price to Retailer			$331.50	
–	Distribution Cost/Mark-up		15%	$ –	$(49.37)
–	Shipping/Logistic Cost to Distribution Center		0%	$ 17.00	$ (17.00)
=	Manufactur's Selling Price			$264.78	
–	Profit Margin		8%	$ –	$ (21.18)
–	Warranty Cost		2%	$ –	$ (5.30)
–	Corporate Allocations		10%	$–	$ (26.48)
–	Business Unit Selling, General and Administrative		12%	$ –	(31.77)
	Non Recurring Development Cost	1200000			
	Estimated Production Volume	200000			
–	Allocated Non Recurring Development Cost			$ 6.00	$ (6.00)
=	Business Unit Target Cost				$ 174.05
–	Overhead		45%	$ –	$ (78.32)
=	Direct Target Cost (Labour and Material				$ 9573

4. *Balance target cost with requirements*: Before the target cost is finalized, it must be considered in conjunction with product requirements. The greatest opportunity to control a product's costs is through proper setting of requirements or specifications. This requires a careful understanding of the voice of the customer, use of conjoint analysis to understand the value that customers place on particular product capabilities, and use of techniques such as quality function deployment to help make these tradeoff's among various product requirements including target cost.
5. *Establish a target costing process and a team-based organization*: A well-defined process is required that integrates activities and tasks to support to support target costing. This process needs to be based on early and proactive consideration of target costs and incorporate tools and methodologies described subsequently. Further, a team-based organization is required that integrates essential disciplines such as marketing, engineering, manufacturing, purchasing, and finance. Responsibilities to support target costing need to be clearly defined.
6. *Brainstorm and analyse alternatives*: The second most significant opportunity to achieve cost reduction is through consideration of

multiple concept and design alternatives for both the product and its manufacturing and support processes at each stage of the development cycle. These opportunities can be achieved when there is out-of-the-box or creative consideration of alternatives coupled with structured analysis and decision-making methods.

7. Establish product cost models to support decision-making. Product cost models and cost tables provide the tools to evaluate the implications of concept and design alternatives. In the early stages of development, these models are based on parametric estimating or analogy techniques. Further on in the development cycle as the product and process become more defined, these models are based on industrial engineering or bottom-up estimating techniques. The models need to be comprehensive to address all of the proposed materials, fabrication processes, and assembly process and need to be validated to insure reasonable accuracy. A target cost worksheet can be used to capture the various elements of product cost, compare alternatives, as well as track changing estimates against target cost over the development cycle.
8. Use tools to reduce costs. Use of tools and methodologies related to design for manufacturability and assembly, design for inspection and test, modularity and part standardization, and value analysis or function analysis. These methodologies will consist of guidelines, databases, training, procedures, and supporting analytic tools.
9. Reduce indirect cost application. Since a significant portion of a product's costs are indirect, these costs must also be addressed. The enterprise must examine these costs, re-engineer indirect business processes, and minimize non-value-added costs. But in addition to these steps, development personnel generally lack an understanding of the relationship of these costs to the product and process design decisions that they make. Use of activity-based costing and an understanding of the organization's cost drivers can provide a basis for understanding how design decisions impact indirect costs and, as a result, allow their avoidance.
10. Measure results and maintain management focus. Current estimated costs need to be tracked against target cost throughout development and the rate of closure monitored. Management needs to focus attention of target cost achievement during design reviews and phase-gate reviews to communicate the importance of target costing to the organization.

Kaizen costing

The process of continual cost reduction that occurs after a product design has been completed and is now in production. Cost reduction techniques can include working with suppliers to reduce the costs in their processes, implementing less costly re-designs of the product, or reducing waste costs.

The Value Chain

To better understand the activities through which a firm develops a competitive advantage and creates shareholder value, it is useful to separate the business system into a series of value-generating activities referred to as the value chain. In his 1985 book Competitive Advantage, Michael Porter introduced a generic value chain model that comprises a sequence of activities found to be common to a wide range of firms.

Porter identified primary and support activities as shown in the following diagram:

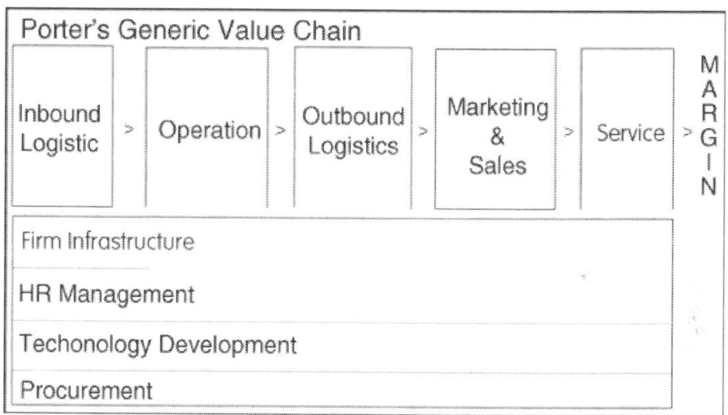

Fig. Porter's Generic Value Chain

The goal of these activities is to offer the customer a level of value that exceeds the cost of the activities, thereby resulting in a profit margin.

The primary value chain activities are:

- *Inbound Logistics*: The receiving and warehousing of raw materials, and their distribution to manufacturing as they are required.
- *Marketing and Sales*: The identification of customer needs and the generation of sales.
- *Operations*: The processes of transforming inputs into finished products and services.
- *Outbound Logistics*: The warehousing and distribution of finished goods.
- *Service*: The support of customers after the products and services are sold to them.

These primary activities are supported by:

- Human resource management: employee recruiting, hiring, training, development, and compensation.
- Procurement: purchasing inputs such as materials, supplies, and equipment.

- Technology development: technologies to support value-creating activities.
- The infrastructure of the firm: organizational structure, control systems, company culture, etc.

The firm's margin or profit then depends on its effectiveness in performing these activities efficiently, so that the amount that the customer is willing to pay for the products exceeds the cost of the activities in the value chain. It is in these activities that a firm has the opportunity to generate superior value. A competitive advantage may be achieved by reconfiguring the value chain to provide lower cost or better differentiation.

The value chain model is a useful analysis tool for defining a firm's core competencies and the activities in which it can pursue a competitive advantage as follows:

- *Cost advantage*: By better understanding costs and squeezing them out of the value-adding activities.
- *Differentiation*: By focusing on those activities associated with core competencies and capabilities in order to perform them better than do competitors.

Cost Advantage and the Value Chain

A firm may create a cost advantage either by reducing the cost of individual value chain activities or by reconfiguring the value chain. Once the value chain is defined, a cost analysis can be performed by assigning costs to the value chain activities. The costs obtained from the accounting report may need to be modified in order to allocate them properly to the value creating activities.

Porter identified 10 cost drivers related to value chain activities:

1. Capacity utilization
2. Degree of vertical integration
3. Economies of scale
4. Firm's policy of cost or differentiation
5. Geographic location
6. Institutional factors
7. Interrelationships among business units
8. Learning
9. Linkages among activities
10. Timing of market entry

A firm develops a cost advantage by controlling these drivers better than do the competitors. A cost advantage also can be pursued by reconfiguring the value chain. Reconfiguration means structural changes such a new production process, new distribution channels, or a different sales approach. For example, FedEx structurally redefined express freight service by acquiring its own planes and implementing a hub and spoke system.

Differentiation and the Value Chain

A differentiation advantage can arise from any part of the value chain. For example, procurement of inputs that are unique and not widely available to competitors can create differentiation, as can distribution channels that offer high service levels. Differentiation stems from uniqueness. A differentiation advantage may be achieved either by changing individual value chain activities to increase uniqueness in the final product or by reconfiguring the value chain.

Porter identified several drivers of uniqueness:

- Institutional factors
- Integration
- Interrelationships
- Learning
- Linkages among activities
- Location
- Policies and decisions
- Scale
- Timing

Many of these also serve as cost drivers. Differentiation often results in greater costs, resulting in tradeoffs between cost and differentiation. There are several ways in which a firm can reconfigure its value chain in order to create uniqueness. It can forward integrate in order to perform functions that once were performed by its customers. It can backward integrate in order to have more control over its inputs. It may implement new process technologies or utilize new distribution channels. Ultimately, the firm may need to be creative in order to develop a novel value chain configuration that increases product differentiation.

Technology and the Value Chain

Because technology is employed to some degree in every value creating activity, changes in technology can impact competitive advantage by incrementally changing the activities themselves or by making possible new configurations of the value chain.

Various technologies are used in both primary value activities and support activities:

- Inbound Logistics Technologies
  - Transportation
  - Material handling
  - Material storage
  - Communications
  - Testing
  - Information systems
- Operations Technologies

  - Process
  - Materials
  - Machine tools
  - Material handling
  - Packaging
  - Maintenance
  - Testing
  - Building design and operation
  - Information systems
- Outbound Logistics Technologies
  - Transportation
  - Material handling
  - Packaging
  - Communications
  - Information systems
- Marketing and Sales Technologies
  - Media
  - Audio/video
  - Communications
  - Information systems
- Service Technologies
  - Testing
  - Communications
  - Information systems

Note that many of these technologies are used across the value chain. For example, information systems are seen in every activity. Similar technologies are used in support activities. In addition, technologies related to training, computer-aided design, and software development frequently are employed in support activities. To the extent that these technologies affect cost drivers or uniqueness, they can lead to a competitive advantage.

Linkages between Value Chain Activities

Value chain activities are not isolated from one another. Rather, one value chain activity often affects the cost or performance of other ones. Linkages may exist between primary activities and also between primary and support activities. Consider the case in which the design of a product is changed in order to reduce manufacturing costs.

Suppose that inadvertantly the new product design results in increased service costs; the cost reduction could be less than anticipated and even worse, there could be a net cost increase. Sometimes however, the firm may be able to reduce cost in one activity and consequently enjoy a cost reduction in another, such as when a design change simultaneously reduces manufacturing costs and improves reliability so that the service costs also are reduced. Through such improvements the firm has the potential to develop a competitive advantage.

Analyzing Business Unit Interrelationships

Interrelationships among business units form the basis for a horizontal strategy. Such business unit interrelationships can be identified by a value chain analysis. Tangible interrelationships offer direct opportunities to create a synergy among business units. For example, if multiple business units require a particular raw material, the procurement of that material can be shared among the business units.

This sharing of the procurement activity can result in cost reduction. Such interrelationships may exist simultaneously in multiple value chain activities. Unfortunately, attempts to achieve synergy from the interrelationships among different business units often fall short of expectations due to unanticipated drawbacks. The cost of coordination, the cost of reduced flexibility, and organizational practicalities should be analysed when devising a strategy to reap the benefits of the synergies.

Outsourcing Value Chain Activities

A firm may specialize in one or more value chain activities and outsource the rest. The extent to which a firm performs upstream and downstream activities is described by its degree of vertical integration. A thorough value chain analysis can illuminate the business system to facilitate outsourcing decisions. To decide which activities to outsource, managers must understand the firm's strengths and weaknesses in each activity, both in terms of cost and ability to differentiate.

Managers may consider the following when selecting activities to outsource:

- Whether the activity can be performed cheaper or better by suppliers.
- Whether the activity is one of the firm's core competencies from which stems a cost advantage or product differentiation.
- The risk of performing the activity in-house. If the activity relies on fast-changing technology or the product is sold in a rapidly-changing market, it may be advantageous to outsource the activity in order to maintain flexibility and avoid the risk of investing in specialized assets.
- Whether the outsourcing of an activity can result in business process improvements such as reduced lead time, higher flexibility, reduced inventory, etc.

THE VALUE CHAIN SYSTEM

A firm may specialize in one or more value chain activities and outsource the rest. The extent to which a firm performs upstream and downstream activities is described by its degree of vertical integration. A thorough value chain analysis can illuminate the business system to facilitate outsourcing decisions. To decide which activities to outsource, managers must understand the firm's strengths and weaknesses in each activity, both in terms of cost and ability to differentiate.

Managers may consider the following when selecting activities to outsource:

- Whether the activity can be performed cheaper or better by suppliers.
- Whether the activity is one of the firm's core competencies from which stems a cost advantage or product differentiation.
- The risk of performing the activity in-house. If the activity relies on fast-changing technology or the product is sold in a rapidly-changing market, it may be advantageous to outsource the activity in order to maintain flexibility and avoid the risk of investing in specialized assets.
- Whether the outsourcing of an activity can result in business process improvements such as reduced lead time, higher flexibility, reduced inventory, etc.

A firm's value chain is part of a larger system that includes the value chains of upstream suppliers and downstream channels and customers.

Porter calls this series of value chains the value system, shown conceptually below:

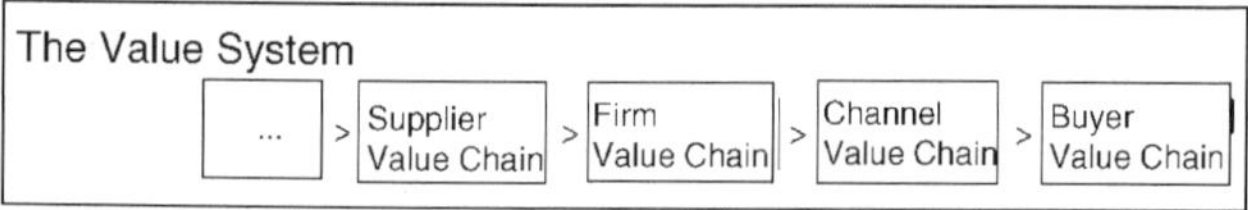

Linkages exist not only in a firm's value chain, but also between value chains. While a firm exhibiting a high degree of vertical integration is poised to better coordinate upstream and downstream activities, a firm having a lesser degree of vertical integration nonetheless can forge agreements with suppliers and channel partners to achieve better coordination. For example, an auto manufacturer may have its suppliers set up facilities in close proximity in order to minimize transport costs and reduce parts inventories. Clearly, a firm's success in developing and sustaining a competitive advantage depends not only on its own value chain, but on its ability to manage the value system of which it is a part.

LIFE-CYCLE COST ANALYSIS

Energy Efficiency and Life-Cycle Cost Analysis

Life-cycle cost (LCC) analysis is the most rational, objective method for selecting the optimum HVAC system for a laboratory facility. Through LCC analysis, all factors that influence total system cost can be identified and quantified. Subjective factors such as fuel cost adjustments, component reliability, and maintenance costs are also included. LCC analysis can be used to assess the economic consequences of any decision by comparing two or more alternatives.

Annual Cost Comparison

Review of the annual cost of space conditioning for a laboratory or cleanroom shows the high impact of energy costs. A Class 10,000 cleanroom system costs five to 10 times as much to operate annually as the conditioning system for the facility's office spaces; a Class 100 laboratory cleanroom system will cost 50 times as much.

In either case, however, the contributions to total cost are:

- Capital costs, *i.e.* interest plus depreciation, contributing 15 to 25 per cent;
- Energy costs, contributing 65 to 75 per cent; and
- Maintenance costs, contributing 10 per cent.

A life-cycle cost analysis does not need to be extremely complex to yield reasonably accurate figures for first and operational costs. A modified LCC, similar to a simple payback, does not account for inflation or cost of money; this modified LCC can give an order-of-magnitude appraisal to help determine whether or not to add an EEM to a system. If LCC computations are easily understood, the analysis is more likely to be used by design teams and accepted by researchers/owners. One approach to simplifying life-cycle cost analysis is to convert facility operating costs to an equivalent annual expense per fume hood. This number can serve as a common denominator for comparing the composite performances of various system designs and for examining the sensitivity of each design alteration. The energy engineer should concentrate on determining realistic values for the most sensitive design factors before selecting the HVAC system type.

LCC Factors

LCC factors that influence a laboratory's HVAC system design can be broken into three categories: design factors, economic factors, and performance factors. Sometimes other factors must be considered; for example, a functional-use factor may be developed based on efficiency studies of personnel in the operations of different laboratory systems or components. Because laboratory personnel LCCs are very high, the more functional a design or system is, the more LCC savings are possible. An example is the workspace flexibility and reduced costs of space planning that can be afforded by a raised floor system.

JUST-IN-TIME

Just-in-time (JIT) is an inventory strategy that strives to improve a business's return on investment by reducing in-process inventory and associated carrying costs. To meet JIT objectives, the process relies on signals or Kanban between different points in the process, which tell production when to make the next part. Kanban are usually 'tickets' but can be simple visual signals, such as the presence or absence of a part on a shelf. Implemented correctly, JIT can improve a manufacturing organization's return on investment, quality, and efficiency. Quick notice that stock depletion requires personnel to order new stock is critical to the inventory reduction at the center of JIT. This saves warehouse space and costs.

However, the complete mechanism for making this work is often misunderstood. For instance, its effective application cannot be independent of other key components of a lean manufacturing system or it can "...end up with the opposite of the desired result.". In recent years manufacturers have continued to try to hone forecasting methods , however some research demonstrates that basing JIT on the presumption of stability is inherently flawed.

Activity-based management

Activity-based management (ABM) is a method of identifying and evaluating activities that a business performs using activity-based costing to carry out a value chain analysis or a re-engineering initiative to improve strategic and operational decisions in an organization. Activity-based costing establishes relationships between overhead costs and activities so that overhead costs can be more precisely allocated to products, services, or customer segments. Activity-based management focuses on managing activities to reduce costs and improve customer value. Kaplan and Cooper. Cost and effect: Using integrated cost systems to drive profitability and performance. (Boston: Harvard Business School Press.)

Divide ABM into operational and strategic:

- Operational ABM is about "doing things right", using ABC information to improve efficiency. Those activities which add value to the product can be identified and improved. Activities that don't add value are the ones that need to be reduced to cut costs without reducing product value.
- Strategic ABM is about "doing the right things", using ABC information to decide which products to develop and which activities to use. This can also be used for customer profitability analysis, identifying which customers are the most profitable and focusing on them more.

A risk with ABM is that some activities have an implicit value, not necessarily reflected in a financial value added to any product. For instance a particularly pleasant workplace can help attract and retain the best staff, but may not be identified as adding value in operational ABM. A customer that represents a loss based on committed activities, but that opens up leads in a new market, may be identified as a low value customer by a strategic ABM process. Managers should interpret these values and use ABM as a "common, yet neutral, ground ... this provides the basis for negotiation". ABM can give middle managers an understanding of costs to other teams to help them make decisions that benefit the whole organisation, not just their activities' bottom line.

Cost-Volume-Profit Analysis

Cost-volume-profit (CVP) analysis expands the use of information provided by breakeven analysis. A critical part of CVP analysis is the point where total revenues equal total costs (both fixed and variable costs). At this breakeven point (BEP), a company will experience no income or loss. This BEP can be an initial examination that precedes more detailed CVP analyses. Cost-volume-profit analysis employs the same basic assumptions as in breakeven analysis.

The assumptions underlying CVP analysis are:

- All units produced are sold.
- Changes in activity are the only factors that affect costs.
- Costs can be classified accurately as either fixed or variable.
- The behaviour of both costs and revenues in linear throughout the relevant range of activity.
- When a company sells more than one type of product, the sales mix will remain constant.

INTERNAL RATE OF RETURN

The Internal Rate of Return (IRR) is the discount rate that generates a zero net present value for a series of future cash flows. This essentially means that IRR is the rate of return that makes the sum of present value of future cash flows and the final market value of a project equal its current market value. Internal Rate of Return provides a simple 'hurdle rate', whereby any project should be avoided if the cost of capital exceeds this rate. Usually a financial calculator has to be used to calculate this IRR, though it can also be mathematically calculated using the following formula:

$$CF_o + \frac{CF_1}{(1+r)^1} + \frac{CF_2}{(1+r)^2} + \frac{CF_3}{(1+r)^3} + \frac{CF_n}{(1+r)_n} + \frac{CF_n}{(1+r)^n} = 0$$

CF is the Cash Flow generated in the specific period. IRR, denoted by 'r' is to be calculated by employing trial and error method. Internal Rate of Return is the flip side of Net Present Value (NPV), where NPV is the discounted value of a stream of cash flows, generated from an investment. IRR thus computes the break-even rate of return showing the discount rate, below which an investment results in a positive NPV. A simple decision-making criteria can be stated to accept a project if its Internal Rate of Return exceeds the cost of capital and rejected if this IRR is less than the cost of capital. However, it should be kept in mind that the use of IRR may result in a number of complexities such as a project with multiple IRRs or no IRR. Moreover, IRR neglects the size of the project and assumes that cash flows are reinvested at a constant rate.

The Modified Internal Rate of Return (MIRR) is an other financial measure used to determine the attractiveness of an investment. In IRR calculations, positive cash flows are assumed to be 'paid' instantly to the investor who can use them immediately to reinvest on a new project. But in reality, the positive cash flows are not paid instantly to the investors, but rather kept by the 'project management entity' until the end of the project. The Modified Internal Rate of Return assumes that the positive cash flows are immediately re-invested until the end of the project. To make these calculations, it is common practice to use the weighted average cost of capital as interest rate on the positive cash flows.

ASPECTS OF DECISION-MAKING

AVERAGE COST

In economics, average cost is equal to total cost divided by the number of goods produced. It is also equal to the sum of average variable costs plus average fixed costs. Average costs may be dependent on the time period considered. Average costs affect the supply curve and are a fundamental component of supply and demand.

$$AC = \frac{TC}{Q}$$

Average cost is distinct from the price, and depends on the interaction with demand through elasticity of demand and elasticity of supply. In cases of perfect competition, price may be lower than average cost due to marginal cost pricing. Average cost will vary in relation to the quantity produced unless fixed costs are zero and variable costs constant. A cost curve can be plotted, with cost on the y-axis and quantity on the x-axis. Marginal costs are often shown on these graphs, with marginal cost representing the cost of the last unit produced at each point; marginal costs are the first derivative of total or variable costs. A typical average cost curve will have a U-shape, because fixed costs are all incurred before any production takes place and marginal costs are typically increasing, because of diminishing marginal productivity.

In this "typical" case, for low levels of production there are economies of scale: marginal costs are below average costs, so average costs are decreasing as quantity increases. An increasing marginal cost curve will intersect a U-shaped average cost curve at its minimum, after which point the average cost curve begins to slope upward. This is indicative of diseconomies of scale. For further increases in production beyond this minimum, marginal cost is above average costs, so average costs are increasing as quantity increases. An example of this typical case would be a factory designed to produce a specific quantity of widgets per period: below a certain production level, average cost is higher due to under-utilised equipment, while above that level, production bottlenecks increase the average cost.

Relationship to Marginal Cost

When average cost is declining as output increases, marginal cost is less than average cost. When average cost is rising, marginal cost is greater than average cost. When average cost is neither rising no average cost.

Other special cases for average cost and marginal cost appear frequently:

- Constant marginal cost/high fixed costs: each additional unit of production is produced at constant additional expense per unit. The average cost curve slopes down continuously, approaching marginal cost. An example may be hydroelectric generation, which has no fuel expense, limited maintenance expenses and a high up-front fixed cost. Industries where fixed marginal costs obtain, such as electrical transmission networks, may meet the conditions for a natural monopoly, because once capacity is built, the marginal cost to the incumbent of serving an additional customer is always lower than the average cost for a potential competitor. The high fixed capital costs are a barrier to entry.
- Minimum efficient scale/maximum efficient scale: marginal or average costs may be non-linear, or have discontinuities. Average cost curves may therefore only be shown over a limited scale of production for a given technology. For example, a nuclear plant would be extremely inefficient for production in small quantities; similarly, its maximum output for any given time period may essentially be fixed, and production above that level may be technically impossible, dangerous or extremely costly. The long run elasticity of supply will be higher, as new plants could be built and brought on-line.
- Low or zero fixed costs / constant marginal cost: since there is no economy of scale, average cost will be close to or equal to marginal cost. Examples may include buy and celling of commodities etc.

Relationship Between AC, AFC, AVC and MC

- The Average Fixed Cost curve starts from a height and goes on declining continuously as production increases.
- The Average Variable Cost curve, Average Cost curve and the Marginal Cost curve start from a height, reach the minimum points, then rise sharply and continuously.

- Marginal Cost curve is the determining curve, while the rest are determined curves.
- The movement in the Marginal Cost curve determines the movement and direction of the other curves.
- The Average Fixed Cost curve nears the Average Cost curve initially and then moves away from it. The Average Variable Cost Curve is never parallel or intersects the Average Cost curve due to the existence of the Average Fixed Cost in all units of production.
- The Marginal Cost curve always passes through the minimum points of the Average Variable Cost and Average Cost curves, though the Average Variable Cost curve attains the minimum point prior to that of the Average Cost curve.

Average fixed cost

Average fixed cost is an economics term used to describe the total fixed costs divided by the quantity (Q) of units produced.

$$AFC = \frac{TFC}{Q}$$

Average fixed cost is a per-unit measure of fixed costs. As the total number of goods produced increases, the average fixed cost decreases because the same amount of fixed costs are being spread over a larger number of units. Average variable cost plus average fixed cost equals average total cost.

$$ATC = AVC + AFC$$

AVERAGE VARIABLE COST

Average variable cost (AVC) is an economics term to describe a firm's variable costs divided by the quantity (Q) of total units of output. It is a cost that a firm must generate from its business if it must continue business because firm must incur it whether it makes profit or not.

$$AVC = \frac{TVC}{Q}$$

Where:

- TVC = Total Variable Cost
- AVC = Average Variable Cost
- Q = Quantity of Units Produced

Average variable cost plus average fixed cost equals average total cost:

$$AVC + AFC = ATC.$$

Cost-minimization analysis

Cost-minimization is the simplest of the pharmaco-economics tools and is applied when comparing two drugs of equal efficacy and equal tolerability.

Therapeutic equivalence must be referenced by the author conducting the study and should have been done prior to the cost-minimization work. Since equal efficacy and equal tolerability is already demonstrated, there is no requirement to find a common efficacy denominator as would be the case when conducting a cost-effectiveness study.

The author is not precluded from doing so through the use of "cost/cure" or "cost/year of life gained". If efficacy and tolerability is demonstrated, however, then a simple comparison of "cost/course of treatment" can suffice for the purpose of comparing two or more therapeutically equivalent treatment alternatives.

How ever when doing so you do run the risk of confusing possible target markets due to the issue of severity of possible deaths occurring. This was the case in New York in 2004 with the well known case 'Murpheys Law' which is now a well known case study for cost minisation. This was all due to severe cost cutting leading to 'Murpheys' death due to a large back lash from his employees resulting in his death! Cost minimisation should be carefully considered before being implomented. When conducting a cost-minimization study, the author needs to measure all costs inherent to the delivery of the therapeutic intervention and that are relevant to the pharmacoeconomic perspective.

COST/BENEFIT ANALYSIS

You may have been intensely creative in generating solutions to a problem, and rigorous in your selection of the best one available. However, this solution may still not be worth implementing, as you may invest a lot of time and money in solving a problem that is not worthy of this effort. Cost Benefit Analysis or CBA is a relatively* simple and widely used technique for deciding whether to make a change.

As its name suggests, you simply add up the value of the benefits of a course of action, and subtract the costs associated with it. Costs are either one-off, or may be ongoing. Benefits are most often received over time. We build this effect of time into our analysis by calculating a payback period. This is the time it takes for the benefits of a change to repay its costs. Many companies look for payback on projects over a specified period of time *e.g.* three years.

How to Use the Tool

In its simple form, cost-benefit analysis is carried out using only financial costs and financial benefits. For example, a simple cost benefit ratio for a road scheme would measure the cost of building the road, and subtract this from the economic benefit of improving transport links. It would not measure either the cost of environmental damage or the benefit of quicker and easier travel to work. A more sophisticated approach to building a cost benefit models is to try to put a financial value on intangible costs and benefits.

This can be highly subjective - is, for example, a historic water meadow worth $25,000, or is it worth $500,000 because if its environmental importance? What is the value of stress-free travel to work in the morning? These are all questions that people have to answer, and answers that people have to defend.

The version of the cost benefit approach we explain here is necessarily simple. Where large sums of money are involved project evaluation can become an extremely complex and sophisticated art. The fundamentals of this are explained in Principles of Corporate Finance by Richard Brealey and Stewart Myers - this is something of an authority on the subject.

Example

A sales director is deciding whether to implement a new computer-based contact management and sales processing system. His department has only a few computers, and his salespeople are not computer literate. He is aware that computerized sales forces are able to contact more customers and give a higher quality of reliability and service to those customers. They are more able to meet commitments, and can work more efficiently with fulfillment and delivery staff.

His financial cost/benefit analysis is shown below:

Costs:

- 10 network-ready PCs with supporting software @ $2,450 each
- 1 server @ $3,500
- 3 printers @ $1,200 each
- Cabling and Installation @ $4,600
- Sales Support Software @ $15,000

Training costs:

- Computer introduction - 8 people @ $400 each
- Keyboard skills - 8 people @ $400 each
- Sales Support System - 12 people @ $700 each

Other costs:

- Lost time: 40 man days @ $200 / day
- Lost sales through disruption: estimate: $20,000
- Lost sales through inefficiency during first months: estimate: $20,000

Benefits:

- Tripling of mail shot capacity: estimate: $40,000 / year
- Ability to sustain telesales campaigns: estimate: $20,000 / year
- Improved efficiency and reliability of follow-up: estimate: $50,000 / year
- Improved customer service and retention: estimate: $30,000 / year
- Improved accuracy of customer information: estimate: $10,000 / year

- More ability to manage sales effort: \$30,000 / year

COST-EFFECTIVENESS ANALYSIS

Cost-effectiveness analysis (CEA) is a technique for selecting among competing wants wherever resources are limited. Developed in the military, CEA was first applied to health care in the mid-1960s and was introduced with enthusiasm to clinicians by Weinstein and Stason in 1977:

- "If these approaches were to become widely understood and accepted by the key decision makers in the health-care sector, including the physician, important health benefits or cost savings might be realised."

Regardless of whether this hope was realised, CEA has since become a common feature in medical literature.

THE BASICS OF CEA

CEA is a technique for comparing the relative value of various clinical strategies. In its most common form, a new strategy is compared with current practice in the calculation of the cost-effectiveness ratio:

$$\text{CE ratio} = \frac{\text{cost}_{\text{new strategy}} - \text{cost}_{\text{currentpractice}}}{\text{effect}_{\text{new strategy}} - \text{effect}_{\text{current pratice}}}$$

The result might be considered as the "price" of the additional outcome purchased by switching from current practice to the new strategy. If the price is low enough, the new strategy is considered "cost-effective." It's important to carefully consider exactly what that statement means. If a strategy is dubbed "cost-effective" and the term is used as its creators intended, it means that the new strategy is a good value. Note that being cost-effective does not mean that the strategy saves money, and just because a strategy saves money doesn't mean that it is cost-effective.

Also note that the very notion of cost-effective requires a value judgment—what you think is a good price for an additional outcome, someone else may not. It's also worthwhile to recognize that CEA is only relevant to certain decisions. The various way a new strategy might compare with an existing approach. Note that a CEA is relevant only if a new strategy is *both* more effective and more costly.

TRANSACTION COSTS

Transaction costs are commissions and processing charges incurred as part of a business transaction. In some cases, this transaction cost is a percentage of the total sale. In other cases, it may be a flat fee. In general, the money spent on the transaction costs is often referred to as a *spread*. Understanding transaction costs is very important for anyone who is looking to buy or sell any financial product, whether it is stocks, bonds, currency or valuable metals. It does not matter whether you are buying or selling assets, transaction costs can be incurred in a number of different situations. It is important to read all policies and agreements of the company executing the transaction in order to have full awareness of which transaction costs you may incur.

One of the most common types of transaction costs is the buy/sell spread. While they can go by several different names, spreads are the costs that an investment manager charges to execute a transaction. To provide a real-world example, let's assume the currency exchange rate is $2 US Dollar for every 1 Euro.

Though someone may expect to get 5 Euros if they pay $10 USD, it is likely that he will receive somewhat less than that. Why is it that a trader may get less than the published rate? Because of the buy/sell spread. The person or agency executing the trade takes out a cut in order to provide the service. The amount charged for that service will likely be different, depending on the person or firm.

Some firms will actually use their transaction costs as an incentive to attract customers. If an investment firm has a competitive rate in their transaction costs, this can lead to a substantial cost savings for an investor, especially if that investor executes a large number of trades as a general practice. Though it is not as prevalent as it once was, several trading firms specializing in online trades advertise their transaction costs regularly.

TOTAL COST

In economics, and cost accounting, total cost describes the total economic cost of production and is made up of variable costs, which vary just as to the quantity of a good produced and include inputs such as labour and raw materials, plus fixed costs, which are independent of the quantity of a good produced and include inputs that cannot be varied in the short term, such as buildings and machinery. Total cost in economics includes the total opportunity cost of each factor of production in addition to fixed and variable costs.

The rate at which total cost changes as the amount produced changes is called marginal cost. This is also known as the marginal unit variable cost. If one assumes that the unit variable cost is constant, as in cost-volume-profit analysis developed and used in cost accounting by the accountants, then total cost is linear in volume, and given by: total cost = fixed costs + unit variable cost * amount.

ABSORPTION COSTING

Absorption costing is a method for appraising or valuing a firm's total inventory by including all the manufacturing costs incurred to produce those goods. These manufacturing costs include.

Product Costs

- *Direct Materials*: These are the raw materials such as wood, metal, bricks, etc that are used in order to create a finished usable good which will be demanded by the market.
- *Direct Labour*: Direct Labour is the manwork and total factory hours put behind assembling the raw materials, creating the finished good, etc.
- *Fixed Manufacturing Overhead*: This includes expenses such as rent of factory where the raw materials are turned into finished goods, amortization of factory building, utilities, etc.
- *Variable Manufacturing Overhead*: These are the general and administrative expenses in the manufacturing process.

Absorption costing is different from the other costing methods because it takes into account fixed manufacturing overhead. It is hard to factor in the fixed manufacturing overhead expenses into calculating the per unit price of goods, therefore other methods such as Variable Costing do not take it into account. One drawback of absorption costing is that managers can increase production levels without taking into account total sales. With higher production levels, this year's expenses can be deferred to next year, thus lowering this year's costs. What does this mean? The managers get a fat bonus and pay raises thanks to more "profits."

Inventory Production and Absorption Costing

When beginning inventory and ending inventory levels are different, profit calculations using the Absorption costing can be difficult. Here are the effects of fluctuating inventory levels:

- If Beginning Inventory = Ending Inventory, then Absorption Costing = Variable Costing
- If Inventory Levels = Low, then Variable Costing Profit > Absorption Costing Profit
- If Inventory Levels = High, then Absorption Costing Profit >Variable Costing Profit

SUNK COSTS

Sunk costs are sums that have already been spent and can not be recovered. The concept is important because sunk costs are irrelevant to financial decisions. Many people tend to feel instinctively that because an investment has been made it is necessary to get a return on it. This can lead to people rejecting one course of action in favour of another that actually generates smaller cash flows. This can happen to business, portfolio investment and personal decisions. Suppose a hotel has calculated that their cost for providing a room is £100 per night, of which £50 covers their rental of the building and £20 covers their other fixed costs and £30 covers the costs that result from having an extra guest. Now suppose the market rate for hotel rooms goes down and they are only able to charge £50 per night. The hotel is committed to remaining open. It appears that the hotel will make a £50 loss on each night per guest so they should not accept bookings until prices rise. Of course this is wrong as the rent and other fixed costs are already committed to and have to be paid anyway.

The hotel should accept bookings at any price it can get above £30, as these make a positive contribution. A common mistake made by investors is reluctance to sell securities at a loss. It does not matter what you paid for shares, if the market price has fallen you have already made that loss. It is a sunk cost and should be forgotten about. What matters is whether the shares are worth holding or not at the current market price. A key question is whether the shares would still be worth buying at current prices. If not, they are probably not worth holding.

SEMI-VARIABLE COSTS

Semi-variable costs are those that have both fixed cost and variable cost elements. For example, a manufacturer's electricity bill may include elements that are fixed and elements that are variable.

SEARCH COST

Search costs are one facet of transaction costs or switching costs. Rational consumers will continue to search for a better product or service until the marginal cost of searching exceeds the marginal benefit. Search theory is a branch of microeconomics that studies decisions of this type. The costs of searching are divided into external and internal costs. External costs include the monetary costs of acquiring the information, and the opportunity cost of the time taken up in searching. External costs are not under the consumer's control. All they can do is choose whether or not to incur them. Internal costs include the mental effort given over to undertaking the search, sorting the incoming information, and integrating it with what the consumer already knows. Internal costs are determined by the consumer's ability to undertake the search, and this in turn depends on intelligence, prior knowledge, education and training.

These internal costs are the background to the study of bounded rationality. The Internet was expected to eliminate search costs. For example, electronic commerce was predicted to cause disintermediation as search costs become low enough for end-consumers to incur them directly instead of employing retailers to do this for them. This would in turn lead to lower prices and less variation between prices quoted by different sellers.

REPUGNANCY COSTS

Repugnancy costs are costs borne by an individual or entity as a result of a stimulus that goes against that individual or entity's cultural mores. The cost could be emotional, physical, mental or figurative.

The stimulus could be anything from food to people to an idea. These costs are perspective-dependent and individual. These costs may be different for different groups of people; countries, states, ethnicities, etc. The term allows for a clear and understandable way of representing the concept of contextual stigma in a literal and applicable sense.

QUALITY COST

Quality cost is the sum of all costs a company invests into the release of a quality product. When developing a software product, there are four types of quality costs: prevention costs, appraisal costs, internal failure costs, and external failure costs.

1. Prevention costs represent everything a company spends to prevent software errors, documentation errors, and other product-related errors. These include requirements and usability analysis, for example. Dollars spent on prevention costs are the most effective quality dollars, because preventing errors from getting into the product is much cheaper than fixing errors later. If there is an error in a requirement or the intended usability, and money is spent on developing the software to the erroneous requirement, the costs of identifying the error, determining how to fix it, and then developing new code to correct it will arise later.
2. Appraisal costs include the money spent on the actual testing activity. Any and all activities associated with searching for errors in the software and associated product materials falls into this category. This includes all testing: by the developers themselves, by an internal test team, and by an outsourced software test organization. This also includes all associated hardware, software, labour, and other costs. Once a product is in the coding phases, the goal is to do the most effective appraisal job, so that internal failure work is streamlined and well-managed and prevents skyrocketing external failure costs.
3. Internal failure costs are the costs of coping with errors discovered during development and testing. These are bugs found before the product is released. The further in the development process the errors are discovered, the more costly they are to fix. So the later the errors are discovered, the higher their associated internal failure costs will be.
4. External failure costs are the costs of coping with errors discovered after the product is released. These are typically errors found by your customers. These costs can be much higher than internal failure costs, because the stakes are much higher. These costs include post-release customer and technical support. Errors at this stage can also be costly in terms of your company's reputation and may lead to lost customers.

The Four Categories of Quality Costs

All the costs can be effectively reduced through smarter test efforts that include a high degree of test automation. Test automation when done right leads to greater test coverage, resulting in higher-quality products. Higher-quality products require less technical support, fewer patches, and lead to greater customer satisfaction. Smarter automated testing also speeds up the release process and incrementally reduces the manual test costs.

But most of all, more test coverage gives you and your customers more confidence in your product. You will feel more comfortable knowing that there are not bugs lurking in your software that have not been exposed yet because of insufficient test coverage.

You will also not have to scramble at the last minute to deal with a problem and fix it to your customer's satisfaction in a rush. The solution to quality cost problems is to get a better understanding of your investment in product quality and manage your costs better. The first place most organizations look for a better understanding is in the highest cost area: the software test effort or lack thereof. For example, if you do not test at all, your testing or appraisal cost is low.

You will ship on time but your external failure costs will skyrocket. Your prevention and appraisal costs will result in finding errors that can be corrected while they are still internal failures, where they are cheaper to deal with than when they are external failures. The goal of understanding quality costs is to analyse where you spend your time and money to get the most bang for the buck.

It is well known that it is faster and cheaper to find and fix a bug during unit testing done by developers early in the development cycle. Should we then spend most of our time/budget on unit testing? No.

here are many limitations to unit testing. Unit testing is not capable of finding many varieties of bugs, including graphical user interface (GUI) bugs, usability problems, end-to-end bugs, and configuration bugs.

For most organizations, getting a better unit test effort will help you release a better product sooner. It is not a replacement for the test effort done by skilled software testers, but it may reduce the time that test effort takes. Understanding quality costs will hopefully help you shift some of your test effort to the most cost-effective places.

The total quality cost is shown in the upper bathtub-shaped curve. On the bottom axis is the quality of performance, ranging from totally defective to zero defects. On the left axis is the cost per good unit of product. You can see that with highly defective software, your prevention and appraisal costs are very low, but your failure costs are very high, yielding a high total quality cost.

With zero defect software, likewise, your failure costs are very low, but your prevention and appraisal costs are very high. To optimize your total quality costs, you want to be between these extremes, at the bottom of the bathtub curve.

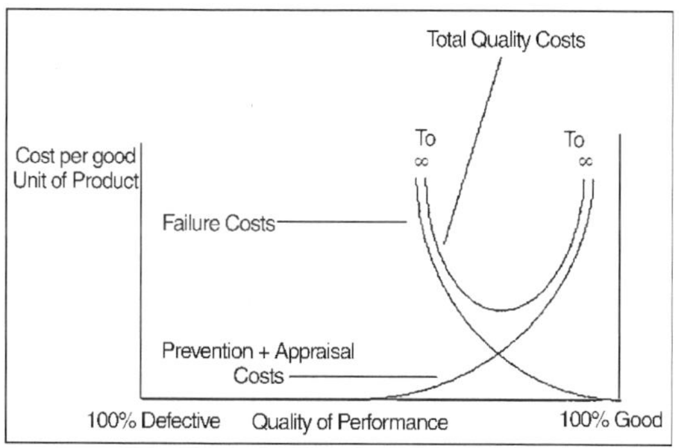

The Oretical Model of Optimum Quality Cost

This offers two challenges: First, a sufficiently sophisticated accounting system allowing a typical mid-sized company to track the total cost of quality has yet to be developed. To optimize total quality cost, you need to have the appropriate categories in your accounting system and keep track of the related costs. Second, you need to be able to track your external quality costs. You may not even have enough information from customers on why the software is not working for them.

How are you going to know what to book into your accounting system for external failure costs? The point here is that while capturing this data is difficult and expensive, you know that the benefit is reducing your overall cost of quality. You need to determine if the benefits of tracking your total quality cost will give you enough of a return on investment to make setting up the appropriate accounting system and paying for the implementation of the programme worthwhile.

ECONOMIC COST

The economic cost of a decision depends on both the cost of the alternative chosen and the benefit that the best alternative would have provided if chosen. Economic cost differs from accounting cost because it includes opportunity cost. As an example, consider the economic cost of attending college. The accounting cost of attending college includes tuition, room and board, books, food, and other incidental expenditures while there. The opportunity cost of college also includes the salary or wage that otherwise could be earning during the period. So for the two to four years an individual spends in school, the opportunity cost includes the money that one could have been making at the best possible job.

The economic cost of college is the accounting cost plus the opportunity cost. Thus, if attending college has a direct cost of $20,000 dollars a year for four years, and the lost wages from not working during that period equals

$25,000 dollars a year, then the total economic cost of going to college would be $180,000 dollars ($20,000 x 4 years + $25,000 x 4 years).

EXPLICIT COST

An explicit cost is an easily accounted cost, such as wage, rent and materials. It can be transacted in the form of money payment and is lost directly, as opposed to monetary implicit costs. Explicit cost are those which the entrepreneur has to pay from his own pocket. Explicit costs require an outlay of money by the firm.

Implicit Costs, Explicit Costs, and Total Costs

Implicit cost + explicit cost = total cost. Implicit cost is not equal to total cost, but a component of it. A simple example: Sean builds a cabinet. He spends 2 hours building the cabinet. He could have been working instead and normally makes $25/hour at his job. Since he was building a cabinet he wasn't paid for this time.

The materials to make the cabinet cost him $20;

- His Explicit Costs are: $20 in materials
- His Implicit Costs are: $25/hr x 2 hrs= $50 of foregone pay
- His Total Costs are: $20 in materials + $50 of foregone pay = $70 Total Costs

INDIRECT COSTS

Indirect costs are costs that are not directly accountable to a cost object. Indirect costs may be either fixed or variable. Indirect costs include taxes, administration, personnel and security costs, and are also known as overhead.

Indirect vs. Direct Costs

Direct costs are those for activities or services that benefit specific projects, *e.g.*, salaries for project staff and materials required for a particular project. Because these activities are easily traced to projects, their costs are usually charged to projects on an item-by-item basis.

Indirect costs are those for activities or services that benefit more than one project. Their precise benefits to a specific project are often difficult or impossible to trace. For example, it may be difficult to determine precisely how the activities of the director of an organization benefit a specific project.

It is possible to justify the handling of almost any kind of cost as either direct or indirect. Labour costs, for example, can be indirect, as in the case of maintenance personnel and executive officers; or they can be direct, as in the case of project staff members.

Similarly, materials such as miscellaneous supplies purchased in bulk—pencils, pens, paper—are typically handled as indirect costs, while materials required for specific projects are charged as direct costs.

ISOCOST

In economics an isocost line represents a combination of inputs which all cost the same amount. Although similar to the budget constraint in consumer theory, the use of the isocost pertains to cost-minimization in production, as opposed to utility-maximization.

The typical isocost line represents the ratio of costs of labour and capital, so the formula is often written as:

$$rK + wL = C$$

Where w represents the wage of labour, and r represents the rental rate of capital.

The slope is:

$$-w / r$$

or the negative ratio of wages divided by rental fees.
The isocost line is combined with the isoquant line to determine the optimal production point.

The Cost Function for a Firm with Two Variable Inputs

Consider a firm that uses two inputs and has the production function F. This firm minimizes its cost of producing any given output y if it chooses the pair (z1, z2) of inputs to solve the problem Min z1,z2w1s conditional input demand functions. The firm's minimal cost of producing the output y is w1z1*(y,w1, w2) + w2z2*(y,w1, w2) (the value of its total cost for the values of z1 and z2 that minimize that cost). The function TC defined by

$$TC(y,w1,w2) = w1z1 * (y,w1,w2) + w2z2 * (y,w1,w2)$$

Which is called the firm's (total) cost function. (Note that the hard part of the problem is finding the conditional input demands; once you have found these, then finding the cost function is simply a matter of adding the conditional input ogether with thc weights w1 and w2.). An Isocost line shows all the combinations of capital and labour that can be bought for a given total cost"

LOCK-IN (DECISION-MAKING)

Lock-in can be seen as the escalating commitment of decision-makers to an ineffective course of action. It concerns institutional lock-in as compared to technical lock-in of which the QWERTY keyboard is a famous example. The decision-making process is characterised by various informal and formal decision-making moments and decision-makers can become committed to the project before the formal decision to build was taken.

The formation of commitment is not necessarily bad, but when commitment turns into lock-in, it has by definition a negative influence on the project performance. Lock-in can occur at the decision-making level or at the project level. There are possibilities to avoid lock-in when decision-makers can be made aware of this phenomenon. However, lock-in can also be used intentionally, in which case, it is much more difficult to prevent and hence manage cost overruns.

Decision Making Process

The decision-making process of large infrastructure projects is marked by the formal decision to build the project. However, there are several possible moments in the decision-making process before the formal decision is taken at which decision-makers are committed to the project.

The extent of which decision-makers are committed to the project is of importance here. Early commitment, commitment to the project before the formal decision to build has been taken, is in itself not necessarily negative. It could be advantageous to the decision-making process as it could enforce a decision.

This eventually could limit delay and contribute to the projects' performance. Early commitment can result in negative outcomes once the commitment turns into escalating commitment and lock-in. As lock-in is based on escalating commitment, it has, by definition, a negative influence on project performance. Lock-in has the potential to explain the large cost overruns in large scale transportation infrastructure projects.

Formation

Lock-in with respect to decision-making is created when sub-optimal policies are used as a consequence of *e.g.* path dependency, even though a better alternative is present. The term refers to the escalating commitment of decision-makers to an ineffective course of action. Escalating commitment itself refers to the style of psychological coping associated with the inability to withdraw from obligations. The process of escalating commitment is also known as "entrapment" , the "sunk-cost effect" , the "knee-deep in the big muddy" effect , and the "too-much-invested-to-quit" effect.

Occurrence

Lock-in can occur both at the decision-making level and can influence the extent of overruns in two ways:

1. The first involves the "methodology" of calculating cost overruns just as to the "formal decision to build". Due to lock-in, however, the "real decision to build" is made much earlier in the decision-making process and the costs estimated at that stage are often much lower than those that are estimated at a later stage in the decision-making process, thus increasing cost overruns.
2. The second way that lock-in can affect cost overruns is through "practice". Although decisions about the project need to be made, lock-in can lead to inefficient decisions that involve higher costs. Sunk costs in terms of both time and money, the need for justification,

escalating commitment , and inflexibility and the closure of alternatives are indicators of lock-in.

Prevention

There are different types of lock-in; conscious/unconscious and intentional/ unintentional lock-in. Some of these types of lock-in can be avoided. Decision-makers can be made conscious about their behaviour, for example by confronting them with the lack of sufficient alternatives. When these decision-makers are willing to change their behaviour and consider other alternatives, they are less likely to become committed to one project alternative and hence, the chance for lock-in can be partly avoided.

However, other types of lock-in are more difficult to control, especially intentional lock-in. Intentional lock-in is the result of specific behaviour of parties that act deliberately in the interest of their project. Cost overruns may thus be partly unnecessary or avoidable if such deliberate creation of lock-in had not taken place, and be partly unavoidable due to the incapacity of decision-makers to make optimal decisions.

MARGINAL COST OF CAPITAL SCHEDULE

Marginal Cost of Capital (MCC) Schedule is a graph that relates the Cost of Capital (MCC) Schedule is a graph that relates the firm's weighted average cost of each dollar of capital to the total amount of new capital raised. The WACC is the minimum rate of return allowable, and still meeting financial obligationts such as debt, interest payments, dividends etc... Therefore, the WACC averages the required returns from all long-term financing sources. The WACC is based on cash flows, which are after-tax. By the same notion then, the WACC should be calculated on an after-tax basis.

MARGINAL COST

In economics and finance, marginal cost is the change in total cost that arises when the quantity produced changes by one unit. That is, it is the cost of producing one more unit of a good. Mathematically, the marginal cost (MC) function is expressed as the first derivative of the total cost (TC) function with respect to quantity (Q). Note that the marginal cost may change with volume, and so at each level of production, the marginal cost is the cost of the next unit produced.

$$MC = \frac{dTC}{dQ}$$

In general terms, marginal cost at each level of production includes any additional costs required to produce the next unit. If producing additional vehicles requires, for example, building a new factory, the marginal cost of those extra vehicles includes the cost of the new factory. In practice, the analysis is segregated into short and long-run cases, and over the longest run, all costs are marginal.

At each level of production and time period being considered, marginal costs include all costs which vary with the level of production, and other costs are considered fixed costs. A number of other factors can affect marginal cost and its applicability to real world problems. Some of these may be considered market failures. These may include information asymmetries, the presence of negative or positive externalities, transaction costs, price discrimination and others.

Cost Functions and Relationship to Average Cost

In the simplest case, the total cost function and its derivative are expressed as follows, where Q represents the production quantity, VC represents variable costs, FC represents fixed costs and TC represents total costs.

$$MC = \frac{dTC}{dQ} = \frac{d(FC + VC)}{dQ} = \frac{dVC}{dQ}$$

Since fixed costs do not vary with production quantity, it drops out of the equation when it is differentiated. The important conclusion is that marginal cost is not related to fixed costs. This can be compared with average total cost or ATC, which is the total cost divided by the number of units produced and does include fixed costs.

$$ATC = \frac{FC + VC}{Q}$$

For discrete calculation without calculus, marginal cost equals the change in total cost that comes with each additional unit produced. For instance, suppose the total cost of making 1 shoe is \$30 and the total cost of making 2 shoes is \$40. The marginal cost of producing the second shoe is \$40 - \$30 = \$10.

Economies of Scale

Production may be subject to economies of scale. Increasing returns to scale are said to exist if additional units can be produced for less than the previous unit, that is, average cost is falling. This can only occur if average cost at any given level of production is higher than the marginal cost. Conversely, there may be levels of production where marginal cost is higher than average cost, and average cost will rise for each unit of production after that point.

This type of production function is generally known as diminishing marginal productivity: at low levels of production, productivity gains are easy and marginal costs falling, but productivity gains become smaller as production increases; eventually, marginal costs rise because increasing output becomes more expensive. For this generic case, minimum average cost occurs at the point where average cost and marginal cost are equal; this point will not be at the minimum for marginal cost if fixed costs are greater than zero.

Externalities

Externalities are costs that are not borne by the parties to the economic transaction. A producer may, for example, pollute the environment, and others may bear those costs. A consumer may consume a good which produces benefits for society, such as education; because the individual does not receive all of the benefits, he may consume less than efficiency would suggest. Alternatively, an individual may be a smoker or alcoholic and impose costs on others. In these cases, production or consumption of the good in question may differ from the optimum level.

Negative Externalities of Production

Much of the time, private and social costs do not diverge from one another, but at times social costs may be either greater or less than private costs. When marginal social costs of production are greater than that of the private cost function, we see the occurrence of a negative externality of production. Productive processes that result in pollution are a textbook example of production that creates negative externalities. Such externalities are a result of firms externalising their costs onto a third party in order to reduce their own total cost.

As a result of externalising such costs we see that members of society will be negatively affected by such behaviour of the firm. In this case, we see that an increased cost of production on society creates a social cost curve that depicts a greater cost than the private cost curve. In an equilibrium state we see that markets creating negative externalities of production will overproduce that good. As a result, the socially optimal production level would be lower than that observed.

Positive Externalities of Production

When marginal social costs of production are less than that of the private cost function, we see the occurrence of a positive externality of production. Production of public goods are a textbook example of production that create positive externalities. An example of such a public good, which creates a divergence in social and private costs, includes the production of education.

It is often seen that education is a positive for any whole society, as well as a positive for those directly involved in the market. We see that such production creates a social cost curve that is less than that of the private curve. In an equilibrium state we see that markets creating positive externalities of production will under produce that good. As a result, the socially optimal production level would be greater than that observed.

Social Costs

Of great importance in the theory of marginal cost is the distinction between the marginal private and social costs. the marginal private cost shows the cost associated to the firm in question. it is the marginal private cost that is used by business decision makers in their profit maximization goals, and by individuals in their purchasing and consumption choices. marginal social cost is similar to private cost in that it includes the cost functions of private enterprise but also that of society as a whole, including parties that have no direct association with the private costs of production.

It incorporates all negative and positive externalities, of both production and consumption. hence, when deciding whether or how much to buy, buyers take account of the cost to society of their actions if private and social marginal cost coincide. the equality of price with social marginal cost, by aligning the interest of the buyer with the interest of the community as a whole is a necessary condition for economically efficient resource allocation.

IMPORTANCE OF OPPORTUNITY COST

The concept of opportunity cost is very important in the following areas of managerial decision making:

1. *Decision-Making and Efficient Resource Allocation:* The concept of opportunity cost is very important for rational decision-making by the producer. Suppose, a producer has to decide whether he should produce black and white T.V. or colour T.V. from his given resources. He can come to rational decision only by measuring opportunity cost of production of both types of T.V. and by comparing these products with existing market prices.
   As a result, efficient allocation of resources will also be possible. A resource will always be used in that business where it will have the highest opportunity cost. For example, if a graduate is receiving ` 3,000 as a shop assistant but can earn ` 5,000 as a clerk, then he will join the job of a clerk leaving the shop because his opportunity cost is high.
2. *Determination of Relative Prices of Goods:* If the same group of resources can produce either a colour T.V. or four black and white T. V.s, the price of a colour T.V. will be kept equal to at least a four-fold price of a black and white T.V. Hence, the concept of opportunity cost is useful in the determination of relative prices of various goods.
3. *Determination of Normal Remuneration of a Factor:* Opportunity cost determines the price for the best alternative use of a factor of production. Suppose a manager can earn ` 20,000 per month as a lecturer in a management school, the firm will have to pay him at least ` 20,000 for continuing his service as a manager.

Hence, it is obvious that the concept of opportunity cost has special importance in management.

Direct Costs and Indirect Costs

Direct costs are the costs that have direct relationship with a unit of operation, *i.e.*, they can be easily and directly identified or attributed to a particular product, operation or plant. For example, the salary of a branch manager, when the branch is a costing unit, is a direct cost. Direct costs directly enter into the cost of production but retain their separate identity.

On the other hand, indirect costs are those costs whose source cannot be easily and definitely traced to a plant, a product, a process or a department, such as electricity, stationery and other office expenses, depreciation on building, decoration expenses, etc. All the direct costs are variable because they are linked to a particular product or department. Therefore, they vary with changes in them. On the contrary, indirect costs may or may not be variable.

Private and Social Costs

Private costs are the costs incurred by a firm in producing a commodity or service. These ^ include both explicit and implicit costs. However, the production activities of a firm may lead to eco-nomic benefit or harm for others. For example, production of commodities like steel, rubber and chemi-cals, pollutes the environment which leads to social costs.

On the other hand, production of such services as education, sanitation services, park facilities, etc. leads to social benefits. Take for instance, education which not only provides higher incomes and other satisfactions to the recipients but also more enlightened citizens to the society. If we add together the private costs of production and economic damage upon others such as environmental pollution, etc., we arrive at social costs.

Incremental Costs and Sunk Costs

Incremental costs denote the total additional costs associated with the marginal batch of output. These costs are the additions to costs resulting from a change in the nature and level of business activity, *e.g.*, change in product line or output level, adding or replacing a machine, changes in distribution channels, etc. In the long-run, firms expand their production, employ more men, materials, machinery and equipment. All these expenses are incremental costs.

Sunk costs are the costs that are not affected or altered by a change in the level or nature of business activity. It cannot be altered, increased or decreased by varying the level of activity or the rate of output. All past or actual costs are regarded as sunk costs. Thus, sunk costs are irrelevant for decision making as they do not vary with the changes expected for future by the management, whereas incremental costs are relevant to the management for business making.

Explicit Costs and Implicit Costs

Explicit costs are those payments that must be made to the factors hired from outside the control of the firm. They are the monetary payments made by the entrepreneur for purchasing or hiring the services of various productive factors which do not belong to him. Such payments as rent, wages, interest, salaries, payment for raw materials, fuel, power, insurance premium, etc. are examples of explicit costs.

Implicit costs refer to the payments made to the self-owned resources used in production. They are the earnings of owner's resources employed in their best alternative uses. For example, a business-man utilises his services in his own business leaving his job as a manager in a company.

Thus, he foregoes his salary as a manager. This loss of salary becomes an implicit cost of his own business. Implicit costs are also known as imputed costs. They are important for calculation of profit and loss account. They play a crucial role in the analysis of business decisions.

Historical and Replacement Costs

The historical cost is the actual cost of an asset incurred at the time the asset was acquired. It means the cost of a plant at a price originally paid for it. In contrast, replacement cost means the price that would have to be paid currently for acquiring the same plant. So historical costs are the past costs and replacement costs are the present costs.

Price changes over time cause a difference between historical costs and replacement costs. For example, suppose that the price of a machine in 1995 was ₹ 1, 00,000 and its present price is ₹ 2, 50,000, the actual cost of ₹ 1, 00,000 is the historical cost while ₹ 2, 50,000 is the replacement cost.

The concept of replacement cost is very useful for the management. It projects a true picture while the historical cost gives poor projection to the management. Historical cost of assets is used for accounting purposes, in the assessment of net worth of the firm, while the replacement cost is used for business decision regarding the renovation of the firm.

Past Costs and Future Costs

Past costs are the costs which have been actually incurred in the past. They are beyond the control of the management because they are already incurred. These costs can be evaluated with retro-spective effect. On the contrary, future costs refer to the costs that are reasonably expected to be incurred in some future periods.

They involve forecasting for control of expenses, appraisal of capital expenditure decisions on new projects as well as expansion programmes and profit-loss projections through proper costing under assumed cost conditions.

The management is more interested in future costs because it can exercise some control over them. If the management considers the future cost too high, it can either plan to reduce them or find out sources to meet them. These costs are also called avoidable costs or controllable costs.

Business Costs and Full Costs

Business costs are the costs which include all the payments and contractual obligations made by the firm together with the book cost of depreciation on plant and equipment.

They are relevant for the calculation of profits and losses in business, and for legal and tax purposes. In contrast, full costs consist of opportunity costs and normal profit. Opportunity costs are the expected earnings from the next best use of the firm's resources. Normal profit is the minimum profit required for the existence of a firm.

Common Production Costs and Joint Costs

Sometimes, two or more than two products emerge from a common production process and from a single raw material. For example, the same piece of leather may be used for slippers or shoes. Such products present some peculiar and important problems for the management. They are identifiable as separate products only at the end of the process. So the costs incurred upto this point are common costs. Thus, common costs are the costs which cannot be traced to separate products in any direct manner.

When an increase in the production of one product results in an increase in the output of another product, such products are joint products and their costs are joint costs. For example, when gas is produced from coal, coke and other products also emerge automatically. Likewise, wheat and straw, cotton and cotton seeds may be its other examples.

Shutdown Costs and Abandonment Costs

Shutdown costs are the costs that are incurred in the case of a closure of plant operations. If the operations are continued, these costs can be saved. These costs include all types of fixed costs, the costs of sheltering plant and equipment, lay-off expenses, employment and training of workers when the operation is restarted. On the other hand, abandonment costs are the costs which are incurred because of retiring altogether a plant from use. These costs are related to the problem of disposal of assets. For example, the costs are related to the discontinuance of tram services in Delhi.

These concepts of costs are very important for the management when they have to make deci-sions regarding the continuance of existing plant, suspension of its operations or its closure.

Out-of-Pocket Costs and Book Costs

The costs which include cash payments or cash transfers that may be recurring or non-recurring are called out-of-pocket costs. All the explicit costs such as rent, wages, interest, transport charges, etc. are out-of-pocket costs. They are also called explicit costs. Book costs are the actual business costs which enter into book accounts but are not paid in cash. They are considered while finalising the profit and loss accounts. For example, depreciation which does not require current cash payments. They are also called imputed costs. Book costs may be converted into out-of-pocket costs. If a factor of production is owned, that is book cost. But, if it is hired, that is out-of-pocket cost.

Urgent Costs and Postponable Costs

Urgent costs are those costs that are necessary for the continuation of the firm's activities. The cost of raw materials, labour, fuel, etc. may be its examples which have to be incurred if production is to take place. The costs which can be postponed for some time, *i.e.*, whose postponement does not affect the operational efficiency of the firm are called postponable costs. For example, maintenance costs which can be postponed for the time-being. This distinction of cost is very useful during war and inflation.

ESCAPABLE COSTS AND UNAVOIDABLE COSTS

Escapable costs are the costs which can be reduced by contraction in business activities. Here, net effect on costs is important. However, it is difficult to estimate indirect effects such as the closure of an unprofitable business unit which will reduce costs but will increase the other related expenses like transportation charges, etc. On the other hand, unavoidable costs are the costs which do not vary with changes in the level of production, but they are unavoidable such as fixed costs.

INCREMENTAL COSTS AND MARGINAL COSTS

There is close relation between marginal cost and incremental cost. But they have difference also. In reality, incremental cost is used in a broad sense in relation to marginal cost. Marginal cost is the cost of producing an additional unit of output, while incremental cost is defined as the change in cost resulting from a change in business activities. In other words, incremental cost is the total additional cost related to marginal quantity of output. The concept of incremental cost is very important in the business world because, in practice, it is not possible to use every unit of input separately.

THE COST FUNCTION:

The cost function expresses a functional relationship between total cost and factors that deter-mine it. Usually, the factors that determine the total cost of production (C) of a firm are the output (0, the level of technology (T), the prices of factors (P_f) and the fixed factors (F). Symbolically, the cost function becomes,

$$C=f\ (Q, T, P_f, F)$$

Such a comprehensive cost function requires multi-dimensional diagrams which are difficult to draw. In order to simplify the cost analysis, certain assumptions are made. It is assumed that a firm produces a single homogeneous good (q) with the help of certain factors of production. Some of these factors are employed in fixed quantities whatever the level of output of the firm in the short run. So they are assumed to be given.

The remaining factors are variable whose supply is assumed to be known and available at fixed market prices. Further, the technology which is used for the production of the good is assumed to be known and fixed. Lastly, it is assumed that the firm adjusts the employment of variable factors in such a manner that a given output Q of the good q is obtained at the minimum total cost, C.

Thus the total cost function is expressed as:

$$C=f\ (Q)$$

Which means that the total cost (C) is a function if) of output (Q), assuming all other factors as constant. The cost function is shown diagrammatically by a total cost (TC) curve. The TC curve is drawn by taking output on the horizontal axis and total cost on the vertical axis, as shown in Figure below.

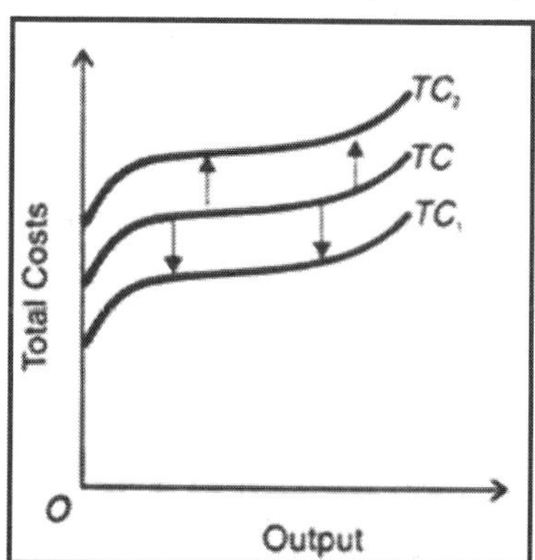

It is a continuous curve whose shape shows that with increasing output total cost also increases. The total cost function and the TC curve relate total cost to output under given conditions. But if any of the given conditions such as the technique of production change, the cost function is changed.

For instance, if there is an improved technique of production, the cost of production for any given out-put will be less than before which will shift the new cost curve TC_1 below the old curve TC, as shown in Figure. On the other hand, if the prices of factors rise, the cost of production will increase which will shift the cost curve upwards from TC to TC_2 as shown in Figure.

COST-OUTPUT RELATION

The Cost-output relation is discussed in the traditional and modem theories of costs under the short-run and long-run cost analysis which are explained as under.

THE TRADITIONAL THEORY OF COSTS

The traditional theory of costs analyses the behaviour of cost curves in the short run and the long run and arrives at the conclusion that both the short run and the long run curves are U-shaped but the long-run cost curves are flatter than the short-run cost curves.

Firm's Short-Run Cost Curves

The short run is a period in which the firm cannot change its plant, equipment and the scale of organisation. To meet the increased demand, it can raise output by hiring more labour and raw materials or asking the existing labour force to work overtime.

Short-Run Total Costs

The scale of organisation being fixed, the short-run total costs are divided into total fixed costs and total variable costs:

$$TC = TFC + TVC$$

Total Costs or TC

Total costs are the total expenses incurred by a firm in producing a given quantity of a commodity. They include payments for rent, interest, wages, taxes and expenses on raw materials, electricity, water, advertising, etc.

Total Fixed Costs or TFC

Are those costs of production that do not change with output. They are independent of the level of output. In fact, they have to be incurred even when the firm stops production temporarily. They include payments for renting land and buildings, interest or borrowed money, insurance charges, property tax, depreciation, maintenance expenditures, wages and salaries of the permanent staff, etc. They are also called overhead costs.

Total Variable Costs or TVC

Are those costs of production that change directly with output. They a rise when output increases, and fall when output declines. They include expenses on raw mate-rials, power, water, taxes, hiring of labour, advertising etc., They are also known as direct costs.

The relation between total costs, variable costs and fixed costs is presented in Table below, where column (1) indicates different levels of output from 0 to

10 units. Column (2) indicates that total fixed costs remain at ₹ 300 at all levels of output. Column (3) shows total variable costs which are zero when output is nothing and they continue to increase with the rise in output.

In the beginning they rise quickly, and then they slow down as the firm enjoys economies of large scale production with further increases in output and later on due to diseconomies of production, the variable costs start rising rapidly. Column (4) relates to total costs which are the sum of columns (2), and (3) *i.e.*, TC – TFC + TVC. Total costs vary with total variable costs when the firm starts produc-tion.

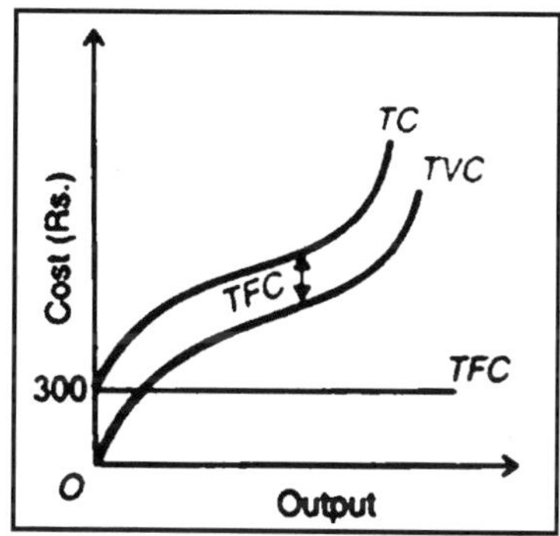

The curves relating to these three total costs are shown diagrammatically in Figure. The TC curve is a continuous curve which shows that with increasing output total costs also increase. This curve cuts the vertical axis at a point above the origin and rises continuously from left to right. This is because even when no output is produced, the firm has to incur fixed costs.

Table. Cost Function in the Short-Run

TO (1)	TFC (2)	TVC (3)	TC (4) (2+3)	AFC (5) (2+1)	AVC (6) (3+1)	ATC (7) (5+6) Or (4+1)	MC (8) (from 4)
	₹	₹	₹	₹	₹	₹	₹
0	300	0	300	300	0	300	–
1	300	300	600	300	300	600	300
2	300	400	700	150	200	350	100
3	300	450	750	100	150	250	50
4	300	500	800	75	125	200	50
5	300	600	900	60	120	180	100
6	30	720	1020	50	120	170	120
7	300	890	1190	42.9	127.1	170	170
8	300	1100	14000	37.5	137.5	175	210
9	300	1350	1650	33.3	150	183.3	470
10	**300**	**2000**	**2300**	**30**	**200**	**230**	650

The TFC curve is shown as parallel to the output axis because total fixed costs are the same (₹ 300) whatever the level of output. The TVC curve has an inverted-S shape and starts from the origin Î because when output is zero, the TVCs are also zero. They increase as output increases.

So long as the firm is using less variable factors in proportion to the fixed factors, the total variable costs rise at a diminishing rate. But after a point, with the use of more variable factors in proportion to the fixed factors, they rise steeply because of the application of the law of variable proportions. Since the TFC curve is a horizontal straight line, the TC curve follows the TVC curve at an equal vertical distance.

Short-Run Average Costs:

In the short run analysis of the firm, average costs are more important than total costs. The units of output that a firm produces do not cost the same amount to the firm. But they must be sold at the same price. Therefore, the firm must know the per unit cost or the average cost. The short-run average costs of a firm are the average fixed costs, the average variable costs, and the average total costs.

Average Fixed Costs or AFC equal total fixed costs at each level of output divided by the number of units produced:

$$AFC = TFC/Q$$

The average fixed costs diminish continuously as output increases. This is natural because when constant total fixed costs are divided by a continuously in-creasing unit of output, the result is continuously diminish-ing average fixed costs. Thus the AFC curve is a downward sloping curve which approaches the quantity axis without touching it. It is a rectangular hyper-bola.

Short-Run Average Variable Costs (or SAVC) equal total variable costs at each level of output divided by the number of units produced:

$$SAVC = TVC/Q$$

The average variable costs first decline with the rise in output as larger quantities of variable factors is applied to fixed plant and equipment. But eventually they begin to rise due to the law of diminishing returns. Thus the SAVC curve is U-shaped, as shown in Figure.

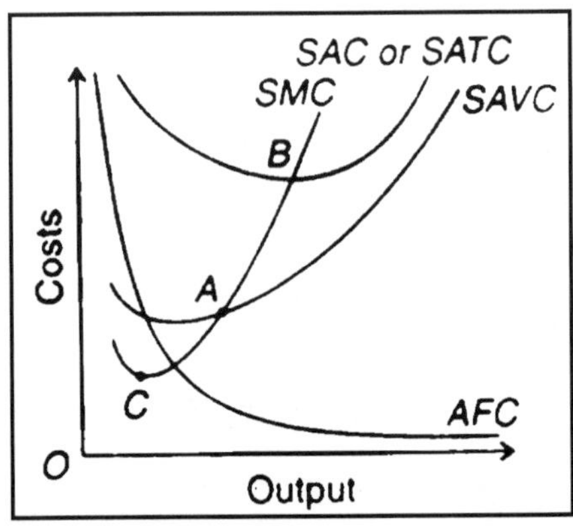

Short-Run Average Total Costs (or SATC or SAC) are the average costs of producing any given output.

They are arrived at by dividing the total costs at each level of output by the number of units produced:

$$SAC \text{ or } SATC = TC/Q\ TFC/Q + TVC/Q = AFC + AVC$$

Average total costs reflect the influence of both the average fixed costs and average variable costs. At first average total costs are high at low levels of output because both average fixed costs and average variable costs are large. But as output increases, the average total costs fall sharply because of the steady decline of both average fixed costs and average variable costs till they reach the minimum point. This results from the internal economies, from better utilisation of existing plant, labour, etc. The minimum point Â in the figure represents optimal capacity. As production is increased after this point, the average total costs rise quickly because the fall in average fixed costs is negligible in relation to the rising average variable costs.

The rising portion of the SAC curve results from producing above capacity and the appearance of internal diseconomies of management, labour, etc. Thus the SAC curve is U- shaped.

Why is SAC curve U-shaped?

The U-shape of the SAC curve can also be explained in terms of the law of variable proportions. This law tells that when the quantity of one variable factor is changed while keeping the quantities of other factors fixed, the total output increases but after some time it starts declining.

Machines, equip-ment and scale of production are the fixed factors of a firm that do not change in the short run. 'On the other hand, factors like labour and raw materials are variable. When increasing quantities of variable factors are applied on the fixed factors, the law of variable proportions operates.

When, say the quanti-ties of a variable factor like labour are increased in equal quantities, production rises till fixed factors like machines, equipment, etc. are used to their maximum capacity. In this stage, the average costs of the firm continue to fall as output increases because it operates under increasing returns. Due to the opera-tion of the law of increasing returns when the variable factors are increased further, the firm is able to work the machines to their optimum capacity. It produces the optimum output and its average costs of production will be the minimum which is revealed by the minimum point of the SAC curve, point Â in Figure.

It the firm tries to raise output after this point by increasing the quantities of the variable factors, the fixed factors like machines would be worked beyond their capacity. This would lead to diminishing returns. The average costs will start rising rapidly. Hence, due to the working of the law of variable proportions the short-run AC curve is U-shaped.

SHORT RUN MARGINAL COST:

A fundamental concept for the determination of the exact level of output of a firm is the marginal cost. Marginal cost is the addition to total cost by producing an additional unit of output:

$$SMC = \Delta TC/\Delta Q$$

Algebraically, it is the total cost of n + 1 units minus the total cost of n units of output $MC_n = TC_{n+1} - TC_n$. Since total fixed costs do not change with output, therefore, marginal fixed cost is zero. So marginal cost can be calculated either from total variable costs or total costs. The result would be the same in both the cases. As total variable costs or total costs first fall and then rise, marginal cost also behaves in the same way. The SMC curve is also U-shaped. Thus the short-run cost curves of a firm are the SAVC curve, the AFC curve, the SAC curve and the SMC curve. Out of these four curves, the AFC curve is insignificant for the deter-mination of the firm s exact output and is, therefore, generally neglected.

FIRM'S LONG-RUN COST CURVES:

In the long run, there are no fixed factors of production and hence no fixed costs. The firm can change its size or scale of plant and employ more or less inputs. Thus in the long run all factors are variable and hence all costs are variable.

The long run average total cost or LAC curve of the firm shows the minimum average cost of producing various levels of output from all-possible short-run average cost curves (SAC). Thus the LAC curve is derived from the SAC curves. The LAC curve can be viewed as a series of alternative short-run situations into any one of which the firm can move.

Each SAC curve represents a plant of a particular size which is suitable for a particular range of output. The firm will, therefore, make use of the various plants up to that level where the short-run average costs fall with increase in output. It will not produce beyond the minimum short-run average cost of producing various outputs from all the plants used together.

Let there be three plants represented by their short-run average cost curves SAC_1 SAC_2 and SAC_3 in Figure. Each curve represents the scale of the firm. $SA\tilde{N}_1$depicts a lower scale while the movement from SAC_2 to SA $\tilde{N}_1$shows the firm to be of a larger size. Given this scale of the firm, it will produce up to the least cost per unit of output. For producing ON output, the firm can use SAC_1or SAC_2 plant.

The firm will, however, use the scale of plant represented by SAC_3since the average cost of producing ON output is NB which is less than NA, the cost of producing this output on the SAC_2 plant. If the firm is to pro-duce OL output, it can produce at either of the two plants. But it would be advantageous for the firm to use the plant SA C_2 for the OL level of output.

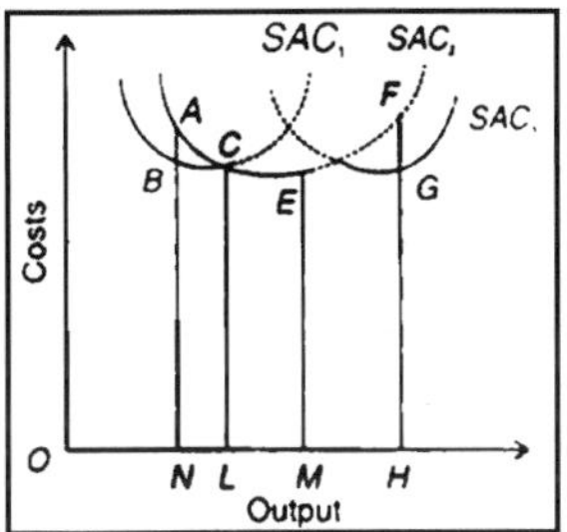

But it would be more profitable for the firm to produce the larger output OM at the lowest aver-age cost ME from this plant. However, for output OH, the firm would use the SAÑ$_1$ plant where the average cost HG is lower than HF of the SAC_2 plant.

Thus in the long-run in order to produce any level of output the firm will use that plant which has the minimum unit cost. If the firm expands its scale by the three stages represented by $SAC_1SAC_2$and SAC_3 curves, the thick wave-like portions of these curves form the long-run average cost curve. The dotted portions of these SAC curves are of no consideration during the long run because the firm would change the scale of plant rather than operate on them. But the long-run average cost curve LAC is usually shown as a smooth curve fitted to the SAC curves so that it is tangent to each of them at some point, where $SAC_{1,}SAC_{2,}$ SAC_3, SAC_4 and $SAC_5$are the short-run cost curves. It is tangent to all the SAC curves but only to one at its minimum point.

The LAC is tangent to the lowest point E of the curve SAC_3 in Figure at OQ optimum output. The plant SAC_3 which produces this OQ optimum output at the minimum cost QE is the optimum plant, and the firm produc-ing this optimum output at the minimum cost with this opti-mum plant is the optimum firm. If thc firm produces less than the optimum output OQ, it is not working its plant to full capacity and if it produces beyond it is overworking its plants. In both the cases, the plants SAC_2 and SAC_4 have higher average costs of production than the plant SAC_3

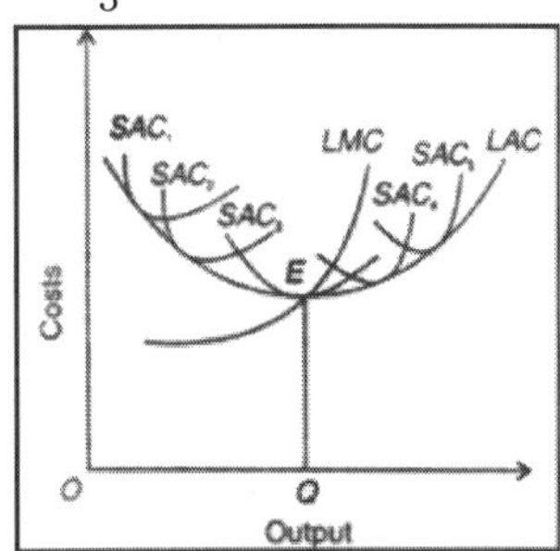

The LAC curve is known as the "envelope" curve because it envelopes all the SAC curves. According to Prof. Chamberlin, "It is composed of plant curves; it is the plant curve. But it is better to call it a "planning" curve because the firm plans to expand its scale of production over the long run."

The long-run marginal cost (LMC) curve of the firm intersects SAC_1 and LAC curves at the minimum point E.

LAC Curve Flatter than SAC Curve:

Though the long-run average cost (LAC) curve is U-shaped, yet it is flatter than the short-run average cost (SAC) curve.

It means that the LAC curve first falls slowly and then rises gradually after a minimum point is reached.

1. Initially, the LAC gradually slopes downwards due to the availability of certain economies of scale like the economical use of indivisible factors, increased specialisation and the use of technologi-cally more efficient machines or factors. The returns to scale increase because of the indivisibility of factors of production.

   When a business unit expands, the returns to scale increase because the indivis-ible factors are employed to their maximum capacity. Further, as the firm expands, it enjoys internal economies of production. It may be able to install better machines, sell its products more easily, borrow money cheaply, procure the services of more efficient manager and workers, etc. All these economies help in increasing the returns to scale more than proportionately.
2. After the minimum point of the long-run average cost is reached, the LAC curve may flatten out over a certain range of output with the expansion of the scale of production. In such a situation, the economies and diseconomies balance each other and the LAC curve has a disc base.
3. With further expansion of scale, the diseconomies like the difficulties of coordination, manage-ment, labour and transport arise which more than counterbalance the economies so that the LAC curve begins to rise. This happens when the indivisible factors become inefficient and less productive due to the over expansion of the scale of production. Moreover, when supervision and coordination become difficult, the per unit cost increases. To these internal diseconomies are added external diseconomies of scale.

These arise from higher factor prices or from diminishing productivities of factors. As the indus-try continues to expand, the demand for skilled labour, land, capital, etc. rises. Transport and marketing difficulties also emerge. Prices of raw materials go up. All these factors lead to diminishing returns to scale and tend to raise costs.

The LAC curves first falls and then rises more slowly than the SAC curve because in the long run all costs become variable and few are fixed. The plant and equipment can be altered and adjusted to the output. The existing factors can be worked fully and more efficiently so that both the average fixed costs and average variable costs are lower in the long run than in the short run. That is why, the LAC curve is flatter than the SAC curve.

Similarly, the LMC curve is flatter than the SMC curve because all costs are variable and there are few fixed costs. In the short-run, the marginal cost is related to both the fixed and variable costs. As a result, the SMC curve falls and rises more swiftly than the LMC curve. The LMC curve bears the usual relation to the LAC curve. It first falls and is below the LAC curve. Then rises and cuts the LAC curve at its lowest point E and is above the latter throughout its length, as shown in Figure below.

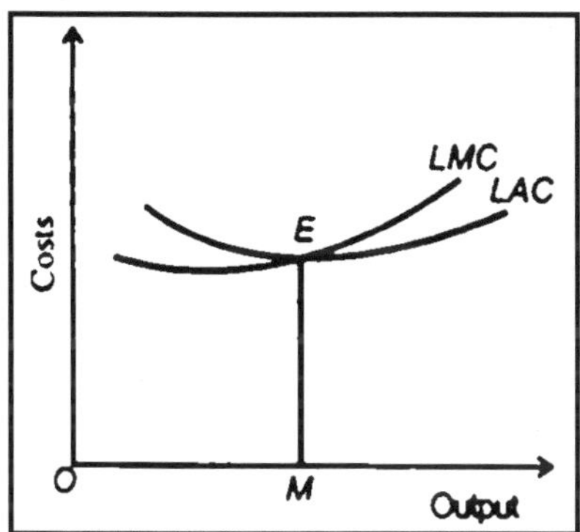

THE MODERN THEORY OF COSTS

The modem theory of costs differs from the traditional theory of costs with regard to the shapes of the cost curves. In the traditional theory, the cost curves are U-shaped. But in the modem theory which is based on empirical evidences, the short-run SAVC curve and the SMC curve coincide with each other and are a horizontal straight line over a wide range of output. So far as the LAC and LMC curves are concerned, they are L-shaped rather than U-shaped. We discuss below the nature of short- run and long-run cost curves according to the modem theory.

SHORT-RUN COST CURVES

As in the traditional theory, the short-run cost curves in the modem theory of costs are the AFC, SAVC, SAC and SMC curves. As usual, they are derived from the total costs which are divided into total fixed costs and total variable costs.

But in the modem theory, the SAVC and SMC curves have a saucer-type shape or bowl-shape rather than a U-shape. As the AFC curve is a rectangular hyperbola, the SAC curve has a U-shape even in the modem version. Economists have investigated on the basis of empirical studies this behaviour pattern of the short-run cost curves.

According to them, a modern firm chooses such a plant which it can operate eas-ily with the available variable direct factors. Such a plant possesses some reserve capacity and much flexibility. The firm installs this type of plant in order to produce the maximum rate of output over a wide range to meet any increase in demand for its product.

The saucer-shaped SAVC and SMC curves are shown in Figure. To begin with, both the curves first fall upto point A and the SMC curvelies below the SAVC curve. "The falling part of the SAVC shows the reduction in costs due to the better utilisation of the fixed factor and the consequent increase in skills and productiv-ity of the variable factor (labour).

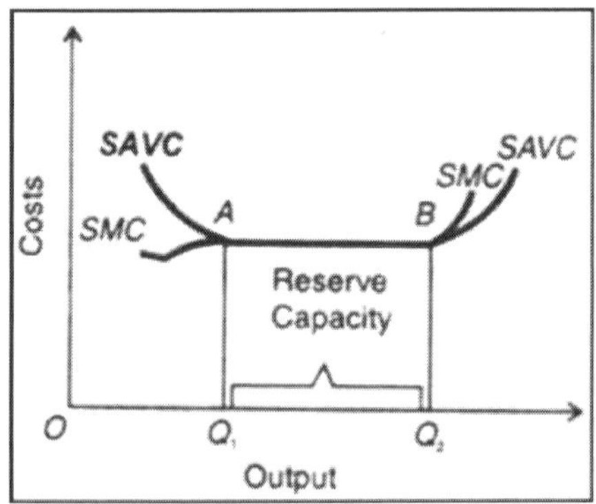

With better skills, the wastes in raw materials are also being reduced and a better utilisation of the whole plant is reached." So far as the flat stretch of the saucer-shaped SAVC curve over $Q_{:1}Q_2$ range of output is concerned, the empirical evidence reveals that the operation of a plant within this wide range exhibits constant returns to scale.

The reason for the saucer-shaped SAVC curve is that the fixed factor is divisible. The SAV costs are constant over a large range, up to the point at which all of the fixed factor is used. Moreover, the firm's SAV costs tend to be constant over a wide range of output because there is no need to depart from the optimal combination of labour and capital in those plants that are kept in operation. Thus there is a large range of output over which the SAVC curve will be flat. Over that range, SMC and SAVC are equal and are constant per unit of output. The firm will, therefore, continue to produce within Q_1Q_2 reserve capacity of the plant.

After point B, both the SAVC and SMC curves start rising. When the firm departs from its normal or the load factor of the plant in order to obtain higher rates of output beyond Q_2, it leads to higher SAVC and SMC.

The increase in costs may be due to the over-time operations of the old and less efficient plant leading to frequent breakdowns, wastage of raw materials, reduction in labour productivity and increase in labour cost due to overtime operations. In the rising portion of the SAVC curve beyond point B, the SMC curve lies above it.

The short-run average total cost curve (SATC or SAC) is obtained by adding vertically the average fixed cost curve (AFC) and the SAVC curve at each level of output. The SAC curve, continues to fall up to the OQ level of output at which the reserve capacity of the plant is fully exhausted.

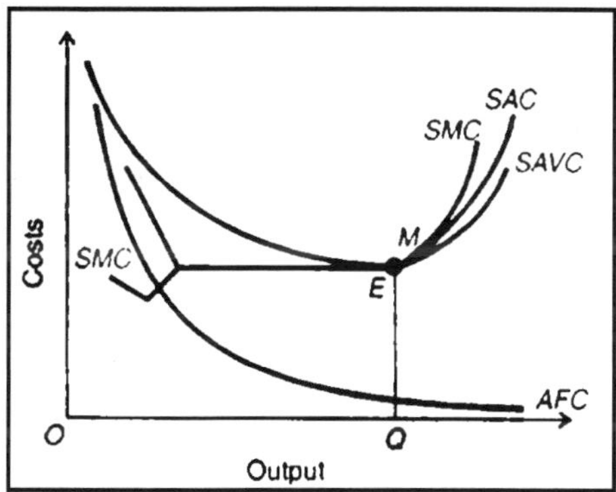

Beyond that output level, the SAC curve rises as output increases. The smooth and continuous fall in the SAC curve upto the OQ level of output is due to the fact that the AFC curve is a rectangular hyperbola and the SAVC curve first falls and then becomes horizontal within the range of reserve capacity. Beyond the OQ output level, it starts rising steeply. But the minimum point M of the SAC curve where the SMC curve intersects it, is to the right of point E of the SAVC curve. This is because the SAVC curve starts rising steeply from point E while the AFC curve is falling at a very low rate.

LONG-RUN COST CURVES

Empirical evidence about the long-run average cost curve reveals that the LAC curve is L-shaped rather than U-shaped. In the beginning, the LAC curve rapidly falls but after a point "the curve remains flat, or may slope gently downwards, at its right-hand end." Economists have assigned the following reasons for the L-shape of the LAC curve.

Production and Managerial Costs

In the long run, all costs being variable, production costs and managerial costs of a firm are taken into account when considering the effect of expansion of output on average costs. As output increases, production costs fall continuously while managerial costs may rise at very large scales of output. But the fall in production costs outweighs the increase in managerial costs so that the LAC curve falls with increases in output. We analyse the behaviour of production and managerial costs in explaining the L-shape of the LAC curve.

Production Costs

As a firm increases its scale of production, its production costs fall steeply in the beginning and then gradually. The is due to the technical economies of large scale production enjoyed by the firm. Initially, these economies are substantial. But after a certain level of output when all or most of these economies have been achieved, the firm reaches the minimum optimal scale or mini- mum efficient scale (MES).

Given the technology of the industry, the firm can continue to enjoy some technical economies at outputs larger than the MES for the following reasons:

(a) From further decentralisation and improvement in skills and productivity of labour;
(b) From lower repair costs after the firm reaches a certain size; and
(c) By itself producing some of the materials and equipment cheaply which the firm needs instead of buying them from other firms.

MANAGERIAL COSTS

In modern firms, for each plant there is a corresponding managerial set-up for its smooth operation. There are various levels of management, each having a separate management technique applicable to a certain range of output. Thus, given a managerial set-up for a plant, its mana-gerial costs first fall with the expansion of output and it is only at a very large scale output, they rise very slowly.

To sum up, production costs fall smoothly and managerial costs rise slowly at very large scales of output. But the fall in production costs more than offsets the rise in managerial costs so that the LAC curve falls smoothly or becomes flat at very large scales of output, thereby giving rise to the L-shape of the LAC curve.

In order to draw such an LAC curve, we take three short-run average cost curves SAC_1 SA $\tilde{N}_2$, and SAC_3representing three plants with the same technology in Figure below. Each SAC curve includes production costs, managerial costs, other fixed costs and a mar-gin for normal profits. Each scale of plant (SAC) is subject to a typical load factor capacity so that points A, Â and Ñ represent the minimal optimal scale of out-put of each plant.

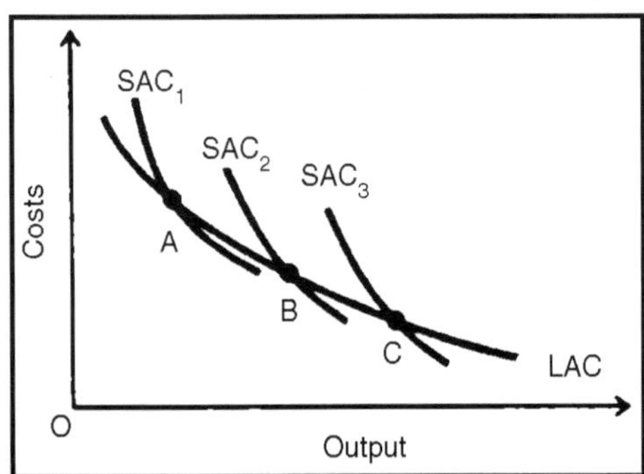

By joining all such points as A, Â and Ñ of a large number of SACs, we trace out a smooth and continuous LAC curve. This curve does not turn up at very large scales of output. It does not envelope the SAC curves but intersects them at the optimal level of output of each plant.

Technical Progress

Another reason for the existence of the L-shaped LAC curve in the modern theory of costs is technical progress. The traditional theory of costs assumes no technical progress while explaining the U-shaped LAC curve. The empirical results on long-run costs conform the widespread existence of economies of scale due to technical progress in firms.

The period between which technical progress has taken place, the long-run aver-age costs show a falling trend. The evidence of diseconomies is much less certain. So an upturn of the LAC at the top end of the size scale has not been observed. The L-shape of the LAC curve due to tech-nical progress is explained in Figure below.

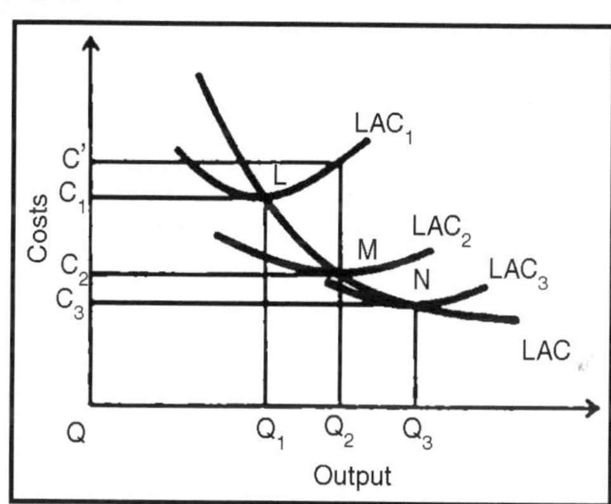

Suppose the firm is producing OQ_1 output on LAC_1curve at a per unit cost of $\hat{I}\tilde{N}_1$ If there is an increase in demand for the firm's product to OQ_2,with no change in technology, the firm will produce OQ_2 output along the LAC_1curve at a per unit cost of $\hat{I}\tilde{N}_2$. If, however, there is technical progress in the firm, it will install a new plant having LAC_2 as the long-run average cost curve. On this plant, it produces OQ_2 output at a lower cost OC_2 per unit.

Similarly, if the firm decides to increase its output to OQ_3 to meet further rise in demand technical progress may have advanced to such a level that it installs the plant with the LAC_3 curve. Now it produces OQ_3output at a still lower cost OC_3 per unit. If the minimum points, L, M and N of these U- shaped long-run average cost curves LAC_1, LAC_2 and LAC_3 are joined by a line, it forms an L-shaped gently sloping downward curve LAC.

Learning

Another reason for the L-shaped long- run average cost curve is the learning process. Learning is the product of experience. If experience, in this context, can be measured by the amount of a commodity produced, then higher the production is, the lower is per unit cost. The consequences of learning are similar to increasing re-turns. First, the knowledge gained from working on a large scale cannot be forgotten. Second, learning increases the rate of productivity. Third, experience is measured by the aggregate output produced since the firm first started to produce the product. Learning-by-doing has been observed when firms start producing new products. After they have produced the first unit, they are able to reduce the time required for production and thus reduce their per unit costs. For example, if a firm manufactures airframes, the fall observed in long-run average costs is a function of experience in producing one particular kind of airframe, not airframes in general.

One can, therefore, draw a "learning curve" which relates cost per airframe to the aggregate number of airframes manufactured so far, since the firm started manufacturing them.

Figure shows a learning curve LAC which relates the cost of producing a given output to the total output over the entire time period. Growing experience with making the product leads to falling costs as more and more of it is produced. When the firm has exploited all learning possibilities, costs reach a minimum level, M in the figure. Thus, the LAC curve is L-shaped due to learning by doing.

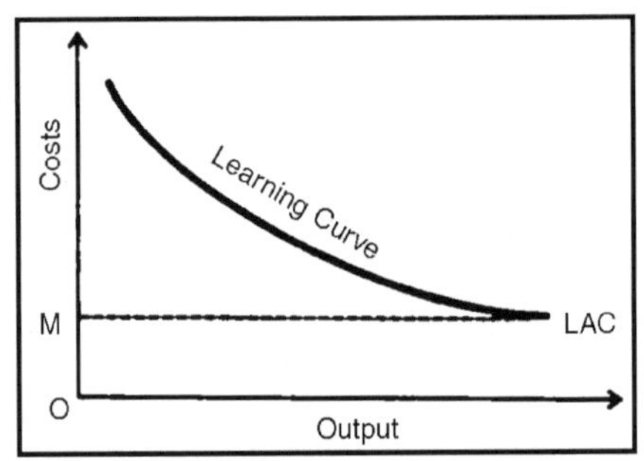

RELATION BETWEEN LAC AND LMC CURVES

In the modern theory of costs, if the LAC curve falls smoothly and continuously even at very large scales of output, the LMC curve will lie below the LAC curve throughout its length, as shown in Figure.

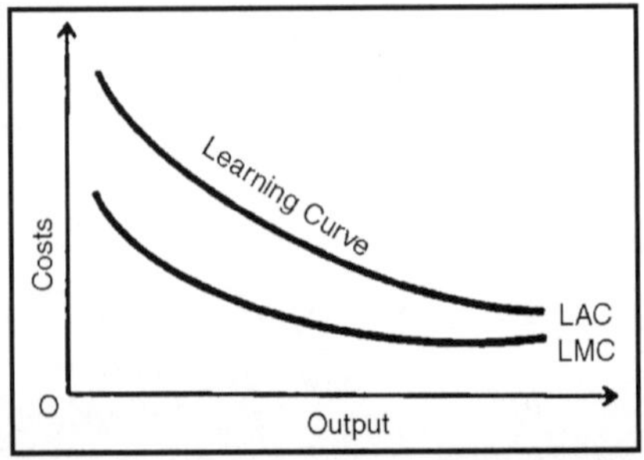

If the LAC curve is downward sloping up to the point of a minimum optimal scale of plant or a mini-mum efficient scale (MES) of plant beyond which no further scale economies exist, the LAC curve becomes horizontal. In this case, the LMC curve lies below the LAC curve until the MES point M is reached, and beyond this point the LMC curve coincides with the LA Ñ curve, as shown in Figure below.

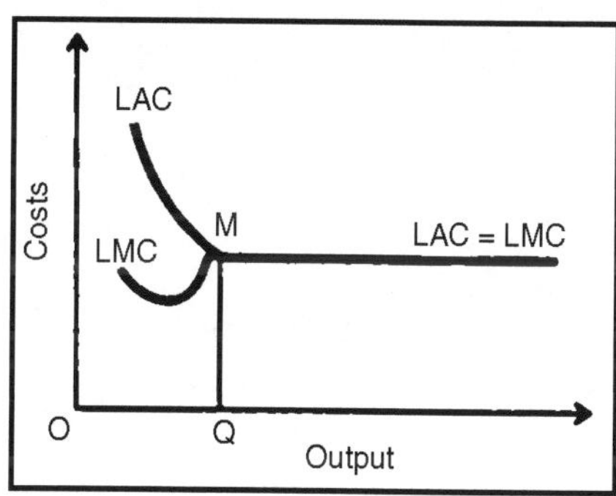

Conclusion

The majority of empirical cost studies suggest that the U-shaped cost curves postulated by the traditional theory are not observed in the real world. Two major results emerge predominantly from most studies. First, the SAVC and SMC curves are constant over a wide-range of output. Second, the LAC curve falls sharply over low levels of output, and subse-quently remains practically constant as the scale of output increases. This means that the LAC curve is L-shaped rather than U-shaped. Only in very few cases diseconomies of scale were observed, and these at very high levels of output.

7

Micro and Macro Economics

DEFINITION OF 'MICROECONOMICS'

The branch of economics that analyses the market behaviour of individual consumers and firms in an attempt to understand the decision-making process of firms and households. It is concerned with the interaction between individual buyers and sellers and the factors that influence the choices made by buyers and sellers. In particular, microeconomics focuses on patterns of supply and demand and the determination of price and output in individual markets (*e.g.* coffee industry).

Macroeconomics studies large-scale phenomena in the national economy, and even in global economies, because they're interrelated. These would include central bank interest rates, national employment numbers, gross national product figures, trade deficits or surpluses, foreign currency exchange rates, and other major economic activity and data.

By contrast, microeconomics studies a limited, smaller area of economics, including the actions of individual consumers and businesses, and the process by which both make their economic decisions – buying, selling, the prices businesses charge for their goods and services and how much of these goods and services they produce and or offer. Microeconomic study reveals how start-up businesses have determined the competitively successful or unsuccessful pricing of their goods and services based on consumer needs and choices, market competition and other financial and economic formulas.

Microeconomics also studies supply-demand ratios and its effect on consumer spending and business decision-making. At the heart of consumer purchasing is the concept of utility, a classic economic idea. Utility is the term applied to a consumer's satisfaction after the purchase of some product or service. Because a consumer's feeling of satisfaction may be impossible to precisely quantify in actual numbers, the concept may seem impractical. But a reasonably close approximation is useful to businesses, and may also be useful to the individual consumer who can probably measure that feeling of satisfaction with a "gut" reaction.

Economics is a social science that examines how people choose among the alternatives available to them. It is social because it involves people and their behaviour. It is a science because it uses, as much as possible, a scientific approach in its investigation of choices.

SCARCITY, CHOICE, AND COST

All choices mean that one alternative is selected over another. Selecting among alternatives involves three ideas central to economics: scarcity, choice, and opportunity cost.

Scarcity

Our resources are limited. At any one time, we have only so much land, so many factories, so much oil, so many people. But our wants, our desires for the things that we can produce with those resources, are unlimited. We would always like more and better housing, more and better education—more and better of practically everything.

If our resources were also unlimited, we could say yes to each of our wants—and there would be no economics. Because our resources are limited, we cannot say yes to everything. To say yes to one thing requires that we say no to another. Whether we like it or not, we must make choices.

Our unlimited wants are continually colliding with the limits of our resources, forcing us to pick some activities and to reject others. Scarcity is the condition of having to choose among alternatives. Ascarce good is one for which the choice of one alternative requires that another be given up.

Consider a parcel of land. The parcel presents us with several alternative uses. We could build a house on it. We could put a gas station on it. We could create a small park on it. We could leave the land undeveloped in order to be able to make a decision later as to how it should be used.

Suppose we have decided the land should be used for housing. Should it be a large and expensive house or several modest ones? Suppose it is to be a large and expensive house. Who should live in the house? If the Lees live in it, the Nguyens cannot. There are alternative uses of the land both in the sense of the type of use and also in the sense of who gets to use it. The fact that land is scarce means that society must make choices concerning its use. Virtually everything is scarce. Consider the air we breathe, which is available in huge quantity at no charge to us. Could it possibly be scarce?

The test of whether air is scarce is whether it has alternative uses. What uses can we make of the air? We breathe it. We pollute it when we drive our cars, heat our houses, or operate our factories. In effect, one use of the air is as a garbage dump. We certainly need the air to breathe. But just as certainly, we choose to dump garbage in it. Those two uses are clearly alternatives to each other. The more garbage we dump in the air, the less desirable—and healthy—

it will be to breathe. If we decide we want to breathe cleaner air, we must limit the activities that generate pollution. Air is a scarce good because it has alternative uses.

Not all goods, however, confront us with such choices. A free good is one for which the choice of one use does not require that we give up another. One example of a free good is gravity. The fact that gravity is holding you to the earth does not mean that your neighbour is forced to drift up into space! One person's use of gravity is not an alternative to another person's use.

There are not many free goods. Outer space, for example, was a free good when the only use we made of it was to gaze at it. But now, our use of space has reached the point where one use can be an alternative to another. Conflicts have already arisen over the allocation of orbital slots for communications satellites. Thus, even parts of outer space are scarce. Space will surely become more scarce as we find new ways to use it. Scarcity characterizes virtually everything. Consequently, the scope of economics is wide indeed.

Opportunity Cost

It is within the context of scarcity that economists define what is perhaps the most important concept in all of economics, the concept of opportunity cost. Opportunity cost is the value of the best alternative forgone in making any choice.

The opportunity cost to you of reading the remainder of this chapter will be the value of the best other use to which you could have put your time. If you choose to spend $20 on a potted plant, you have simultaneously chosen to give up the benefits of spending the $20 on pizzas or a paperback book or a night at the movies. If the book is the most valuable of those alternatives, then the opportunity cost of the plant is the value of the enjoyment you otherwise expected to receive from the book.

The concept of opportunity cost must not be confused with the purchase price of an item. Consider the cost of a college or university education. That includes the value of the best alternative use of money spent for tuition, fees, and books. But the most important cost of a college education is the value of the forgone alternative uses of time spent studying and attending class instead of using the time in some other endeavour. Students sacrifice that time in hopes of even greater earnings in the future or because they place a value on the opportunity to learn. Or consider the cost of going to the doctor. Part of that cost is the value of the best alternative use of the money required to see the doctor. But, the cost also includes the value of the best alternative use of the time required to see the doctor. The essential thing to see in the concept of opportunity cost is found in the name of the concept. Opportunity cost is the value of the best opportunity forgone in a particular choice. It is not simply the amount spent on that choice.

The concepts of scarcity, choice, and opportunity cost are at the heart of economics. A good is scarce if the choice of one alternative requires that another be given up. The existence of alternative uses forces us to make choices. The opportunity cost of any choice is the value of the best alternative forgone in making it.

NATURE OF MICROECONOMICS

Microeconomics represents the study of how members in a society use available resources to make choices in the marketplace. Those choices refer to purchases of goods and services from business providers. As a business, part of your role is to provide and promote products that are demanded by a target market group within the population. In essence, you want to influence the choices of consumers who have limited budgets to spend on various products and services.

SUPPLY AND DEMAND

Supply and demand is one of the most critical concepts at the microeconomic level. This is the comparison of the level of consumer demand for particular goods to the available supply in the marketplace. In a highly competitive industry in which consumers possess many choices, supply might exceed demand. Over time, this can cause some businesses to fail. In a more niche market with few providers, your opportunity to succeed in meeting demand may be higher if you offer and promote a quality product with desired benefits.

Pricing

Business pricing strategies correlate strongly with microeconomic factors. The ideal, or equilibrium price point exists at the point at which quantity supplied in the market exactly equals demand. The higher your prices, the lower the size of the population who will buy them. However, if you offer lower prices than the market demand dictates, you leave money on the table and you might also end up with shortages of your product or services. This can cause customer alienation and negatively affect the business in the long term.

Research and Promotion

Understanding microeconomics helps in effectively researching and promoting products. Research is useful in investigating potential customer demand and in developing products that best match desired benefits. This benefits you once you pay for advertising and use other promotional techniques to promote your brand and its benefits. These marketing techniques are critical in achieving competitive advantages over other companies trying to optimize performance as customers make choices based on their needs and budgets.

ASSUMPTIONS AND DEFINITIONS

The fundamentals of Microeconomics lies in the analysis of the preference relations. Preference relations are defined simply to be a set of different choices that an actor can choose (a k-cell metric space) that actors can also compare between any two bundles of choices (completeness of the relationship.) In order to analyse the problem further, the assumption of transitivity is added to the mix. These two assumptions of completeness and transitivity that is imposed upon the preference relations are what is termed rationality. Microeconomic analysis are conducted mainly through imposition of additional constraints on the preference relations or even relaxation of the above stated assumptions (most often transitivity) although such relaxation makes the problem much harder to analyse.

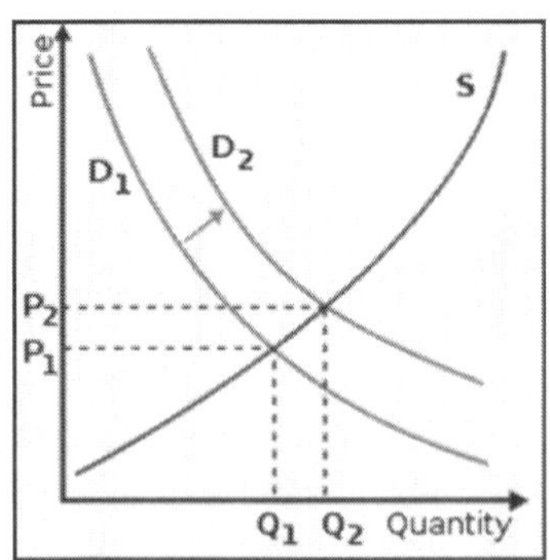

Fig. The supply and demand model describes how prices vary as a result of a balance between product availability at each price (supply) and the desires of those with purchasing power at each price (demand). The graph depicts a right-shift in demand from D_1 to D_2along with the consequent increase in price and quantity required to reach a new market-clearing equilibrium point on the supply curve (S).

The theory of supply and demand usually assumes that markets are perfectly competitive. This implies that there are many buyers and sellers in the market and none of them have the capacity to significantly influence prices of goods and services. In many real-life transactions, the assumption fails because some individual buyers or sellers have the ability to influence prices. Quite often, a sophisticated analysis is required to understand the demand-supply equation of a good model. However, the theory works well in situations meeting these assumptions.

Mainstream economics does not assume *a priori* that markets are preferable to other forms of social organization. In fact, much analysis is devoted to cases where so-called market failures lead to resource allocation that is suboptimal by some standard (defence spending is the classic example, profitable to all for use but not directly profitable for anyone to finance). In such cases, economists may attempt to find policies that avoid waste, either directly by government control, indirectly by regulation that induces market participants to act in a manner consistent with optimal welfare, or by creating "missing markets" to enable efficient trading where none had previously existed.

This is studied in the field of collective action and public choice theory. "Optimal welfare" usually takes on a Paretian norm, which in its mathematical application of Kaldor–Hicks method. This can diverge from the Utilitarian goal of maximizing utility because it does not consider the distribution of goods between people. Market failure in positive economics (microeconomics) is limited in implications without mixing the belief of the economist and their theory.

The demand for various commodities by individuals is generally thought of as the outcome of a utility-maximizing process, with each individual trying to maximize their own utility under a budget constraint and a given consumption set.

OPPORTUNITY COST

Opportunity cost of an activity (or goods) is equal to the best next alternative uses/foregone. Although *opportunity cost* can be hard to quantify, the effect of opportunity cost is universal and very real on the individual level. In fact, this principle applies to all decisions, not just economic ones.

Opportunity cost is one way to measure the cost of something. Rather than merely identifying and adding the costs of a project, one may also identify the next best alternative way to spend the same amount of money. The forgone profit of this *next best alternative* is the opportunity cost of the original choice. A common example is a farmer that chooses to farm their land rather than rent it to neighbours, wherein the opportunity cost is the forgone profit from renting. In this case, the farmer may expect to generate more profit alone. This kind of reasoning is a very important part of the calculation of discount rates in discounted cash flow investment valuation methodologies. Similarly, the opportunity cost of attending university is the lost wages a student could have earned in the workforce, rather than the cost of tuition, books, and other requisite items (whose sum makes up the total cost of attendance). Note that opportunity cost is not the *sum* of the available alternatives, but rather the benefit of the single, best alternative.

Possible opportunity costs of a city's decision to build a hospital on its vacant land are the loss of the land for a sporting centre, *or* the inability to use the land for a parking lot, *or* the money that could have been made from selling the land, *or* the loss of any of the various other possible uses — but not all of these in aggregate. The true opportunity cost would be the forgone profit of the most lucrative of those listed.

One question that arises here is how to determine a money value for each alternative to facilitate comparison and assess opportunity cost, which may be more or less difficult depending on the things we are trying to compare. For example, many decisions involve environmental impacts whose monetary value is difficult to assess because of scientific uncertainty. Valuing a human life or the economic impact of an Arctic oil spill involves making subjective choices with ethical implications.

It is imperative to understand that no decision on allocating time is free. No matter what one chooses to do, they are always giving something up in return. An example of opportunity cost is deciding between going to a concert and doing homework. If one decides to go the concert, then they are giving up valuable time to study, but if they choose to do homework then the cost is giving up the concert. Any decision in allocating capital is likewise: there is an opportunity cost of capital, or a hurdle rate, defined as the expected rate one could get by investing in similar projects on the open market. Opportunity cost is vital in understanding microeconomics and decisions that are made.

APPLIED MICROECONOMICS

Applied microeconomics includes a range of specialized areas of study, many of which draw on methods from other fields. Industrial organization examines topics such as the entry and exit of firms, innovation, and the role of trademarks.

Labour economics examines wages, employment, and labour market dynamics. Financial economics examines topics such as the structure of optimal portfolios, the rate of return to capital, econometric analysis of security returns, and corporate financial behaviour. Public economics examines the design of government tax and expenditure policies and economic effects of these policies (*e.g.*, social insurance programmes).

Political economyexamines the role of political institutions in determining policy outcomes. Health economics examines the organization of health care systems, including the role of the health care workforce and health insurance programmes. Urban economics, which examines the challenges faced by cities, such as sprawl, air and water pollution, traffic congestion, and poverty, draws on the fields of urban geography and sociology. Law and economics applies microeconomic principles to the selection and enforcement of competing legal regimes and their relative efficiencies. Economic history examines the evolution of the economy and economic institutions, using methods and techniques from the fields of economics, history, geography, sociology, psychology, and political science.

DEVELOPMENT

Traditional marginalism

The modern field of microeconomics arose as an effort of neo-classical economics school of thought to put economic ideas into mathematical mode. An early attempt was made by Antoine Augustine Cournot in *Researches on the*

Mathematical Principles of the Theory of Wealth (1838) in describing a spring water duopoly that now bears his name. Later, William Stanley Jevons's *Theory of Political Economy* (1871), Carl Menger's Principles of Economics (1871), and Léon Walras's *Elements of Pure Economics: Or the theory of social wealth* (1874–77) gave way to what was called the Marginal Revolution.

Some common ideas behind those works were models or arguments characterized by rational economic agents maximizing utility under a budget constrain. This arose as a necessity of arguing against the labour theory of value associated with classical economists such as Adam Smith, David Ricardo and Karl Marx. Walras also went as far as developing the concept of general equilibrium of an economy.

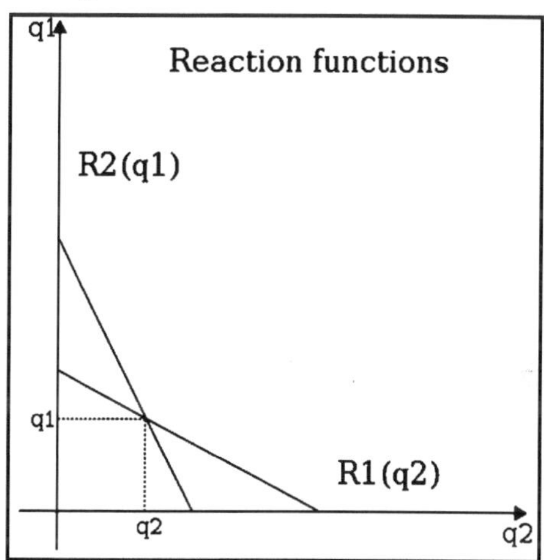

Fig. Classic duopoly model of Cournot:reaction functions of both firms are derived by imposing profit maximization, the Nash equilibrium is given by intersection of R1 and R2. At equilibrium no firm has a rational self-interest in changing produced quantities.

Alfred Marshall's textbook, *Principles of Economics* was published in 1890 and became the dominant textbook in England for a generation. His main point was that Jevons went too far in emphasizing utility as an attempt to explain prices over costs of production. In the book he writes: "There are few writers of modern times who have approached as near to the brilliant originality of Ricardo as Jevons has done. But he appears to have judged both Ricardo and Mill harshly, and to have attributed to them doctrines narrower and less scientific than those they really held.

Also, his desire to emphasize an aspect of value to which they had given insufficient prominence, was probably in some measure accountable for his saying, "Repeated reflection and enquiry have led me to the somewhat novel opinion that value depends entirely upon utility."

This statement seems to be no less one-sided and fragmentary, and much more misleading, than that into which Ricardo often glided with careless brevity, as to the dependence of value on cost of production; but which he never regarded as more than a part of a larger doctrine, the rest of which he had tried to explain. " In the same appendix he further states:

"Perhaps Jevons' antagonism to Ricardo and Mill would have been less if he had not himself fallen into the habit of speaking of relations which really exist only between demand price and value as though they held between utility and value; and if he had emphasized as Cournot had done, and as the use of mathematical forms might have been expected to lead him to do, that fundamental symmetry of the general relations in which demand and supply stand to value, which coexists with striking differences in the details of those relations. We must not indeed forget that, at the time at which he wrote, the demand side of the theory of value had been much neglected; and that he did excellent service by calling attention to it and developing it. There are few thinkers whose claims on our gratitude are as high and as various as those of Jevons: but that must not lead us to accept hastily his criticisms on his great predecessors."

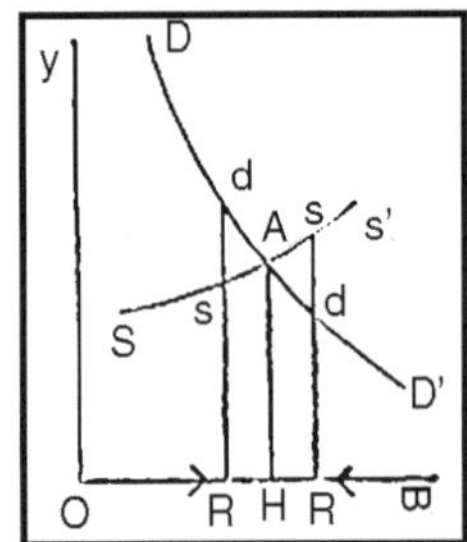

Fig. Marshall's diagram: SS′ is the supply curve, DD′ is the demand curve and A is the equilibrium

Marshall's idea of solving the controversy was that the demand curve could be derived by aggregating individual consumer demand curves, which were themselves based on the consumer problem of maximizing utility. The supply curve could be derived by superimposing a representative firm supply curves for the factors of production and then market equilibrium would be given by the intersection of demand and supply curves. He also introduced the notion of different market periods: mainly short run and long run. This set of ideas gave way to what economists call perfect competition, now found in the standard microeconomics texts, even though Marshall himself had stated:

"The process of substitution, of which we have been discussing the tendencies, is one form of competition; and it may be well to insist again that we do not assume that competition is perfect. Perfect competition requires a perfect knowledge of the state of the market; and though no great departure from the actual facts of life is involved in assuming this knowledge on the part of dealers when we are considering the course of business in Lombard Street, the Stock Exchange, or in a wholesale Produce Market; it would be an altogether unreasonable assumption to make when we are examining the causes that govern the supply of labour in any of the lower grades of industry. For if a man had sufficient ability to know everything about the market for his labour, he would have too much to remain long in a low grade. The older economists, in constant contact as they were with the actual facts of business life, must have known this well enough; but partly for brevity and simplicity, partly because the term "free competition" had become almost a catchword, partly because they had not sufficiently classified and conditioned their doctrines, they often seemed to imply that they did assume this perfect knowledge. "

An early formulation of the concept of production functions is due to Johann Heinrich von Thünen, which presented an exponential version of it. The standard Cobb–Douglasproduction function found in microeconomics textbooks refers to a collaborative paper between Charles Cobb and Paul Douglas published in 1928 in which they analised U.S. manufacturing data using this function as the basis of a regression analysis for estimating the relationship between inputs (labour and capital) and output (product): this discussion takes place through the concept of marginal productivity. The mathematical form of the Cobb–Douglas function can be found in the prior work of Wicksell, Thünen, and Turgot.

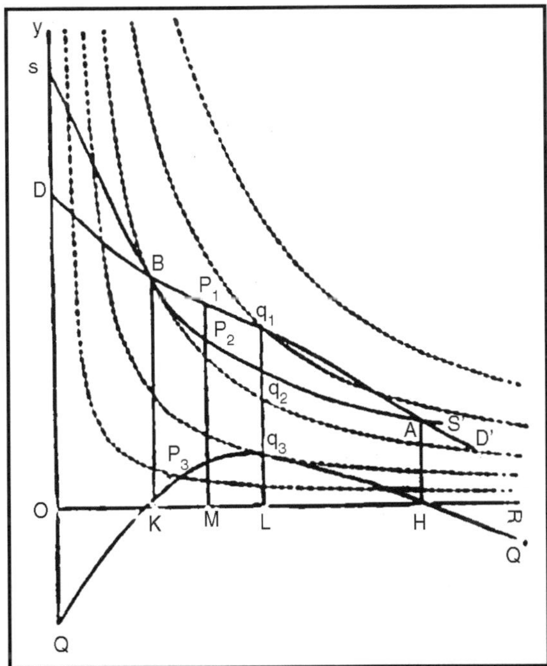

Fig. One of Marshall's diagrams formonopoly: DD′ is the demand curve, SS′ the supply curve, QQ′ is the monopoly revenue curve and q3 the maximum revenue point. Cournot had already considered the mathematics of monopoly in the Mathematical Principles of the Theory of Wealth but he draw no diagram

Jacob Viner presented an early procedure for constructing cost curves in his "Cost Curves and Supply Curves" (1931), the paper was an attempt to reconcile two streams of thought when dealing with this issue at the time: the idea that supplies of factors of production were given and independent of rate of remuneration (Austrian School) or dependent on rate of remuneration (English School, that is followers of Marshall). Viner argued that, "The differences between the two schools would not affect qualitatively the character of the findings," more specifically, "...that this concern is not of sufficient importance to bring about any change in the prices of the factors as a result of a change in its output."

In Viner's terminology—now considered standard—the *short run* is a period long enough to permit any desired output change that is technologically possible without altering the scale of the plant—but is not long enough to adjust the scale of the plant. He arbitrarily assumes that all factors can, for the short run, be classified in two groups: those necessarily fixed in amount, and those freely variable. *Scale of plant* is the size of the group of factors that are fixed in amount in the short-run, and each scale is quantitatively indicated by the amount of output that can be produced at the lowest average cost possible at that scale.

Costs associated with the fixed factors are *fixed costs*. Those associated with the variable factors are *direct costs*. Note that fixed costs are fixed only in their aggregate amounts, and vary with output in their amount per unit, while direct costs vary in their aggregate amount as output varies, as well as—ordinarily, at least—in their amount per unit.

He explains that if the law of diminishing returns holds that output per unit of variable factor falls as total output rises, and that if the prices of the factors remain constant—then average direct costs increase with output. Also, if atomistic competition prevails—that is, the individual firm output won't affect product prices—then the individual firm short-run supply curve equals the short run marginal cost curve. In the long run, the supply curve for industry can be constructed by summing individual marginal cost curves abscissas. He also explains that internal economies of scale are primarily a long-run phenomenon and are due either to reductions in the technical coefficients of production (technical economies=increasing productivity) or to discounts resulting from larger size (pecuniary economies). Externaleconomies of scale are also either technical or pecunary, but in this case are due to aggregate behaviour of the industry. It should be made clear that these long-run results only hold if producer are rational actors, that is able to optimize their production so as to have an *optimal scale of plant*.

Imperfect competition and game theory

In 1929 Harold Hotelling published "Stability in Competition" addressing the problem of instability in the classic Cournout model: Bertrand criticized it for lacking equilibrium for prices as independent variables and Edgeworth constructed a dual monopoly model with correlated demand with also lacked stability. Hotteling proposed that demand typically varied continuously for relative prices, not discontinuously as suggested by the later authors.

Following Sraffa he argued for "the existence with reference to each seller of groups who will deal with him instead of his competitors in spite of difference in price", he also noticed that traditional models that presumed the uniqueness of price in the market only made sense if the commodity was standardized and the market was a point: akin to atemperature model in physics, discontinuity in heat transfer (price changes) inside a body (market) would lead to instability. To show the point he built a model of market located over a line with two sellers in each extreme of the line, in this case maximizing profit for both sellers leads to a stable equilibrium.

From this model also follows that if a seller is to choose the location of his store so as to maximize his profit, he will place his store the closest to his competitor: "the sharper competition with his rival is offset by the greater number of buyers he has an advantage". He also argues that clustering of stores is wasteful from the point of view of transportation costs and that public interest would dictate more spatial dispersion.

A new impetus was given to the field when around 1933 Joan Robinson and Edward H. Chamberlin, published respectively, *The Economics of Imperfect Competition* (1933) and *The Theory of Monopolistic Competition* (1933), introducing models of imperfect competition. Although the monopoly case was already exposed in Marshall's Principles of Economics and Cournot had already constructed models of duopoly and monopoly in 1838, a whole new set of models grew out of this new literature. In particular themonopolistic competition model results in a non efficient equilibrium. Chamberlin defined monopolistic competition as, "...challenge to traditional viewpoint of economics that competition and monopoly are alternatives and that individual prices are to be explained in terms of one or the other." He continues, "By contrast it is held that most economic situations are composite of both competition and monopoly, and that, wherever this is the case, a false view is given by neglecting either one of the two forces and regarding the situation as made up entirely of the other."

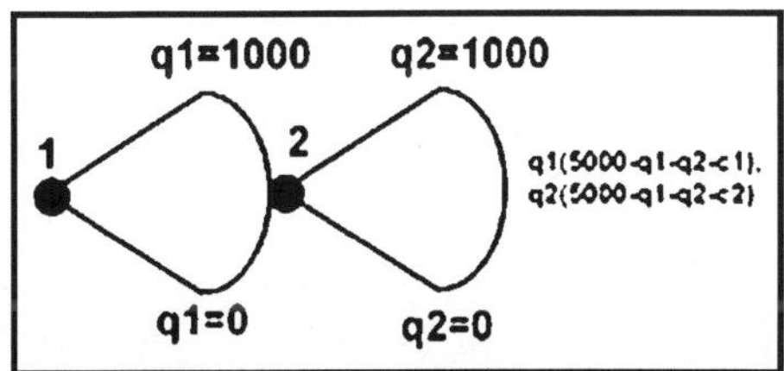

Fig. Stackelberg competition represented as an extensive formgame with Infinite action space.

Later, some market models were built using game theory, particularly regarding oligopolies. A good example of how microeconomics started to incorporate game theory, is the Stackelberg competition model published in 1934, which can be characterized as a dynamic game with a leader and a follower, and then be solved to find a Nash Equilibrium.

William Baumol provided in his 1977 paper the current formal definition of a natural monopoly where "an industry in which multiform production is more costly than production by a monopoly" (p. 810): mathematically this equivalent to subadditivity of the cost function. He then sets out to prove 12 propositions related to strict economies of scale, ray average costs, ray concavity and transray convexity: in particular strictly declining ray average cost implies strict declining ray subadditivity, global economies of scale are sufficient but not necessary for strict ray subadditivity.

In 1982 paper Baumol defined a contestable market as a market where "entry is absolutely free and exit absolutely costless", freedom of entry in Stigler sense: the incumbent has no cost discrimination against entrants. He states that a contestable market will never have an economic profit greater than zero when in equilibrium and the equilibrium will also be efficient. According to Baumol this equilibrium emerges endogenously due to the nature of contestable markets, that is the only industry structure that survives in the long run is the one which minimizes total costs.

This is in contrast to the older theory of industry structure since not only industry structure is not exogenously given, but equilibrium is reached without add hoc hypothesis on the behaviour of firms, say using reaction functions in a duopoly. He concludes the paper commenting that regulators that seek to impede entry and/or exit of firms would do better to not interfere if the market in question resembles a contestable market.

Externalities and market failure

In 1937, "The Nature of the Firm" was published by Coase introducing the notion of transaction costs (the term itself was coined in the fifties), which explained why firms have an advantage over a group of independent contractors working with each other. The idea was that there were transaction costs in the use of the market: search and information costs, bargaining costs, etc., which give an advantage to a firm that can internalize the production process required to deliver a certain good to the market. A related result was published by Coase in his "The Problem of Social Cost" (1960), which analyses solutions of the problem of externalities through bargaining, in which he first describes a cattle herd invading a farmer's crop and then discusses four legal cases: *Sturges v Bridgman*, *Cooke v Forbes*, *Bryant v Lejever*, and *Bass v Gregory*. He then states:

"In earlier sections, when dealing with the problem of rearrangement of legal rights through the market, it was argued that such a rearrangement would be made trough the market whenever this would lead to an increase in the value of production. But this assumed costless market transactions. Once the costs of carrying out market transactions are taken into account it is clear that such rearrangement of rights will only be undertaken when the increase in the value of production consequent upon the rearrangement is greater than the costs which would be involved in bringing it about. When it is less, the granting of an injunction (or the knowledge that it would be granted) or the liability to pay damages may result in an activity being discontinued (or may prevent its being started) which would be undertaken if market transactions were costless. In these conditions the initial delimitation of legal rights does have an effect on the efficiency with which the economic system operates. One arrangement of rights may bring about a greater value of production than any other. But unless this is the arrangement of rights established by the legal system, the costs of reaching the same result by altering and combining rights through the market may be so great that this optimal arrangement of rights, and the greater value of production which it would bring, may never be achieved."

This then becomes relevant in context of regulations. He argues against the Pigovian tradition:

"...The problem which we face in dealing with actions which have harmful effects is not simply one of restraining those responsible for them. What has to be decided is whether the gain from preventing the harm is greater than the loss which would be suffered elsewhere as a result of stopping the action which produces the harm.

In a world in which there are costs of rearranging the rights established by the legal system, the courts, in cases relating to nuisance, are, in effect, making a decision on the economic problem and determining how resources are to be employed. It was argued that the courts are conscious of this and that they often make, although not always in a very explicit fashion, a comparison between what would be gained and what lost by preventing actions which have harmful effects. But the delimitation of rights is also the result of statutory enactments. Here we also find evidence of an appreciation of the reciprocal nature of the problem. While statutory enactments add to the list of nuisances, action is also taken to legalize what would otherwise be nuisances under the common law. The kind of situation which economists are prone to consider as requiring Government action is, in fact, often the result of Government action. Such action is not necessarily unwise. But there is a real danger that extensive Government intervention in the economic system may lead to the protection of those responsible for harmful being carried too far."

This period also marks the beginning of mathematical modelling of public goods with Samuelson's "The Pure Theory of Public Expenditure" (1954), in it he gives a set of equations for efficient provision of public goods (he called them collective consumption goods), now know as the Samuelson condition.

He then gives a description of what is know called the free rider problem: "However no decentralized pricing system can serve to determine optimally these levels of collective consumption. Other kinds of "voting" or "signalling" would have to be tried. But, and this is the point sensed by Wicksell but perhaps not fully appreciated by Lindahl, now it is in the selfish interest of each person to give false signals, to pretend to have less interest in a given collective consumption activity than he has, etc."

Around the 1970s the study of market failures again came into focus with the study of information asymmetry. In particular three authors emerged from this period: Akerlof, Spence, and Stiglitz. Akerlof considered the problem of bad quality cars driving good quality cars out of the market in his classic "The Market for Lemons" (1970) because of the presence of asymmetrical information between buyers and sellers.

Spence explained that signalling was fundamental in the labour market, because since employers can't know beforehand which candidate is the most productive, a college degree becomes a signalling device that a firm uses to select new personnel. A synthesizing paper of this era is "Externalities in Economies with Imperfect Information and Incomplete Markets" by Stiglitz and Greenwald: the basic model consists of households that maximize a utility function, firms that maximize profit—and a government that produces nothing, collects taxes, and distributes the proceeds. An initial equilibrium with no taxes is assumed to exist, a vector x of household consumption and vector z of other variables that affect household utilities (externalities) are defined, a vector π of profits is defined along with a vector E of households expenditures. Since the envelope theorem holds, if the initial non- taxed equilibrium is Pareto optimal then it follows that the dot products Π (between π and the time derivative of z) and B (between E and the time derivative of z) must equal each other. They state:

"Except in the special case (which is unlikely to hold generically) where Π and B exactly cancel each other out, the existence of these externalities will make the initial equilibrium inefficient and guarantee the existence of welfare-improving tax measures." One application of this result is to the already mentioned Market for Lemons, which deals with adverse selection: households buy from a pool of goods with heterogeneous quality considering only average quality, since in general the equilibrium is not efficient, any tax that raises average quality is beneficial (in the sense of optimal taxation). Other applications were considered by the authors, such as tax distortions, signalling, screening, moral hazard, incomplete markets, queue rationing, unemployment and rationing equilibrium.

Behavioural Economics

Kahneman and Tversky published a paper in 1979 criticizing the very idea of the rational economic agent. The main point is that there an asymmetry in the psychology of the economic agent that gives a much higher value to losses than to gains. This article is usually regarded as the beginning of behavioural economics and has consequences particularly regarding the world of finance. The authors summed the idea in the abstract as follows:

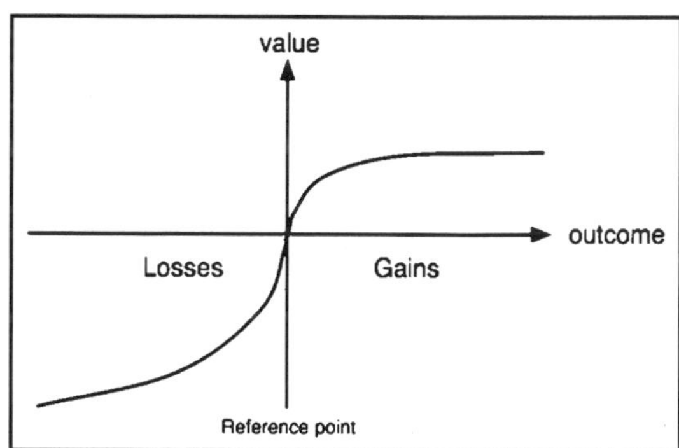

Fig. Asymmetric value function inprospect theory: big losses have a much bigger psychological impact than big gains

"...In particular, people underweight outcomes that are merely probable in comparison with outcomes that are obtained with certainty. This tendency, called certainty effect, contributes to risk aversion in choices involving sure gains and to risk seeking in choices involving sure losses. In addition, people generally discard components that are shared by all prospects under consideration. This tendency, called the isolation effect, leads to inconsistent preferences when the same choice is presented in different forms."

Great Recession and executive compensation

More recently, the Great Recession and the ongoing controversy on executive compensation brought the principal–agent problem again to the centre of debate, in particular regarding corporate governance and problems with incentive structures.

THE FIELD OF ECONOMICS

THE ECONOMIC WAY OF THINKING

Economists study choices that scarcity requires us to make. This fact is not what distinguishes economics from other social sciences; all social scientists are interested in choices.

An anthropologist might study the choices of ancient peoples; a political scientist might study the choices of legislatures; a psychologist might study how people choose a mate; a sociologist might study the factors that have led to a rise in single-parent households. Economists study such questions as well. What is it about the study of choices by economists that makes economics different from these other social sciences?

Three features distinguish the economic approach to choice from the approaches taken in other social sciences:

1. Economists give special emphasis to the role of opportunity costs in their analysis of choices.
2. Economists assume that individuals make choices that seek to maximize the value of some objective, and that they define their objectives in terms of their own self-interest.
3. Individuals maximize by deciding whether to do a little more or a little less of something. Economists argue that individuals pay attention to the consequences of small changes in the levels of the activities they pursue.

The emphasis economists place on opportunity cost, the idea that people make choices that maximize the value of objectives that serve their self-interest, and a focus on the effects of small changes are ideas of great power. They constitute the core of economic thinking. The next three sections examine these ideas in greater detail.

OPPORTUNITY COSTS ARE IMPORTANT

If doing one thing requires giving up another, then the expected benefits of the alternatives we face will affect the ones we choose. Economists argue that an understanding of opportunity cost is crucial to the examination of choices.

As the set of available alternatives changes, we expect that the choices individuals make will change. A rainy day could change the opportunity cost of reading a good book; we might expect more reading to get done in bad than in good weather. A high income can make it very costly to take a day off; we might expect highly paid individuals to work more hours than those who are not paid as well. If individuals are maximizing their level of satisfaction and firms are maximizing profits, then a change in the set of alternatives they face may affect their choices in a predictable way.

The emphasis on opportunity costs is an emphasis on the examination of alternatives. One benefit of the economic way of thinking is that it pushes us to think about the value of alternatives in each problem involving choice.

Individuals Maximize in Pursuing Self-Interest

What motivates people as they make choices? Perhaps more than anything else, it is the economist's answer to this question that distinguishes economics from other fields.

Economists assume that individuals make choices that they expect will create the maximum value of some objective, given the constraints they face. Furthermore, economists assume that people's objectives will be those that serve their own self-interest. Economists assume, for example, that the owners of business firms seek to maximize profit. Given the assumed goal of profit maximization, economists can predict how firms in an industry will respond to changes in the markets in which they operate. As labour costs in the United States rise, for example, economists are not surprised to see firms moving some of their manufacturing operations overseas.

Similarly, economists assume that maximizing behaviour is at work when they examine the behaviour of consumers. In studying consumers, economists assume that individual consumers make choices aimed at maximizing their level of satisfaction. In the next chapter, we will look at the results of the shift from skiing to snowboarding; that is a shift that reflects the pursuit of self-interest by consumers and by manufacturers.

In assuming that people pursue their self-interest, economists are not assuming people are selfish. People clearly gain satisfaction by helping others, as suggested by the large charitable contributions people make. Pursuing one's own self-interest means pursuing the things that give one satisfaction. It need not imply greed or selfishness.

Choices Are Made at the Margin

Economists argue that most choices are made "at the margin." The margin is the current level of an activity. Think of it as the edge from which a choice is to be made. A choice at the margin is a decision to do a little more or a little less of something.

Assessing choices at the margin can lead to extremely useful insights. Consider, for example, the problem of curtailing water consumption when the amount of water available falls short of the amount people now use. Economists argue that one way to induce people to conserve water is to raise its price. A common response to this recommendation is that a higher price would have no effect on water consumption, because water is a necessity. Many people assert that prices do not affect water consumption because people "need" water. But choices in water consumption, like virtually all choices, are made at the margin. Individuals do not make choices about whether they should or should not consume water. Rather, they decide whether to consume a little more or a little less water. Household water consumption in the United States totals about 105 gallons per person per day. Think of that starting point as the edge from which a choice at the margin in water consumption is made. Could a higher price cause you to use less water brushing your teeth, take shorter showers, or water your lawn less? Could a higher price cause people to reduce their use, say, to 104 gallons per person per day? To 103? When we examine the choice to consume water at the margin, the notion that a higher price would reduce consumption seems much more plausible. Prices affect our consumption of water because choices in water consumption, like other choices, are made at the margin.

The elements of opportunity cost, maximization, and choices at the margin can be found in each of two broad areas of economic analysis: microeconomics and macroeconomics. Your economics course, for example, may be designated as a "micro" or as a "macro" course. We will look at these two areas of economic thought in the next section.

MICROECONOMICS AND MACROECONOMICS

The field of economics is typically divided into two broad realms: microeconomics and macroeconomics. It is important to see the distinctions between these broad areas of study.

Microeconomics is the branch of economics that focuses on the choices made by individual decision-making units in the economy—typically consumers and firms—and the impacts those choices have on individual markets. Macroeconomics is the branch of economics that focuses on the impact of choices on the total, or aggregate, level of economic activity.

Why do tickets to the best concerts cost so much? How does the threat of global warming affect real estate prices in coastal areas? Why do women end up doing most of the housework? Why do senior citizens get discounts on public transit systems? These questions are generally regarded as microeconomic because they focus on individual units or markets in the economy.

Is the total level of economic activity rising or falling? Is the rate of inflation increasing or decreasing? What is happening to the unemployment rate? These are questions that deal with aggregates, or totals, in the economy; they are problems of macroeconomics. The question about the level of economic activity, for example, refers to the total value of all goods and services produced in the economy. Inflation is a measure of the rate of change in the average price level for the entire economy; it is a macroeconomic problem. The total levels of employment and unemployment in the economy represent the aggregate of all labour markets; unemployment is also a topic of macroeconomics.

Both microeconomics and macroeconomics give attention to individual markets. But in microeconomics that attention is an end in itself; in macroeconomics it is aimed at explaining the movement of major economic aggregates—the level of total output, the level of employment, and the price level.

We have now examined the characteristics that define the economic way of thinking and the two branches of this way of thinking: microeconomics and macroeconomics. In the next section, we will have a look at what one can do with training in economics.

PUTTING ECONOMICS TO WORK

Economics is one way of looking at the world. Because the economic way of thinking has proven quite useful, training in economics can be put to work in a wide range of fields. One, of course, is in work as an economist. Undergraduate work in economics can be applied to other careers as well.

Careers in Economics

Economists working for business firms and government agencies sometimes forecast economic activity to assist their employers in planning. They also apply economic analysis to the activities of the firms or agencies for which they work or consult. Economists employed at colleges and universities teach and conduct research.

Peruse the web site of your college or university's economics department. Chances are the department will discuss the wide variety of occupations that their economics majors enter. Unlike engineering and accounting majors, economics and other social science majors tend to be distributed over a broad range of occupations.

Applying Economics to Other Fields

Suppose that you are considering something other than a career in economics. Would choosing to study economics help you?

The evidence suggests it may. Suppose, for example, that you are considering law school. The study of law requires keen analytical skills; studying economics sharpens such skills. Economists have traditionally argued that undergraduate work in economics serves as excellent preparation for law school. Economist Michael Nieswiadomy of the University of North Texas collected data on Law School Admittance Test (LSAT) scores for undergraduate majors listed by 2,200 or more students taking the test in 2003. Table below "LSAT Scores and Undergraduate Majors" gives the scores, as well as the ranking for each of these majors, in 2003 and in two previous years in which the rankings were compiled. In rankings for all three years, economics majors recorded the highest scores.

Table. LSAT Scores and Undergraduate Majors

Major field	LSAT average 2003–2004	2003–2004 Rank	1994–1995 Rank	1991–1992 Rank
Economics	156.6	1	1	1
Engineering	155.4	2	4	2
History	155.0	3	2	3
English	154.3	4	3	4
Finance	152.6	5	6	5
Political science	152.1	6	9	9
Psychology	152.1	7	7	8
Accounting	151.1	8	8	6
Communications	150.5	9	10	10
Sociology	150.2	10	12	13
Bus. Administration	149.6	11	13	12
Criminal Justice	144.7	12	14	14

Here are the average LSAT scores and rankings for the 12 undergraduate majors with more than 2200 students taking the test to enter law school in the 2003–2004 academic year.

MACROECONOMICS

The behaviour of aggregate economic Variables, such as total investment, total consumption, govt. expenditures and taxation, unemployment, inflation, economic growth..... etc.

Macroeconomics can be best understood in contrast to microeconomics which considers the decisions made at an individual or firm level. Macroeconomics considers the larger picture, or how all of these decisions sum together. An understanding of microeconomics is crucial to understand macroeconomics.

To understand why a change in interest rates leads to changes in real GDP, we need to understand how lower interest rates influence decisions, such as the decision of how much to save, at the firm or household level. Once we understand how an individual, on average, will change their behaviour we will then understand the large scale relationships in an economy.

MACRO-ECONOMIC THEORY

Macro-economics is traditionally broken down into macro-economic *theory* and macro-economic *policy*. Macro-economic theory involves the construction and use of models of the whole, 'macro', economy. Economists build such models so that they can explain the structure of an economy, and the role and significance of the parts that make up this structure. Macro-economic models also help the economist understand how the separate components of the macro-economy are related.

Macro-economic models are also used to help economists and policy makers make predictions, or forecasts, about the economy, and about the effect of changes in one economic variable, such as exchange rates, on other variables, such as prices and output.

MACRO-ECONOMIC POLICY OBJECTIVES

Macro-economic policy refers to how governments and other policy makers compensate for market failures in order to improve economic performance and well-being. Improvements in performance begin with the setting of policy objectives, which include the achievement of sustainable economic growth and development, stableprices and full employment. Some of the objectives set are potentially in conflict with each other, which means that, in attempting to achieve one objective, another one is 'sacrificed'. For example, in attempting to achieve full employment in the short-term price inflation may occur in the longer term.

Policy Targets

In order to achieve policy objectives, policy makers will set targets to aim for. Targets are often fixed, and widely known, such as the current UK inflation target of 2 per cent, but they may also be flexible and less widely known, such as exchange rate and employment targets.

Policy Instruments

Once policy objectives and targets are established, policy makers need to choose between alternative policy tools, or instruments. These instruments are the *levers of control* of the macro-economy and include monetaryinstruments such as interest rates, and fiscal instruments such as tax rates and government spending.

Policy Disagreements

Policy disagreements occur for a number of reasons. Macro-economic policy is often shaped by long heldnormative beliefs about what is essential, and this influences the choice of model, objective, target, and instrument. For example, some economists put the eradication of poverty above the maximisation of corporate profits, and this will strongly influence their belief about how the tax system should be used. In addition, different economists may use different economic models and forecasting techniques, and this may lead them to disagree about the need for, size of, or timing of policy changes.

THE TERMINOLOGY OF BUSINESS CYCLES

ECONOMY RESOURCES OF TROUGH

When the economy is at a trough, there are lots of unemployed resources, the level of output is low in relation to the economy's capacity to produce. There is thus a substantial amount of unused productive capacity. Business profits are low; for some individual companies, they are negative. Confidence about the economy in the immediate future is lacking and, as a result, many firms are unwilling to risk making new investments.

CHARACTERISTICS OF RECOVERY

The characteristics of a recovery, or expansion, are many: old equipment is replaced; employment, income, and consumer spending all begin to rise; and expectations become more favourable, as a result of increases in production, sales, and profits. Investments that once seemed risky may be undertaken as the climate of business starts to change from one of pessimism to one of optimism. Production can be increased with relative ease merely by reemploying the existing unused capacity and unemployed labour.

PEAK CYCLE

A peak is the top of a cycle. At the peak, existing capacity is used to a high degree; labour shortages may develop, particularly in categories of key skills; and shortages of essential raw materials are likely. As shortages develop in more and more markets, a situation of general excess demand develops. Costs rise, but because prices rise also, business remains profitable.

CONTRACTION AND RECESSION

A recession, or contraction, is a downturn in economic activity. Common usage defines a recession as a fall in the *real* GDP for two successive quarters. Demand falls off, and, as a result, production and employment also fall. As employment falls, so do households' incomes. Profits drop, and some firms encounter financial difficulties. Investments that looked profitable with the expectation of continually rising demand now appear unprofitable. It may not even be worth replacing capital goods as they wear out because unused capacity is increasing steadily. In historical discussions, a recession that is deep and long-lasting is often called a depression. The most famous depression in modern history was the one that took place during 1929-1933.

MACROECONOMICS: ECONOMIC PERFORMANCE AND GROWTH

Income is one of the most significant factors in measuring economic performance, and gross domestic product (GDP) is the most commonly used measure of a country's economic activity. In short, GDP reflects the value of all final goods and services legally produced in an economy in a given time period. The distinction between final goods and intermediate goods is an important one. A tomato sold to a ketchup manufacturer would NOT be included in the GDP number, while a tomato sold in a store as produce would be included, as it represents the final use of that good. It is also worth noting that trade in illegal goods and services are also excluded from GDP figures.

There are two ways of approaching GDP – the expenditure approach and the resource cost-income approach. The expenditure approach totals the amount spent on goods and services during a year, while the resource cost-income approach adds up the payments made to suppliers of resources and other inputs that go into goods and services.

The expenditure approach is arguably more common, and it breaks GDP into four commonly watched components – personal consumption, gross profit domestic investment, government spending, and net exports to foreigners. Personal consumption has long been the largest component of GDP in the United States and is made of household spending on goods and services. Domestic investment refers to spending on fixed assets (capital expenditures) and additions made to inventories during the year.

By comparison, under the resource cost-income approach, compensation paid to employees is the largest component of GDP, with depreciation, indirect taxes, interest, corporate profits, and the income of the self-employed following. (To learn from the past, check out *A Review Of Past Recessions*.) Going a step further, there are other types of analysis that can be applied to GDP. Real GDP is the broadest view of an economy's output, and the one most widely used by economists. Real GDP differs from nominal GDP in that it attempts to adjust for rising price levels to determine what amounts to changes in the volume of activity in an economy. Economists observe not only the absolute level of GDP, but its growth over time. In fact, most discussions of GDP are undertaken in terms of growth. Going another step further, it is often useful to examine GDP in the context of its relationship to the number of participants in an economy. GDP per capita often correlates to the standard of living and the extent of economic development in a country. The U.S., and China, for instance, have similar GDPs in absolute terms, but the per capita GDP in each country is much different and reflects the much higher standard of living in the United States. There are some drawbacks and limitations to the use of GDP. GDP excludes any unpaid activity as well as illegal activity, so it cannot account for the value of all economic activity in a nation. GDP also fails to account for reductions in quality of life and losses to natural disasters or crime. The destruction wrought by an earthquake, for instance, would not be accounted for in GDP accounting, but the rebuilding efforts would be counted. Likewise, even per-capita GDP does not necessarily reflect the wealth of the typical citizen, as a majority of low-earning citizens could be offset by a small group of very high earners. (For more on GDP, read *High GDP Means Economic Prosperity, Or Does It?*)

There are other significant measures of income to consider. National income refers to the total income paid to owners of human capital (wages for labour) and physical capital, and includes both domestic and foreign income. National income can also be calculated as the sum of wages, interest, self-employment income, rent and business profits. Personal income, in contrast, is the income received by individuals; it excludes corporate profits and social security taxes, but adds back transfer payments (like Social Security), interest and dividend. Disposable income is personal income that is actually available for spending or saving; it is personal income net of personal income taxes.

MODELS OF GROWTH

While the large majority of economists basically agree with the use of metrics like GDP and GDP per capita as measures of growth, there is considerably less agreement in how to explain how economies grow over time.

Some models hold that growth is exogenous – long-term growth is determined by factors external to the economy. Other models post that growth is endogenous – long-term growth is determined by factors within the system. More specifically, there are models like the Harrod-Domar model that examine the consequences of fixed capital and labour ratios and the propensities to save. This model highlights the problems of rigidities in the capital/labour ratio and savings rate. By comparison, theSolow model holds that growth in GDP is explained by population increases, technical progress and increased investment.

As with many economic models, these are not so much predictive as explanatory; seeking to identify the impact of certain variables and conditions. While economic growth is clearly an important objective for most governments, most economies do not operate at their full potential. Often there is a gap between the amount of GDP actually produced and the potential GDP that the economy could produce with full employment and full resource utilisation – this gap is called the output gap (or the GDP gap).

POST KEYNESIAN MACROECONOMICS OR "EVOLUTIONARY KEYNESIANISM"

The dominant paradigm in mainstream macroeconomics is a synthesis of New Keynesian and New Endogenous Growth economics, which has modified the New Classical and monetarist-based neo-liberal macroeconomics known as the "Washington Consensus." The same model appears dominant in the UK, and perhaps in Euroland's European Central Bank and the EU countries as well. Evolutionary/Institutionalist and Post Keynesian economics (IPK) offers a very different approach to policy making which could be characterised as "evolutionary Keynesianism." This paper compares and contrasts the two approaches to macroeconomics.

Dominant (or hegemonic) in the mainstream means:

1. The view of most policy advisors (Federal Reserve, Council of Economic Advisors, IMF, World Bank, Bank of England, European Central Bank).
2. Appears in the most widely adopted textbooks and taught in the universities.
3. Taught and supported in the elite graduate schools.
4. Accepted by the majority of the profession.

The history of macroeconomics over last 50 years can be interpreted as a dialectical struggle between two opposing visions of the economy (as in Schumpeter's "pre-analytic visions" with which economists begin their work):

1. Stable, tending towards short run equilibrium at the natural rate of unemployment and potential output; tending towards a "steady state" long run rate of growth determined by the rate of technological change and growth in inputs. Business cycles are caused by external disturbances or supply shocks. The role of the state should be limited to providing the necessary institutional infrastructure, especially property rights, money and competitive markets. This approach originated in classical economics and reappeared in New Classical Economics (NCE); it also underlies Solovian growth theory.
2. Inherently unstable, with unemployment usually greater than optimal, and capacity utilisation lower than optimal. The actual growth rate is determined by short run cycles in production as well as the factors

cited in classical, NCE and Solovian growth theory; the growth rate is usually lower than optimal. Demand is unstable and usually insufficient. Macro policy can improve performance greatly. Marx, Keynes and Institutionalist-Post Keynesian economists share this view of the economy.

3. New Keynesian economics (NKE) emerged in the 1980s; it occupies a 3rd, intermediate position.

CONCEPT OF NEW KEYNESIAN ECONOMICS

NKE accepts most of the NCE microeconomic core: flexible wages, prices and interest rates lead the economy to the "natural rate" of unemployment (usually termed the NAIRU or "non-accelerating rate of inflation unemployment rate"), which can be described as a Walrasian and Hicksian general equilibrium. But the adjustment process may take a long time due to "coordination failures" caused by inflexible wages and prices. The level of GDP fluctuates around the "potential" GDP which is produced when unemployment is at the natural rate. Business cycles are temporary deviations from the long run trend growth rate, caused by supply or demand shocks. The trend growth rate and the natural rate of unemployment are both "strong attractors" dominated by the rate of technological change and the institutional and historical factors which influence labour markets.

Large demand gaps can and should be offset by demand management policies, using monetary policy. Fiscal policy is too clumsy a tool because the political and implementation time lags are too long, and the multiplier effects of fiscal policy are small. Therefore, fiscal policy is only useful for extreme crises and monetary policy should be used for normal stabilisation situations; although "fine tuning" is impossible, "rough tuning" is possible. This represents a modification of the extreme laissez-faire/non-intervention approach supported by NCE. NKE recognises the social costs of recessions and the importance of demand factors; it defends countercyclical monetary policy and advocates demand management using "constrained rules" such as (John) Taylor's rule. In most versions, the procedure is to estimate (or forecast) potential GDP and any demand gap, then adjust (nominal and real) interest rates to move actual GDP to its potential; target interest rates rather than the money stock, since the velocity of money is unstable and the money supply is endogenous. Fiscal budgets should be balanced over the business cycle.

The principal contribution of NKE has been to provide microeconomic foundations that explain why wages and prices are sticky in modern economies (imperfect competition, management strategy, menu costs, information costs, contracts, efficiency wages are often cited) and to model the implications of this market behaviour for macroeconomics. NKE rationalises state intervention to improve short period macroeconomic performance. Reducing the natural rate of unemployment requires restructuring labour markets (increasing labour market "flexibility").

ACCEPTS OF NEW ENDOGENOUS GROWTH THEORY

Most NKE economists also accept New Endogenous Growth theory (NEG), which first appeared in the late 1970s, early 1980s. NEG accepts the NCE/NKE vision of the natural rate of unemployment and the Solow growth model equilibrium steady state growth rate (the latter determined primarily by technological change) as the normal states which the economy tends towards. NEG also accepts the NCE/Solow argument that savings finances investment, so that an increase in the savings rate leads to more investment and at least temporarily a higher growth rate. But NEG rejects the NCE/Solow proposition that diminishing marginal returns to capital occurs as the capital/labour (K/L) ratio increases. Increasing returns are possible, so that the growth rate does not necessarily tend towards Solow's rate of technological change, the "steady state" growth rate for per capita real income.

Institutionalist and Post Keynesian Economics

Institutionalist and PK economists tell similar macro stories. The macroeconomics of first and second generation evolutionary or Institutionalist economists such as Commons, Veblen, and Mitchell were similar to Keynes's in many respects. Many of the recent contributors to Institutionalist macroeconomics published in the JEI, such as John Cornwall, Paul Davidson, Hyman Minsky, Basil Moore, and Randy Wray also contributed to Post Keynesian economics. Institutionalist and Post Keynesian economists argue that economic development is conditioned by and transforms economic institutions such as money, markets and property rights: transformational growth leads to structural and institutional change. Economies should be understood as complex systems with emerging properties that successively develop different laws of motion and pose different problems.

State intervention to create or change institutions is often necessary to promote the goals of full employment, economic growth, equity, social justice and harmony. Given the emphases on institutional change, full employment and demand management, "evolutionary Keynesianism or evolutionary macroeconomics" are appropriate terms for the IPK approach and models.

There are some similarities between IPK and NKE (the importance of aggregate demand is the chief common element) and IPK is consistent with much of NEG, there are however important distinctions between IPK and the orthodox consensus with respect to ultimate goals, assumptions, method, analysis and policy.

Differences Between IPK and NK/NEG

IPK – especially PK – emphasizes the importance of "fundamental" or "absolute uncertainty," Paul Davidson's "non-ergodicity," as a characteristic of the real world which has important implications for both theory and policy. NCE and NKE economics both assume "probabilistic risk," which is more tractable but unrealistic. The economy is inherently unstable because of this profound uncertainty-which implies great risk for many crucial decisions- and the resultant instability of expectations regarding profits from investment and the future price of assets. Financial instability and economic instability are dialectically interactive and must be constrained with appropriate institutions. Instability is not as important a concern in NKE economics, and financial markets are discussed largely as an afterthought. Financial markets and money are central to IPK macro (following Keynes's attempt to develop a "monetary theory of production." Economies are best understood as "complex systems" which are "self organising" and exhibit "emerging properties" as they develop - using the insights and language of complexity analysis.

This proposition is a modern version of a core concept in original evolutionary economics: since institutions and economies evolve through historical time, theory must be institutionally specific if it is to be useful. Since the behaviour of a complex system is not simply the outcome of the behaviour of its components, the complexity proposition also means that we can't adequately understand an economy (a complex system) by observing the behaviour of a component and extrapolating that behaviour to the system as a whole (as Keynes observed in his "paradox of thrift" argument). Rather than the "microeconomic foundations of macroeconomics" (as in NCE and NKE) we need to understand the "macroeconomic foundations of microeconomics."

External shocks and inflexible wages and prices explain recessions and deviations from trend for NKE; IPK argues that even if wages and prices were flexible, full employment is not guaranteed. There is no unique natural rate or NAIRU which the economy gravitates towards and which acts as a strong attractor. IPK argues that flexible wages and prices would enhance instability since falling wages and prices in a recession would probably reduce profits, investment and employment. Sticky wages, prices and interest rates are a good thing; institutions which stabilise these are useful and should be developed (national collective bargaining; incomes policy).

IPK emphasizes insufficient aggregate demand as a cause for low growth as well as recessions (NKE only recessions). IPK advocates demand enhancing policy, including inequality reducing tax, transfer and expenditure systems, low interest rates, and employer of last resort programmes. Most IPK economists favour Lerner's "functional finance" theory of fiscal policy: the levels of taxation and government expenditure should be consistent with full employment and price stability. Money is not neutral: changes in the price and availability of liquidity have powerful effects on the real economy; macroeconomics should begin with an analysis of the roles of liquidity in the economy, as in Keynes's "monetary theory of production." But IPK economists are skeptical regarding the power of monetary policy by itself and see fiscal policy as a more powerful tool for demand management. They are skeptical re "rules," in favour of "discretion" in policy. IPK follows Keynes and Kalecki in arguing that savings do not finance or determine investment. Profit expectations, interest rates, the availability and the cost of finance are the important influences on investment - not the flow of savings - since the former variables are largely independent of saving. Savings are determined by the level of income, itself determined by aggregate demand. The NK/NEG argument that policy should encourage higher saving is generally incorrect: high saving can mean low aggregate demand, capacity utilisation and investment. IPK puts a higher priority on full employment than on low inflation; full employment is understood as the rate of unemployment that obtains when everyone who desires employment and is willing to work at the going wage rate for workers with comparable skills is employed. Inflation is seen as the result of distributional struggles between capital and labour which can lead to "cost push" inflation. Again, institutions which socially control wages, prices and the distribution of income are necessary for full employment and price stability – some form of incomes policy. Many (but not all) IPK economists argue for government employer of last resort programmes as necessary for full employment. IPK sees a strong reinforcing link between demand, cycles and growth: high demand leads to high employment and capacity utilisation which leads to high investment which leads to higher productivity in the next period (higher growth).

The distribution of income influences aggregate demand. More equality is demand, investment, profit and growth enhancing. IPK proposes "demand-led" growth economics; propositions 7, 8, 9 and 10 are not in NKE/NEG; IPK is richer, has more explanatory power and more usefulness in informing the design of macro policy. Most IPK economists favour some form of exchange rate regime which would reduce exchange rate instability; most NKE economists accept flexible ER systems. IPK economists favour financial market regulation and see unregulated markets as instability enhancing; most NK economists see financial instability and crises as occasional episodes which can be handled on an *ad hoc* basis.

Bibliography

Abhay Kumar Srivastava : *Abbreviation of Physical Education and Sports*, B R International Publication, Delhi, 2002.

Ajay Kumar Attri : *Adult Education*, APH Publication, Delhi, 2012.

Ajoy Chatterjee : *Adult Education and Rural Development*, Commonwealth Publication, Delhi, 2008.

Amrish Kumar Ahuja : *Economics of Education : Strictly on the Basis of Prescribed Syllabus with Modern Trends*, Authorspress Publication, Delhi, 2007.

Anil Kumar Thakur and Md Abdus Salam : *Economics of Education and Health in India*, Deep and Deep Publication, Delhi, 2008.

Brijesh Upadhya and Yogesh Kumar Singh : *Advanced Educational Psychology*, APH Publication, Delhi, 2007.

D. Pulla Rao : *Economics of Education And Human Development in India*, Akansha Publishing House, Delhi, 2010.

Hemant Kumar Panda : *Public Financing and Economics of Education in India*, Academic Excellence, Delhi, 2008.

I. Sundar and R. Jawahar : *Principles of Economics of Education*, Sarup Book, Delhi, 2009.

Jeilu Oumer Hussein : *Economics of Education*, Discovery Publication, Delhi, 2007.

N Ramnath Kishan : *Economics of Education*, APH Publication, Delhi, 2008.

N. Nagarajan : *Economics of Education Family Life Education*, Publication, Delhi, 2010.

Saroj and S.P. Sharma : *Adult Education and Economic Reforms*, Vista Publication, Delhi, 2012.

Upendra Bhakta : *Advanced Educational Psychology*, Random Publication, Delhi, 2011.

Usha Rao : *Advanced Educational Psychology*, Himalaya Publishing House, Delhi, 2008.

Foss, Nicolai J., and Peter G. Klein.: *"Entrepreneurship and the Economic Theory of the Firm: Any Gains from Trade"* In Rajshree Agarwal, Sharon A. Alvarez, and Olav Sorenson, eds., Handbook of Entrepreneurship: Disciplinary Perspectives.Norwell,

Mass: Kluwer, 2005.

Foss, Nicolai J.: "*Misesian Ownership and Coasian Authority in Hayekian Settings: The Case of the Knowledge Economy*" Quarterly Journal of Austrian Economics 4, 2001.

Foss, Nicolai J.: "*The Theory of the Firm: The Austrians as Precursors and Critics of Contemporary Theory*" Review of Austrian Economics 7, 1994.

Ghoshal, Sumantra, Peter Moran and Luis Almeida-Costa.: "*The Essence of the Megacorporation: Shared Context, not Structural Hierarchy*" Journal of Institutional and Theoretical Economics 151, 1995.

Ionnanides, Stavros.: "*Towards an Austrian Perspective on the Firm*" Review of Austrian Economics 11, 1999.

Jensen, Michael C. and William H. Meckling.: "*Specific and General Knowledge and Organizational Structure*" In Lars Werin and Hans Wijkander, eds., Contract Economics, Oxford: Blackwell, 1992.

Klein, Peter and Sandra Klein.: "*Do Entrepreneurs Make Predictable Mistakes? Evidence from Corporate Divestitures*" Quarterly Journal of Austrian Economics, 2001.

Klein, Peter G.: "*Economic Calculation and the Limits of Organization*" Review of Austrian Economics 9, 1996.

Klein, Peter G.: "*Entrepreneurship and Corporate Governance*" Quarterly Journal of Austrian Economics 2, 1999.

Klein, Peter G.: "*Opportunity Discovery, Entrepreneurial Action, and Economic Organization*" Strategic Entrepreneurship Journal 2, 2008.

M.Madana Mohan and P.Premchand Babu.: *Managerial Economics and Financial Analysis*, Himalaya Publishing House, Delhi, 2011.

M.S. Bhat and A.V. Rau.: *Managerial Economics and Financial Analysis*, BS Publications, Delhi, 2008.

R.K. Tailor.: *Principles of Managerial Economics*, RBSA Publication, 2012.

Robert Waschik, Timothy C.G. Fisher and David Prentice.: *Managerial Economics : A Strategic Approach*, Routledge India, 2011.

S.P. Gupta.: *Managerial Economics*, Deep and Deep Publication, Delhi, 2012.

Shipra Chawla.: *A Textbook of Managerial Economics*, Dominant Publication, Delhi, 2012.

V.P. Raghavan.: *Managerial Economics : The Economic Way of Thinking of Managerial Decisions Theories Applications and Cases*, Kunal Books, Delhi, 2010.

W. Bruce Allen, Neil A. Doherty, Keith Weigelt and Edwin Mansfield.: *Managerial Economics : Theory, Applications and Cases*, Viva Books, 2011.

Index

A

B

C

D

E

F

G

H

I

K

L

M

O

P

Q

R

S

T

U

V